The Government of Social Life in Colonial India

From the early days of colonial rule in India, the British established a two-tier system of legal administration. Matters deemed secular were subject to British legal norms, while suits relating to the family were adjudicated according to British understandings of Hindu or Muslim law, known as personal law. This important new study analyzes the system of personal law in colonial India through a reexamination of its emphasis on women's rights. Focusing on Hindu law in western India, it challenges existing scholarship, showing how – far from being a system based on traditional values, or a system that operated in isolation from secular law – Hindu law was developed around ideas of liberalism, and this framework encouraged questions about equality, women's rights, the significance of bodily difference, and more broadly the relationship between state and society. Rich in archival sources, wide-ranging, and theoretically informed, the book illuminates how social life, emblematized by the system of personal law, came to function as an organizing principle of colonial governance and of nationalist political imaginations.

Rachel Sturman is Associate Professor of History and Asian Studies at Bowdoin College. Her writing has appeared in many journals, including *Comparative Studies in Society and History*, *The Journal of Asian Studies*, *Economic & Political Weekly*, and *Gender & History*.

Cambridge Studies in Indian History and Society 21

Cambridge Studies in Indian History and Society publishes monographs on the history and anthropology of modern India. In addition to its primary scholarly focus, the series includes work of an interdisciplinary nature which contributes to contemporary social and cultural debates about Indian history and society. In this way, the series furthers the general development of historical and anthropological knowledge to attract a wider readership than that concerned with India alone.

A list of titles which have been published in the series is featured at the end of the book.

The Government of Social Life in Colonial India

Liberalism, Religious Law, and Women's Rights

RACHEL STURMAN

Bowdoin College, Maine

CAMBRIDGE
UNIVERSITY PRESS

CAMBRIDGE UNIVERSITY PRESS
Cambridge, New York, Melbourne, Madrid, Cape Town,
Singapore, São Paulo, Delhi, Mexico City

Cambridge University Press
32 Avenue of the Americas, New York, NY 10013-2473, USA

www.cambridge.org
Information on this title: www.cambridge.org/9781107010376

First published 2012

Printed in the United States of America

A catalog record for this publication is available from the British Library.

Library of Congress Cataloging in Publication data
Sturman, Rachel Lara, 1969–
The government of social life in colonial India : liberalism, religious law,
and women's rights / Rachel Sturman.
p. cm. – (Cambridge studies in Indian history and society)
Includes bibliographical references and index.
ISBN 978-1-107-01037-6
1. Women's rights – India – History. 2. India – Social conditions. 3. Religious
law – India – History. 4. Great Britain – Colonies. I. Title.
HQ1742.S7888 2012
954–dc23   2012000798

ISBN 978-1-107-01037-6 Hardback

To my parents,
Audrie and Larry Sturman,
Who opened my eyes to a broader world,
lived the values of social justice, and
taught me the power of ideas.

Contents

Acknowledgments

In writing a book that concerns itself with the metaphorics of value and the impossibility of absolute recompense, my own intellectual, personal, and professional debts have remained powerfully before me, as has the inevitably partial nature of any accounting. This book is the product of many acts of kindness as well as kismet over many long years.

This book began as a dissertation under the direction of Barbara Metcalf at the University of California, Davis. The initial research and writing were made possible through an American Institute of Indian Studies Junior Research Fellowship, the Mellon Fellowship in the Humanities, the University of California President's Fellowship, the Mabel McLeod Lewis Fellowship, and a Phi Beta Kappa Award. Further support from the University of Michigan Society of Fellows, the University of Michigan Rackham Faculty Research Grant, and the Bowdoin College Sabbatical Fellowship saw the transformation of the project into the present book.

I am grateful for the research assistance provided by the archive and library staff at the Maharashtra State Archives in Mumbai and in Pune, at the Mumbai High Court Archives and Advocates' Library and Reading Room, and at the Asian and African Studies Reading Room of the British Library. Special thanks also to Pune District Judge S. R. Khanzode, and to the staff at the District Court, for their generosity with their time and knowledge of the court's functioning and its history. At Bowdoin, critical phases of research were made possible through the indefatigable efforts of the ILL staff, particularly Guy Saldanha, who consistently went above and beyond.

In India, the friendship, warmth, and generosity of many helped make Mumbai an adopted home. Reena Martins provided an endless supply of witty sarcasm coupled with love and care. Pratibha Mehra was a generous and urbane companion. Rusheed Wadia gave of his time and expertise, showing me many Mumbais, sharing his knowledge of the archives, stepping in to help out in so many ways, and trusting in our friendship. Manju in the Mumbai High Court Advocates' Library helped me navigate the court with her classic finesse, while providing a running critique of each and every dominant "system" with warmth and good humor. The women of Stree Sangam – Bina, Gomathi, Shalini, Chaynaka, Sonu, and others, and especially Geeta Kumana – made me feel welcome. Felicia Dias opened up her home to me for the long duration of my research.

Some of my foremost debts are to my teachers and mentors who launched me on this path and who saw this project to completion. My study of colonialism, of gender, and of South Asia began at the University of Chicago through formative experiences working with Leora Auslander, Barney Cohn, Ron Inden, John Kelly, and Gyan Pandey, among others.

At UC-Davis, Barbara Metcalf's wisdom, intellectual acuity, and deep historical sensibility guided this work in its early stages and beyond, continually pushing me to clarify and strengthen my arguments. To this day, her call to "write for people" remains a goal that I strive toward. Barbara's devotion to the larger aims of the historical profession, her unwavering ethical commitments, her intellectual curiosity, and her abundant warmth and generosity showed me ways of being a historian in the broadest sense.

Tom Metcalf likewise played an important role in this project, probing and questioning its aims, and ever nudging me toward the pragmatic value of completion. I have long benefited from his knowledge and skepticism, and enjoyed his proclivities for pushing the envelope. The intellectual community that Barbara and Tom fostered through the Colonialism and Culture reading group created an invaluable space for exploring arguments and ideas, and for cultivating friendships. Carina Johnson and Lisa Trivedi especially became important friends and interlocutors who have provided valued comradeship and perspective for many years.

Susan Mann offered a model of intellectual and personal engagement, a delight in people and in the world, and a tremendous ability to laugh that long served as touchstones for my own development as a scholar, teacher, and colleague.

At the University of Michigan, I benefited from the remarkable intellectual community forged by a dynamic group of faculty and graduate students. I am grateful to Jim Boyd White for his stewardship of the Society of Fellows, and for his sensitivity to bringing the interpretive methods of the humanities to the study of law. Thanks are also due to my fellow Fellows at Michigan for their readings of early chapters and for their companionship. Faculty in the Department of History and in the Anthro-History Program made Michigan a truly exceptional place to begin the process of writing this book, combining brilliance, warmth, and intellectual generosity in equal measure. I am especially grateful for the support I received from Fred Cooper, Geoff Eley, Gillian Feeley-Harnik, Rebecca Scott, Ann Stoler, Tom Trautmann, and the late Fernando Coronil, as well as other members of the Comparative Study of Social Transformations working group and the Marxist Study Group. Also critical to these years were the friendship and intellectual ferocity of Lee Schlesinger. Lee's intellectual rigor, his commitment to Maharashtra and Marathi studies, and the vibrant social sphere he and Lisa created in their home, especially through Kitab Mandal, remain dear to me. Sharad Chari and Christi Merrill were trusted colleagues and friends, who dazzled (and continue to dazzle) me with their creativity, analytical verve, and fabulousness, and who provided effortless camaraderie.

This work – and the span of my life spent working on it – have been vastly enriched through numerous conversations and patient readings by brilliant interlocutors, and through critical support provided at key moments. I am grateful to Dipesh Chakrabarty, Uma Chakravarti, Sharad Chari, Sandra Comstock, Rochona Majumdar, Uday Mehta, Christi Merrill, Radhika Mongia, Gyanendra Pandey, Anupama Rao, Mitra Sharafi, Radhika Singha, Gopika Solanki, Andrea Zemgulys, and the late Sujata Patel. Several people stand out for their exceptional role: David Gilmartin did yeoman's service in reading multiple chapter drafts and providing ever-incisive comments that truly "got" what the book was about even when I wasn't sure. Minnie Sinha read several early incarnations of portions of this work and engaged with it with seriousness, and with sparkling and provocative critique. Her support has made a crucial difference. Raji Sunder Rajan has been remarkable both in her reading and engagement with this work, and in her broader presence and support. For seeing the possible, and also for overlooking the limitations of the actual, I am ever grateful.

A group of extraordinary friends and fellow travelers have sustained me through many years and many vicissitudes. For everything their friendship has meant to me, I am grateful to Cherie Barkey, Durba Ghosh, Marlé Hammond, Larissa Heinrich, Anne Keary, Michelle Mancini, Karin Martin, and Elaine Meckenstock. Anupama Rao has long been an important friend and exceptional interlocutor, demanding of my work its highest potential and seeing what it was about long before I did. I am grateful for her rigor, commitment, generosity, and loyalty. Andrea Zemgulys remains in a category all her own: for years of dear friendship, for her singular humor, and for abiding in the same universe, as she knows.

I have been fortunate to find at Bowdoin College a supportive and generous community that sustained me through the long process of writing this book. Among many wonderful colleagues, several deserve special mention: Connie Chiang, David Gordon, and David Hecht created a helpful early writing group. Allen Wells has been both informal mentor and consummate mensch from the beginning. In Sara Dickey I found both kindred spirit and welcome mentor and interlocutor, whose unpretentious and generous sociability has made all the difference. Belinda Kong, Jayanthi Selinger, Jeff Selinger, and Hilary Thompson provided intellectual and personal camaraderie, brilliant conversation, trusted friendship, and invaluable assistance with the final stages of writing.

Portions of this work were presented to numerous audiences at conferences, workshops, and invited lectures over the years, and I am grateful for the many helpful comments I received in these venues. They have certainly helped me make this a better book. Special thanks are due to Frank Conlon for an early intervention, and to the conveners and participants in "The Concept of the Political" workshop at Columbia University, in the University of Chicago Department of Anthropology Monday Lecture Series, and in the University of Michigan Department of History Faculty Seminar Series.

I wish to thank Marigold Acland, my editor at Cambridge University Press, for her support for this project from the beginning; Joy Mizan for her assistance throughout the process; Alison Auch of PETT Fox, Inc., for her excellent copyediting; Bindu Vinod for expert management; and the production team at Newgen Knowledge Works that worked on this book. I am also grateful to the anonymous reviewers for Cambridge University Press for their careful and generous reading of my lengthy manuscript and for their helpful suggestions for revision.

An early version of portions of Chapter 3 was previously published as "Property and Attachments: Defining Autonomy and the Claims of Family in Nineteenth-Century Western India" in *Comparative Studies in Society and History* 47, 3 (July 2005): 611–637, and is reproduced with permission of Cambridge University Press. Portions of an early version of Chapter 4 were previously published as "Marriage and the Morality of Exchange: Defining the Terrain of Law in Late Nineteenth

Century Western India" in *Decentering Empire: Britain, India, and the Transcolonial World*, edited by Durba Ghosh and Dane Kennedy (Hyderabad: Orient Longman, 2006: 51–75). These selections are reproduced with permission of Orient Blackswan. The frontispiece image is reproduced with kind permission from Noshir Gobhai. My thanks are also due to the late Sharada Dwivedi for her gracious assistance in facilitating this permission.

Finally, it has been a pleasure to be a part of a large and growing family. My parents, Audrie and Larry Sturman, and siblings Serena, Nicole, and David ("Bro") have proven a tremendous source of support, humor, and goodwill throughout the writing process. The Hoffmans opened up to me with warmth and generosity from the beginning, making me a part of their family. My immediate family has literally lived the writing of this book. To Sylvie, whose birth ushered in utterly unimagined joy, I am grateful for your patience, determination, and exuberance, and for letting me see your world. To Sasha, whose birth hastened this book's completion, thank you for your uniqueness and for showing me the boundlessness of love all over again. My greatest debts are to Paul Hoffman, my unwavering source of strength and solace, who knew me from the beginning, and who has always understood. For your wysiwyg self, for making me laugh, and for innumerable hours of child care and so much more, I am forever grateful.

Abbreviations

BLR	*Bombay Law Reports*
GD	General Department
HD	Home Department
ILR	*Indian Law Reports*
JD	Judicial Department
MIA	*Moore's Indian Appeals*
MSA	Maharashtra State Archives
OIOR	Oriental and India Office Records, British Library
RD	Revenue Department
RNP	Reports on Native (News)Papers

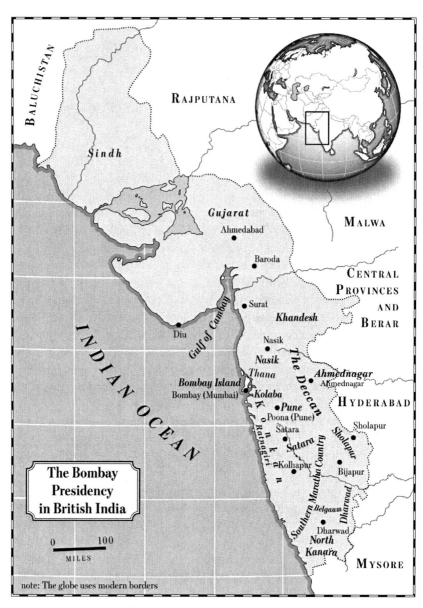

Map of the Bombay Presidency in British India.

Introduction

The British colonial state in India was continually forced to grapple with the forms of law and governance appropriate to Indian society. This question of the necessary, possible, and desirable relationship between colonial law and Indian social life produced a plethora of policies and dilemmas. It also created a new political significance for issues demarcated as social, particularly those related to religion, to women and the family, and to property and economic production and exchange.

This is a book about the practices of government that emerged as the colonial state delineated and engaged with this arena of Indian social life during the long century between the 1810s and the 1940s. It is also about how a group of largely elite Indians responded to and reworked these ideas and practices, shaping Indian political modernity in the process. Focusing on the dominant forms of Hindu law and the Hindu family, this study traces the increasing importance of governing society and the family to the work of the state in this era.[1] At the same time, it explores the uneven ways in which this modern state marked the significance of social differences understood as grounded in the body or defined by birth. Most pointedly, it places colonial debates on religious law, the history of the family, and women's rights within this framework of analysis.

The question of women's rights has a long genealogy in India, dating to the early colonial era. In the late eighteenth and early nineteenth

---

[1] It is because of the central place that the Hindu family has occupied in colonial, anticolonial, and postcolonial theorizing on the relationship between colonial law and Indian society that this book focuses on the formation and operation of colonial Hindu law, rather than exploring the systems of personal law more generally (including Muslim, and eventually also Parsi and Christian personal law).

centuries, many British commentators on Indian culture and "civilization" – missionaries, East India Company officials, liberals, and Utilitarians – articulated an idea of women as a universal category and the rights of women as indicative of a given civilization's hierarchical status in a ladder of civilizations.[2] Despite the significant legal and social subordination of British women at this time, these analyses typically placed Britain at the apex of the civilizational ladder, and India in a low and degraded position. By the 1820s, the colonial state began to identify for itself a moral imperative of protecting Indian women from their own customs and culture. This "obligation" established the grounds for intervention into Hindu religion, culture, and the family – first and most famously by prohibiting *sati*, or widow immolation – but eventually also in seeking to curtail high-caste prohibitions on widow remarriage, as well as female infanticide and the widespread practice of child marriage.

For postcolonial feminist scholars, this colonial history of women's rights has posed at least three dilemmas: (1) that the issue of women's rights was from its inception linked to a justification for colonial rule;[3] (2) that the colonial state articulated the issue of women's rights and enacted various measures putatively to advance those rights, and yet remained committed to retaining and consolidating patriarchal power in a variety of ways;[4] and (3) that because colonial governance placed matters relating to the family under the jurisdiction of Hindu and Muslim religious laws (as defined and enforced by the colonial state), women were and continue to be positioned "between community and state."[5]

---

[2] These ideas are most closely associated with James Mill, *History of British India*, Vol. I (1817), reprint of 2nd ed., London: Baldwin, Gradock & Joy, 1920 (New Delhi: Associated Publishing House, 1982). Yet they formed part of a broader stream of discourse and were widely recapitulated. For later Victorian feminist uses of this model, see Antoinette Burton, *Burdens of History: British Feminists, Indian Women and Imperial Culture, 1865–1915* (Chapel Hill, NC: University of North Carolina Press, 1994).

[3] Lata Mani, *Contentious Traditions: The Debate on Sati in Colonial India* (Berkeley: University of California Press, 1998); Mrinalini Sinha, *Specters of Mother India: The Global Restructuring of an Empire* (Durham, NC: Duke University Press, 2006).

[4] Ibid. Also: Flavia Agnes, *Law and Gender Inequality: The Politics of Women's Rights in India* (New Delhi: Oxford University Press, 1999); Uma Chakravarti, *Rewriting History: The Life and Times of Pandita Ramabai* (Delhi: Kali for Women, 1998); Janaki Nair, *Women and Law in Colonial India: A Social History* (New Delhi: Kali for Women, 1996); Samita Sen, "Offences against Marriage: Negotiating Custom in Colonial Bengal," in *A Question of Silence? The Sexual Economies of Modern India*, edited by Mary E. John and Janaki Nair (New Delhi: Kali for Women, 1998), pp. 77–110; Radhika Singha, *A Despotism of Law: Crime and Justice in Early Colonial India* (Delhi: Oxford University Press, 1998).

[5] Rajeswari Sunder Rajan, *The Scandal of the State: Women, Law and Citizenship in Postcolonial India* (Durham, NC: Duke University Press, 2003).

This last issue has meant that attaining equal rights for women in relation to men has been perceived as achievable only by limiting the operation of (or violating) the norms and prescriptions of the religious communities of which women are a part. Yet even positioning women in a direct relationship to the state has not produced equal rights or personhood but has rather rendered them vulnerable to other forms of state intervention, violence, and "protection."[6]

This ambivalent legacy of rights, coupled with the implications of a uniform or universal rights framework for further marginalizing minority communities (especially Muslims) in India today, has produced a debate about the value of rights as a feminist goal. Such concerns have been amplified by the overwhelming evidence that the enactment of legal rights does not necessarily change social practice: Progressive laws do not directly transform existing values or common sense and indeed often remain a dead letter.[7] In this context, some feminist scholars and activists have articulated powerful critiques of the liberal rights framework, while others have insisted on the value of rights, even as they recognize the dilemmas that such a framework sustains.[8]

This book emerges out of this context of debate, and it both draws on and seeks to extend the latter argument. Yet it does so by pursuing a line of analysis that has hitherto remained largely undeveloped: linking the question of women's rights to the broader dilemmas of the colonial state as a distinctive form of modern liberal state. Liberalism in its colonial incarnation has been famously characterized as adopting an attitude of "not quite, not yet," placing the colony within the perpetual "waiting room of history," with the educative, temporal deferral of political rights always securing colonial rule for an indefinite future.[9] Nonetheless,

[6] Ibid. Also, Ashwini Tambe, *Codes of Misconduct: Regulating Prostitution in Late Colonial Bombay* (Minneapolis: University of Minnesota Press, 2009).

[7] Bina Agarwal, *A Field of One's Own: Gender and Land Rights in South Asia* (Cambridge: Cambridge University Press, 1994); Srimati Basu, *She Comes to Take Her Rights: Indian Women, Property, and Propriety* (Albany: State University of New York Press, 1999).

[8] Nivedita Menon, *Recovering Subversion: Feminist Politics Beyond the Law* (New Delhi: Permanent Black, 2004), articulates a version of the former position. Some examples of the latter include Ratna Kapur and Brenda Cossman, *Subversive Sites: Feminist Engagements with Law in India* (New Delhi: Sage Publications, 1996); Sarkar, "A Pre-History of Rights: The Age of Consent Debate in Colonial Bengal," *Feminist Studies* 26, 3 (Fall 2000): 601–622; Sinha, *Specters of Mother India*; Sunder Rajan, *Scandal of the State* and "Rethinking Law and Violence: The Domestic Violence (Prevention) Bill in India, 2002," *Gender & History* 16, 3 (Nov. 2004): 769–793.

[9] Dipesh Chakrabarty, *Provincializing Europe: Postcolonial Thought and Historical Difference* (Princeton, NJ: Princeton University Press, 2000), p. 8. See also Uday Singh Mehta, *Liberalism and Empire: A Study in Nineteenth-Century British Liberal Thought*

elements of a liberal theory of personhood, society, and the state strongly shaped colonial state practice, and its assumptions structured the terms of debate, such that even institutional structures and policies grounded in different principles were framed explicitly in relation to liberal models, and often themselves collapsed into the paradoxes of liberalism, for example, rejecting liberal models as inapposite to Indian social life *in its present state.*[10]

The paradoxes intrinsic to liberalism took on acute form in the colonial context. At the core of these paradoxes was the powerful postulate of abstract human equivalence, but an equivalence grounded in the attribution of qualities and capacities that were nonetheless not viewed as universal. This simultaneous denial and reinstantiation of the significance of bodily difference at once produced new universal categories of difference (e.g., gender, race) and suggested new potentialities for overcoming them. Likewise, such potentialities produced a horizon supporting new struggles for political and social equality (and eventually also state policies). At the same time, they also heightened the paradoxical nature of such efforts at commensuration, which lessened inequalities but relied on and intensified the attribution of difference.[11]

A critique of colonial liberalism has shaped postcolonial theory and analysis, and likewise underlies this work.[12] Yet rather than seeking out dimensions of thought and experience that historically exceeded colonial liberalism, this book seeks to engage with its multifaceted operation. It does so by focusing on two aspects of liberal state power, both of which

(Chicago: University of Chicago Press, 1999); Homi Bhabha, *The Location of Culture* (London: Routledge, 1994). Certainly the fulfillment of the liberatory promises of liberalism, and even the existence of the autonomous individual rights-bearing subject that formed its philosophical foundation, remained quite attenuated, even in the West, for much of the nineteenth century. And in the colonial context, it was explicitly denied.

[10] Mehta, *Liberalism and Empire.* In addition to Mehta, see Joan Scott, *Only Paradoxes to Offer: French Feminists and the Rights of Man* (Cambridge, MA: Harvard University Press, 1996).

[11] Scott, *Only Paradoxes to Offer*; Elizabeth Povinelli, *The Cunning of Recognition: Indigenous Alterities and the Making of Australian Multiculturalism* (Durham, NC: Duke University Press, 2002); Anupama Rao, *The Caste Question: Dalits and the Politics of Modern India* (Berkeley: University of California Press, 2009); Sinha, *Specters of Mother India.*

[12] See, for example, Dipesh Chakrabarty, *Provincializing Europe* and *Habitations of Modernity: Essays in the Wake of Subaltern Studies* (Chicago: University of Chicago Press, 2002); Partha Chatterjee, *The Politics of the Governed: Reflections on Popular Politics in Most of the World* (New York: Columbia University Press, 2004); Mehta, *Liberalism and Empire*; Gauri Viswanathan, *Outside the Fold: Conversion, Modernity, and Belief* (Princeton, NJ: Princeton University Press, 1998).

centered on the core problem of the relationship of persons to the state and of the state to its people. First, it examines the paradoxes of liberalism as they took shape within colonial state practice; in particular the ways in which Indian social life was at once depoliticized *and* rendered politically significant, as impinging on the possibility of recognizing persons as abstract bearers of universal legal and/or political rights. Second, it explores the elaboration of new modalities of governance that brought everyday social life to the attention of the state, in a manner that most closely approximates what Foucault described as "governmentality."[13] Governmentality references the simultaneous processes by which modern state power came to extend itself to diverse aspects of the life, health, welfare, and social functioning of the people, now viewed as potentially distinctive and crosscutting demographic populations, even as such concerns were increasingly absorbed by agencies outside the state (e.g., in the fields of economics, statistics, sociology, urban planning, public health, and, eventually, in NGOs) and internalized by individuals as matters of self-discipline or self-regulation.[14] This book thus examines how liberal political and political economic ideas, and their concomitant forms of governance, pervaded the colonial state's engagements with the family.

COLONIAL LAW AND INDIAN SOCIETY

The relationship between the colonial state and Indian society formed a – perhaps *the* – foundational question for colonial governance throughout the entire era of colonial rule. A question first and foremost about the legitimacy of an external, colonial rule founded on violent conquest, it initially resolved into a matter of the proper (legitimate and pragmatic) forms of colonial law and administration.[15]

[13] Michel Foucault, "Governmentality," in *The Foucault Effect: Essays in Governmentality*, edited by Graham Burchell, Colin Gordon, and Peter Miller (Chicago: University of Chicago Press, 1991), pp. 87–104.

[14] Ibid. See also Hannah Arendt, "The Public and the Private Realm," in *The Human Condition*, 2nd ed. (Chicago: University of Chicago Press, 1998; orig. 1958); Mary Poovey, *Making a Social Body: British Cultural Formation, 1830–1864* (Chicago: University of Chicago Press, 1994); Gyan Prakash, "The Colonial Genealogy of Society: Community and Political Modernity in India," in *The Social in Question: New Bearings in History and the Social Sciences*, edited by Patrick Joyce (London: Routledge, 2002), pp. 81–96.

[15] This was clearly at issue in the much-analyzed attack by Edmund Burke on Warren Hastings during the latter's impeachment trial. See Mithi Mukherjee, "Justice, War, and the Imperium: India and Britain in Edmund Burke's Prosecutorial Speeches in the Impeachment Trial of Warren Hastings," *Law and History Review* 23, 3 (Fall 2005): 589–630; Nicholas

Institutionally, from the earliest days of British trade and residence in Indian ports in the seventeenth century until the 1860s, a dual system of courts adjudicated disputes in areas of British residence and eventually conquest. Crown courts, eventually designated Supreme Courts, had civil and criminal jurisdiction over British subjects residing in what became the Presidency Towns of Calcutta, Madras, and Bombay, as well as over Indians residing there with whom these British subjects were engaged.[16] They operated essentially according to the procedure of British courts, and they applied British common law and English statutes. Beginning in 1772, in the countryside – or *mofussil* – outside of the Presidency Towns, East India Company courts had jurisdiction over disputes among non-British subjects in areas ceded to the Company. These courts applied a combination of British laws and procedures and British understandings of preexisting Indian legal systems. During this era of "Company Raj," it was the Company courts that formed the primary colonial arena for adjudicating disputes among Indians.[17]

Inseparable from the institutional structures of colonial law and administration was the question of whether the colonial state could and should enforce Indian or British laws and legal imaginations. As is widely known, the first governor-general of British India, Warren Hastings, argued strongly for a form of government that respected Indians' own laws; by this he meant primarily religious laws. In 1772, while governor

B. Dirks, *The Scandal of Empire: India and the Creation of Imperial Britain* (Cambridge, MA: Harvard University Press, 2006); Sara Suleri Goodyear, *The Rhetoric of English India* (Chicago: University of Chicago Press, 1992).

[16] These courts included the Mayor's Courts, first established in 1726, the Recorder's Courts (which briefly replaced the Mayor's Court in Madras and Bombay), as well as the Supreme Court (which definitively replaced the Mayor's and Recorder's Courts) established in Calcutta in 1773, in Madras in 1800, and in Bombay in 1823. This narrative is drawn from B. B. Misra, *The Administrative History of India, 1834–1947, General Administration* (New Delhi: Oxford University Press, 1970), pp. 501–511.

[17] The Company courts relied on the labor of Indian personnel from the beginning, employing Indians as judges and pleaders at the lower levels, as well as in virtually all aspects of their everyday operation. Nevertheless, until the second half of the nineteenth century, the judges at the appellate level – District Courts, Sadr Adalats, as well as the Privy Council in London – were exclusively British. See Richard Clarke, ed., *The Regulations of the Government of Bombay in Force at the End of 1850; to Which Are Added, The Acts of the Government of India, in Force in That Presidency*, Reg. 2, chapter 2, S. 30 and 31 of 1827 (London: J. & H. Cox, 1850), pp. 13–14; Herbert Cowell, *The History and Constitution of the Courts and Legislative Authorities in India*, 6th rev. ed. (Calcutta: Thacker, Spink & Co., 1936), pp. 249–254; Chittaranjan Sinha, *The Indian Judiciary in the Making, 1800–33*, chapter 2 (New Delhi: Munshiram Manoharlal, 1971); John Jeya Paul, *The Legal Profession in Colonial South India* (Bombay: Oxford University Press, 1991), pp. 12–13.

of Bengal (prior to his appointment as governor-general the following year), Hastings issued a Plan for the Administration of Justice, which ultimately formed the basis for the distinctive system that was put into place.[18] This plan established a bifurcated system of civil law, in which British law would form the basis for most matters of law – territorial law, as well as an edifice of procedural or adjectival law. In matters of a "religious" nature, however, Indians would be governed by their own religious laws, or what was termed "personal law," so denominated because it applied to persons regardless of domicile; it was the law inherent to their personal status.[19] This system of personal law construed Indians as essentially defined by religion and as divided into two religious categories: Hindu and Muslim. At the same time, it delimited the jurisdiction of religious law to matters relating to religion, caste, and especially the family. In Hastings's renowned words, "In all suits regarding inheritance, marriage, caste, and other religious usages, or institutions, the laws of the Koran with respect to Mahomedans, and those of the Shaster with respect to Gentoos [Hindus], shall be invariably adhered to."[20] These matters would be adjudicated in the colonial courts according to (British understandings of) the relevant dictates of Hindu or Muslim law.

Hastings's original 1772 plan had involved several presumptions: that religions constituted discrete entities and systemic structures of law and belief that directly governed people's everyday practice; that these religious laws primarily centered on the family (and on caste in the Hindu context), so that territorial laws grounded in British legal principles could be applied in other matters of civil law without significant violation of the core of religious law; and that the content of these systems of religious law was specified in religious texts.[21] Each of these presumptions

---

[18] Peter J. Marshall, *Bengal: The British Bridgehead, 1740–1828*, The New Cambridge History of India, II, 2 (Cambridge: Cambridge University Press, 1988); Ranajit Guha, *A Rule of Property for Bengal: An Essay on the Idea of Permanent Settlement* (Durham, NC: Duke University Press, 1996; orig. Paris: Mouton, 1963); Robert Travers, *Ideology and Empire in Eighteenth Century India: The British in Bengal* (Cambridge: Cambridge University Press, 2007).

[19] This original use of the term "personal" was thus not a reflection of the sensibility that religion was a private matter.

[20] Cited in Sir Courtenay Ilbert, *The Government of India: Being a Digest of the Statute Law Relating Thereto, with Historical Introduction and Explanatory Matter*, 3rd ed. (Oxford: Clarendon Press, 1915; reprint, Delhi: Neeraj Publishing House, 1984), p. 278. The word "succession" was later added to the list of covered topics.

[21] Travers argues that Hastings had a common-law or ancient-constitution view of personal law, not grounded exclusively in texts. Nonetheless, the projects in legal scholarship that Hastings initiated were those of textual translation and compilation. Travers, *Ideology and Empire*, 188–190.

had implications for the structure of colonial personal law, and historians have shown how the colonial system enacted a fundamental break, transforming preexisting social practices and legal forms.[22] Crucially, while the system was conceptualized as applying to Indians their own religious laws in matters related to inheritance, marriage, and the like, the state took on the role of defining and adjudicating that religious law. Personal law was thus construed at once as an integral part of the colonial legal system, adjudicated in colonial courts by colonial legal personnel, and as an arena of nonintervention by the colonial state.[23] That despite this explicit colonial model of nonintervention, the state inevitably did intervene in these "religious" matters, was widely recognized during the colonial era itself, and has also been a subject of considerable scholarly inquiry.

Such a focus on the dual problem of the law's inadequate reflection of Indian society and its intervention therein has drawn critical attention to the colonial nature of the systems of religious law. The system institutionalized a colonial sociology of India that perceived India as an agglomeration of communities, with religion and caste forming the primary building blocks of Indian society.[24] Because of the critical implications of this system, which first rendered religious community rather than the individual the unit of legal and political recognition, which in addition constituted Hindus and Muslims as separate legal subjects governed by different sets of laws, and which moreover enforced a variety of legal disabilities on women according to their religious community, scholars have typically underscored the particular features of this system and its divergence from secular civil law.[25]

This book instead insists on connecting the system of personal law to the broader context of colonial civil law and administration. As this work

---

[22] Bernard S. Cohn, "Law and the Colonial State in India," in *Colonialism and Its Forms of Knowledge: The British in India* (Princeton, NJ: Princeton University Press, 1996), pp. 57–75; J. D. M. Derrett, *Religion, Law and the State in India* (London: Faber & Faber, 1968; reprint, Delhi: Oxford University Press, 1999); Marc Galanter, *Law and Society in Modern India*, edited and introduction by Rajeev Dhavan (Delhi: Oxford University Press, 1989).

[23] A system that left these matters to adjudication by Indians in preexisting legal forums would have produced fundamentally different results, but ones no less colonial, as the system of indirect rule in Africa suggests. See Martin Chanock, *Law, Custom and Social Order: The Colonial Experience in Malawi and Zambia* (Cambridge: Cambridge University Press, 1985); Mahmood Mamdani, *Citizen and Subject: Contemporary Africa and the Legacy of Late Colonialism* (Princeton, NJ: Princeton University Press, 1996).

[24] Dirks, *Castes of Mind*; Prakash, "Colonial Genealogy."

[25] Cohn, "Law and the Colonial State"; Derrett, *Religion, Law and the State*; Marc Galanter, "The Displacement of Traditional Law," in *Law and Society in Modern India*, 15–36. An important exception is Singha, *Despotism of Law*.

shows, in that broader context of law and administration, debates in the field of liberal political economy profoundly shaped colonial visions, and the policies that emerged from those debates sought to redefine and secularize existing property forms and to render existing social relations of obligation more economical. This book contends that those coordinates of a liberal theory of property likewise became embedded within the system of personal law. Focusing on colonial Hindu law, this study shows how questions concerning the nature of individual ownership, the power to alienate property, or the nature of liability for contracts became the dominant terms of reference within the system of personal law. It argues that what was produced out of this was what might be termed a modern, "secular" Hindu law: a Hindu law that largely dispensed with questions of ritual status and the like in favor of an almost exclusive focus on property rights; a Hindu law that both implicitly and explicitly grappled with the ethics of reinforcing difference and inequality, in ways that resonated with the paradoxes of egalitarianism within liberal political thought.

The colonial system of personal law entailed a particular kind of secular stance, involving a claim by the colonial state at once to religious neutrality, to a sovereign ethical position above the various systems of religious law from which it would evaluate the substantive terms of those systems, and to sovereign jurisdictional reach to enforce (its interpretations of) the terms of religious laws. Thus, the system of personal law in some sense encapsulated in its most vivid form the broader and specifically liberal dilemmas of the relationship between colonial law and Indian society. It claimed to enforce Indian societal norms, but it also operated by distinguishing which elements and institutions of Indian legal sensibilities, values, and norms – that is, which elements of Indian *nomos* – would constitute law and which would simply have social force. Defining Indian social life from the perspective of law thus involved a doubled movement of integration into the state and distinction from it.

The colonial state thus posited itself as a secular agency, and yet it deployed religious values and governed via religious norms in a variety of ways. For some scholars, this suggests the nonsecular character of the state, and many have critiqued the colonial model of modernization as secularization in any case.[26] While this book finds any pronouncement on

---

[26] Talal Asad, *Formations of the Secular: Christianity, Islam, Modernity* (Stanford, CA: Stanford University Press, 2003); Nandini Chatterjee, "English Law, Brahmo Marriage, and the Problem of Religious Difference: Civil Marriage Laws in Britain and India," *Comparative Studies in Society and History* 52, 3 (2010): 524–552; David Scott and

the secular or nonsecular character of the colonial state inherently unresolvable and unilluminating,[27] it nonetheless utilizes the terms "secular" and "secularization" as valuable for describing three distinct and at times countervailing processes: (1) the legal emptying out of ritual or hieratic significance from concepts of property and personhood, which involved less a Weberian process of disenchantment than a shift toward an inexorable focus on questions of comparative value, equality, or commensurability as the primary politico-legal mode through which persons and things signify; (2) the absorption of theological power by the state; and (3) the development of the category of social life as a residuum of the politico-legal domain, where matters of ritual significance would remain operative, but to which they would also now remain consigned. Thus, rather than a separation of religion from the state, one might think of secularization in the colonial Indian context as a process in which the state operated through religious law, shedding the ritual significance of that law into the domain of social life while absorbing its governing functions into the state. Such a process nonetheless remained unstable in its configuration of social life: If social life was to become the proper delimited domain of religion, it was also itself conceptualized as a domain where the operation of such beliefs, values, and norms was potentially and properly steadily diminishing. The secularizing force of the colonial state thus involved at once the development of the category of society or social life as distinct from state power and the potential transformation of social life through state norms that emphasized human rather than divine agency and ends. Secularism was (and is) an intrinsically ambiguous concept in its vision of religion and of social life.

This distinction between social life and the state posed a version of the problem that Karl Marx identified in contemporary mid-nineteenth-century European processes of state secularization: that the emergence of abstract political subjecthood – the model of the universal political equivalence of men – was effected through a political designification of social distinctions, such as birth, rank, education, property, and occupation, that nonetheless preserved those distinctions as operative within social life.[28] Abstract political subjecthood and the secular, universal claims of the

Charles Hirschkind, eds., *Powers of the Secular Modern: Talal Asad and His Interlocutors* (Stanford, CA: Stanford University Press, 2006).

[27] See the important piece, Hussein Ali Agrama, "Secularism, Sovereignty, Indeterminacy: Is Egypt a Religious or a Secular State?" *Comparative Studies in Society and History* 52, 3 (2010): 495–523.

[28] Karl Marx, "On the Jewish Question," in *The Marx-Engels Reader*, 2nd ed., edited by Richard Tucker (New York: W. W. Norton & Co., 1978; orig. 1844), p. 33.

state were thus premised on the ongoing social significance of bodily differences, religion, property, and the like. Such modes of thought rendered the vulnerabilities of persons within social and intimate life stubbornly insurmountable. This model of abstract universal political subjecthood was integrally connected to liberal theories of property.

PROPERTY AND POLITICAL THEORY

In the tradition of British political thought, property had long been connected to theories of individual rights and to the power of states.[29] These ideas had developed a heightened significance since the early modern era, when political philosophers from Hobbes to Locke posited property as foundational to their divergent theories of the origin of the state and the nature and possibility of political liberty. The philosophical writings of John Locke perhaps proffered in the most vivid and influential terms a theory that linked property to natural rights and political liberty, postulating that every man has "a property in his own person" in the form of his labor. For Locke, this universal form of masculine self-ownership likewise established a universal male right to political liberty.[30] A theory of property and of universal human acquisitiveness equally undergirded Hobbes's quite different views of the conditions and aims that led men to agree to cede some of their liberty for the protection afforded by the state.[31]

These ideas became salient in a seventeenth-century context in which the development and expansion of new forms of commerce and exchange were linked to the emergence of new theories of the universal motivation of selfish interest, as well as of the possibilities of human empathy and of international law.[32] These ideas of the universal operation of interest,

[29] Richard Tuck, *Natural Rights Theories: Their Origin and Development* (Cambridge: Cambridge University Press, 1979), pp. 5–29. See also David Armitage, *The Ideological Origins of the British Empire*, Ideas in Context, vol. 59 (Cambridge: Cambridge University Press, 2000); Lisa Levy Peck, "Kingship, Counsel and Law in Early Stuart Britain," in *The Varieties of British Political Thought, 1500–1800*, edited by J. G. A. Pocock (Cambridge: Cambridge University Press, 1993), pp. 80–115.

[30] John Locke, "The Second Treatise of Government," in *Two Treatises of Government*, Cambridge Texts in the History of Political Thought, edited by Peter Laslett (Cambridge: Cambridge University Press, 1988), chapter 4, S. 27, 287. Tuck brings into relief the conservative origins of natural rights theories: Locke and later liberal theorists thus reflect an anomalous development. Tuck, *Natural Rights Theories*, 3.

[31] Thomas Hobbes, *Leviathan*, Cambridge Texts in the History of Political Thought, edited by Richard Tuck (Cambridge: Cambridge University Press, 1996).

[32] Peck, "Kingship, Counsel and Law"; Emma Rothschild, *Economic Sentiments: Adam Smith, Condorcet and the Enlightenment* (Cambridge, MA: Harvard University Press, 2001); Steve Pincus, "Neither Machiavellian Moment Nor Possessive Individualism: Commercial

rationality, and sentiment (and of their not-entirely-universal extension to some peoples), became embedded in new legal formations of
property and contract that further facilitated these forms of exchange.[33]
Some sense of the connectedness of these new economic forms, new
legal instruments, and the concerns of contemporary political philosophy emerges in the pervasive philosophical reflections of the era on the
importance of keeping one's obligations, and indeed on the obligation
itself (or contract) as the modality by which political communities are
formed and bound.[34]

These new conceptualizations of the political significance of property
and ownership both resonated with and jostled up against classical republican ideas that linked ownership of land to the political virtue that alone
made possible the rights and duties of citizenship.[35] Indeed the social
contract theories of both Hobbes and Locke treated as politically insignificant the republican (and broader early modern common sense) view
that particular forms of property (e.g. land, or money) were linked to
particular qualities of persons. Yet this emergent liberal political theory,
particularly in its Lockean incarnation, retained a core connection linking
property ownership, the qualities or capacities of persons, and political
rights: It was the putatively universal quality of masculine self-ownership
that undergirded the claim to political rights.

In Britain, by the nineteenth century this connection at once strengthened claims to political rights by men of the new urban industrial working
class, and highlighted the connection between British women's legal and
political incapacity. Married women in particular were placed in a position of legal incapacity through the doctrine of coverture, which held that
the married couple constituted a single legal personality, in which women
were "covered" by the legal personality of their husbands. In practice,

Society and the Defenders of the English Commonwealth," *American Historical Review*
103, 3 (June 1998): 705–737.

[33] James Gordley, *The Philosophical Origins of Modern Contract Doctrine* (Oxford:
Clarendon Press, 1991); Pincus, "Neither Machiavellian Moment"; J. G. A. Pocock,
Virtue, Commerce, History: Essays on Political Thought and History (Cambridge:
Cambridge University Press, 1985); Deborah Valenze, *The Social Life of Money in
English Past* (Cambridge: Cambridge University Press, 2006); Tuck, *Natural Rights
Theories*; Peck, "Kingship, Counsel and Law."

[34] Locke, *Two Treatises*; Hobbes, *Leviathan*. See Tuck's discussion of Selden and his follow-
ers, as well as Hobbes, in *Natural Rights Theories*; also Pincus, "Neither Machiavellian
Moment."

[35] J. G. A. Pocock, *The Machiavellian Moment: Florentine Political Thought and the Atlantic
Republican Tradition* (Princeton, NJ: Princeton University Press, 1975); Pincus, "Neither
Machiavellian Moment."

this meant that unless special legal instruments had been executed prior to a woman's marriage, the act of marriage effectively transferred control over all her property and earnings to her husband. A married woman could not singly execute contracts or be sued for debts, nor could she be called upon to testify in court against her husband.[36]

During the second half of the nineteenth century, English feminists waged major campaigns to reform marriage law. These included efforts to expand women's rights and opportunities for divorce, and to establish married women's independent property rights.[37] Although an initial Married Women's Property Bill was defeated in 1856, by the late 1860s, advocates of female suffrage were explicitly linking women's political incapacity to their legal incapacity as property holders, while they also saw women's independent property rights as key to the possibility of transforming marriage from a relationship of dominance and subordination into a relationship between equals. Throughout the 1870s and early 1880s, the connection between women's property rights and women's suffrage both spurred feminist campaigns and complicated the passage of women's property rights.[38] The eventual passage of the Married Women's Property Act of 1882 empowered married women to act as autonomous legal persons, capable of legal agency over their own separate property. Yet even this legislation did not fully abolish the principle of coverture, retaining key distinctions between the rights of married and unmarried or widowed women.[39] Such distinctions were retained precisely due to fear that abolishing coverture and granting women full property rights would lead to the abolition of women's political disabilities and to the granting of suffrage as well.[40] Thus in England, the gradual process of winning autonomous property rights for married women was historically linked to and formed a critical ground for feminist claims to political subjecthood.

The contemporaneous colonial interest in Hindu women's property rights both reflected and inflected these Victorian feminist campaigns.[41] Throughout the nineteenth century, colonial legal scholarship and

---

[36] Mary Lyndon Shanley, *Feminism, Marriage and the Law in Victorian England, 1850–1895* (Princeton, NJ: Princeton University Press, 1989), pp. 8–9; Lee Holcombe, *Wives and Property: Reform of the Married Women's Property Law in Nineteenth-Century England* (Toronto: University of Toronto Press, 1983).

[37] This paragraph draws from Shanley, *Feminism, Marriage and the Law.*

[38] Ibid., 104.

[39] Ibid., 126–130.

[40] Ibid., 129–130.

[41] Burton, *Burdens of History.*

jurisprudence focused relentlessly on defining the peculiarities and limitations of Hindu women's property ownership in comparison with the
male form. This legal treatment worked to produce women at once as
a universal and as a particular category within the operation of colonial law: not as defined by and defining the multiple differences of caste,
status, and religious community as they previously had, but as defined
by their distinction from the universal category of men, as was the case
in Britain.[42] Although colonial administrative policies and jurisprudence
regularly bolstered and sought to extend both old and new patriarchal
forms, they framed women's legal status in terms of female inequality
and legal incapacity in ways that drew attention thereto and that ultimately produced a variety of efforts at legal adjustment. Nonetheless, the
implications of this emergence of women as a universal category were
ultimately quite different in India because of the colonial system of religious law.[43]

PROPERTY IN COLONIAL LAW AND GOVERNMENTALITY

Alongside the significance of property within liberal political theory, property also came to serve a critical function in the development and expansion of political economy and new forms of state power. While classical
liberal political thought ultimately preserved the significance of bodily
difference for determining differential capacities and rights, the liberal
orientation toward governance likewise vested the differences of bodies
with political significance.[44] In the colonial context, this took concrete
form in the institutions of law and administration themselves, which created separate jurisdictions for Hindus and Muslims, and which eventually
rendered castes, tribes, lineages, religions, and the like the administrative
units of governance.[45] Yet it also involved colonial interest in bodily qualities, and in the meanings and uses to which bodies could be put. The
attention the colonial state accorded to Hindu women's sexuality and
oppression must be understood at least partially in this frame.

[42] Rachel Sturman, "Family Values: Refashioning Property and Family in Colonial Bombay
Presidency, 1818–1937," Ph.D. diss. (University of California, Davis, 2001). This point is
also mentioned in Sinha, *Specters of Mother India*, 50.

[43] Sinha, *Specters of Mother India*.

[44] Michel Foucault, *The History of Sexuality*, Vol. *1*, translated by Michael Hurley (New
York: Vintage Books, 1990); Giorgio Agamben, *Homo Sacer: Sovereign Power and Bare
Life*, translated by Daniel Heller-Roazen (Palo Alto, CA: Stanford University Press,
1998).

[45] Cohn, "Law and the Colonial State"; Dirks, *Castes of Mind*.

Relatedly, the quite continual colonial interest in inheritance (and to some extent also debt), which had long linked differential property rights and obligations to the particular qualities of birth, likewise steadfastly maintained the connection between physical qualities and material goods that got passed down. By the early twentieth century, this connection enabled a politicization of forms of property and inheritance, which could now be understood as marking the differential social and political value of bodies. In this sense, colonial governmentality at once retained and transformed the core liberal linkage between property and personhood, mobilizing bodily qualities and differences as the basis for a new attentiveness to the economic, social, and political value of persons.

Moreover, as the British expanded their conquests in the subcontinent and reduced most of the remaining areas to political dependency, questions concerning the local forms and rights of property became integral to theorizing the nature of colonial sovereignty (connected to the state's right to collect the land revenue), and eventually to debates about the implications of these property forms for colonial governance and Indian economic expansion. The dictates of political economy regarding human self-interest, the efficacies of free markets, and the desirability of expansive commoditization all relied upon a particular, juridically-sustained, property regime, which the colonial power sought both to implement and to restrain in certain ways.

The prevailing scholarly narratives on the vicissitudes of colonial governance tell of an initial period, exemplified by Hastings's tenure, of British interest in and respect for Indian laws and forms of knowledge, particularly as embodied in the Sanskrit and Perso-Arabic textual traditions. By the early nineteenth century, however, such efforts to govern Indians "by their own laws" were beset by challenges from two directions. On the one hand, a new generation of colonial officials – Mountstuart Elphinstone in Bombay, along with Thomas Munro and Colin Mackenzie in southern India, John Malcolm in southern and western India, and Charles Metcalfe in northern India – deprecated the earlier focus on textual dictates, viewing custom and social practice rather than ancient texts as the proper source of law and as the basis for its legitimacy. On the other hand, British missionaries, liberals, and Utilitarians increasingly attacked both customary and textual Indian traditions, denigrating them for their divergence from the universalist claims of Western and Protestant forms of knowledge and sociopolitical organization.

According to this narrative, the emergent dominance of the Utilitarian ethos within official circles in turn produced a heightened degree of colonial intervention into Indian society from the 1820s through the 1850s. The major rebellion of 1857, which nearly pushed the British out of northern and central India, caused a fundamental change of course, however. In the aftermath of their reconquest, the British consolidated their rule through two countervailing strategies. On the one hand, they dispensed entirely with the scaffolding of the East India Company state and assumed direct Crown Rule over Indian territories. In the decades that followed, they enacted a variety of measures aimed at modernizing and extending the colonial administration, not least in adopting a variety of measures of legal rationalization and codification. In 1861, the High Courts Act dissolved the dual system of Crown courts and Company courts that had prevailed until that time, abolishing the Supreme Court and the Sadr Diwani Adalats and replacing them with a unified High Court in each Presidency or major administrative division.[46] High Courts were accordingly established in Bombay, as well as in Madras and Bengal, in 1862. In the wake of the establishment of the High Courts, in 1864 the government also "superseded" or abolished the position of Indian law officers – Hindu *shastris* and Muslim *maulvis* who had offered textual interpretations and advised European judges on matters of Hindu and Muslim personal law. From this point forward, the courts treated the existing translations and digests of personal law, along with the body of case law, as sufficient for British judges to satisfactorily render decisions according to Hindu and Muslim personal law. On the other hand, the colonial state moved away from efforts to transform Indian society, seeking instead to preserve security and stability by empowering putatively traditional authorities and modes of social organization – castes, tribes, "feudal" lords, religious authorities, customary practice, and the like – as a bulwark against sociopolitical instability and fragmentation.

In attempting to understand the simultaneously modernizing and rationalizing late-nineteenth-century colonial state on the one hand and its conservative, racializing ethos on the other, historians have characterized the colonial state in the era extending from 1858 to the First World War alternately as a Janus-faced state, simultaneously modernizing and traditionalizing in orientation, or as an "ethnographic state," in which modern colonial forms of governmentality operated through categories of Indian primordiality.[47]

---

[46] Kailash Rai, *History of the Courts, Legislature and Legal Profession in India*, reprint of 2nd ed. (Faridabad, Haryana: Allahabad Law Agency, 2000), p. 261; Eric Stokes, *The English Utilitarians and India* (Oxford: Clarendon Press, 1959).

[47] For the former, see David Washbrook, "Law, State, and Agrarian Society in Colonial India," *Modern Asian Studies* 15, 3 (1981): 649–721; Thomas Metcalf, *Ideologies of*

In the analysis of property law and administration presented here, however, a somewhat different narrative emerges. From this perspective, the impact of the Utilitarian ethos that began to pervade colonial administration in the 1820s and 1830s remained quite attenuated and uncertain during that early era. In contrast, the decades spanning the 1860s to the 1880s saw a movement toward a degree of systematization and uniformity that was previously unknown in the institutions and practices of colonial law, spanning issues from professionalizing the education of legal personnel[48] to regularizing judicial procedure,[49] and from the enunciation of property law,[50] to the reporting of judicial precedents

the Raj, The New Cambridge History of India, III, 4 (Cambridge: Cambridge University Press, 1994). For the latter, Nicholas B. Dirks, *Castes of Mind: Colonialism and the Making of Modern India* (Princeton, NJ: Princeton University Press, 2001).

[48] Srivastava, *Development of Judicial System in India under the East India Company, 1833–1858* (Lucknow: Lucknow Publishing House, 1971), pp. 31–53, 183–186; Bakhshi Tek Chand and Harbans Lal Sarin, eds., *The Law of Legal Practitioners in British India, Being an Exhaustive, Up-to-Date and Critical Commentary on the Legal Practitioners' Act (XVIII of 1879), as Amended Up-to-Date...* (Calcutta: Eastern Law House, 1935); Samuel Schmitthener, "A Sketch of the Development of the Legal Profession in India," *Law and Society Review* 3, 2–3 Special Issue Devoted to Lawyers in Developing Societies with Particular Reference to India (Nov. 1968–Feb. 1969): 337–382; Paul, *Legal Profession*, 82–84; C. E. A. Birdwell, "Conditions for Admission to the Legal Profession throughout the British Empire, Part II," *Journal of the Society of Comparative Legislation*, n.s., 13, 1 (1912): 130–131. For the broader context, see Peter Stein, "Maine and Legal Education," in *The Victorian Achievement of Sir Henry Maine: A Centennial Reappraisal*, edited by Alan Diamond (Cambridge: Cambridge University Press, 1991), pp. 195–208; Nowrozjee Furdoonjee, *On the Civil Administration of the Bombay Presidency* (London: John Chapman, 1853), esp. pp. 11–33; Indian Official, *Judicial System of British India, Considered with Especial Reference to the Training of Anglo-Indian Judges* (London: Pelham Richardson, 1852), esp. p. 37ff., and the additional writings they cite.

[49] James Fitzjames Stephen, *Selections from the Records of the Government of India*, Home Dept. No. LXXXIX, "Minute on the Administration of Justice in British India" (Calcutta, 1872).

[50] The third Law Commission, headed by Henry Maine from 1862 to 1869 and by James Fitzjames Stephen from 1869 to 1872, and the fourth Law Commission, headed by Whitley Stokes from 1879 to 1882 and by Courtenay Ilbert from 1882 to 1886, produced a stream of legislation: the Indian Succession Act (X of 1865); the Hindu Wills Act (XXI of 1870); the Registration Act (VIII of 1871), the Law of Evidence (I of 1872); the Special Marriage Act (III of 1872); the Indian Contract Act (IX of 1872); the Limitation Act (XV of 1877); the Negotiable Instruments Act (XXVI of 1881); the Indian Trusts and Companies Acts (II and VI of 1882); the Transfer of Property Act (IV of 1882); and the Inventions and Designs Act (V of 1888). Misra, *Administrative History*, 541. These acts largely reflected attempts to remove property from the jurisdiction of personal law, and to relocate and redefine it within a colonial capitalist property regime. Nonetheless, Sir Courtenay Ilbert argued at the time that despite the considerable extent of codification, in practice, much of this legislation remained limited in jurisdiction, and thus limited in effects. Courtenay Ilbert, "Application of European Law to Natives of India," *Journal of the Society of Comparative Legislation*, 1 (1896–1897): 212–226; see also

and to the statistical recording of judicial administration. [51] Likewise, and
of perhaps even greater importance, this book argues in contrast to much
existing scholarship that at a substantive level as well, during the decades
from the 1860s to the early twentieth century, liberal norms and dilemmas acquired expansive force across the domains of secular civil law and
colonial Hindu law.

Perhaps nowhere were these dilemmas articulated as strongly and influ-
entially as in the writings of Henry Sumner Maine and James Fitzjames
Stephen, both of whom served as law member on the Governor-General's
Council between the early 1860s and early 1870s. As key thinkers whose
work enunciated and shaped the terms of colonial debate throughout the
era of Crown rule, their writings underscore the ways in which liberal legal
norms, interpretive frameworks, and modes of expanding state power
became integral to quite divergent political philosophies of colonial rule.

LAW AND COLONIAL LIBERAL THOUGHT: HENRY SUMNER MAINE AND JAMES FITZJAMES STEPHEN

Henry Maine published *Ancient Law: Its Connection with the Early
History of Society and its Relation to Modern Ideas* in 1861. Although
he had not yet had any experience in India, his book proposed a typology
of Indo-European societies and a model of historical jurisprudence that
linked contemporary India, ancient Rome, and contemporary Britain in
a single arc.[52]

Maine's treatment of law as a subject of historical inquiry immediately
engaged him in questions about the world-historical nature of sovereignty, property, and the family. Drawing on the archive of early colonial
Hindu law and linking it to Roman law, his treatise advanced a theory
of the patriarchal family, defined by the absolute power of the father, or
patria potestas, as the earliest form of human society and the earliest
polity. Families, in this model, were originally little dominions, in which

---

"Indian Codification," *The Law Quarterly Review* 5, 20 (Oct. 1889): 347–369; "Sir
James Stephen as a Legislator," *The Law Quarterly Review* 10 (July 1894): 222–227.

[51] These were compiled in annual *Reports on the Administration of Civil and Criminal
Justice*, beginning in 1864 in Bengal and in 1878 in Bombay. Stokes traces this kind of
statistical collection back to the 1850s reports on the administration of Punjab. Stokes,
English Utilitarians, 245.

[52] Henry Sumner Maine, *Ancient Law: Its Connection with the Early History of Society
and Its Relation to Modern Ideas* (London: Murray, 1861). All quotations are from 1st
American (2nd London) edition (New York: Scribner, Armstrong & Co., 1872).

sons, wives, and other dependents labored under the despotic power of the father.[53] This was the ancient law. From this original political kinship, in which families embedded within themselves the earliest legal relations, Maine suggested that gradually larger states had emerged, and the domain of the latter's jurisdiction slowly usurped the power of the father, expanding the rights of persons. In Maine's most famous dictum, "Starting, as from one terminus of history, from a condition of society in which all the relations of Persons are summed up in the relations of Family, we seem to have steadily moved towards a phase of social order in which all these relations arise from the free agreement of individuals.... We may say that the movement of the progressive societies has hitherto been a movement from Status to Contract."[54]

This stirring enunciation proposed a developmental model in which an originary despotic family-as-state was depoliticized and privatized, alongside other relations of status, to produce a society of contracting individuals. Such a theory aimed to refute the claims of liberal political theorists from Locke to Rousseau to Bentham, who posited an original state of nature peopled by autonomous individuals, and who imagined the origins of the state in their collective social compact. Against these visions with their basis in a priori reasoning, Maine called for a methodology based on the historical examination of early forms and their subsequent development.

Maine's vision in *Ancient Law* proved powerfully influential in colonial policy and jurisprudence. It called for attention to local custom or practice, and for the preservation of indigenous systems, rather than the creation of a new system of colonial law based in principles of modern rationality.[55] Yet it also articulated the quintessential secular liberal model of modernization as the progressive evacuation of legal force from societal orders of authority, and the gradual vesting of such power in the higher-order state.

---

[53] See discussion also in Rosalind Coward, *Patriarchal Precedents: Sexuality and Social Relations* (London: Routledge & Kegan Paul, 1983), esp. chapter 1.

[54] Maine, *Ancient Law*, 163–165.

[55] Clive Dewey, "The Influence of Sir Henry Maine on Agrarian Policy in India," in Diamond, ed., *Victorian Achievement*, 353–375; Karuna Mantena, "Law and 'Tradition': Henry Maine and the Theoretical Origins of Indirect Rule," in *Law and History*, edited by Andrew Lewis and Michael Lobban (Oxford: Oxford University Press, 2004), pp. 159–188, and *Alibis of Empire: Henry Maine and the Ends of Liberal Imperialism* (Princeton, NJ: Princeton University Press, 2010). See also C. A. Bayly, "Maine and Change in Nineteenth Century India," in *Victorian Achievement*, 389–397.

The success of *Ancient Law* led to Maine's appointment as law member of the third Indian Law Commission, a position he held for seven years, from 1862–1869. His experience in India was reflected in his later volume, *Village Communities in the East and West*, which was published in 1871.[56] In this book, Maine was attentive to the changes that colonial administration had already effected within Indian society, particularly in the realm of law. In Maine's view, in the early Crown courts, whose judges were British barristers who came to India after long experience in English law, "The rule of native law dissolved and, with or without [the Judges'] intention, was to a great extent replaced by rules having their origin in English law-books,"[57] while in the Company courts, whose judges were civil servants of the East India Company who had come to India as teenagers, "The native rules hardened and contracted a rigidity which they never had in real native practice."[58] In particular, the preference for Brahminical texts over customary practice, and the arresting of the process of scholarly commentary that historically enabled classical textual reinterpretation to suit contemporary contexts, led to a Brahminized and ossified system of law.[59] Moreover, the same was true even where the colonial government had attempted to operate according to native custom. Maine viewed this as an ironic and unintended turn of events, a revolution in the very nature of custom, set in motion by the mere establishment of local courts by the colonial state:[60]

The customs at once altered their character. They are generally collected from the testimony of the village elders; but when these elders are once called upon to give their evidence, they necessarily lose their old position. They are no longer a half-judicial, half-legislative council. That which they have affirmed to be the custom is henceforward to be sought from the decisions of the Courts of Justice, or from official documents which those courts receive as evidence.... Usage, once recorded upon evidence given, immediately becomes written and fixed law. Nor is it any longer obeyed as usage. It is henceforth obeyed as the law administered by a British Court, and has thus really become a command of the sovereign.[61]

In this narrative, despite the intentions of British judges and administrators, the mere establishment of colonial legal institutions ultimately

[56] Henry Sumner Maine, *Village Communities in the East and West: Six Lectures Delivered at Oxford* (London: Murray, 1871). Quotes are from 3rd and enlarged edition (New York: Henry Holt & Co., 1889).
[57] Maine, *Village Communities*, 44.
[58] Ibid., 45.
[59] Ibid., 47.
[60] Ibid., 70–72.
[61] Ibid., 72.

led to the replacement of a system of customary law in which antiquity established legitimacy, by a system in which law was the command of the sovereign, as Jeremy Bentham and John Austin had argued.

For these reasons, in *Village Communities*, Maine ultimately rejected efforts to preserve Indian customary law that seemed to follow from his propositions in *Ancient Law*, and instead recommended codification, like the Utilitarians he so abhorred, "formed for the most part upon the best European models."[62] Thus, Maine argued, despite the most noble of colonial aims, "it is by indirect and for the most part unintended influence that the British power metamorphoses and dissolves the ideas and social forms underneath it; nor is there any expedient by which it can escape the duty of rebuilding upon its own principles that which it unwillingly destroys."[63] It was this approach that prevailed in Maine's support for codification as law member.

In this pragmatic reconciliation with the ideas of Bentham and Austin, Maine's work held an affinity with that of Utilitarian James Fitzjames Stephen, who replaced him as law member on the Governor-General's Council in 1869 and remained in that position until 1872. Stephen is best known for his unsuccessful attempt to produce a Code of Criminal Law for England, and for his vitriolic refutation of J. S. Mill's brand of liberalism, *Liberty, Equality, Fraternity*, drafted on his return journey from India. At the core of Stephen's thought was the Hobbesian conviction that force is the foundation of law and the ultimate source of its authority. His experience in India solidified these ideas, and he regarded as hypocritical and illusory any attempt to extend democratic institutions to India, as well as British efforts to preserve custom as the basis for colonial law. Indeed, British rule in India only revealed in balder form the coercive foundation of the state that was true everywhere: "[As the British became rulers of India,] they found, as every one who has to do with legislation must find, that laws must be based on principles, and that it is impossible to lay down any principles of legislation at all unless you are prepared to say, I am right, and you are wrong, and your view shall give way to mine, quietly, gradually, and peaceably; but one of us two must rule and the other must obey, and I mean to rule."[64] In contrast to Maine's writing,

---

[62] Ibid., 76. Mantena emphasizes the distinctive logic of Maine's approach to codification – i.e., as necessitated by colonial circumstances, rather than as universally valid, as in the view of liberal Utilitarians such as Stephen. Mantena, *Alibis of Empire*, 112.

[63] Ibid., 27–28.

[64] James Fitzjames Stephen, *Liberty, Equality, Fraternity*, reprint of second 1874 edition (Cambridge: Cambridge University Press, 1967), p. 90.

which suggested that empire produced a historical aberration in the relationship between law and social custom, for Stephen, the empire laid bare the general truth of law that had been disguised and distorted in the West, principally owing to the wrongheaded social contract and philosophical positivist doctrines of the younger Mill, August Comte, and Jean-Jacques Rousseau. Furthermore, whereas Maine urged an understanding of the historical nature of law, and of history or custom as the source spring of its legitimacy, Stephen extolled the virtues of a singular, visible, definitive positive law. Thus, for Stephen, in the India before British rule,

> Nothing could or did exist beyond a set of customs endlessly varying both in their substance and in the degree in which they were observed; and this, again, led to violence in the shape of blood feuds and boundary disputes settled by the strong hand, and surviving from generation to generation. Loose customs, village communities, and violence in order to settle disputes... are as inevitably connected together on the one hand, as are strict law, an organized government, and the rigid administration of justice on the other.... In a word, peace and law go together, just as elastic custom and violence go together. But every one admits that, whatever else we do in India, we must keep the peace; and this is strictly equivalent to saying that we must rule by law.[65]

Far from those who saw in custom a mild and well-regulated organic social order, for Stephen the rule of custom was essentially equivalent to the rule of violence. Yet Stephen's Austinian view of law as the command of the sovereign nonetheless also emphasized force as the foundation of law. In this context, the foundational violence of law was distinguished from the anarchic violence of custom primarily by the ethical, principled claims of law and order. The command of the sovereign was a normative one.

This insight had significant implications for Stephen: Morality inherently derived from religious principles, and thus British claims to religious neutrality in India were false and damaging. Stephen argued that the very assertion of religious neutrality, as well as British abhorrence of religious violence and legislation on liberal principles, such as the 1829 abolition of *sati* and the Caste Disabilities Removal Act of 1850, involved acts of coercion and the delegitimation of Hindu and Muslim ethics.[66] Thus, in his view, the British Empire in India "governs, not indeed on the principle that no religion is true, but distinctly on the principle that no native

---

[65] James Fitzjames Stephen, "Legislation under Lord Mayo," in *The Life of the Earl of Mayo, Fourth Viceroy of India*, V. II, edited by W. W. Hunter, 2nd ed., 143–226 (London: Smith, Elder, & Co., 1876), pp. 166–167.

[66] Stephen, *Liberty, Equality, Fraternity*, 89.

religion is true."[67] For Stephen, colonial secularism – whether understood as religious neutrality or as the evacuation of religion from the affairs of state – merely obscured the reality that the colonial state promoted Western Christian values (and negated Hindu and Muslim values), as indeed it must do.

Thus, like later critics of liberalism on both the political Right and Left, Stephen argued that the democratic/populist liberalism of his day attempted to paper over the fundamentally coercive nature of sovereign power, and that secularism and humanitarianism were particularistic Western principles, backed by force:

The main fact to bear in mind is that there are and there must be struggles between creeds and political systems, just as there are struggles between different nations and classes if and in so far as their interests do not coincide. If Roman and Christian, Trinitarian and Arian, Catholic and Protestant, Church and State, both want the allegiance of mankind, they must fight for it. No peace is possible for men except upon one of two conditions. You may purchase absolute freedom by the destruction of all power, or you may measure the relative powers of the opposing forces by which men act and are acted upon, and conduct yourself accordingly. The first of these courses is death. The second is harmonious and well-regulated life; but the essence of life is force, the exertion of force implies a conflict of forces, and the conflict of forces is the negation of liberty in so far as either force restrains the other.[68]

Stephen thus advanced a theory of the essentially political and agonistic nature of social life. Although he argued pragmatically against active state interference in India in the "social habits or religious opinions of the country," except in conditions of "extreme necessity,"[69] nonetheless like Maine he believed that "in the long run, the mere introduction of peace, law, order, unrestricted competition for wealth, knowledge, and honours, and an education to match, will produce a social revolution throughout every part of India, modifying every part of the daily life of the natives, and changing every article of all their creeds."[70]

Neither Stephen nor Maine engaged directly with colonial Hindu law, or with personal law more generally, although Maine's vision of Indian society drew heavily from that law. For Maine, society as an entity had emerged through the privatization of the family and the development

---

[67] Ibid.

[68] Ibid., 118.

[69] For discussion of the law of exception, see Nasser Hussain, *The Jurisprudence of Emergency: Colonialism and the Rule of Law* (Ann Arbor: University of Michigan Press, 2003).

[70] Stephen, "Legislation under Lord Mayo," 174.

of separate institutions of the state. Society was produced through the same progressive movement that ultimately consecrated the modern individual. In this vision, the debilitating and oppressive forms of social regulation that structured Indian society as it was hitherto known – family, lineage, caste, village, and religion – would eventually be reduced to forms of private (and hence insignificant) subjectification. In contrast, particularly in the colonial context, Stephen viewed the society conceptualized by the liberal theory of jurisdiction (and articulated by Maine) – in which a limited state power eschewed interfering in the separate arenas of civil society, public sphere, market, social relations, religion, and the family – as an impossibility and an unethical obfuscation. While both thinkers emphasized the impossibility of limiting the impacts of colonial law on Indian society, Maine viewed such impacts as embodying a process of secularization and modernization, whereas Stephen viewed them as demonstrating the falsehood or impossibility of colonial claims to secularism. These divergent models of the oppressive political power of society and of the necessary political domination of society by the state would prove highly resilient in both colonial and anti colonial legal thought, and indeed the problematics they identified have continued to resonate to the present.

THE CENTRALITY OF THE FAMILY IN THE POLITICS OF SOCIETY

In the colonial context, as in the West, while the family never became a site for the formulation of abstract rights, the question of *particular* and differential rights within the family and of the possibilities for forms of state protection became an immediate colonial concern. It also eventually became a subject of social reformist and nationalist agitation, and of Indian feminist activism.[71] These rights were addressed to persons (and especially to women) in their particularity – for example, rights to protection from violence, or to basic sustenance – which highlighted women's doubled vulnerability, in that it was not women's condition as abstract persons in general, but their particular embodiment as women that called forth state protection.[72] Such particular rights may be thought of as

---

[71] Mrinalini Sinha's *Specters of Mother India* offers a superlative account of the latter historical process.

[72] Shani D'Cruze and Anupama Rao, "Violence and the Vulnerabilities of Gender," in *Violence, Vulnerability and Embodiment: Gender and History* (Oxford: Blackwell, 2005), pp. 1–18.

forming a foundation for the possibility of abstract rights – as Tanika Sarkar has suggested, a "pre-history of rights"[73] – and simultaneously as reinforcing women as non-abstract, embodied subjects. Such particular, non-abstract legal rights reflected the realities of women's social vulnerability and political disability, but they also highlighted the impediments to rendering the concrete pluralities of human life into a foundation for human rights. The basic corporeality of persons – their fundamentally non-abstract character – constituted the limit to rather than the foundation of their claim to universal humanity.[74] At the same time, however, such particular rights extended the meaningfulness of women as beings whose concrete embodied existence would subject them to new forms of governance.

The same may be said of the family more generally. The liberal theory of the human not only emphasized abstract politico-legal equality, but also the recognition of human irreplaceability and uniqueness; that is, nonequivalence. Such incommensurability was located particularly within the family.[75] And as with women, the family, in constituting the limit of abstract rights – that is, in constituting the domain of humanity beyond commensurability – also formed the grounds for the development and extension of state power. This pivotal treatment of the family as limit of abstract subjecthood and as node of application of state power proved crucial to the development of colonial modalities of governance. The privatization of the family, the cultivation within it of new forms of intimacy, and its subjection to new forms of state scrutiny formed part of a single movement, which likewise undergirded new formations of the political.

In India, as in the West, the family was positioned as a new kind of political object even as it was also construed as the crucial residuum of politics.[76] In both contexts, while the family was separated literally

[73] Sarkar, "Pre-History of Rights."

[74] I draw especially on the work of Hannah Arendt for this formulation. Hannah Arendt, "The Decline of the Nation-State and the End of the Rights of Man," in *The Origins of Totalitarianism*, 2nd enlarged ed. (New York: Meridian Books, 1958; orig. 1951), pp. 291–293, 299–301.

[75] Arendt, *Human Condition*, 8, and "Decline of the Nation-State," 301. See also Peg Birmingham, *Hannah Arendt and Human Rights: The Predicament of Common Responsibility* (Bloomington: Indiana University Press, 2006).

[76] A number of scholars of the precolonial eighteenth century and of the colonial transition have shown how the precolonial political order was grounded in the logics of family – in principles of lineage and in the extension of alliances, dependencies, modes of incorporation, and the like. In this narrative, the family as it has come to be recognized only emerged out of a process of depoliticization that produced it as a

and metaphorically from state power, it became a critical site for its operation.[77] Yet the significance of the family in the colonial context also took shape through the distinctive forms of colonial governance, and particularly through the system of personal law, in which the regulation of the family according to Hindu and Muslim law came to signify the state's recognition of religious community. This emphasis also reflected the centrality of the principle of endogamy to defining religious and caste communities, and the longstanding and widespread significance of the sexual regulation of women (women's sexual honor) as signifying the status of the community. Thus, the significance of the family, birth, and women's sexuality flowed imperceptibly between colonial governance and putatively Indian primordiality. At the same time, the seemingly explicit Indian recognition of the family as a jural entity – not as a set of relationships prior to legal and political forms, but indeed as existing insofar as it was constituted in or as law[78] – solidified countervailing visions at once of the societal origins of law and of the juridical nature of social life. It also suggested more expansive regulatory possibilities: That laws and policies regarding the family might effectively act on society. Such a notion held promise not only to colonial officials, but also to Indian reformers and nationalists.

These modes of colonial state power thus had crucial implications for Indian nationalism. The seminal work of Partha Chatterjee has unraveled both how Indian nationalists dialectically appropriated colonial modes of thought, and the limitations or blockages that prevented a full dialectical

---

private, affective realm. While crucial to our understanding of the precolonial political space, this narrative does not account for the new modes of political investment centered on the family in the nineteenth century. Indrani Chatterjee, ed., *Unfamiliar Relations: Family and History in South Asia* (New Brunswick, NJ: Rutgers University Press, 2004); Malavika Kasturi, *Embattled Identities: Rajput Lineages and the Colonial State in Nineteenth-Century North India* (New Delhi: Oxford University Press, 2002); Sreenivas, *Wives, Widows, Concubines*. For a related narrative that emphasizes the colonial continuities in the operation of these earlier modalities, see Pamela Price, *Kingship and Political Practice in Colonial India* (Cambridge: Cambridge University Press, 1996).

[77] Foucault, "Governmentality"; Lynn Hunt, *The Family Romance of the French Revolution* (Berkeley: University of California Press, 1992); Ernst Kantorowitz, *The King's Two Bodies: A Study in Medieval Political Theology* (Princeton, NJ: Princeton University Press, 1957).

[78] This conception is also integral to William Blackstone's *Commentaries on the Laws of England*, 4 vols. (Oxford: Clarendon Press, 1765–1769; reprint, from the 21st London edition, with notes by G. Sweet, and notes by John L. Wendell, New York: Harper and Bros., 1859). Thomas Trautmann makes this critical observation in *Lewis Henry Morgan and the Invention of Kinship* (Berkeley: University of California Press, 1987).

transformation.[79] This book traces a similar structural dynamic, albeit with a different inflection, foregrounding the conundrums of representing and transforming Indian society to produce an ethical state, rather than the paradox of constructing a nationalism that could be culturally authentic.[80] At the same time, however, the positioning of the family in colonial law that this study traces forces a reassessment of Chatterjee's analysis of the "Nationalist Resolution of the Women's Question," by far the most widely cited formulation of the nationalist imaginary. Chatterjee's analysis traces how Bengali nationalist Hindus at the turn of the twentieth century utilized and recast the colonial binary of public and private to claim the domain of the family as the sovereign terrain of the proleptic Indian nation.[81] Yet while his conclusions may effectively capture the intellectual work of these nationalists at this particular historical juncture, this book argues that it obscures the significance of the family as a terrain of colonial state power from the beginning, and therefore as a site of *ongoing* contestation and exchange between colonial and anti-colonial politics.[82] In this vein, elite nationalist Hindus of all political stripes sought to *utilize* colonial personal law in forging their vision of the nation. Unlike the Muslim religious orthodoxy that largely sought Muslim withdrawal from the institutions of the colonial state, conservative as well as reformist Hindu elites sought to enforce their visions of the dominant religious community within and through the colonial legal edifice.[83] They sought state enforcement of (their vision of) Hindu personal law, not the removal of its legal force.

THE PROBLEM OF ADEQUATION: A QUESTION OF METHOD

This book may be read as a historical ethnography of colonial state practice, but it is not an ethnography of the colonial courts or of colonial

---

[79] Partha Chatterjee, *Nationalist Thought and the Colonial World: A Derivative Discourse* (London: Zed Books, 1986; reprint, Minneapolis: University of Minnesota Press, 1993).

[80] See also Partha Chatterjee, *The Nation and Its Fragments: Colonial and Post-Colonial Histories* (Princeton, NJ: Princeton University Press, 1993); Andrew Sartori, *Bengal in Global Concept History: Culturalism in the Age of Capital* (Chicago: University of Chicago Press, 2008).

[81] Partha Chatterjee, "The Nationalist Resolution of the 'Women's Question,'" in *Recasting Women: Essays in Indian Colonial History*, edited by Kumkum Sangari and Sudesh Vaid (New Brunswick, NJ: Rutgers University Press, 1990), pp. 233–253, also *The Nation and Its Fragments: Colonial and Post-Colonial Histories* (Princeton, NJ: Princeton University Press, 1993).

[82] See, for example, Chakravarti, *Rewriting History*; Singha, *Despotism of Law*; Sinha, *Specters of Mother India*.

[83] See also Chatterjee, "English Law, Brahmo Marriage."

justice.[84] Perhaps especially in the colonial context, such projects tend to produce a narrative focused on the inadequacy or injustice of colonial justice.[85] At the same time, such analyses tend to obscure how the problem of adequation is integral to the legal arena (especially in the era of global capitalism), as the legal system continually poses the question of what forms and quantities of value are equivalent to, or adequate for, what forms of loss, suffering, or damages.

Particularly in the context of family disputes, the law produced a doubled rhetoric – at once juridical and affective – of suffering, loss, damages, and betrayal as the grounds for acts of compensation or commensuration.[86] Such a rhetoric at least partially mirrored (if only in a distorted sense) the affective states that brought families to court, even if what people sought through the law was not attainable thereby. Thus, the problem of adequation was posed not only within colonial law, but within intimate relations: whether from a liberal or a non-liberal frame, the problem of the setting right of relationships, of what was emotionally as well as materially due, continually suggested the incomplete equation of suffering and recompense, and the affective instability of any settlement. The repetition and insistence of this frame of adequation across intimate and legal terrains suggests something of the pathos of lived experience, as well as of the modalities of modern state practice. Thus, rather than the historian adopting the problem of adequation as an intellectual disposition, this past thinking of the problem of adequation merits historical analysis.

From this perspective, while specific cases and their resolution do appear throughout the pages that follow, and with some reflection on their implications in people's lives, the focus of this work is on the problem of the adequacy of colonial law to Indian social life as a question that the colonial state, as well as emergent nationalists and their critics,

---

[84] Ann Laura Stoler, *Along the Archival Grain: Epistemic Anxieties and Colonial Common Sense* (Princeton, NJ: Princeton University Press, 2009), p. 45.

[85] See, for example, Elizabeth Kolsky, *Colonial Justice in British India: White Violence and the Rule of Law* (Cambridge: Cambridge University Press, 2010).

[86] Dipesh Chakrabarty has distinguished between "the subject of law" and "the subject of narratives," the former defined as a domain of legal rights and compensation and the latter as a domain of interiority and affect. While sympathetic to Chakrabarty's overarching project of locating spaces and forms of modernity that exceed or disrupt the global logics of capitalism and the liberal subject, this book suggests that such a distinction cannot be maintained, most importantly in that the forms of suffering and recompense that seek expression in literary narrative are likewise – and crucially – enfolded into the law. Dipesh Chakrabarty, "The Subject of Law and the Subject of Narratives," in *Habitations of Modernity*, 101–114.

continually posed and sought to resolve, and on the kinds of scrutiny as well as areas of obscurity that this form of questioning produced. Integral to such a study is a recognition of the ways in which colonial law itself gave new meanings to the existing forms of regulation, interpellation, and affinity that shaped social and familial life. The presence of colonial law recalibrated the significance of other modes of coercion; its justice resignified other visions of justice, and its operation suggested the possibilities of producing different kinds of subjects. These new visions formed the basis for nationalist appropriations, which claimed legitimacy for a law and a state that would both reflect and transform Indian society.

In addition, although this work highlights court cases and political campaigns that suggest something of women's agency in these transformations, the agency of women is not its primary focus. This is in part because especially in legal cases, it is impossible to know the situations and interests that produced women's legal action, as British and Indian patriarchal commentators were fond of asserting at the time. Yet it is also because this is not a history of feminist political action, but rather a study of the significance of women and the family for colonial and nationalist legal and political formations – a significance, the book suggests, that was not readily articulated or shaped by women until well into the twentieth century.

REGION, COLONY, AND NATION

This book illuminates this complex history of governing social life through an in-depth study of the colonial Bombay Presidency, a region in western India that comprised most of the contemporary states of Maharashtra and Gujarat, portions of contemporary Karnataka, the province of Sind, as well as (for administrative purposes) Aden in Yemen and the island of Zanzibar. Within this vast area, while it draws on evidence from throughout the regions of Gujarat, Karnataka, and Maharashtra, it attends especially to material drawn from the city of Bombay (now Mumbai) and from the Maharashtra cultural region, comprising a narrow littoral, the Konkan districts of Kolaba and Ratnagiri, and dry upland districts of the Deccan Plateau – Ahmednagar, Nasik, Khandesh, Pune, and Satara (see map). This region saw the rise in the seventeenth century of a peasant-warrior kingdom under the leadership of Shivaji Bhonsle. Shivaji both repeatedly engaged with and more famously challenged Mughal rule in the region, establishing a kingdom by rallying support for an emergent Maratha identity in opposition to external rule, grounded in

Marathi language, Maratha country or place, and the peasant-warrior lifestyle.[87] In the eighteenth century, de facto leadership of the kingdom passed to the ruler's Brahmin chief minister, or Peshwa. The Peshwa regime, which would become the most powerful successor state to the Mughal Empire, was distinctive in its expansion of Brahminical power to the domains of government, military, and financial administration.[88] This unusual rule "by, for, and of Brahmins" also involved the extraordinary regulation of caste boundaries, in particular through regulating the sexuality of Brahmin women.[89] Following the definitive colonial conquest of the region in 1818, from the second half of the nineteenth century, the region was also shaped by the increasing prominence of the city of Bombay, as the preeminent site of the emergence of an Indian industrial capitalist class, as well as of new forms of working-class and subaltern-caste politics.[90]

---

[87] Prachi Deshpande, *Creative Pasts: Historical Memory and Identity in Western India, 1700–1960* (New York: Columbia University Press, 2007; Stuart Gordon, *The Marathas, 1600–1818*, The New Cambridge History of India, II, 4 (Cambridge: Cambridge University Press, 1993).

[88] Ibid.; Hiroshi Fukazawa, *The Medieval Deccan: Peasants, Social Systems and States, Sixteenth to Eighteenth Centuries* (Delhi: Oxford University Press, 1991).

[89] Uma Chakravarti, "Wifehood, Widowhood and Adultery: Female Sexuality, Surveillance and the State in Eighteenth-Century Maharashtra," *Contributions to Indian Sociology*, n.s., 29, 1–2 (Jan. 1995): 3–21, also *Rewriting History*; Prachi Deshpande, "Caste as Maratha: Social Categories, Colonial Policy and Identity in Early Twentieth-Century Maharashtra," *Indian Economic and Social History Review* 41, 1 (Jan.–March 2004): 7–32; V. S. Kadam, "The Institution of Marriage and the Position of Women in Eighteenth-Century Maharashtra," *Indian Economic and Social History Review* 25, 3 (July–Sept. 1988): 341–370; Rosalind O'Hanlon, *Caste, Conflict, and Ideology: Mahatma Jotirao Phule and Low Caste Protest in Nineteenth-Century Western India* (Cambridge: Cambridge University Press, 1985); Rao, *The Caste Question*; Sharmila Rege, "The Hegemonic Appropriation of Sexuality: The Case of the Lavani Performers of Maharashtra," *Contributions to Indian Sociology*, n.s., 29, 1–2 (Jan. 1995): 23–38; N. K. Wagle, "Women in the Kotwal's Papers, Pune 1767–1791," in *Images of Women in Maharashtrian Society*, edited by Anne Feldhaus (Albany: State University of New York Press, 1998), pp. 15–60, and "The Government, the Jati, and the Individual: Rights, Discipline, and Control in the Pune Kotwal's Papers, 1766–1794," *Contributions to Indian Sociology* 34, 3 (Sept.–Dec. 2000): 321–360.

[90] Rajnarayan Chandavarkar, *The Origins of Industrial Capitalism in India: Business Strategies and the Working Classes in Bombay, 1900–1940* (Cambridge: Cambridge University Press, 1994), and *Imperial Power and Popular Politics: Class, Resistance, and the State in India, 1850–1950* (Cambridge: Cambridge University Press, 1998); Deshpande, *Creative Pasts*, chapters 5 and 7. Rao, *The Caste Question*, chapter 1; Ashwini Tambe, "Brothels as Families: Reflections on the History of Bombay's *Kothas*," *International Feminist Journal of Politics* 8, 2 (June 2006): 219–242. For a similar phenomenon in north India, see Nandini Gooptu, *The Politics of the Urban Poor in Early Twentieth-Century India* (Cambridge: Cambridge University Press, 2001), esp. chapter 6.

Several recent studies, including of Maharashtra, have explored the dialectical co-formation of region and nation.[91] This historical process took shape across several arenas. From the perspective of felt experience and identification, it occurred perhaps most critically through the burgeoning of vernacular public spheres that developed in multiple languages in the nineteenth century, which played a critical role in cultivating new religious politics and affective identifications, iconographies, and sensibilities of place. At an infrastructural level, however, it occurred through the institutions and practices of the colonial state, which linked region and colony at once materially and conceptually through the railways, the army, the bureaucratic structure of the colonial state, and the treatment of India as a unitary political economic whole made up of its regional parts.[92] Critical to this study, a similar logic structured the operation of the colonial courts and administration. Although there were some regional differences in the treatment of the source of law, as well as in administrative structures at the lower levels, in general parallel systems of courts were established across the provinces of British-ruled India. These developed their own sets of positive coordinates, standard and oft-repeated planks marking out the distinctive features of the law and custom in their region, which perforce referenced and recognized a broader generality of law applying to the whole. Thus similarly to these other infrastructural arenas, within the legal domain, each region was treated as unique in its particulars, and yet recognizably *of* a larger whole. This imbrication of the singular and the exemplary in the construction of region and nation was of course critical to larger nationalist projects. In this context, this study is interested in the regional instantiations of processes that occurred in one shape or another across British India and beyond, highlighting the regional formations of personhood, property, society, and politics, and their inevitable links to broader terrains.

PLAN OF THE BOOK

This book is divided into two parts: Part I examines the embedding of liberal political and political economic theory and new modes of

---

[91] Deshpande, *Creative Pasts*; Manu Goswami, *Producing India: From Colonial Economy to National Space* (Chicago: University of Chicago Press, 2004); Sartori, *Bengal in Global Concept History*.

[92] Deshpande, *Creative Pasts*; Goswami; *Producing India*; Veena Naregal, *Language Politics, Elites and the Public Sphere: Western India under Colonialism* (New Delhi: Permanent Black, 2001); Christopher Pinney, *'Photos of the Gods': The Printed Image and Political Struggle in India* (London: Reaktion Books, 2004).

governance within colonial law and administration. In Part II, the book shows how these liberal norms and dilemmas came to pervade colonial Hindu law, and how early reformist nationalists and those marginalized by mainstream nationalism in turn politicized the forms of personhood, value, and rights created by the operation of personal law.

Chapter 1 traces the redefinition of Indian property forms through the overlapping perspectives of political economy and jurisprudence. Centering on the early colonial treatment of land and hereditary offices, it highlights the early modes of apprehending, regulating, and transforming these property forms. Chapter 2 turns to mid- and late-nineteenth-century concerns with property as a broader problem of economic expansion and social progress. Focusing on the problems of rural credit and indebtedness, and on ongoing policy debates concerning hereditary offices, it examines colonial and Indian reformist efforts to supersede the oppressions of existing social relations and to analyze the effects of colonial capitalism and state policy on Indian society.

In Chapter 3, the focus turns directly to the joint Hindu family and its changing juridical meaning within Hindu personal law. This chapter examines in detail how key coordinates of liberal political and political economic thought came to pervade Hindu law. Chapter 4 traces how customs of Hindu marriage became the grounds for distinctive concerns with women's humanity that at once drew the regulation of women and girls more tightly to the state, and also became the basis for Indian reformist nationalist visions of a re-ethicized national Hindu society. Chapter 5 considers the politicization of the dominant nationalist vision of society and the state during the interwar period by Muslim, Dalit, and liberal feminist activists. Juxtaposing several case studies of community mobilization in the interwar era, the chapter examines how the law of inheritance became a critical site for the formation of new kinds of community and for their struggles for politico-legal recognition. It thus foreshadows the implications of the system of personal law for citizenship and equality in postcolonial India.

PART I

ECONOMIC GOVERNANCE

I

Property between Law and Political Economy

> There is nothing which so generally strikes the imagination, and engages the affections of mankind, as the right of property; or that sole and despotic dominion which one man claims and exercises over the external things of the world, in total exclusion of the right of any other individual in the universe; and yet there are very few that will give themselves the trouble to consider the original and foundation of this right.
>
> – William Blackstone, *Commentaries on the Laws of England*, 1765

Blackstone's musings on property, opening the second book of his expansive compendium on the English common law, drew his reader at once to property's multivalent qualities and to its strange opacity in everyday social life. In Blackstone's account, the generative nature of property – its connection to sovereignty, to the imagination, and to affect and desire, which animated each man in contradistinction to the totality of others – rendered it an object of enchantment that obscured its legal origins and significance. In this context, Blackstone highlighted property as a specifically *legal* relationship that fostered subjectivity and social relations, and one that required historical excavation to elucidate its foundations.

Blackstone's dual orientation at once toward the "magical" nature of property and toward its specific origins would become characteristic of early colonial engagements with Indian property forms. Yet by the early nineteenth century, in India as in Britain, a juridical focus on the origins of rights became entwined with emergent political economic theorizing on the intrinsic agency of property, which tended to recast the magic of property as a matter of universal human nature and of predictable expectations and outcomes – of the producible future rather than the legitimating past.[1] Law and political economy thus came to operate as dual dominant registers of colonial thought, conceptualizing property increasingly in secular terms as a question of rights on the one hand, and of value on the other. These registers produced both distinctive and overlapping models that utilized property to theorize the person as legal and economic subject.

Scholarship on the nature and effects of the colonial property regime has focused on the question of how the colonial state apprehended or transformed Indian property forms and broader social life.[2] This chapter proceeds instead from the recognition that a depiction of a precolonial Indian concept of property that truly diverged from the dominant Western formulation of property as a "bundle of rights" has yet to emerge, reminding us of the global reach of the historical forms through which we think of property's histories. From this perspective, although official opinions on how the colonial state should treat Indian property forms regularly

---

[1] Mary Poovey, *A History of the Modern Fact: Problems of Knowledge in the Sciences of Wealth and Society* (Chicago: University of Chicago Press, 1998).

[2] For the contours of this scholarly debate, see the work of C. A. Bayly; Bernard Cohn, *An Anthropologist among the Historians and Other Essays* (Delhi: Oxford University Press, 1987), and *Colonialism and Its Forms of Knowledge*; Dirks, *Castes of Mind*; Sumit Guha, *The Agrarian Economy of the Bombay Deccan, 1818–1941* (Delhi: Oxford University Press, 1985); Ravinder Kumar, *Western India in the Nineteenth Century: A Study in the Social History of Maharashtra* (London: Routledge & Kegan Paul, 1968); Metcalf, *Ideologies of the Raj*; Price, *Kingship and Political Practice*; Eric Stokes, *The English Utilitarians and India* (Oxford: Clarendon Press, 1959); Travers, *Ideology and Empire*; among others. This argument dates to the colonial era itself, as seen in the writings of Maine and Stephen, discussed in this book's Introduction, and also in Jotirao Phule, *Slavery: In the Civilized British Government, under Cloak of Brahminism* (Bombay: Government of Maharashtra Education Department, 1991). A generation of recent scholars has focused on the ironies of colonial misrecognition – the ways in which colonial translations of Indian lifeworlds inevitably failed to capture their meanings. However, what scholars have typically identified as the misrecognized features of Indian property – its nonabsolute, nonprivate character, and the multiple, layered, and partial claims that it bore – were also at least to some extent recognized as part of the English Common Law in Blackstone's time. Blackstone, *Commentaries on the Laws of England, Vol. II, The Laws of Things*. Moreover, these analyses reproduce the dominant Western formulation of property as "a bundle of rights," only in this case with the various "sticks" held by different owners. See, for example, Cohn, *An Anthropologist*, and *Colonialism and Its Forms of Knowledge*; Stephen Pierce, *Farmers and the State in Colonial Kano: Land Tenure and the Legal Imagination* (Bloomington: Indiana University Press, 2005); André Wink, *Land and Sovereignty in India: Agrarian Society and Politics under the Eighteenth-Century Maratha Svarajya* (Cambridge: Cambridge University Press, 1986). Indeed, attentiveness to the problems of misrecognition dates to the colonial era itself. See, for example, B. H. Baden-Powell, *The Land Systems of British India: Being a Manual of the Land-Tenures and of the Systems of Land-Revenue Administration Prevalent in the Several Provinces, Vol. III* (Oxford: Clarendon Press, 1892), pp. 217ff.

intertwined countervailing and seemingly contradictory ideological formations even at the level of individual thought, the assumptions of liberal political economy became increasingly mobile and pervasive. Indeed, the very centrality of the category (though not the everyday experience) of social life was itself an artifact of this process.[3]

The two parts of this chapter each examine an issue and property form that occasioned dense theorizing and critical policy formation during the early decades of British rule in the region, from 1818 to the early 1860s: the development of the colonial land revenue settlement, and the treatment of existing state revenue grants (*inam*), especially hereditary offices (*vatan*). These histories trace the various significations of what was recognized in British law as "real" property (land and offices) in early colonial law and practice, tracking how colonial administration worked toward resignifying these property forms, producing new models of how property linked to personhood, forged subjectivities, and operated within social life.

PART I: LAND AS AN OBJECT OF VALUE AND RIGHT: THE COLONIAL REVENUE SETTLEMENT

For nearly a century after the British East India Company's conquests in Bengal, the revenues of this commercial empire in India ironically derived largely from the taxation of land. In 1835, W. H. Sykes, former statistical reporter to the Bombay government, estimated that the land revenue accounted for some 82 percent of the Deccan's entire revenue.[4] Ideologically as well, the Company state drew on powerful British common law and "country" sensibilities, as well as on Mughal and pre-Mughal precedents, to focus on the role of land in generating the wealth of empires.[5] The foundational nature of land revenue to the Mughal Empire and to the post-Mughal successor states formed the basis for British claims that their own system of taxation on land followed

---

[3] This point concerning the contradictions in official thought is also made by Neeladri Bhattacharya, "Colonial State and Agrarian Society," in *The Making of Agrarian Policy in British India, 1770–1900*, edited by Burton Stein (Delhi: Oxford University Press, 1992), pp. 119–120; Guha, *Rule of Property*, 9–10; Travers, *Ideology and Empire*, 15; although none of them explores it in detail.

[4] This included small amounts collected through various government lands, quit-rents, fees, and extra cesses. W. H. Sykes, *Land Tenures of the Dekkan* (London: James Moyes, 1835), p. 13.

[5] Travers, *Ideology and Empire*, chapter 4; "'The Real Value of the Lands': The *Nawabs*, the British and the Land Tax in Eighteenth-Century Bengal," *Modern Asian Studies* 38, 3 (2004): 517–558.

from these earlier imperial forms. These forms, which derived from Arab and Central Asian precedents, were initially developed in the thirteenth and fourteenth centuries under Sultanate rule. These had been elaborated and extended by the Mughal emperor Akbar in the mid-sixteenth century, and they had placed exactions from the produce of land at the center of earlier imperial economies.[6] Historians have widely argued that the Mughal system developed complex forms and symbologies of property around the right to collect revenues from the land, and that the British, by rendering the land an object of private property, thereby transformed preexisting concepts of property, sovereignty, and value.[7] At the same time, scholars have argued that markets in a variety of tenancies dated to at least the eighteenth century.[8] The symbolic significance of land revenue and tenancies existed alongside, and at times hand in hand with, its exchangeability. Although the impact of the colonial revenue settlements on rural cultivators and agricultural society has formed one of the most persistent and unresolved subjects of historiographical debate, most historians have concluded that it led to the significant emiseration of vast numbers of cultivators, and some have further argued that it produced increasing socioeconomic stratification and the emergence and consolidation of a class of wealthy farmers.[9]

[6] For debates regarding the Mughal and post-Mughal land revenue system, see Irfan Habib, *The Agrarian System of Mughal India, 1556–1707* (London: Asia Publishing House, 1963); Tapan Raychaudhuri, "The Agrarian System of Mughal India: A Review Essay," in *The Mughal State, 1526–1750*, edited by Muzaffar Alam and Sanjay Subrahmanyam (Delhi: Oxford University Press, 1998), pp. 259–283; N. A. Siddiqi, *Land Revenue Administration under the Mughals, 1700–1750* (New York: Asia Publishing House, 1970); Wink, *Land and Sovereignty.*

[7] See Bernard Cohn, "Representing Authority in Victorian India," in *The Invention of Tradition*, edited by Eric Hobsbawm and Terence Ranger (Cambridge: Cambridge University Press, 1983), pp. 165–210; Nicholas Dirks, *The Hollow Crown: Ethnohistory of an Indian Kingdom*, Cambridge South Asian Studies (Cambridge: Cambridge University Press, 1987).; Guha, *Rule of Property*; Kumar, *Western India*; Sudipta Sen, *Empire of Free Trade: The East India Company and the Making of the Colonial Marketplace* (Philadelphia: University of Pennsylvania Press, 1998); Wink, *Land and Sovereignty.*

[8] Sumit Guha, "Weak States and Strong Markets in South Asian Development, c. 1700–1970," *Indian Economic and Social History Review*, Special Issue on Markets in History: Concepts and Outcomes of Commercialization in South Asia, edited by Jairus Banaji and Tirthankar Roy, 36, 3 (1999): 335–353, and "Society and Economy in the Deccan, 1818–1850," in Stein, ed., *Making of Agrarian Policy*, 187–214; Travers, "'The Real Value of the Lands.'"

[9] Kumar, *Western India*; Neil Charlesworth, "Rich Peasants and Poor Peasants in Late-Nineteenth Century Maharashtra," in *The Imperial Impact: Studies in the Economic History of Africa and India*, edited by Clive Dewey and A. G. Hopkins (London: Athlone Press for the Institute of Commonwealth Studies, 1978), pp. 97–113, and "The Russian Stratification Debate and India," *Modern Asian Studies* 13, 1 (1979): 61–95.

The extensive colonial engagement with the revenue settlement also had other effects. It rendered questions of property rights and sovereignty inseparable from determinations of land as an object of economic value. At the same time, it also recalibrated earlier perspectives that construed antiquity and status as the source of both value and rights, illuminating instead the magic of political economy in producing value. This new political economic discourse preserved the social as a locus of relations of status and hierarchy, while it also construed the social as the arena par excellence of market relations, relations which themselves at once enacted universal human nature and remained susceptible to human intervention, not least by the state.

The Special Character of Land

During the late eighteenth and early nineteenth centuries, major strands of both political economy and law emphasized the special nature of land as a property form. In the arena of law, Blackstone's mid-eighteenth-century *Commentaries on the Laws of England* attested to the centrality of landed property within the British common law tradition, devoting some three-quarters of the volume *The Rights of Things* to the discussion of the nature of real (immovable) property, particularly property in land. In contrast, as David Lieberman has noted, Blackstone's attention to commercial law was slight. Although Blackstone saw the English as a "commercial nation," according to Lieberman, he viewed the law of real property as the appropriate basis for deriving an emergent law of commerce.[10] Similarly, something of the special quality of land as a property form also animated contemporary country Whig and classical republican ideology, whose proponents viewed it as the very precondition for virtuous citizenship in the face of challenges from commercial men.[11] In British India, as in Britain, the judicial administration throughout this era assiduously maintained the distinction between real and personal property, drawing as well on medieval Hindu textual commentaries and on ethnographic evidence.

Alongside this juridical theorizing on land as the quintessential object of rights, in the young field of political economy the French physiocrats,

[10] David Lieberman, "Property, Commerce, and the Common Law: Attitudes to Legal Change in the Eighteenth Century," in *Early Modern Conceptions of Property*, edited by John Brewer and Susan Staves (London: Routledge, 1995), pp. 144–158.

[11] J. G. A. Pocock, "The Mobility of Property and the Rise of Eighteenth-Century Sociology," in *Virtue, Commerce, History*, 103–124; Pincus, "Neither Machiavellian Moment."

whose thinking about capitalist agriculture was so central to early
colonial policy in Bengal, remained wedded in key ways to earlier economic thinking in which value was understood as an inherent quality of
particular objects such as land or precious metals.[12] Although the physiocrats emphasized the centrality of labor and capital to the production
of surplus value, they nonetheless conceptualized land as the source of all
value and the key to national wealth. As Henry Pattullo expressed in his
apocalyptic 1772 treatise, *Essay upon the Cultivation of the Lands, and
the Amelioration of the Revenues of Bengal*,

Lands and agriculture are the subsistence of all ranks, and the source of all revenues. Their produce are the only real riches. Without their regular reproduction,
all other riches can be of no value. Banks and bankers might shut up, or even
might lye open. Their treasures can neither feed nor clothe. The rarest of jewels
would appear bubbles of folly; high and low would be brought upon a level, and
the world would soon be at an end.[13]

It was in opposition to such conceptualizations of value as inherent to
particular objects – which characterized both mercantilism and physi-
ocracy – that Adam Smith had argued that labor and the operation
of markets, not the intrinsic nature of objects, produced the wealth of
nations, a formulation that Marx later drew on for his own labor theory of value.[14] Smith, and in the early-nineteenth-century David Ricardo,
developed detailed formulations of the nature of agricultural production, the role of markets, and the way in which agriculture generated
profits for the capitalist farmer and rent for the landlord. Yet even this
focus on the role of labor in generating value did not entirely supersede
a conceptualization of the special nature of land. Thus, in *The Wealth of
Nations*, although Smith recognized that land varied in fertility and situation, he argued that virtually all land naturally produces food whose
value exceeds the costs of the inputs of labor and capital, and thus always
generates a rent for the landlord.[15] Although Ricardo refuted this thesis,

[12] Guha, *Rule of Property*.
[13] Henry Pattullo, *An Essay upon the Cultivation of the Lands, and the Amelioration of the
Revenues of Bengal* (London, 1772), p. 24, cited in ibid., 42.
[14] Fernando Coronil, *The Magical State: Nature, Money, and Modernity in Venezuela*
(Chicago: University of Chicago Press, 1997), pp. 30–34.
[15] Adam Smith, *An Inquiry into the Nature and Causes of the Wealth of Nations* (1776;
reprint, the Modern Library edition, edited, with an introduction and notes by Edwin
Cannan, introduction by Max Lerner, New York: Random House, 1937), Book I, chapter
XI, "Of the Rent of Land," Part I: On the Produce of Land Which Always Affords Rent,
pp. 146–161.

his theory of surplus value – the idea that rent existed as pure profit (the "unearned increment") for the landlord that did not affect the costs of production – continued to suggest something of the magical quality of land, despite his explicit theorizing to the contrary.

These layered theorizations on the special nature of land even within a capitalist theory of agricultural production found resonance within colonial policy debates and took shape within the colonial administration.[16] In the Bombay Presidency, efforts to determine the nature of regional property forms date to the years following the definitive British conquest of the Maratha/Peshwa regime and the assumption of power in 1818. These efforts sought to ascertain the basis for legitimate claims to property as well as the defining features of existing property forms. An initial inquiry into property in the Deccan opened with the following questions: "Is the actual possessor the absolute master of his property[;] can he of what so *ever sort it may be* give, sell, or will it away? Is the Consent of the immediate Heir or Heirs requisite before such property can be disposed of or alienated? ... Does a person acquire a right to Property by possessing it for a certain number of years, if so, how many years of possession is requisite to form a Prescriptive Right?"[17] These queries, reflecting British emphases on autonomy, alienability, and possession as critical dimensions of property, explicitly placed property within a comparative ethnographic frame, but they also pointed to uncertainties concerning the translatability of a Blackstonean model of property. The questionnaire itself involved a wide-ranging inquiry, turning from these issues to the nature of property held by religious institutions, women's capacity for property, and the treatment of property of uncertain owner, such as discovered treasure, among other issues.[18]

The Bombay officials who traced contemporary forms of property in land reanimated earlier debates in Bengal concerning the divergent foundations of property.[19] As in those earlier debates, despite continual reference to the evidence of "Muslim" or "pre-Muslim" forms, the

---

[16] Guha, *Rule of Property*.

[17] MSA, Pune, Marathi Daftar, Deccan Commissioner's Files, Rumal No. 136, Loose Papers (no date; probably 1818–1826 based on other papers in same collection). Questions posed by Mr. Thackeray, Collector of the Southern Maratha Country, probably to pandits or other local authorities (replies not included). Emphasis in original (unpaginated).

[18] These queries reflected an underlying comparison with such provisions in the common law. See Blackstone, *Commentaries*, Vol. I, *The Laws of Persons*, 290–299.

[19] Thus, compare the discussion that follows in this section with the debates among Hastings, Francis, Dow, and others in Guha, *Rule of Property*, and Travers, *Ideology and Empire*.

underlying reference of these official queries and positions was to competing European social contract theories and to the history of British agriculture, with colonial officials attempting to translate or assimilate Indian into English, Scots, or Irish histories.[20] Furthermore, as in British law, where antiquity of title formed a key criterion of rights, and one that had only relatively recently begun to be challenged by liberal and Utilitarian ideas of rights grounded in effective use,[21] each of the district collectors who submitted evidence to Mountstuart Elphinstone when he served as Deccan commissioner speculated on the antiquity and origins of the primary property forms as a central legitimating feature thereof.[22]

Most pointedly, officials debated whether within Indian political traditions property preceded the state (e.g., it was created by occupancy or cultivation), or whether conquest lodged all property rights in the sovereign. Answering this question became critical both to the colonial legitimation of the revenue settlement and to determining its specific form.

Beginning in the era of Warren Hastings and the early Company state, two opposing theories of the nature of property in India had shaped colonial policy. The official Company position drew on a long lineage of European travel writings, most notably François Bernier's seventeenth-century *Travels in the Mogul Empire*, to argue that traditionally in India all land belonged to the sovereign, as an integral feature of the "despotic" character of Asiatic governments.[23] Warren Hastings thus claimed

[20] The British referents of colonial land and land revenue policy have long been noted – see, for example, Guha, *Rule of Property*; Travers, *Ideology and Empire*, chapter 4. These debates also reflected a much longer European history of theorizing on the nature and origin of property, dating to medieval thinkers who had drawn upon the history of Roman law to formulate a theory of natural rights; Tuck, *Natural Rights Theories*.

[21] Although more fully developed by the Utilitarians, the Lockean notion that a right to property emerges from the application of labor to the natural environment involved an early formulation of this idea. See also Peck, "Kingship, Counsel and Law" for an exceptional early example of this logic.

[22] See Letters of Captain Briggs, Political Agent at Khandesh; Captain Pottinger, Provisional Collector of Ahmednagar; Captain Grant, Political Agent at Satara; Captain Macleod, Assistant Collector of Pune; in Mountstuart Elphinstone, *Report on the Territories Conquered from the Paishwa* (Calcutta: A. G. Balfour, Government Gazette Press, 1821; reprinted as *Territories Conquered from the Paishwa, A Report*, with introduction by J. C. Srivastava, Delhi: Oriental Publishers, 1973), appendix. For scholarship on antiquity as creating legitimacy, see Sumit Guha, "Wrongs and Rights in the Maratha Country: Antiquity, Custom and Power in Eighteenth-Century India," in *Changing Concepts of Rights and Justice in South Asia*, edited by Michael R. Anderson and Sumit Guha (Delhi: Oxford University Press, 1998), pp. 14–29; Travers, *Ideology and Empire*, 8–9, 154.

[23] François Bernier, *Travels in the Mogul Empire, A.D. 1656–1668*, translated and annotated by Archibald Constable, 2nd ed., revised by Vincent A. Smith (Delhi: Low Price Publications, 1989), pp. 163–167. See discussions in Guha, *Rule of Property* and Travers, *Ideology and Empire*.

that the British colonial state was following Mughal precedent in asserting the state as universal landlord, whose grants, or *sanads*, bestowed subordinate and conditional landholding rights on regional and local lords and peasants.[24] In opposition to this view, however, others, such as Philip Francis, Hastings's nemesis and member of his governing council, argued that the Mughal state had always recognized the private property rights of a native aristocracy. Francis's argument that permission of the Mughal emperor for the inheritance of estates constituted nothing more than a "feudal fiction," which the emperor in practice never abridged, implicitly placed the Mughal emperor within a British common law tradition. In other words, the king ultimately held dominion over all the lands of his kingdom, but this right was never asserted against the holders of freehold estates.[25] The right of inheritance thus served as a key marker of the existence of private property and of the limits of state power. It constituted the quintessential individual right as well as societal right against the state.

The debate among officials in early-nineteenth-century Bombay highlighted the uncertain legal relationship among British, Mughal, pre-Mughal, or post-Mughal forms of property.[26] At the village level, colonial ethnography construed the primary and privileged village agricultural tenure as *miras*, from the Arabic *mirashi*, meaning inheritance or patrimony.[27] Yet the nature of this holding remained a subject of

---

[24] See discussion in Guha, *Rule of Property*, 100–102.

[25] Blackstone, *Commentaries, Vol. II, The Laws of Things*, 51, 53, 105. See discussions in Guha, *Rule of Property*, 103ff.; Travers, *Ideology and Empire*, 168. For the early modern ideological expansion of English/British state power, see Armitage, *The Ideological Origins of the British Empire*, 90–99 and chapter 4; Peck, "Kingship, Counsel and Law," 91–93, 102–113.

[26] A number of officials (including Elphinstone, Robertson, and Sykes) emphasized the evidence of what they termed "pre-Muslim" forms left largely untouched by later conquest regimes. Nonetheless, the regional property forms they encountered bore the strong imprint of the administration of the Sultanates that ruled the region from the fourteenth century, followed by that of the Mughals from the seventeenth century. Hiroshi Fukazawa, *The Medieval Decca*; Frank Perlin, "Of White Whale and Countrymen in the Eighteenth-Century Maratha Deccan: Extended Class Relations, Rights, and the Problem of Rural Autonomy under the Old Regime," *Journal of Peasant Studies* 5, 2 (1978): 172–237.

[27] The other major category of agricultural cultivator, which was regularly contrasted with *mirasdars*, was known as *upris*, literally "strangers," who typically cultivated lands on a short-term lease, called an *ukti* lease, in which they agreed to an assessment for a single year, potentially renegotiating the amount year by year. According to all accounts, the respective rights and tenures of *mirasdars* and *upris* were also clear: Whereas *mirasdars* were privileged holders who had a voice within village affairs, *upris* were weak tenants who did not. However, in a variety of circumstances, the *upris* of one village might in fact be the *mirasdars* of another.

controversy. H. D. Robertson, the collector of Pune, construed *mirasdars* as essentially yeomen farmers – farmer-cultivators with freehold property in their lands.[28] In contrast, when Commissioner of the Deccan William Chaplin wrote his 1822 *Report Exhibiting a View of the Fiscal and Judicial System of Administration Introduced into the Conquered Territory above the Ghauts*, he moved from the problem of the origins of *miras* in time immemorial to a theory of the origins of the state as universal landlord, and in fact also to a labor theory of value:

This was doubtless the original foundation of all landed property. But subsequent conquest and the revolution of centuries must often have caused it to change hands, and confounded all original titles. Hence property in the soil became at length vested in the Sovereign power; but as the state could derive no benefit from land, till it had acquired a value through labour, an enlightened ruler would see the advantage of allowing the labourer to enjoy a permanent interest, without which there could be no incentive to improve it. To this sense of mutual interest between the Government and the Peasant, we may ascribe the revival of landed property, rather than to any positive institution of it, which we may search for in vain in the history of Indian Government.[29]

In this narrative, the natural laws of political economy were woven into the history of regional property forms, despite the shortcomings attributed to previous Indian governments. Moreover, Chaplin's account provided for dual origins: This was at once a form of property that preceded the dominion of the state, and it was also returned to the peasant in a more secure version of that original form through the joint interests of the peasant and the state. Such an account ultimately supported rather than negated "the allodial right of the Prince in the Soil."[30] In this speculative historical narrative, sovereignty, by creating property as a protected right, established the critical conditions that enabled labor to establish value. Moreover, such a convergence or intertwining of historical ethnography and political

---

[28] Chaplin derided H. D. Robertson's support for the idea of pre-Muslim origins of this tenurial form. See William Chaplin, *Report Exhibiting a View of the Fiscal and Judicial System of Administration, Introduced into the Conquered Territory above the Ghauts, under the Authority of the Commissioner in the Dekhan* (reprint, Bombay: Government Society Press, 1838; orig., Bombay: Courier Office, 1824), para. 137. Nonetheless, such depictions would continue to exert considerable power throughout the century, most notably in the aftermath of the Deccan Riots and the passage of the Deccan Agriculturalists' Relief Act, discussed in Chapter 2.

[29] Chaplin, *Report Exhibiting*, para. 108 (p. 34).

[30] Chaplin, *Report Exhibiting*, para. 144. This position seems to have held sway with Governor-General Mountstuart Elphinstone, who characterized *miras* property as "hereditary and saleable," but nonetheless as merely a hereditary occupancy claim, with ultimate dominion residing in the state. Elphinstone, *Report on the Territories*, 24.

economy in some sense exemplified the broader pattern of colonial debate and practice on the question of property during this era: an emphasis on preserving existing property forms was joined (albeit unevenly) with an effort to place them within the framework of liberal political economy.[31]

The Bombay government saw itself as essentially preserving these historical tenures intact; nonetheless, it did attempt to modify their value. *Mirasi* claims were highly esteemed; they were typically taxed at the full rate of assessment, and they were treated as inviolable as long as the *mirasdar* paid the government revenue. Even in cases where the *mirasdar* had mortgaged or deserted the land for long periods, he could typically recover it on payment of the mortgage or assessment. Nevertheless, the fact that there was little market for *miras* lands in the early nineteenth century, despite the symbolic value associated with such holdings, led to state efforts to enhance their marketability by limiting the letting out of village wastelands on more favorable leases, as well as by rendering *mirasi* lands subject to attachment for the repayment of debts, thereby facilitating their commoditization.[32]

Most important, however, the state sought to enhance the value of *miras* lands through the land revenue assessment. Under Sultanate, Mughal, and Maratha/Peshwa regimes the land revenue survey and settlement both presumed and produced particular relations of property. The same was true under the British. The effects of the revenue settlement on the social relations of property had formed one of the primary lessons of the Permanent Settlement of Bengal enacted by Governor-General Lord Cornwallis in 1793,[33] and it was with the Bengal example in mind that officials sought to devise an appropriate revenue settlement in Bombay.

---

[31] Both Ranajit Guha and Travers make similar observations. See Guha, *Rule of Property*, 103–109; Travers, *Ideology and Empire*, chapter 4. For a somewhat different narrative concerning the nature and origin of this property form, and one that changed over time, see W. H. Sykes, *Land Tenures of the Dekkan* (London: James Moyes, 1835), 1–4, 10, and *Special Report on the Statistics of the Four Collectorates of the Dukhun, under the British Government* (London: Richard & John E. Taylor, 1838), 280.

[32] Chaplin asserted that the sale of *miras* land "when it does occur, does not fetch much money, except where it has been greatly improved." He argued, too, that the "circumstance of it's [*sic*] being so little a marketable commodity, notwithstanding the many advantages of the tenure, proves that the assessment is usually so high as to leave but a small residue to the proprietor.... My enquiries lead me to think it does not average more than two or three [years' purchase]." Chaplin, *Report Exhibiting*, paras. 122–123.

[33] Baden-Powell emphasized the lack of scientific or empirical investigation in the Bengal Permanent Settlement, but these would form prominent features of the Bombay Settlement. B. H. Baden-Powell, *A Short Account of the Land Revenue and Its Administration; with a Sketch of the Land Tenures* (Oxford: Clarendon Press, 1894), pp. 247ff.

Political Economy and the Conundrums of Local Knowledge

By the time of the conquest of western India, the Permanent Settlement of Bengal was already notorious for enacting a revolution in landholding in that region.[34] In response, in the Bombay Presidency, as in the bulk of the Madras region, the Company state put into place a revenue system based on direct settlement with peasant-holders, or *ryots*, known as the ryotwari settlement.[35] Whereas Cornwallis's Permanent Settlement established the *zamindars* – regional lords who under the Mughals had collected revenue from particular territories on behalf of the state – as the owners of the land, the ryotwari settlement (as well as later settlements in northern and northwestern regions that operated at the level of the male lineage, or *biradari*), retained the "Asiatic" principle of the state as universal landlord. Nevertheless, as Eric Stokes has argued, the early ryotwari settlements also aimed to establish private property in land, held primarily at the level of the cultivator-farmer, with ultimate proprietary right reserved for the state, much along the lines of English freehold property.[36] The state's claim to the position of universal landlord was thus ultimately

---

[34] The extent of the transformation has been a major subject of historiographical dispute and revision, however, dating from the era of the institution of the Permanent Settlement itself. Baden-Powell, *Land Systems of British India*, 207–210; Guha, *Rule of Property*; Sirajul Islam, *The Permanent Settlement in Bengal: A Study of Its Operation, 1790–1819* (Dacca: Bangla Academy, 1979); Harasankar Bhattacharyya, *Zamindars and Patnidars: Study of Subinfeudation under Permanent Settlement* (Burdwan: University of Burdwan, 1985). Despite these effects, the government of India did not fully repudiate Permanent Settlement as the basis for the colonial land revenue until 1871, and it was only "laid to rest" by the secretary of state in 1882. Stokes, *English Utilitarians*, 83–87, 118. Moreover, in western India in the 1870s and 1880s, Indian liberals such as M. G. Ranade would seek to resuscitate it in modified form to establish greater property rights in land for Bombay cultivators. M. G. Ranade, "Mr. Wedderburn and His Critics on a Permanent Settlement for the Deccan," in *Ranade's Economic Writings*, edited by Bipan Chandra (New Delhi: Gian Publishing House, 1990), pp. 80–97. Ranade also critiqued in liberal terms the Bengal Tenancy Act (Act VIII of 1885), which sought to redress the legal vulnerability of the *ryots* produced by the Permanent Settlement, arguing that it discouraged the growth of private property rights, trampled the property rights of *zamindars*, and entrenched feudal relationships. Ranade preferred instead a plan by which the *ryots* would gradually purchase their holdings from the *zamindars*, cultivating qualities of thrift and independence, and thereby become landowners in their own right. M. G. Ranade, "Prussian Land Legislation and the Bengal Tenancy Bill," in *Ranade's Economic Writings*, 212–236.

[35] Dirks argues that this represented less an acknowledgment of different preexisting systems of land tenure in the region than an effort to use custom to provide a justification for what was really an attempt to bring the state machinery more deeply to the level of the individual cultivator. Dirks, *Castes of Mind*, 113–116.

[36] Stokes, *English Utilitarians*, 83–87.

quite compatible with a powerful strain of official opinion that sought to recast local cultivators as yeoman farmers on the English model.[37]

This model was ultimately undermined, however, in the knitting together of such theories of property with the theory of political economy. The works of Ricardo, which defined the landlord's right to the "unearned increment" as a right to the total surplus beyond the factors of production (subsistence for the cultivators and capital inputs), proved particularly significant when linked to the conceptualization of the state as the universal landlord. Such a landlord was thus entitled to – although it might not claim – the full rent of the land.[38] James Mill, as assistant examiner from 1819 for the East India Company in London (and examiner from 1830), adopted this analysis, and staunchly supported the state's claim to the full rent as the proper basis for setting its revenue demand.[39] Indeed, this position was highly influential among officials at all levels of the Company bureaucracy: The arguments and rhetoric of liberal political economy pervaded the communications among assistant district collectors, district collectors, revenue commissioners, and the Bombay government. Thus, Ricardian rent theory has rightly formed a subject of considerable scholarly scrutiny, particularly for the effects it had on the setting of revenue assessments at severely exorbitant rates during this era.[40] Yet it also merits attention as a theory of the way that land (or more pointedly, the labor upon it) produces value for the state. In other words, the productive powers of land and labor automatically accrued to the state, forging the wealth of empires. In this sense, a juridical theory of state right undergirded the operation

---

[37] Stokes, *English Utilitarians*, 122*ff.*, and "The Land Revenue Systems of the North-Western Provinces and Bombay Deccan 1830–1880: Ideology and the Official Mind," in Stein, ed., *Making of Agrarian Policy*, 84–112. Stokes also noted that the Bombay government was virtually unique in claiming uncultivated wastelands as the property of the state rather than belonging to the village community, with the state retaining the right to set the terms of leases for its cultivation. Stokes, *English Utilitarians*, 107. See the arguments put forward to support these claims in Chaplin, *Report Exhibiting*, para. 144.

[38] Stokes, *English Utilitarians*, 87–93, and "Land Revenue Systems," 86–87. See the latter for a revised assessment of his earlier claims on the dominance of rent theory, showing it as more uncertain, as facing challenges from within, and as at times a rhetorical cover for very different government policies in practice.

[39] Ibid.

[40] In addition to Stokes, see Guha, *Agrarian Economy*; Neeraj Hatekar, "Information and Incentives: Pringle's Ricardian Experiment in the Nineteenth Century Deccan," *Indian Economic and Social History Review* 33, 4 (1996): 437–457; Meera Singh, *British Revenue and Judicial Policies in India: A Case Study of Deccan (1818–1826)* (New Delhi: Har-Anand Publications, 1994).

of economic laws, again entwining the legal relations of property with the generation of wealth.

Despite the early official turmoil in grounding the nature and legitimacy of the state's revenue claim, by the late 1830s or 1840s, questions of the theoretical or customary rights between the state and the peasants were treated as essentially settled, and the land revenue assessment became largely a question of accurate calculation. This outcome was to some extent unintended, however: It occurred through a confrontation with the problems of local knowledge and the resignification thereof.

Initially, British officials in the Deccan had contemplated relying on the revenue assessments that had prevailed during the Peshwa regime as the basis for the colonial assessment. Two types of survey, known as *kamal* and *rivaj*, had set different rates in the eighteenth century, with *kamal* signifying the "standard," or a theoretical, rate of assessment, and *rivaj* the customary assessment. In addition, in some places, the *tankha* rate, which had been established in areas under Malik Ambar's administration in the early seventeenth century, and which amounted to a fixed proportion of one-third of the gross produce, prevailed. Yet because of the widespread turmoil of the late eighteenth century, colonial officials deemed these various rates and the actual collections during these years an unreliable measure of the actual productivity of the land and the rate of assessment it could bear. Thus, despite their divergent views on the historical nature of property and right, Deccan Commissioner Chaplin and most of the district collectors supported a colonial revenue survey of the Deccan, which they thought of as a means of collecting information that would enable them to reestablish a locally legitimate system of revenue settlement on correct terms.[41]

In 1825, Robert Keith Pringle, who had been assistant collector to Robertson at Pune, and who had gained the confidence of Chaplin for his work in the Indapur *taluk* (division), was appointed to conduct a survey of the Deccan.[42] Pringle, who had been a student of Thomas Malthus at Haileybury and who had become strongly influenced by the Ricardian theory of rent, emphasized determining the differential qualities of land, which Ricardo had posited as the foundation of rent. Rent, Ricardo had argued, consisted in the differential in the value that could be generated from all land that exceeded the poorest quality.[43] Pringle's survey, which

---

[41] Singh, *British Revenue and Judicial Policies*, 93–96; Elphinstone, *Report on the Territories*, appendix.

[42] Singh, *British Revenue and Judicial Policies in India*, pp. 96–98; Hatekar, "Information and Incentives," 439.

[43] Stokes, *English Utilitarians*, 88.

was conducted between 1826 and 1828, focused on minute calculations of soil quality, productivity, and the net produce. Thus, although the collectors and the commissioner aimed to merely set the preexisting revenue institutions on proper footing, the colonial survey was welded to new forms of knowledge production, as the development of scientific techniques of soil assessment, cadastral surveying, and historical statistical analysis became integral to the process of determining potential agricultural productivity and setting the revenue demand.[44]

Thus, while Bombay officials were among the most committed to preserving precolonial systems intact, Pringle's revenue assessment embodied one of the most orthodox surveys throughout British India, hewing as closely as possible to the dictates of political economy. Almost immediately after it was completed, however, Pringle's assessment was considered a failure – a judgment that has not changed with the passage of time. Coming into effect in some districts in 1829 to 1830 and in others in 1830 to 1831, cultivators abandoned their villages on a large scale. In the words of a later administrative report, "The country was exhausted and deserted."[45] All that remained was "ruined."[46] In the aftermath of Pringle's experiment, the Bombay government was alone among the British territories in abandoning completely the principle of assessing revenue according to theoretical principles, in favor of rough calculations based on what the land had customarily been able to sustain.[47]

In enacting this change of direction, H. E. Wingate and George Goldsmid were appointed in 1836 to develop a new survey and settlement, which at the time was (and since has been) contrasted with Pringle's as based solely on empirical determinations rather than on the theoretical claims of political economy.[48] Nevertheless, as Stokes has argued, Ricardian rent theory remained the dominant way of conceptualizing the revenue settlements throughout the nineteenth century, even in Bombay. According to Stokes, despite the explicit abandonment of the theoretical principles of political economy as a matter of policy, Wingate repeatedly depicted his

---

[44] Kumar, *Western India* focuses on the abandonment and loss of earlier forms. Dirks, *Castes of Mind* attends to the production of new colonial knowledges as integral to the process of governance.

[45] Government of Bombay, *Gazetteer of the Bombay Presidency, Poona District*, Vol. 18, part 2 (hereafter *Poona Gazetteers*) (Bombay: Government Central Press, 1885; reprint, Pune: Government Photozincographic Press, 1992), p. 401; drawing from Bombay Government Revenue Record 666 of 1835.

[46] Letter of J. D. Bellassis to G. Wingate, January 26, 1839, MSA, RD 1840, 114/1198, quoted in Kumar, *Western India*, 111.

[47] Stokes, *English Utilitarians*, 103–107, 122–123; and "Land Revenue Systems," 88.

[48] Stokes, *English Utilitarians*, 104.

efforts as adhering to the Ricardian theory of rent.[49] Indeed, the element
that is often cited as characteristic of Wingate and Goldsmid's survey –
minute classification of soil types – had also formed the distinctive feature of Pringle's earlier survey, and derived from Ricardian attentiveness
to the differential quality of the soil as the basis for any calculation of
net produce.

In this process, complex precolonial systems of measuring and categorizing the land were utilized unevenly. The colonial surveys of both
Pringle and his successors retained many of the existing local categories and terms, although at times with different meanings and as part
of different ordering systems.[50] In the words of Goldsmid, Wingate, and
Davidson, authors of the revenue settlement that ultimately operated for
much of the nineteenth century, "There are numerous varieties of soil,
known amongst cultivators by peculiar characteristics and distinguishing names; but as many of these differ little, if at all, in fertility, and our
classification has reference to the latter consideration alone, it would be
out of place to notice in it anything beyond the mere question of value."[51]
In this frank exclusive focus on "value," value itself was construed as a
matter of definitive calculation, reducible to a question of quantifiable
productivity. Such a conceptualization of value dispensed with experiential knowledge of the soils, as well as with other facets that shaped
the terms of local valuation, in an attempt to establish value as a stable,
universalizable measure. Goldsmid and Wingate's thirty-year assessment
came into operation in most places in the late 1840s and early 1850s, and
despite the continued severity of rural poverty, the assessment was considered a success by the colonial power, and Wingate was involved in the
revisions to the assessments in the 1870s and 1880s.

The turn to empirical measures in Goldsmid and Wingate's settlement
also effectively shifted the valorization of knowledge from one form of
local knowledge to another. From a desire for authentic customary local
knowledge, such as Robertson and Chaplin had sought, the revenue

[49] Ibid., 103–107, 122–127.
[50] The categorization of land as "wet," "dry," or "garden" land, and distinctions concerning
    access to water (e.g., irrigation, wells, rainfall) and the like were retained, as in some ways,
    were the concepts of the measured field, or *bigha*, and of the survey number, although
    these latter terms were used to refer to multiple ways of measuring or demarcating land.
    See Baden-Powell, *Short Account*, 213.
[51] H. E. Goldsmid, G. Wingate, D. Davidson, *Selections from the Records of the Bombay
    Government Papers of the Joint Report of 1847*, No. DXXXII, n.s., "Measurement and
    Classification Rules of the Deccan Gujarat, Konkan and Kanara Surveys" (Nagpur:
    Government Press, 1975), p. 11.

survey both under Pringle and under Goldsmid and Wingate turned to a search for the local specifics of universal knowledge (e.g., annual rainfall, soil depths), or for local knowledge largely shorn of cultural significance (e.g., forms of irrigation, standard crops, average yields, and so forth).

This shift was at once epistemological and pragmatic. Alongside the debates over the proper intellectual basis for the assessment, this shift to a large extent reflected a colonial effort to overcome their dependence on local village officials, district officers, and other Indian intermediaries, whose venality, dishonesty, and corruption had long formed an integral part of administrative discourse and whom British officials blamed for the widespread inaccuracies that led to the failure of Pringle's assessment. The pervasive colonial emphasis on the untrustworthiness of "native officers" and their role in widespread defalcation and falsification of accounts became integral to the development of a land revenue policy that many colonial officials viewed as simultaneously protecting the cultivators and securing the state its due. In the words of Deccan Commissioner Chaplin regarding the district officers [*deshmukhs* and *deshpandés*], "It has long, and I believe pretty universally, been found that the services which these Officers are capable of rendering to the state, do not in any degree compensate for the abuses which almost invariably arise from their mismanagement and malversation."[52] Chaplin further quoted with approbation the findings of the Ahmednagar revenue collector, Captain Pottinger, to the effect that "the only object of these persons was to plunder both Government and the Ryut."[53]

Such official depictions were widespread.[54] Sumit Guha has highlighted the role that this rhetoric of Indian perfidy played in shaping colonial administrative policies, linking it to broader colonial efforts

[52] Chaplin, *Report Exhibiting*, para. 180.
[53] Ibid.
[54] The narrative they produced has also shaped historical analysis in a variety of ways. Thus, Ravinder Kumar's important study of the colonial Deccan to some extent confirms the colonial analysis, arguing that at the village level local officials and prosperous landholders colluded to shift the burden of the revenue assessment onto the backs of the marginal cultivators. This was also the official narrative. Kumar, *Western India*, 108–111. In addition to Kumar's account thereof, see *Poona Gazetteers*, 401–410. Similarly, in a recent article, Neeraj Hatekar suggests that superior cultivators bribed local officials, but as a rational response to their loss of an earlier informational advantage that had benefited them under the precolonial settlements. Hatekar, "Information and Incentives." Nevertheless, one of Hatekar's main goals is to refute Kumar's claims that the precolonial distribution of the land revenue was largely equitable and based on collective responsibility, and that the colonial system removed such collective responsibility, thus opening the way for bribery and a widening differentiation of wealthy from marginal cultivators.

to delegitimize and undermine Indian authorities, and hence to colonial racism and domination. What bears further analysis, however, is the way in which this derogatory rhetoric construed the challenges of the colonial land revenue administration as fundamentally a problem of information. As such, it charged supposedly dishonest Indian personnel with preventing the colonial power from acquiring the empirical data necessary to set the revenue assessment on just and moderate terms.[55] This disciplinary emphasis on empirical and numerical data unseated both the earlier focus on ethnographic narratives of customary rights as well as the utility of local knowledge.[56] This was in no sense natural or inevitable. As John Brewer has characterized the late-eighteenth-century English context, tax collecting in this era "focused to an unusual degree on the routines of quantification."[57] In this modality, physical data became construed as universal knowledge distinct from and oppositional to cultural or local knowledge.

These new forms of universal secular knowledge relied on a complex model of the social – as a field at once of rational analysis and calculation, of private contract, and of state policy. Such characterizations further shaped the legal register, in which property was conceptualized as the primary and original right, as integral to private social relations beyond the purview of the state, and also as enforced and sustained by state action. These complex understandings of the social surfaced prominently in the colonial engagement with hereditary offices. Coincidentally, this was the form of property held by those "native officers" who were the object of so much contemporary British calumny.

PART II: HEREDITARY OFFICES AND THE USES OF THE SOCIAL

The hereditary offices held by persons involved in the revenue establishment were known as *vatan*, from the Arabic meaning "native place" or

---

[55] This may be identified as part of a history of British concern with governance as a problem of information, emerging in the long eighteenth century. See John Brewer, *The Sinews of Power: War, Money and the English State, 1688–1783* (New York: Alfred A. Knopf, 1989), esp. chapter 8. For the history of colonial information gathering, see C. A. Bayly, *Empire and Information: Intelligence Gathering and Social Communication in India, 1780–1870* (Cambridge: Cambridge University Press, 1996). Compare also with Foucault, "Governmentality."

[56] These were never entirely distinct, as for example in the gathering and use of ethnographic statistics in Sykes, *Special Report*.

[57] Brewer, *Sinews of Power*, 128–129. Notably, Brewer makes this assertion in the context of a discussion of the relative lack of state concern with pursuing smugglers, suggesting something of a difference in state concern with various modes of tax evasion in the colonial context.

"homeland." Although some colonial officials (as well as later historians) recognized that *vatan* was the general term for a variety of hereditary positions, including, for example, all different kinds of village artisans, the colonial government was primarily interested in those *vatan* that were directly connected to the state system of revenue administration.[58] These were the district head (*deshmukh*), district accountant (*deshpandé*), village headman (*patil*), village accountant (*kulkarni*), and village menial servant (*mahar*).

Vatan, as a form of property, was a type of *inam*,[59] or hereditary grant by the state. Typically involving the right to the revenues of a particular parcel of land, *inam* was found widely throughout regions that had at one time been incorporated into the Mughal Empire or other Turkic, Persianate, or Central Asian styles of governance, where it took on several different forms.[60] *Vatan*, or what was sometimes referred to as "*vatan inam*" typically involved a grant in which the holder, who performed particular services for the village and for the state, was thereby entitled to retain the revenue of a parcel of village land (or a portion thereof). If the *vatandar* (*vatan* holding) family cultivated it themselves, the entire produce and revenue of such lands remained in their hands; if they hired others to cultivate it, the share ordinarily claimed by the state would belong to the *vatandar*.

The colonial treatment of *vatan* took shape as part of broader colonial efforts to address *inam* property in general. Colonial concern with *inam*

---

[58] See Chaplin, *Report Exhibiting*; Elphinstone, *Report on the Territories*; R. N. Goodine, *Report on the Deccan Village Communities (Selections from the Records of the Bombay Government, No. IV) – With Special Reference to the Claims of the Village Officers in the Ahmednugger Collectorate to "Purbhara Huks," or Remuneration from Their Villages, Independent of What They Receive from Government* (Bombay: Education Society's Press, 1852). The extensive correspondence in the Revenue Department concerning "Wuttuns" also confirms this.

[59] The term is derived from the Arabic *in'am*, (from the inf. n. iv of *in'am*, "to be good, agreeable") meaning: benefaction, donative, gratuity, largesse, favor, gift, present. John T. Platts, *A Dictionary of Urdu, Classical Hindi and English*, 4th printing (London: Crosby Lockwood and Son, 1911; reprint, Lahore: Sang-E-Meel Publications, 1994).

[60] The historian of western India Hiroshi Fukazawa distinguishes three categories of objects granted in *inam* in the region: (1) *inam* village, in which all or most of the revenues of the village were held hereditarily by persons or institutions; (2) "mere" *inam*, which were hereditary grants of a fixed portion of the revenue of a village; and (3) *inam* lands, which were hereditary grants to occupy and cultivate particular lands within a village on a revenue-free basis or with a light *inam* tax. Fukazawa, *The Medieval Deccan*. See also Guha, *Agrarian Economy*; Wink, *Land and Sovereignty*. Colonial officials identified two broad categories of *inam* in the region: *sanad inam* and *gaon nisbat inam*. The former referred to *inam* lands granted by *sanad* (deed), which were typically made on unclaimed or fallow land, while the latter was land set aside in the village for those performing various village services, such as *vatandars*. Each of these two types was divided into multiple sorts. *Poona Gazetteers*, 356.

derived from their interest in revenue collection because lands that were classed as *inam* paid revenue to their holder, or *inamdar*, rather than to the state. The colonial state thus ultimately sought to limit the prevalence of this property form, seeking to abolish potentially spurious grants as a means of enhancing government revenues and "cleaning up" government administration. At the same time, and from a somewhat different perspective, colonial investigations into *inam* also reflected an interest in solidifying the power of these superior holders so as to preserve rural stability and bolster a class of rural landholders on the model of English aristocratic gentry.[61]

In relation to both *inam* in general and *vatan* in particular – as in the context of land revenue administration – political economy and ethnography formed both competing and entangled discourses of policy and of rights. Yet in contrast to the treatment of land revenue, despite the pervasive rhetoric of liberal political economy within colonial administration by the 1830s, in the regulation of *vatan* and *inam* its dictates remained controversial, and its implementation in practice remained uneven. Large *inams* as well as the most elite district-level *vatans* were ultimately separated from their special connection to the state and transformed into regular private property in the 1860s. Village level *vatans*, however, remained a subject of countervailing policies until well into the twentieth century.

Inam: From Sovereignty to Property

Under Sultanate, Mughal, and post-Mughal regimes, *inams* had given the holder (*inamdar*) the same position in relation to his *inam* as the sovereign had in relation to the areas under his control: the claim to the revenues therefrom. *Inamdars* who held entire villages also frequently exercised forms of judicial power over their domains, while being personally exempt from judicial inquiry, in the same way as the sovereign.[62]

---

[61] Scholars have noted this tension in numerous contexts. See, for example, Cohn, *An Anthropologist*; Thomas R. Metcalf, *Land, Landlords and the British Raj: Northern India in the Nineteenth Century* (Berkeley: University of California Press, 1979); Bhattacharya, "Colonial State and Agrarian Society."

[62] See also Burton Stein's model of the segmentary state in medieval south India. Burton Stein, *Peasant State and Society in Medieval South India* (Delhi: Oxford University Press, 1980). The "segmentary" character of these forms of power and property refers primarily to the ways in which a model or form is replicated at diverse levels of society. This is central to André Wink's argument that the eighteenth-century Maratha *svarajya* legitimated itself through Persianate (Mughal) conceptions of sovereignty and resistance (particularly through the concept of *fitna*). Wink, *Land and Sovereignty*. See also Lynn Hunt's discussion of the French Revolution, in which the model of sovereignty was linked to the model

As both André Wink and Stewart Gordon have suggested for the Deccan region, this segmentary or modular form of sovereignty could at times form the basis for breakaway claims to independence. This was particularly the case with regional or district lords/officials (*deshmukhs*), who were often chiefs in their own right, with their own independent powers to grant *inams*.[63]

In the eighteenth century, *inams* had been used for a variety of purposes – as a way of signaling political favor, as a claim to sovereignty on the part of the person granting the *inam*, and as a way of structuring social relations. An early colonial list of existing *inams* in the southern Dharwad district included grants to drumbeaters, temple dancers, those supplying flowers to decorate the temple image, the Qazi of a Mosque, the Kutib for reading the Qur'an, the Mullah, the astrologer, the wrestlers, performers, conjurers, tricksters, actors, dancers, storytellers, musicians, those who provide water to travelers, the builders and repairers of tanks, *zamindars* (*deshmukhs* and *deshpandés*) and other officers for their daughters' betrothal ceremonies, beggars, and others.[64]

Inam had been integral to a system in which relational transactions and claims both symbolized and materially reinscribed relations of superiority and inferiority, dominance and subordination. Transactions in money, produce, gifts, and loans played a central role in signifying and enacting complex hierarchical relations.[65] Thus, for example, the colonial list of *inams* from Dharwad cited above ended with the official comment that "of these Enams some have been granted by the Paishwa, Sirsoobedars, Dessyes of districts and Sewusthans … [illegible]

---

of the family. Lynn Hunt, *The Family Romance of the French Revolution* (Berkeley: University of California Press, 1992), and Foucault's discussion of the transformation of the modular relationship between the sovereign and the family in "Governmentality."

[63] Gordon's and Wink's works suggest a form of political struggle and negotiation in which those incorporated under a higher level of sovereignty would both acknowledge that higher level and resist it to claim their own sovereignty, while asserting their claim within the idiom that legitimated the higher level. Wink, *Land and Sovereignty*, 238–250; Stewart Gordon, *Marathas, Marauders, and State Formation in Eighteenth-Century India* (Delhi: Oxford University Press, 1994).

[64] MSA, Pune, List No. 14, Rumal No. 1, File No. 5 (1819?), pp. 10–17. For later investigations into such claims, see, for example, MSA, Pune, List No. 14, Rumal No. 35, File No. 327, pp. 110–111, Letter of Alexander Gray to William Hart, August 14, 1861. The list includes as recipients: musicians, dancing girls, head shepherd, drum beater, village peon, bearer of an umbrella, priests, money tester, and others.

[65] For two provocative accounts of the role of the gift and the loan in reinscribing such relations, see Indrani Chatterjee, *Gender, Slavery and Law in Colonial India* (New Delhi: Oxford University Press, 1999), and Gyan Prakash, *Bonded Histories: Genealogies of Labor Servitude in Colonial India* (Cambridge: Cambridge University Press, 1990).

interior officers, who had no right to do so, but who were at the time Mamlutdars. Others by disobedient chiefs affording under authority of Government. Others by Village and other Officers with the conniv-ance of their Superiors. Some possess Sunnuds or old Accounts, others not, some are for a limited period."[66] Although colonial research into these *inams* reflected a primary concern with the potential spuriousness of the claims, historically the problem of authority had to do with the question of sovereignty at stake in who had the legitimate power to give.[67] This divergent view of legitimacy was eventually incorporated into the official treatment of *inams*, as detailed by the inam commis-sioner Alfred Thomas Etheridge in his 1873 *Narrative of the Bombay Inam Commission*. According to Etheridge, "To confer grants of land and pensions was, of all other rights of sovereignty, *the* privilege which the new ruler jealously exercised and by which he knew he could best make the arm of his authority felt."[68]

In the 1840s, colonial policy efforts to deal with *inams* coalesced in the creation of an Inam Commission, headed first by H. E. Goldsmid and then by William Hart, with the mandate of investigating and defin-ing existing claims.[69] Those who held *sanads* or other strong evidence of their claims were confirmed in their holdings with the issuance of new *sanads*. In those cases where the Commission called for state revocation of the *inam*, however, this determination typically did not involve a loss of hereditary connection to those lands if the lands were held directly by the *inamdar*. Such lands became regular private property, subject to the colonial revenue demand (land tax), but they were not taken from their holder, who now became a simple landlord. Yet in cases where the

---

[66] MSA, Pune, List No. 14, Records of the Commissioner, Central Division, Relating to Alienation and Sardars, Rumal No. 1, File No. 5 (1819?), pp. 10–17.

[67] Wink, *Land and Sovereignty* makes a similar point, as does Chatterjee, *Gender, Slavery and Law* for the Nizamat of Murshidabad, pp. 126*ff*.

[68] A. T. Etheridge, *Narrative of the Bombay Inam Commission and Supplementary Settlements*, Selections from the Records of the Bombay Government, No. CXXXII n.s. (Poona: Deccan Herald Press, 1873), p. 9. See also the discussion of R. N. C. Hamilton, the British Resident at the Native State of Indore (under the rule of the Holkar family), as early as 1845, MSA, Pune, List No. 12/64, Rumal No. 21, File No. 753, p. 47. Although colonial officials at times incorporated the symbolic importance of certain forms of giv-ing into their own attempts to assert legitimacy for themselves, the overwhelming trend in colonial adjudication of *inams* in the Bombay Presidency was to treat them with all of the ambivalence reserved for feudal tenures. See Cohn, "Representing Authority in Victorian India," 165–210.

[69] Initially established to examine *inams* in the districts of Dharwad and Belgaum in 1842–1843, Act XI of 1852 extended the Inam Commission to the whole of the Bombay Presidency. Etheridge, *Narrative of the Bombay Inam Commission*, 19–20.

inamdar merely claimed the revenues of a village, resumption did involve an absolute loss and corresponding gain for the state.

Due to the slow progress of the Commission, in 1863 the government enacted Summary Settlement Acts (Acts II and VII of 1863). These acts enabled those *inams* that were still to be adjudicated to be subjected to what was termed, using the feudal language, a "quitrent" – a liability to pay a portion of the revenues – in exchange for foregoing an inquiry into the validity of title, which could potentially result in the wholesale resumption of the *inam*. Such a settlement "cured" any defects of title and allowed holders to retain the remainder of the revenues.[70] The Inam Settlement thus had the dual benefit for the state of seeming to preserve rural stability and of enhancing the state revenues. According to official calculations, in 1873 the operations of the Inam Commission had led to the resumption of Rs. 37,17,121 out of a total value of alienated lands amounting to Rs. 87,75,319, or more than 40 percent of the total value. At the same time, it also produced a new form of privileged landholding defined by the terms of private property, rather than by its relationship to sovereignty.

Vatan: Hereditary Identity and Colonial Bureaucracy

Vatan was a form of *inam*, but differed from other kinds of *inam* in its connection to a particular occupation. Holding a *vatan* entailed a hereditary claim to perform a particular social labor and to receive revenues from a grant of land (*inam*), as well as other honors and perquisites (*manpan*). Frank Perlin's work has shown that in the eighteenth century, control of *vatans* became a key strategy for the intensification of power by rural elites. According to Perlin, regional lords extended their control in the countryside by gaining access to village-level offices.[71] This process of vertical extension seems to have reflected a context of struggle between regional lords and the Peshwa state, in which the Peshwa attempted to centralize his power and rein in these lords by obviating their position at

---

[70] The Summary Settlement also enabled these *inamdars* as well as those whose *inams* had already been adjudicated to transform their *inams* into regular private property through an additional payment, or *nazarana*. In the Mughal and Peshwa eras, unlike in the gift of *inam*, the gift of *nazarana* marked the giver as inferior to, loyal to, and recognized by the sovereign. For some of the vicissitudes of colonial treatment of *nazarana*, see MSA, RD 1835, Vol. 33/655, Comp. 102, pp. 257–263; RD 1838, Vol. 4/864, Comp. 166, pp. 125–127; MSA, RD 1859, 170/1442, pp. 149–258, esp. pp. 151–152, 190. See also Cohn's discussion of *nazarana* in "Representing Authority."

[71] Perlin, "Of White Whale."

the regional level, thereby spurring them to link their power more tightly to the villages.[72] As with *inam* in general, *vatan* was central to politics and political maneuvering in the eighteenth century.[73]

Under the eighteenth-century Peshwa government, the holders of *vatan* had been routinely confirmed and occasionally divested by the state.[74] While the early colonial administration, first under Mountstuart Elphinstone and then under John Malcolm, aimed to continue this function, such efforts foundered on the problems of defining what *vatan* entailed as a form of property. Neither entirely private, nor entirely public, from the official perspective *vatan* entailed an anomalous – or an ominously feudal – property form.

Although colonial officials developed divergent opinions regarding *vatan*, they overwhelmingly viewed it as made up of three parts: first, the office, or *vatan* service; second, the remuneration, or *vatan* property (which typically involved a combination of revenue-free [*inam*] lands, government cash payments, as well as payments in cash and kind from the villagers); and third, additional honors and perquisites. This conceptualization suggested that *vatan* property was essentially payment for *vatan* service, in which case the added honors and perquisites appeared to be an inappropriate and irrational excess. *Vatan* was thus consistently represented as an inappropriately paid government office: an office in which the holder was overpaid (or sometimes underpaid), but at any rate imprecisely paid for his labor.[75] Indeed, as was the case with *miras*, *vatan* seemed an object of irrational valuation – embodying an exchange value that remained at once unmoored from actual economic worth and also tied to its resistance to exchange.[76] Nonetheless, the colonial government also sought to marshal such existing "irrational" forms of value to the ends of liberal political economy.

As a claim to a particular set of hereditary social relations, forms of sociality, and community belonging, *vatan* was connected to that more

---

[72] Kenneth Ballhatchet, *Social Policy and Social Change in Western India, 1817–1830* (London: Oxford University Press, 1957), pp. 121–123.

[73] Hiroyuki Kotani has recently gone further, describing the "Vatan system" as the very basis of village social relations, encompassing the work of revenue administration, agricultural tenancy (*miras*), and village artisanal occupations (*bara balutédar*). Hiroyuki Kotani, *Western India in Historical Transition: Seventeenth to Early Twentieth Centuries* (Delhi: Manohar, 2002), pp. 1–7, 27–30, 39–48, 52–61.

[74] See Fukazawa, *Medieval Deccan*; Stewart Gordon, *Marathas, Marauders, and State Formation*; and Wink, *Land and Sovereignty*.

[75] See, for example, MSA, Pune, List No. 12/64, Rumal No. 21, File No. 753, p. 7.

[76] For an early analysis of value associated with resistance to exchange emerging out of the vast anthropological literature on the gift, see Annette Weiner, *Inalienable Possessions: The Paradox of Keeping-While-Giving* (Berkeley: University of California Press, 1992).

renowned set of Indian social relations, which has come to be known as caste. While not all members of an occupational caste community held a *vatan* for their form of labor, holding a *vatan* was typically connected to particular caste identification. In general, *vatan* exemplified the connection between property forms and forms of personhood, where property instantiated and reproduced social identities and modes of sociality. As Sumit Guha has noted, the term *haq*, used for claims to produce, artisanal goods, and perquisites associated with *vatan* and also more broadly, was generally translated by the colonial power as "right." Yet such rights were also historically associated with the "properties" and intrinsic faculties of particular forms of personhood or embodiment. Thus, Guha quotes an example in the definition provided in Molesworth's early-nineteenth-century Marathi-English dictionary: "Climbing trees is the monkey's haq"; that is, an action appropriate to the monkey's character.[77] *Haq* and *vatan* were part of a conceptual system, not unlike that of eighteenth-century Britain, in which differential forms of property and rights denoted the particular intrinsic qualities of different beings. *Vatans* in general were greatly prized and were considered a mark of high social standing. This was true even of *vatans* connected to stigmatized labor, such as the Mahar *vatan*: Although Mahars were considered Untouchables, those who held the *vatan* commanded higher status within the community than those who did not.

As with other property, ownership of a *vatan* was held collectively among males within the family, with every lineal male member of the family entitled to share equally therein. Although in the case of *patils* (village headmen), usually the eldest member of the lineage of the eldest male performed the service, in other offices – especially that of *kulkarni* (village accountants) – service was typically performed by rotation among all eligible sharers. Moreover, even in contexts where a single family member performed the service, such as with the office of *patil*, each holder was considered an equal sharer in the *vatan* and likewise entitled to share in its wealth and perquisites, except for a few special honors reserved for the person who performed the service. This meant that any given *vatan* was typically held among several, and frequently dozens, of sharers. In addition, in times of financial distress, *vatandars* frequently mortgaged or sold portions of their *vatans*, so that a given *vatan* might be split in

---

[77] Guha, "Wrongs and Rights," 19. Notably, this usage is no longer included in the 1857 second edition of the dictionary. J. T. Molesworth and George and Thomas Candy, *Molesworth's Marathi and English Dictionary*, 2nd revised ed. (Bombay: Education Society's Press, 1857; reprint, New Delhi: Asian Educational Services, 1989), 881. Interestingly, this also resonates with Richard Tuck's description of the medieval European usage in *Natural Rights Theories*, 25–26.

two or more "divisions" (*taksim*), each of which was then held among the numerous co-sharers of the family. This collective form of ownership seemed inherently inimical to British notions of efficient office holding: Not only was the claim to serve in office based on heredity rather than merit, but the rewards of office were dispersed among numerous persons who played no role in performing the service.

The history of colonial adjudication of *vatan* is easy to read as a straightforward narrative of the secularization or modernization of property and social relations, of the shift from status to contract. Indeed, *vatan* does not exist anymore, and reading the thousands of pages that it generated in the nineteenth and early twentieth centuries is thus like following a dead end of history, tracing its path to obsolescence. Nevertheless, for much of the nineteenth century, colonial policy did not aim to abolish *vatan*, despite its feudal resonances. Rather, one of the central questions that emerged in colonial adjudication of village (as opposed to district) *vatans* was whether these offices could be used to strengthen the administrative capabilities of the colonial government, thereby transforming *vatan* from a form of property that signaled and signified hereditary social identities and social status, to a form of salaried – albeit hereditary – employment, an effective civil service.

Such concerns about the nature and potentialities of office holding in part reflected the contemporary British context of recent and ongoing reform of offices from corrupt and inefficient personal sinecures to a professionalized state bureaucracy. As John Brewer has shown, the nineteenth-century reformist rhetoric that railed against the "Old Corruption" of office in Britain at once reflected the ongoing realities of office holding – whose lucrative character emerged vividly with the expansion of revenues that accompanied the Revolutionary and Napoleonic Wars – and the reformist perspective itself that denigrated eighteenth-century practices in order to elevate its own model for an ideal reformed polity.[78] The colonial treatment of *vatan* must be understood as integral to this wider nineteenth-century context of reform, whose comparative dimension – the seeming similarities between *vatan* and European feudal offices, the latter recently (yet incompletely) transformed with the expansion and professionalization of state bureaucracy in the eighteenth century – framed the meanings of these offices for colonial officials.

By the second half of the century, colonial policies aimed to privatize the relations of status that formed the core of *vatan* holding by relocating

---

[78] Brewer, *Sinews of Power*, 71–72.

them within the ambiguous terrain of the social, separate from the activities and interests of the state, even if they might still prominently structure the relations of social life. In the case of district officers, the framing of *vatan* as transparent payment for labor ultimately became the basis for a colonial policy of superseding these elite forms of *vatan* altogether, making it a form of private property by ending the connection of *vatan* holding to the activities of the state, as had occurred and was occurring with elite *inams* more generally during this era.[79] In contrast, in the case of the stigmatized village Mahar *vatan*, as discussed in Chapter 6, even into the mid-twentieth century the colonial government strongly resisted ending this system that ensured the performance of various denigrated forms of labor on behalf of the state and the village community. Ultimately, the colonial treatment of *vatan* worked to limit and supersede *vatandars'* hereditary connections to the state, but it nonetheless preserved such hereditary status relations as appropriate to the domain of social life. Indeed, inheritance as perhaps the central mechanism for the transfer of property and as the primary terms for defining bodily difference remained largely operative, confirmed by, albeit separated from, the state. This involved not so much a shift in the meanings of heredity per se in this period than a form of secularization in which the operation of heredity was removed in certain ways from the sphere of government.

Defining Vatan: Lessons from Political Economy for Elite Village Officers

Debates over colonial *vatan* policy in relation to elite village officers likewise played out larger arguments within contemporary political economy concerning the behaviors that would predictably result from various policies. For example, one of the primary terms through which the Bombay government attempted to regulate *vatan* was by considering that key British marker of private property, alienability: its ability to be gifted, mortgaged, or sold by an individual sharer or by all the sharers in the

---

[79] This occurred through what became known as Gordon's Settlement, the product of a commission composed of civil servant Stewart St. John Gordon, along with Vithal Vinchurkar, a wealthy *inamdar* of high status (whose own *vatan* became subject to the vicissitudes of colonial administration), and Keshav Ramchandra Jog, a retired agent in the colonial Survey Department. MSA, RD 1863–1885, Selection No. CLXXIV, "Extracted from the Proceedings of the Government of Bombay, 7th March 1863," pp. 1–446.

vatan. Regulation XVI of 1827, with the goal of preserving rural stability, prohibited the alienation of *vatan* property from a *vatandar* family beyond the lifetime of the holder.[80] This provision limited the length of mortgages of *vatans* and effectively banned their sale, although both multigenerational mortgages and sales of *vatans* had occurred with some regularity under the Peshwas, and continued to occur on occasion, despite this regulation, until the middle of the century, when new administrative policies redefined the meaning of *vatan* holding.[81]

Moreover, despite the terms of this regulation, throughout the decades that followed, colonial revenue commissioners, district collectors, assistant collectors, as well as the Bombay governor and the government of India, played out alternate scenarios considering the impact of potential policies regarding alienation. If a *patil* could mortgage or sell the revenue portion of his office, while still retaining responsibility for performing the service, the governor reasoned in 1836 that this would saddle him – and his descendants – with an onerous burden; such a headman would thus poorly attend to the service, and would be tempted to enrich himself through bribes and coercion.[82] Then again, if a village headman could alienate the whole *vatan*, the colonial government would have little control over who ended up heading the village.[83] In the late 1830s, the government of Bombay itself supported limited sales of *vatans* in cases where all the co-sharers joined together to sell the whole of the *vatan* to a single individual. It advocated this policy as a means of curbing the increasing subdivision of *vatans* from generation to generation.[84] Due to the reticence of the government of India to legalize *vatan* sale under any circumstances, however, it dropped the matter in 1840.[85] In the late 1850s, J. D. Inverarity, revenue commissioner of the Southern Division, returned to the issue, seeking to make *vatan* subject to regular market transactions. Inverarity cited the opinions of W. S. Boyd, the collector of Khandesh, who

---

[80] Regulation XVI of 1827, Section XX, Clauses 1 and 2; cited in MSA, RD 1859, 170/1442, pp. 149–258. See also discussion at MSA, RD 1859, 170/1442, pp. 238–239.

[81] The multifarious forms of mortgage and incomplete sale that were legitimated under the previous Peshwa regime, and the regular occasions of mortgage and sale of *vatans* or *vatan* shares, perquisites, and so forth, suggests both the mobility and marketability of rights and privileges during the eighteenth century, and also the value attached to this form of property. Kumar, *Western India*, 134–135; Perlin, "Of White Whale."

[82] See, for example, the debates in MSA, RD (1859), 170/1442, pp. 149–258, esp. pp. 183–184.

[83] See opinion submitted by the Madras Board of Revenue on the issue to this effect. Ibid., p. 197.

[84] MSA, RD 1859, 170/1442, pp. 164–165.

[85] Ibid., 202–203.

argued simultaneously on the grounds of tradition and of political economy that traditionally *vatans* had been alienable, and that the Regulations of 1827 had been having deleterious effects on rural social relations:

> It is notorious that the offices of Patels and Coolcurnees in the smaller Villages have greatly been lowered in estimation by the knowledge that they cannot be sold. The same hold upon the members of these families cannot be maintained; their credit suffers, because the great security they could always offer – "their wuttun" – is no longer available as a pledge, and they will gradually sink into still greater decay.[86]

Inverarity likewise argued that the fact that *vatan* included "social immunities, honors and dignities," rather than simply payment for service, legitimated the treatment of all these "excess" elements as regular private property, available for market transactions.[87] The Bombay government countered, however, that "if the social rights which are so highly valued be separated by sale from the official emoluments, the office will be less sought after & the influence of its holder would be impaired. So that the very object of maintaining hereditary village officers would be defeated."[88] The question of alienability thus fit into larger debates about how colonial policy might regulate the value of this property form and produce desirable outcomes within Indian society.[89] These arguments marshaled the languages of political economy and of historical rights side by side, and to a variety of ends.

Alongside the question of alienability of *vatans* came efforts to transform *vatan* into a merit-based system of government employment and an efficient form of property holding. Thus in 1838, British local and district officials in the Southern Maratha Country supported the petition of one Girreapa, a clerk (*karkoon*) who performed village accountant, or *kulkarni*, duties in a few villages in Belgaum District, and who requested to be permitted to hold permanently an unclaimed *kulkarni vatan* that had lapsed to the state.[90] Drawing on this petition, officials developed a proposal for expanding the hereditary office system by awarding lapsed *vatans* to "deserving native servants."

The logic of this proposal was to reward the best clerks, to provide an incentive for them to work at their highest level of performance, and simultaneously to improve the administration of villages by ensuring that

---

[86] Ibid., 153–157.
[87] Ibid., 184–185. Citing Report of Government dated October 1, 1836.
[88] Ibid., 247–258.
[89] Ibid., 164–165, 202–203.
[90] MSA, RD 1838, Vol. 40/900, Comp. 352, pp. 235–266.

the work of village administration was performed by someone who had a permanent interest in the welfare of the village, rather than by a traveling clerk who had no real knowledge of, or connection to, the village. Thus, Assistant Collector of Belgaum Randolph Barrett, in forwarding Girreapa's petition to the collector, John Dunlop, wrote:

> By constituting the Petitioner an owner of this Wuttun on the same terms as tho' it fell to him by inheritance, Government will derive benefit, and that the general condition of the Village be improved … should the Petitioner's request be complied with, either he himself or his representative will be continually on the spot.… The Petitioner is moreover a man of excellent character and if constituted a wuttundar intends planting trees, sinking a well if requisite, making a garden and cultivating Khalsat [unassessed wastelands].… In making this application for the Petitioner I have in view (should this meet with approbation), a proposition for the similar disposal of several other unclaimed Wuttuns, in the districts under my charge.[91]

Barrett's vision of the traveling clerk transformed into an improving landlord gained the approval both of the revenue commissioner and of the government of Bombay. At the government of India level, however, the proposal ground to a halt, as the central government feared that the practice "would be open to much abuse."[92] Yet, in rejecting this proposal, the colonial government did not dismiss the logic of creating vested interests in improved cultivation; rather it sought to create such an outcome through economic incentives in cash or produce, instead of through bestowing hereditary privileges.[93] As this position suggests, divergent policy positions to some extent obscured a shared official assumption as to the power of "interest" in shaping behavior, and the capacity of the colonial rulers to remake Indian society on more desirable terms through the manipulation thereof.

This effort to restructure *vatan* as a form of employment became prominent by the late 1830s and early 1840s, and it shaped the administration of village *vatans* through the third quarter of the century. The primary emphasis of such efforts was to tie *vatan* holding more tightly to the labor of *vatan* service, so that as far as possible, the *vatan* property would belong to those responsible for the labor. Thus, successive pieces of legislation placed increasing emphasis on what colonial officials termed

---

[91] Ibid., 239–241. Bracketed comments added.

[92] Ibid., 258.

[93] Ibid., 259. Moreover, although the government of India's reticence prevented Barrett's proposal from being implemented at that time, by the late 1870s the state had sanctioned the possibility of conferring such offices on "deserving native servants." See, for example, MSA, RD 1895, 294/549, pp. 87–98; RD 1938, File No. 8677/33, pp. 16–19, which specifies that such appointment can be made under a combination of the Vatan Act of 1874 and the Land Revenue Code of 1879.

the "officiator" of the *vatan*, attempting to make *vatandar* status more isomorphic with *vatan* service, and rendering control over officiating – performing the service – key to reaping the benefits of *vatandar* status.[94]

These policies reflected ongoing and countervailing efforts at once to respect preexisting rights and to make *vatan* part of a system of efficient and merit-based liberal governance that was ultimately responsible to the state. Some officials went even further, emphasizing a notion of public service at once to the people and to the state that needed to be ingrained in these officers. Thus R. N. Goodine, in his 1845 *Report on the Deccan Village Communities*, which dealt primarily with claims to *haqs* by village officers, reflected extensively on the proper form of remuneration for village officers, arguing that the form of remuneration structured the nature of the system as a whole. Fundamentally, he urged that "to ensure the fidelity and zeal of Native subordinates, it is necessary that their interests should be so bound up with those of government, that injury or success may be reciprocal."[95] Goodine argued further, however that this involved a necessary choice concerning what colonial governance would mean:

There are two methods of procedure, diametrically opposite to each other: the first is, by continuing the former method of remuneration, to preserve the spirit

---

[94] The two primary pieces of legislation were Act XI of 1843 and Act III of 1874; the latter is discussed in Chapter 2. Holding the position of officiator did not necessarily imply performing the labor directly. Especially in the case of the most elite *vatandars*, the actual service was performed by an agent, or *gumasta*. For a farcical presentation of some of the effects of this act, see MSA, RD 1844, Vol. 56/1613, Comp. 1203, pp. 13–17. Act XI of 1843 also confirmed an 1839 resolution by the governor that enabled widows to hold their husbands' *vatans* for the duration of their lifetimes, appointing male agents to perform the *vatan* service or officiate the *vatan* on the widows' behalf. The Regulations of 1827 had explicitly prohibited women from holding *vatans*; the change with the new legislation occurred as a result of petitions by widows, accompanied by a mass of evidence provided by district collectors and their assistants that showed that under the precolonial regime, widows had regularly inherited their husbands' share of *vatans* and other *inams*, and in families without male heirs, they had disposed of them as they saw fit. See MSA, RD 1839, Vol. 47/1010, Comp. No. 29, pp. 1–139. Also segments of the report submitted to the Inam commissioner at MSA, Pune, List No. 12, Records of Captain Gordon, Rumal No. 21, File 754 (entire), 1838–1853, pp. 143–149. Act XI of 1843 also formally established the right of government to intervene in the naming of an officiator, while it legally enshrined the principle of regulating *vatans* through registers containing lists of the co-sharers in each *vatan*. The new positive power of the register would take on increasing importance in the policies established in the second half of the century, as discussed in Chapter 2. See also Kumar, *Western India*, 141–147; Richard Saumarez Smith, *Rule by Records: Land Registration and Village Custom in Early British Panjab* (Delhi: Oxford University Press, 1996).

[95] Goodine, *Report on the Deccan Village Communities*, 29. This also resonates with what Steve Pincus has identified as an earlier political economic articulation of the necessary unity of personal (commercial) and state interests, dating to the tract wars of the mid-seventeenth century. See Pincus, "Neither Machiavellian Moment."

of the ancient system, and the influence of its officials; the second is, by making these officials purely Government servants, and throwing more of the domestic management of a community into the hands of its members, to teach the people to think and act for themselves, and to lay the foundation of those domestic institutions so necessary for their improvement.[96]

In this model, cash salaries would render these officials proper public servants, whose responsibility was to the people and to the state. The feudal property form had hitherto curbed this development; changing the mode of remuneration would bring in its wake the series of necessary transformations in thought and in social relations that formed the precondition for Indians to become full political subjects. Yet notably, the effects that Goodine attributed to salaried income bore a strong resemblance to those that Whigs and classical republicans had previously attributed to landholding: the virtues of civic engagement that formed the basis for citizenship. The use of cash salaries to remunerate village *vatandars* was formalized in 1853 as part of Wingate's Settlement.[97]

Producing Vatan as Social Relations: A View from the Margins

Some of the complex implications of colonial *vatan* policy in reformulating the relationship between social life and the state emerge in the context of those positions at the margins of state interest – those offices not connected to revenue collection and administration, but that operated at the heart of village social relations. These were the *bara balutedars* ("twelve entitled to receive *baluta*,"[98] or portions of grain in exchange for their service or crafts), whose positions were customarily considered a type of *vatan*. British reports and records classed these *balutedars*, and others who held small *inam* grants, into two types: "village servants useful to the community," such as carpenters and blacksmiths, and "useless

---

[96] Goodine, *Report on the Deccan Village Communities*, 39.

[97] See also MSA, Pune, List No. 14, Rumal No. 5, File No. 52-A (no page numbers). Letter from the Court of Directors, London, dated November 6, 1850, to the Governor in Council, Bombay.

[98] Different villages included slightly different occupations in the list of twelve, and sometimes there were fourteen counted instead of twelve. See discussion in Molesworth's *Marathi-English Dictionary*, 2nd ed., 567. The *baluta* system was a prescriptive or formal system – often *balutedars* did not receive the share to which they were prescriptively entitled, as demonstrated in the longstanding disputes between *kunbis* (agriculturalists) and Mahars dating even from precolonial times, where *kunbis* accused Mahars of poisoning their cattle, and Mahars accused *kunbis* of not paying their *baluta*. See Sumit Guha, *Agrarian Economy*, and "Civilisations, Markets and Services: Village Servants in India from the Seventeenth to the Twentieth Centuries," *Indian Economic and Social History Review* 41, 1 (2004): 79–101; Kotani, *Western India in Historical Transition*.

village servants." Yet by the 1860s, the direction of government policy was similar for both types, aiming to limit the state connection to these positions and to define them as "purely social." These efforts resonate with the contemporary process of detoothing the district officers, as well as with the Inam Settlement more generally, but in the context of these village servants, unyoking them from the state did not imply an end to their hereditary positions, or to the hereditary forms of labor these positions entailed, but simply located them beyond the reach of the state. Thus, by mid-century, even as proposals concerning *patils* and *kulkarnis* aimed to create a professionalized labor core (specifically, in the logic of the day, ensuring adequate remuneration in order to prevent rampant bribery and embezzlement and promote efficient labor), proposals regarding what were classed as "useless village servants" attempted to transform and curtail their holdings, while "useful village servants" were treated as engaged in a type of contractual relationship outside of the state.[99] In both of the latter cases, the state effort was to make these social rather than state liabilities. In this sense, "useful and useless village servants" together marked out a space of social life that produced and made claims to a particular political and socioeconomic order based on the hierarchies of birth, but one that ironically was now recast as a matter of private contract.[100]

At a general level, the state thus confirmed the principle of heredity at the core of *vatan*, but it sought (albeit unevenly and contradictorily) to separate from the state the ways in which heredity structured social life. These efforts dealt differently with different offices: District offices and those of "useful (to the village)" and "useless" village servants were transformed into private property, while village offices "useful to government" (particularly in the work of revenue collection) were integrated in a variety of ways into the colonial bureaucracy. Moreover, the form of privatization that rendered *vatan* a matter of hereditary – but purely

---

[99] In the case of "useless village servants," the proposal entailed resuming half of their revenues from land (making such lands subject to payment of half the revenue assessment), defining it as fully transferable private property, and ending cash payments by the state by purchasing them at the rate of twenty years' value. In A. T. Etheridge's words, "The class of individuals referred to is that which is found in the enjoyment of certain State emoluments for doing nothing." Further, "This can scarcely be regarded as an act of compulsion.... But, if necessary, compulsion may very properly be resorted to." MSA, Pune, List No. 14, Rumal No. 44, File No. 91, pp. 106–710; also in MSA, RD 1868, 7/429, pp. 361–366. For "useful village servants," see MSA, RD 1881, 199/703 pp. 99–134; RD 1883, 259/1486, pp. 37–57; RD 1885, 349/1486, pp. 253–254; RD 1889, 79/820, pp. 27–47.

[100] For a unified discussion of the treatment of these various forms of *vatan*, see Etheridge's later *Narrative of the Bombay Inam Commission*, 38–41.

social – relations of power, nonetheless preserved it as subject to state cognizance. The treatment of "useful and useless" village servants thus underscores how this form of privatization of *vatan* implied both the continuation of hereditary social roles outside of the state and potential state enforcement thereof, even as it also sought to enact a fundamental transformation in preexisting sociopolitical modes of power.

CONCLUSION

During the early decades of colonial rule in the Bombay Presidency, the presumptions and modalities of political economic thought came to pervade official theorizing on matters of law and rights. At the same time, the logics and principles of political economy were highly mobile, and became embedded in a variety of different kinds of arguments, deployed in unpredictable and seemingly contradictory ways. This emergent official theorizing and policy produced a complex construal of the arena of social life: at once as subject to rational analysis and empirical calculation, as the domain of private contracts outside of (but enforced by) the state, as an arena of ethical civic cultivation, and as the space where nonsecular modes of social relations would continue to hold sway.

If the work of land revenue administration largely became a matter of scientific data collection and political economic and statistical calculation, this involved both a reconceptualization of the property nature of land, the wealth and value it generated, and the nature of ownership thereof, as well as ironically a "settlement" and bracketing of those very questions of sovereignty and ethnographic-historical rights that undergirded this transformation. Moreover, land remained a distinctive property form in this era – the dominion and succor of the state – yet its valuation nonetheless increasingly became subject to new theories of value.

In contrast to the land revenue, *vatan* remained inseparable from questions of rights and the very structure of local governance. As such, *vatan* as a property form involved the administration in the recognition and enforcement of hereditary social relations, even when it attempted to remove such relations from the workings of the state. Moreover, the administration of *vatan* during these decades continued to confirm that property established differential forms of personhood, marking the appropriateness of different bodies for various forms of labor, even if increasingly as a matter of private social relations. The effective privatization of some *vatans* during this era produced an uneven relationship of this form of property to the state, but it did not address this relationship between property and personhood; it merely divorced the question from matters of state interest.

Yet if *vatan* administration in this period eventually sought to privatize hereditary social relations, it also remained enmeshed in theorizing how this office might operate within the state, as well as in questions concerning the nature, rights, and motivations of the person as property holder. Thus *vatan* administration posed fundamental questions concerning the extent to which an arena of social life could in fact be bracketed off from the concerns of the state.

This issue became prominent during the second half of the century, in the emergence of what was at the time sometimes referred to as "social economy," the problem of producing efficient and just social relations. In this context, the very relations that had been cast as properly social rather than matters of state functioning or policy became a problem as such. How should the state address the encumbrances, the modes of domination and oppression that structured social life? This was a problem that came to animate both official British reflections and the efforts of Western-educated Indian reformers.

2

The Dilemmas of Social Economy

In all civilized societies there is a vast amount of suffering and destitution, very lamentable to contemplate, but which it is wholly out of the powers of the State by any direct action to eradicate.

– Lord Cranbrook, Secretary of State for India, 1878

The system of distributing work according to ancient hereditary rights of service with practically no regard to the capacities of the workers ... can tend only to inefficiency. These ancient rights now conflict with the rights of the public to have the public service efficiently administered through a well-selected, properly-trained, and adequately-paid subordinate staff.... The hereditary rights of privileges of individuals must give way to the needs of the public.

– James McNeill, Acting Collector of Pune District, 1913

While reassessing the ignorant farmers' lands every thirty years, the European workers, blindly worshipping our virtuous government, do not say "Amen" until they have raised the taxes at least a little.

– Jotirao Phule, *The Cultivator's Whipcord*, 1883

During the decades following the massive Indian Rebellion of 1857 and the establishment of Crown Rule in 1858, the mandate of ensuring colonial security and economy provided the framework for renewed official examination of the social relations of property in India. Whereas in north India, the colonial government sought to further entrench the power of major landholders, or "loyal *taluqdars*," in western India, where this form of estate did not prevail, official attention came to focus instead on issues of rural indebtedness and the economic viability of small holdings.[1] These

[1] For north India, see Thomas Metcalf, *The Aftermath of Revolt: India, 1857–1870* (Princeton, NJ: Princeton University Press, 1964).

concerns, along with continued attention to the system of hereditary offices, reflected efforts to produce what was occasionally referred to as "social economy"; that is, flourishing social and economic relations characterized by efficiency and cohesion.[2] As the epigraphs to this chapter suggest, the question of the nature and plasticity of Indian society – its misery and deprivation, its morality or immorality, its stability, instability, or improvability – framed unresolved debates about what a social economy for India would entail.

The question of whether the colonial state could and should regulate Indian social relations or shape Indian society dominated official debate on all relevant policy issues at this time.[3] While ideological differences produced divergent responses to this question, the question itself reflected a shared conceptualization of Indian society as an object potentially – and also not inevitably – acted on by the state, and as susceptible to material and moral amelioration or decline.[4]

This context – at once political, material, and intellectual – compelled new arguments and theorizing on individual and social need and benefit, in which, however unevenly and paradoxically, the state sought to replace the burdens of existing social relations and to inculcate a new experiential understanding of social obligation. In its treatment of the rural structures of power that coalesced into patterns of indebtedness and in hereditary office holding, the colonial state sought to define a public interest that sutured society and state, even as it also sought continually to demarcate a sphere of social life that remained distinct from the interests of state.

These colonial debates and policies, and Indian engagements with them, reflected new questions concerning the social operation of political

---

[2] The transformation of the original meaning of *oikos*, the household or domestic economy, into a societal scale and public affair is discussed in Arendt, *The Human Condition*, esp. 28–49, and further extended in Foucault, "Governmentality."

[3] Despite the implementation of new technologies of government associated with the census, the famine commissions and famine works, and public health campaigns, these often highly coercive activities did not accompany or produce complex models of contemporary Indian society. In India, in contrast to the theorization of society in Europe, society was largely conceptualized in binaristic terms – as riven between tradition and modernity. David Arnold, *Colonizing the Body: State Medicine and Epidemic Disease in Nineteenth-Century India* (Berkeley: University of California Press, 1993); Bernard Cohn, "The Census, Social Structure and Objectification in South Asia," in *An Anthropologist among the Historians*, 224–54; Dirks, *Castes of Mind*; N. G. Barrier, ed. *The Census in British India* (Delhi: Manohar, 1981).

[4] See Sudipta Kaviraj and Sunil Khilnani, "Introduction: Ideas of Civil Society," in *Civil Society: History and Possibilities*, edited by Sudipta Kaviraj and Sunil Khilnani (Cambridge: Cambridge University Press, 2001), pp. 1–6; Prakash, "The Colonial Genealogy of Society."

economy and the potential of state policies to shape individual behavior and to produce complex aggregate effects. Integral to these diverse efforts to refashion the relations or conditions of social life was a new problematization of the family, especially of the impediments that the joint Hindu family posed to producing a more economical social order. At the same time, these efforts sought to redefine the existing and desirable interaction among various modes of compulsion – economy, law, ethics, and violence – that shaped individual subjects in their social environment. These efforts thus also highlighted the entangled relationship between autonomy and compulsion, in which autonomy was not categorically inimical to compulsion, but rather involved an unstable distinction between legitimate and illegitimate modes of compulsion. In this vein, contemporary commentators debated the ethics and pragmatics of economic rather than legal compulsion, of law rather than violence or economic immiseration, and of internalized discipline and moral obligation rather than law. Such theorizing on the forces that did and should animate individual action thus also foregrounded and problematized the relationship between the state and societal modes of power.

PART I: DEBT, LEGAL OBLIGATION, AND THE CRISIS OF RURAL SOCIETY

The Compulsions of Credit

When colonial officials began to focus on the issue of debt in the mid-nineteenth century, they did so within a broader Victorian context in which debt solidified concerns both about social degeneration and about the individual debtor as a nonautonomous and potentially contaminating economic and moral subject.[5] In the colonial context, those concerns became layered with a colonial focus on the effects of widespread indebtedness on social and political stability, and on the extraordinary forms of subjection of debtors to creditors. In colonial depictions, the extremity of debt in India operated against the very possibility of political economy, undermining the industriousness of the debtor entirely: As one major report argued, since work though he might, all the peasant's profits

---

[5] The figure of the debtor was a prominent one across a variety of textual genres in nineteenth-century Britain as well as India, expressing the anxieties provoked by the contemporary expansion of finance, speculation, and credit as property forms. Pocock, "Mobility of Property"; Mary Poovey, "Speculation and Virtue in *Our Mutual Friend*," in *Making a Social Body*, 155–181.

would go to his creditor, he had no incentive to labor or improve his cultivation.[6] Likewise, in colonial policy debates, the figure of the debtor highlighted a core dilemma within liberal political economy concerning the putative legal equality and autonomy of the contracting subject. In the words of J. D. Inverarity, revenue commissioner of the Northern Division, in 1858, "It is the law which is at fault in assuming debtor and creditor in this country to be equal, whereas they are actually in the position of master and slave."[7] Although these arguments were presented in terms of the specific cultural character of Indian debtors and creditors, in fact virtually identical arguments shaped nearly concurrent legislative efforts in Britain, as some colonial commentators observed.[8] The unequal and unfree condition of the debtor (whether English or Indian) thus inherently suggested his disability or lack, and hence his need for external protection.[9] Such state protection would perhaps ironically seek to secure the autonomy of the debtor – both against the ravages of the market and against the oppressive structures of social life.

Credit and Debt in Early Colonial State Practice

Credit and debt, although conceptualized by the colonial state as private interests, were closely tied to the state land revenue demand, in that both the requirement of paying the revenue in specie and the timing when payments were due, formed the primary conditions that produced the widespread and longstanding relationships of indebtedness among the majority of the population in the countryside.

---

[6] *Report of the Committee on the Riots in Poona and Ahmednagar, 1875, with Appendices*, 3 vols. (Bombay: Government Central Press, 1876), p. 41 (hereafter *Deccan Riots Commission Report*).

[7] Cited in ibid., 32. Inverarity would later (while revenue commissioner of the Southern Division) seek to subject *vatan* to market relations, as discussed in Chapter 1.

[8] Minute on the Debtor's Bill, 1886, by W. E. Hart, Chief Judge of the Court of Small Causes, Bombay, MSA, JD 1886, 19/953, unpaginated. Hart cited J. S. Mill's *Principles of Political Economy* and W. J. Law's "Supplementary Paper on Bankruptcy and Insolvency" as examples. This argument is also supported by V. Markham Lester, *Victorian Insolvency: Bankruptcy, Imprisonment for Debt, and Company Winding-up in Nineteenth-Century England* (New York: Oxford University Press, 1995).

[9] For many, the greatest mark of the subjection of the debtor (particularly in Britain) was his liability in his own person, such that he could be arrested and imprisoned at the instance of the creditor, suggesting moreover that a quasi-penal regime operated in this realm of civil faults. In India, although efforts to abolish imprisonment for debt formed a major subject of official debate during the late nineteenth century, these efforts were largely unsuccessful until the early twentieth century, in contrast to Britain, except as folded into the provisions of the Deccan Agriculturalists' Relief Act, discussed in the next section.

Such features long predated the British conquest, and highly developed monetary instruments, as well as formal and informal money lending practices, had long been associated with extensive mercantile networks throughout the region, as well as with the state revenue demand. These preexisting forms became the subject of initial colonial ethnographic inquiries, as had occurred with both land and offices, discussed in Chapter 1. Compared to those property forms, however, administrative engagement with the relations between creditors and debtors remained less developed until the 1840s and 1850s. And only in the last decades of the century, in the aftermath of what became known as the Deccan Riots in 1875, did these concerns emerge as a major object of policy and debate.

Questions concerning the legal relations between creditors and debtors had formed part of the initial colonial inquiries into regional property forms. The wide-ranging early official questionnaire discussed in the Chapter 1 included the following queries:

May [a] Creditor seize Debtors Wife, children or Goods – may he seize Debtor person & beat, or otherwise violently coerce him without legal authority?; What caste persons may be compelled to work out a Debt by daily labour, and what kind of work may be imposed on each Caste; When there are several creditors of the four different Casts [*sic*] – is the priority of these debts, – the validity of their deeds, or the superiority of their Casts, of most Weight – show the order in which each is considered; If [a] Debtor be confined, state the rules under which he is allowed to return to his Meals, and satisfy the causes of nature, and the degree of latitude allowed for Ceremonies, etc.[10]

These questions suggest that colonial interest centered on two issues: first, on the personal liabilities of debt, the ways one's own body (or the bodies of one's wife and children) might be liable for the extraction of payment; and second, on the extent to which personal status (e.g., lineage, caste) might define a person's legal liabilities and claims. Given that in Britain, this was an era of public debate on the morality of credit and the dangers of insolvency, and eventually of legislative reform leading to the formal abolition of imprisonment for debt in 1869, these questions also reflected contemporary British uncertainties about the nature of personal liability and legitimate forms of repayment, and about the wealth that inhered in bodies.[11]

[10] Pune Archives, Marathi Daftar, Deccan Commissioner's Files, Rumal No. 136, Loose Papers.

[11] See Lester, *Victorian Insolvency*; G. R. Rubin, "Law, Poverty and Imprisonment for Debt, 1869–1914," in *Law, Economy and Society, 1750–1914: Essays in the History of English Law*, edited by G. R. Rubin and David Sugarman (Abingdon: Professional Books, 1984), pp. 241–299.

Such concerns would also eventually shape judicial reflections on the liabilities of debt in India.[12]

Most early official ethnographic inquiries included at least brief treatments of the social role of moneylenders and the conditions of the people with respect to indebtedness.[13] Although at times widely divergent in detail, from these inquiries emerged a number of principles that formed the basis for government policies: the near-universality of rural indebtedness, particularly among cultivators, often passed from generation to generation according to the tenets of Hindu law; the oppressive rates of interest, combined with the illiteracy of most debtors, that tended to make debt a permanent condition, although customarily the interest charged on money debts could not exceed the principal; and the reliance of moneylenders on informal or private modes of compulsion to induce repayment, particularly *takazi*, or dunning, which included forcing the debtor to squat in contorted positions, or with a stone on his head under the hot sun, until payment was forthcoming.[14]

Elphinstone's Regulations of 1827 attempted to address these circumstances in several ways. Regulation IV sought to make the courts, rather than informal compulsion, the primary agency for the recovery of debts, while confirming existing practice that exempted the cattle and tools of cultivators from attachment for repayment of debts. Regulation V limited the annual rate of interest to 9 percent, and for debts contracted prior to the Regulations coming into force, it limited the annual rate recoverable in the courts to 12 percent. Yet Elphinstone's code also regularized the charging of compound interest, enabled imprisonment for debt, and rendered immovable property subject to attachment for repayment. This last provision was little availed of, however, at least initially, since what the cultivator could sell – typically at most a *mirasi* title – was usually of little interest to moneylenders, especially given the low market value of *miras* at this time.[15]

Official concern with the effects of colonial policies on agricultural debtors emerged by 1841,[16] and the first detailed inquiry into agricultural indebtedness occurred in 1843 under J. D. Inverarity.[17] Inverarity's

[12] Bhattacharya, "Colonial State and Agrarian Society."

[13] Notably, these inquiries treated the property nature of money (or of movable property more generally, such as grain, jewels, or precious metals) and the nature of ownership therein, as a subject of little interest – in stark contrast to the treatment of land and offices.

[14] See the divergent official analyses in *Poona Gazetteers*, Part II, 107.

[15] *Poona Gazetteers*, Part II, 112. Miras is discussed in Chapter 1.

[16] MSA, JD 1841, 25(715)/417, pp. 43–51.

[17] *Poona Gazetteers*, Part II, 112.

inquiry focused on the prevalence of usurious rates of interest.[18] While virtually all officials confirmed the widespread and oppressive burden of debt among most of the rural population, the government ultimately concluded that any legal enactment would be counterproductive, largely following the laissez-faire principle articulated by Pune Collector P. Stewart, and ultimately by Inverarity himself, that "all enactments to fix a lower than the market rate of interest had the effect of enhancing it."[19]

In 1855, the Bombay government not only declined to further regulate interest rates, but in fact repealed the existing restrictions on interest in Elphinstone's Code.[20] This principle of subjecting debt to the regulation of the market was further embodied in the India-wide Code of Civil Procedure, passed in 1859, which not only expedited cases for the repayment of debt through the courts, but rendered cultivators' cattle and tools subject to attachment. The Limitation Act passed that same year aimed to protect debtors somewhat from this new power of creditors by limiting the use of the civil courts to cases brought within three years of the bond (rather than the previous six years for oral or twelve for written agreements). Ironically, however, the working of the act seemed to demonstrate Stewart and Inverarity's premise: It resulted in creditors using the threat of legal action to force debtors to pass new written bonds at compound rates, and often with an additional premium attached, every two or three years. The Limitation Act's effect was thereby to intensify both the indebtedness and the legal subjection of the debtor, given the authority of a written contract if the case came to court.[21]

As all of this suggests, the courts themselves thus came to play a primary – if at times unintended – role in reshaping the social relations of debt. Therefore, what was presented as the quite limited and ineffectual intervention by the state into credit relations at the level of legislation was belied by the courts' active role in enhancing the power of creditors. Such effects of the courts on the social relations of credit also formed a contemporary object of official inquiry and analysis.

---

[18] Replies from officials suggested that prevailing annual rates of interest in the Deccan ranged from 30 to 60 percent, depending on the financial condition of the borrower. Ibid.

[19] Ibid., 112–113.

[20] Ibid., 114.

[21] Sumit Guha argues that the expansion and intensification of indebtedness during the period 1858–1862 was only secondarily due to the Limitation Act. Rising prices and a strong labor market during these years would have put pressure on the money market and led moneylenders to pursue their debtors more avidly at this time. Guha, *Agrarian Economy*, 75.

The contemporary statistics on the operation of the courts offered information on the number of cases brought for recovery of debts, the castes of the plaintiff and the defendant, the amounts sued for, and the outcome of the suits. These statistics suggested that by the 1840s, the courts had become a major mechanism for the recovery of petty (as well as great) debts. According to an 1842 letter by Pune Judge John Warden, official returns showed nearly 9,000 suits annually, of which, in nearly 16 out of 17, the amount claimed was less than Rs. 100.[22] In the city of Bombay as well, the operation of the Court of Small Causes suggested a similar urban story. Although new rules passed in 1847 extended the jurisdiction of the Small Causes Court to Rs. 600, the vast majority of cases filed in this court were for claims less than Rs. 100, and the vast majority of cases were either decided in favor of the plaintiff, or struck off and compromised.[23] The principal plaintiffs of the court were Marwaris, or moneylenders, although as was recognized at the time, moneylending was widely practiced across most castes by anyone who had any financial resources. Thus to a great extent it was moneylenders who used this court to enforce debt repayment. The role of the courts in compelling defaulting petty debtors to repay their creditors points to expanding state involvement in regulating the petty credit system and the formalization of personal liability and modes of compulsion. It also suggests the extent to which the court's conceptualization of the contractual nature of loans worked to the benefit of creditors.[24]

Such statistics formed the basis for further administrative inquiries and policy debates concerning rural agriculturalists. In the early 1850s, Survey Commissioner Wingate argued that the favorable treatment of creditors in the courts, and the effectiveness of the state in executing its decrees, were themselves expanding the ranks and the rapacity of moneylenders to poor agriculturalists. Similarly, in 1858, Bombay governor Lord (John) Elphinstone suggested that the civil courts were the object of widespread popular antipathy because of their role in serving the

---

[22] The numbers were 8,310 out of 8,813 suits for the previous year. Extract Letter of John Warden, November 4 1842, in MSA, JD 1851, 12/518, pp. 41–45.

[23] In 1853–1854, suits for less than Rs. 100 stood at approximately 9,500 out of 11,000. Of those cases, some 5,000 were decided in favor of the plaintiff and 4,500 were struck off and compromised. It is unclear whether the use of the colonial courts reflected instances where personal connections between debtor and creditor were weaker and thus involved less opportunity for the use of personal and symbolic modes of compulsion, such as *takazi* and debt bondage, or whether the legal mechanism was simply added to the existing repertoire.

[24] *Poona Gazetteers*, Part II, 115.

moneylenders' greed.[25] Such analyses of statistics, along with new inquiries into family economy, would become increasingly important during the last decades of the century.

Rural Stability and the Deccan Agriculturalist

During the last decades of the nineteenth century, debates concerning the conditions of indebtedness and the relations between creditor and debtor in western India coalesced around events that became known as the Deccan Riots. These events entailed some thirty-three uprisings across the villages and towns of Pune and Ahmednagar Districts in the summer of 1875.[26] In a period of agricultural downturn caused in part by the end of the cotton boom (a boom produced by the disruption of cotton exports from the southern United States during the American Civil War), as well as in the context of the revision of the Revenue Settlement and imposition of a higher revenue demand, peasants attacked the homes and shops of Gujarati and Marwari moneylenders. Although they left the moneylenders themselves largely unscathed, in each case, the peasants targeted the moneylenders' account books, burning or destroying the papers that constituted legal records of their bonds.

The colonial army and police rapidly put down this unrest, but it nonetheless proved incendiary in official circles. In part, this reaction reflected an official stance of alarm and concern with "readiness" in response to any outbreak of rural violence in the aftermath of the 1857 Rebellion. In this case, however, the highly limited and targeted nature of the violence suggested specific causes of discontent that in fact meshed with prevailing interpretations of the causes of the massive 1857 revolt itself. From the time of its suppression, the dominant interpretation in official British circles of the underlying causes of the 1857 Rebellion had focused on the discontent produced by colonial intervention in indigenous society, and particularly on the "rapid transfer of landed property from old to new hands" since the early 1830s.[27]

---

[25] Ibid.

[26] For now-classic analyses of the colonial construction of the "riot," see Shahid Amin, *Event, Metaphor, Memory: Chauri Chaura, 1922–1992* (Berkeley: University of California Press, 1995); Ranajit Guha, "The Prose of Counter-Insurgency" in *Subaltern Studies, Vol. II: Writings on South Asian History and Society*, edited by Ranajit Guha (Delhi: Oxford University Press, 1983), pp. 1–42; Gyanendra Pandey, "The Colonial Construction of the Indian Past," in *The Construction of Communalism in Colonial North India* (Delhi: Oxford University Press, 1990), pp. 23–65.

[27] I. C. Bernard, Officiating Secretary to the Government of India, Reviewing the Opinion of Secretary of State Lord Stanley, Extract from the Proceedings of the Government of India

In the context of the Deccan unrest, inquiries followed, and the Report of the Deccan Riots Commission was issued the following year. It concluded – in familiar terms that in fact recapitulated analyses from the 1840s and 1850s – that a vast social transformation had been occurring in the countryside: Peasants, who had always been indebted to moneylenders, had become increasingly so in the context of the expansion of commercial agriculture, itself produced by the revenue settlement of Goldsmid and Wingate, which had dramatically increased the market value of land.[28] In this process of commodification, both agriculturalists' desire to expand their holdings and the value of their collateral for loans that might enable them to do so, increased markedly, leading to further expansion of rural indebtedness.[29] More dangerously, moneylenders had increasingly turned to the colonial courts to force debt repayment, and the courts had overwhelmingly confirmed the claims of the creditors.[30] This had ultimately resulted, according to the Commission, in the large-scale transfer of lands from peasant cultivators to Gujarati and Marwari moneylenders (*sowcars*), whose foreignness was seen as exacerbating their rapacity. In a pattern that was viewed as both socially undesirable and politically dangerous, formerly yeoman peasants were now rapidly becoming tenants on lands they had previously owned.[31]

These explanations promoted a critique of Utilitarianism and of the market, and concomitant support for preserving "traditional" modes of power in Indian society. The influence of Henry Maine's *Ancient Law* in colonial administrative circles during this era has been frequently

in the Home Dept. (Judicial) Nos. 9–608 to 9–618, May 27, 1879, in *Selections from the Records of the Government of India*, Home Department, No. CLV, "Correspondence Regarding the Law of Land Sale," 1879.

[28] *Poona Gazetteers*, 110–123; *Deccan Riots Commission Report*, 39.

[29] Charlesworth, *Peasants and Imperial Rule*, 42–43, 83–94, chapters 4 and 6; S. Guha, *Agrarian Economy*, 70–78, 83; *Poona Gazetteers*, 113–114.

[30] "Correspondence Regarding the Law of Land Sale."

[31] This analysis is also adopted by Kumar, *Western India in the Nineteenth Century*. Given the familiarity of much of this rhetoric, it is not surprising that revisionist scholars of several decades ago, including Neil Charlesworth and Ian Catanach, began to question both the importance of the riots as well as the effects of the legislation it produced. Both scholars ultimately suggested that the riots fitted neatly into existing debates within the government, and formed the basis for desired shifts in policy, even though that policy itself was in some ways limited in its effects. Both scholars do point to an expansion in the class of "agriculturalist money-lenders" however; that is, rich peasants who were presumably increasingly able to take the place of Gujarati *vanias* and Marwaris. Neil Charlesworth, "The Myth of the Deccan Riots of 1875," *Modern Asian Studies* 6, 4 (Oct. 1972): 401–421; I. J. Catanach, *Rural Credit in Western India, 1875–1930: Rural Credit and the Co-operative Movement in the Bombay Presidency* (Berkeley: University of California Press, 1970), pp. 10–55, esp. p. 26.

cited to suggest a widespread shift in colonial policy along these lines.[32] As with the Maine of *Ancient Law*, however, many of those supporting such changes in colonial policy viewed the market as natural and inevitable, but as inappropriate to the conditions of social existence in late-nineteenth-century India. For example, in an 1874 Minute, Law Member Sir Arthur Hobhouse summarized the now widely held belief that although the transfer of land from "the military to the trading classes" was a natural and inevitable feature of the progress of peace and civilization, the problem in India was that change was "being compressed into so short a period of time." For Hobhouse, the very benefits of British government in India had created the contemporary dilemma:

In the first place, by keeping the peace, by securing that he who sows shall reap, and by ascertaining and limiting the amount of taxation, we have given to land a kind of value which it did not possess before, and have made it an object of desire to those who possess money. In the second place, we have set up a powerful machine for doing justice and holding people to their obligations, so that a debtor must pay to the extent of his means, and cannot, however lawless or remote, set his creditor at defiance.... Two essential elements of civilization and national growth – a system of revenue and a system of legal administration – have been brought to bear upon society before it has made corresponding advances in general intelligence, in habits of prudence, or in its sense of the importance of enforcing obligations.[33]

Hobhouse thus viewed the blessings of a benevolent British rule as posing problems of structural adjustment for a society unprepared for such strong winds of progress. Yet, like Maine, he considered it impossible and undesirable to attempt to return to a status quo ante. Moreover, as the secretary of state for India Lord Cranbrook confirmed, many of the difficulties faced by cultivators in India as a whole and in the Deccan in particular offered "no opening on which the legislator can enter with effect." In the words of Lord Cranbrook cited in the epigraph to this chapter, "In all civilized societies there is a vast amount of suffering and destitution, very lamentable to contemplate, but which it is wholly out of the powers of the State by any direct action to eradicate."[34] Nonetheless, officials from the Bombay government as well as the government of India now converged in seeing potential room for amelioration in the

[32] Clive Dewey, "Influence of Sir Henry Maine"; Karuna Mantena, "Law and 'Tradition,'" and *Alibis of Empire*.

[33] Minute by Sir Arthur Hobhouse, dated April 28, 1874, in "Correspondence Regarding the Law of Land Sale," 408–409.

[34] Secretary of State to the Government of Bombay, No. 4 (Legislative), dated December 26, 1878, in ibid., 416.

law of land sale and in the operation of the courts in favor of creditors. As Lord Cranbrook himself further noted, "It is abundantly manifest to me, on the evidence collected by the [Deccan Riots] Commissioners, that no evil has been so loudly, and I must say so justly, complained of by the people as the action of the courts."[35] This near-exclusive emphasis on the role of the courts in enforcing debts, obscuring the role of the land revenue assessment in producing them, would form a major object of critique by liberal Indian reformer and nationalist M. G. Ranade, as will be seen.

Prominent in the group calling for adjustments in colonial policy was Sir Raymond West (1832–1912), scholar of Hindu law and justice of the Bombay High Court, who wrote a tract in 1873, predating the Deccan Riots, on the necessity of protecting agricultural land from sale for the repayment of debts. *The Land and the Law in India* was ultimately not so much about land, however, as about contracts, and "the right exercise of the State's authority in India in giving or refusing to give effect to private obligations."[36] Colonial law and the judicial system had hitherto operated disproportionately to the advantage of creditors; the question was the social and political costs of continuing to do so.

Strongly influenced by Maine's historical jurisprudence, West argued that in an expanding society, "when a community is passing from a very low state of organization, to one of comparative complication and refinement," the laws of the state could create an excess of power in the hands of the creditor: "The creditor practically has the person of his debtor as a pledge for the debt, and enjoying this advantage is legally relieved from all that care and circumspection which morality, if not self-interest, ought to make him exercise."[37] It was just such a condition that West identified in the India the British had created. Tracing the history of Aryan society in India, West argued that both imprisonment for debt and the attachment of a debtor's land in execution of a decree were unknown in Hindu law and under the major eighteenth-century regimes, such as the Maratha state and the Mysore of Tipu Sultan. Given these conditions, "to impose on such people the rule of punctual payment on the appointed day, with the alternative of law proceedings, costs, and eviction from house and land, was to condemn the mass of them to ruin."[38] West went

---

[35] Ibid., 417.
[36] Sir Raymond West, *The Land and the Law in India: An Elementary Inquiry and Some Practical Suggestions* (Bombay: Education Society's Press, 1873), p. 6.
[37] Ibid., 10.
[38] Ibid., 21–24.

on to excoriate the application of the principles of contemporary English society to an Indian society that had yet to go through the necessary stages to attain the apex that was the English present:

> Our English Government, taking for universal principles a set of prejudices directly the reverse of these, has built up its system on the rule of "Laissez faire," assumed a complete practical equality amongst its subjects in bargain making, thought little of the corporate character of the family, nothing of the tie between it and its lands. Yet in many of its measures it might well have borne in mind, that as the principles it was applying were but of recent discovery or demonstration, there was at least a possibility that in the older time they had never been hit upon, simply because of the existence of conditions which prevented the possibility of a beneficial practice in accordance with them suggesting a sound and fruitful theory.[39]

West thus articulated a theory of historical difference, at once decrying the universalism of the ideologues of laissez-faire and also suggesting that it was material conditions that enabled the emergence of what were properly local, not universal, principles as theory. The application of such theory or principles to India was already producing significant consequences. Ironically, West drew on a familiar strand of classical republican rhetoric to depict British rule as effectively causing the replacement of a sturdy yeoman peasantry with capitalists entirely lacking in civic virtue:

> The Rajput or Maratha yeomen disappearing or sinking into indigence and despair are replaced, as the Roman freeholders were, by a class of mere cultivators living from hand to mouth, without strong local attachments, or the sturdiness which independence gives. Above these come the new race of capitalists; men possessed by no ennobling ideas of public duty, cowards as a rule by caste and confession, citizens in no sense beyond that of benefiting society by selfish accumulation. A country with such a class of landlords must soon afford a caricature that should rather startle the advocates of economics and self-adjustment as the sole or chief basis of polity.[40]

West's concerns about the uncertain political virtue of a society of merchants, which harkened back to earlier debates in Bengal and in England, reflected an effort to establish a desirable "political community,"[41] characterized at once by economic independence and by the attachments of birth and locality.[42] What was not at issue for West, however, nor for that

---

[39] Ibid., 31–32.

[40] Ibid., 36.

[41] Ibid., 54–55. See Ranade's critique of West's proposals, specifically those aiming to restrict the alienability of land, M. G. Ranade, "Land Law Reform and Agricultural Banks," in Ranade, *Ranade's Economic Writings*, p. 156.

[42] Pocock, "Mobility of Property"; Rothschild, *Economic Sentiments*.

matter for the colonial officials who ultimately drafted the legislation on rural indebtedness, was the importance of the market and of institutions (including the courts) for the regulation of property and finance.

The 1879 Deccan Agriculturalists' Relief Act aimed to respond to these perceived conditions. The provisions of the act tried to ease the effects of rural indebtedness by protecting agricultural land from sale for the repayment of debts (except in cases where it had been explicitly pledged, and even then only as a last resort). It also sought to limit the pressure of exorbitant interest rates and the charging of compound interest, and it exempted agriculturalists from imprisonment for debt. In addition, it promoted conciliation and payment by installment to satisfy the needs of both debtors and creditors, and it sought to make a more benevolent version of the courts' justice accessible to rural debtors by granting the local government the power to vest village *patils* with the position of village *munsif*, or local judge, enabling them to decide suits of this nature for a value of up to Rs. 10.[43]

The act has long been understood as part of a broader ideological shift against liberalism in the aftermath of the 1857 rebellion. It imposed restrictions on the transfer of peasant land; it attempted to fix social identities and the social relations they entailed (i.e., it sought to prevent "non-agriculturalists" from acquiring the land of "agriculturalists");[44] and it created a significant role for the state in regulating and overseeing the loans that peasants undertook. One of the central and most onerous provisions of the legislation for the subordinate judges, village *munsifs*, and others engaged in enforcing it was the requirement to "go behind the bond" in certain subsets of cases, to trace the history of the relationship between the debtor and the creditor when a given case came before the court. These features represented a movement away from laissez-faire ideology.

Yet those who took this putatively traditionalist position nonetheless sought to regularize and expand the money economy, to limit liability

---

[43] The limitations the act imposed on the transferability of land were modest: It did not restrict any such transfer when the land was specifically pledged, and it enabled the court to direct the collector to take possession of any lands in excess of those required for subsistence and to manage them for the benefit of the creditor for seven years at a time. See also Thomas Metcalf, "The British and the Moneylender in Nineteenth-Century India," *Journal of Modern History* 34, 4 (Dec. 1962): 390–397.

[44] This impulse was ultimately most fully developed in the Punjab and embodied in the Punjab Land Alienation Act of 1901, which prohibited such transfers altogether. This distinction perhaps derived from the same grounds as the distinction in English bankruptcy law between "traders" and "non-traders," which was abolished only with the English bankruptcy reforms of the late nineteenth century. See Lester, *Victorian Insolvency*.

from extending to the bodies of the debtor and his family, and to ensure the functioning of a social economy in which relations of production and exchange could be seen as operating in the interests of a "mutual benefit" that forged the public good.[45] Moreover, the debates and the framing of the act consistently posited debt not as enmeshing entire structures of social relations, but as an antagonistic encounter of two individuals: debtor and creditor.[46] It was this relationship that needed to be made socially economical. The emphasis on preserving traditional social relations and the crucial protective role of the state therein thus went hand in hand with attentiveness to the expansion of the money economy in the countryside, and with a model of the acquisitive subject, drawn to support his neighbors in order that the economic welfare of each might benefit all. What was necessary was not only loosening the most egregious traditional forms of compulsion and obligation, but also instilling a proper sense of social obligation within the debtor. Hence, by the mid-1880s, in the context of contemporary proposals to abolish imprisonment for debt, West argued *against* such measures, despite the earlier views articulated in *The Land and the Law in India*: "If the ordinary native of India could be trained to a scrupulous fulfilment [*sic*] of his obligations, that would do him infinitely more good than a morbid sense of the sacredness of his person.... There is nothing essentially wrong ... in pledging one's person as security for the fulfilment of an obligation."[47] As this opinion suggests, for West, the liberal opposition between economic and legal modes of compulsion broke down in the recognition that the law played a critical role in "giving or refusing to give effect" to financial obligations. From this perspective, securing bodily autonomy appeared less important than inculcating personal discipline and a new sense of social responsibility. The educative process to achieve this result would necessarily involve some form of compulsion. Unsurprisingly, these concerns to establish the

---

[45] Among the key proposals both of those who took this putatively traditionalist position, as well as of Indian liberals such as Ranade, was the establishment of government agricultural banks or eventually cooperative societies to ensure adequate credit facilities in the countryside. Such proposals envisioned a role for the state in rural financing that violated liberal principles of laissez-faire to be sure, but nonetheless retained a capitalist market orientation. MSA, JD 1885, 43/1276; Kumar, *Western India*, 228–263; Catanach, *Rural Credit*, 10–55.

[46] For discussion of the conceptualizations of the individual and society implicit in such usage of "mutual benefit," see Mary Poovey, "The Liberal Civil Subject and the Social in Eighteenth-Century British Moral Philosophy," in Joyce, ed., *The Social in Question*, 44–61.

[47] Minute by Chief Justice of the Supreme Court Raymond West on the Bill to Amend the Law Regarding Imprisonment for Debt, MSA, JD 1886, 19/953, unpaginated.

social relations of property on their proper footing took on a different hue from the perspective of Indian commentators.

The Crisis of Agricultural Society in Indian Reformist Analyses and Critiques

Contemporary Indian reformers drew on these colonial methodologies and perspectives, but turned them to different analyses of the crisis of rural society. For reformers as distinctive as renowned elite social reformer, scholar, judge, and eventually High Court justice M. G. Ranade, and major non-Brahmin writer and activist Jotirao Phule, the fundamental problem was the way that colonial institutions both operated and failed to operate within rural society. Despite the distance between their perspectives, both developed a historical method of analysis for understanding the present woes of rural society, and both ultimately sought a prominent, developmentalist role for the colonial state, identifying the current role of the state in structuring social relations as both oppressive and inadequate.

Ranade, a Chitpavan Brahmin educated in the elite colonial institutions of the time, spoke directly to contemporary debates within the colonial administration; his writings addressed issues such as the Deccan Agriculturalists' Relief Act, rural credit and the law regarding land sale, the colonial revenue settlement, and the application of liberal political economy to India.[48] The voluntary society he helped form in Pune in 1870, the Sarvajanik Sabha (All People's Society), regularly addressed itself to the colonial government, and selections from one of its reports was included in the Report of the Deccan Riots Commission.[49] Indeed, Ranade was appointed special judge under the Deccan Agriculturalists' Relief Act in 1887, prior to his appointment to the High Court in 1895.

Ranade's major economic writings spanned some fifteen years, from the late 1870s through the early 1890s. This was also a critical period of his social reformist labors, although he continued those actively until his death in 1901, as discussed in Chapter 4. Ranade sustained several key arguments during this era: first and foremost, he relentlessly identified the extreme and ever-increasing colonial land revenue assessment as

[48] Most of Ranade's writings on contemporary Indian economics appeared in the *Journal of the Poona Sarvajanik Sabha*. Chandra, ed., *Ranade's Economic Writings, v.*

[49] "Extract from the Report of the Committee of the Poona Sarvajanik Sabha, Chapter III," Miscellaneous Papers, *Deccan Riots Commission Report*, 1875, 123–125.

the major cause of the rural agriculturalists' woes.[50] Refuting the state's claim to the status of universal landlord, he used the evidence of the Deccan Riots Commission Report itself to show the "one-sidedness" of the colonial emphasis on the responsibility of creditors and of the colonial courts, which ignored the responsibility of the land revenue exaction for the prevailing condition of the peasantry.[51] It was the necessity of paying the revenue that drove the peasant to the *sowcar*. This was the fundamental economic fact that underlay the coercive relations between creditor and debtor.[52] Perhaps ironically, Ranade argued that the *only* way to solve the "agrarian problem" was to establish a version of permanent settlement.[53] In other words, occupants needed to be converted into landowners.

Ranade thus simultaneously drew upon and critiqued the dictates of liberal political economy. As early as 1879, he railed against the Ricardian theory of rent, lashing out against the idea of the unearned increment: "It is a public misfortune that theorists, who find no scope for their hobbies in England, are allowed to inflict their mischievous fallacies upon this country with unrestricted freedom."[54] Yet at the same time, he situated his arguments within the iron laws of capital and markets. For example, he assessed the operation of the recently enacted Deccan Agriculturalists' Relief Act, drawing on classical liberal arguments concerning wealth and thrift:

In all countries property, whether in land or other goods, must gravitate towards that class which has more intelligence, and greater foresight, and practices abstinence, and must slip from the hands of those who are ignorant, improvident, and hopeless to stand on their own resources. This is a law of Providence, and can never be wisely or safely ignored by practical Statesmen for any fancied political or sentimental considerations.[55]

This inevitable evolutionary development, and what he elsewhere called the "natural union of capital and land,"[56] had clear implications both for

[50] Ranade, "The Agrarian Problem and Its Solution," "The Law of Land Sale in British India," "Land Law Reform and Agricultural Banks," and "Proposed Reforms in the Resettlement of Land Assessments," in *Ranade's Economic Writings*, 18; 78; 174–176; 254.

[51] Ranade, "The Deccan Agriculturists Bill," and "Mr. Wedderburn and His Critics on a Permanent Settlement for the Deccan," ibid., 22–23, 44; 81.

[52] Ranade, "The Deccan Agriculturists Bill," ibid., 40–41.

[53] Ranade, "The Agrarian Problem and Its Solution," "The Deccan Agriculturists Bill," and "Proposed Reforms in the Resettlement of Land Assessments," ibid., 13–16, 18; 39, 41; 254–255.

[54] Ranade, "The Agrarian Problem and Its Solution," ibid., 18.

[55] Ranade, "The Law of Land Sale in British India," ibid., 78.

[56] Ranade, "The Agrarian Problem and Its Solution," ibid., 17.

the power and limits of state action. The state's proper role in the context of the current agrarian crisis was necessarily both limited and developmentalist: to raise the level of the agriculturalist class so as to enable it to benefit more from these natural tendencies. This could be achieved only by limiting the revenue assessment, establishing proprietary rights, expanding education, and supporting rural credit institutions such as cooperative banks that would enable capital to flow to these hitherto economically parched regions.[57] Moreover, integral to the real economic advancement of the country was industrialization and the redevelopment of manufacturing, in order to reverse the nineteenth-century trend that saw artisanal producers pushed into agriculture, further crowding the ranks thereof.[58] If Ranade viewed economic inequalities as to some extent inevitable, he nonetheless called upon the state to play a significant and necessary role in enhancing the economic potential of Indian society.[59]

Ranade thus critiqued what he termed "dogmatic" free trade ideology, but retained a certain ambivalence regarding the universality claimed by and for political economy. He began to develop a comparative historicist methodology in his early writings, and by the early 1890s, he explicitly articulated his arguments within a historicist framework.[60] However, as was true of Maine, whose methodology Ranade adopted, this comparative historicism nonetheless assumed a universal historical trajectory.[61] Thus, in his 1881 essay on land law reform and agricultural banks, where he first utilized the comparative method, he also argued that "human nature is everywhere the same, and it cannot logically be maintained that the same incentives and guarantees, which the English planters require in their own interests, are out of place in the case of Native farmers."[62] Indeed, it was this universalism that *enabled* the comparative method through which he could examine the operation of state

---

[57] Ranade, "Mr. Wedderburn and His Critics," "Land Law Reform and Agricultural Banks," and "Reorganization of Real Credit in India," ibid., 97; 167–174, 177–178; 304.

[58] Ranade, "Industrial Conference," ibid., 277.

[59] Bhabatosh Datta, "The Background of Ranade's Economics," *Indian Journal of Economics* 22, 3 (1942): 261–275.

[60] For an early example of the comparativist model, see "Land Law Reform and Agricultural Banks," in *Ranade's Economic Writings*, 169ff. For his later explicit arguments, see "Indian Political Economy," ibid., 322–349. For a discussion of Ranade's use of German historicism, see Ajit Dasgupta, *A History of Indian Economic Thought* (London: Routledge, 1993), 90ff.

[61] This blending of the two frameworks is noted also in Dasgupta, *Indian Economic Thought*, 87–119, 116–117.

[62] Ranade, "Land Law Reform and Agricultural Banks," in *Ranade's Economic Writings*, 176.

policies in Hungary, France, and the like. In other words, human nature was the same, but history produced important differences. By 1893, Ranade fully articulated his historicist framework, arguing, in a critique of British writers who viewed self-government and democracy as inappropriate to India, but nonetheless ruthlessly applied to the colony the dictates of liberal political economy, "If in Politics and Social Sciences, time and place and circumstances, the endowments and aptitudes of men, their habits and customs, their laws and Institutions, and their previous History, have to be taken into account, it must be strange indeed, that in the Economical aspect of our life, one set of general principles should hold good everywhere for all time and place, and for all stages of Civilization."[63] Yet alongside this critique, Ranade left unquestioned the universal necessity of capital for agricultural (and industrial) development, and the essential role of what he called "the magic of property" in creating investment in land.[64]

Ultimately, Ranade developed a nationalist version of social economy in which, in a movement that sought to extend beyond the status-to-contract trajectory forecast by Maine, the relations of individuals would give way to the interests of society, and the needs of society in turn would draw out an expansive role for the state. Accordingly, in his 1893 essay, "Indian Political Economy," he argued,

Modern Thought is veering to the conclusion that the Individual and his Interests are not the centre round which the Theory should revolve, that the true centre is the Body Politic of which the Individual is a member, and that Collective Defense and Well-being, Social Education and Discipline, and the Duties, and not merely the Interests, of men, must be taken into account, if the Theory is not to be merely Utopian.[65]

These concerns of the "Body Politic" in turn necessitated a more active role in governance for the state:

The State is now more and more recognized as the National Organ for taking care of National needs in all matters in which individual and co-operative efforts are

---

[63] Ranade, "Indian Political Economy," ibid., 324.

[64] Ranade, "Land Law Reform and Agricultural Banks" and "The Re-Organization of Real Credit in India," ibid., 177–178; 304ff. Andrew Sartori argues that such blending of universalism and historical differentiation by elite Indian observers entailed an effective analysis of contemporary global capitalism as they witnessed it, which suggested both universal truths about economic production, but also the limitations, disjunctures, and failures thereof in the colonial context. Sartori, *Bengal in Global Concept History*.

[65] Ranade, "Indian Political Economy," in *Ranade's Economic Writings*, 336. Ranade's depiction is highly reminiscent of the seventeenth-century English merchants discussed in Pincus, "Neither Machiavellian Moment."

not likely to be so effective and economic as National effort. This is the correct view to take of the true functions of a State.... The question is one of time, fitness, and expediency, not one of liberty and rights."[66]

Thus, in Ranade's model, the freedom of the individual itself opened out to the question of society, or the nation as a whole, and to the critical role of the state in enhancing that society's capacities and securing its interests. In this sense, despite his critique of the actual workings of the colonial state, Ranade articulated a view of the necessity of an expansive state to safeguard the body politic.[67]

Such a view of the necessary power and socially transformative potential of the state also shaped the vision of Jotirao Phule. Phule was one of the earliest modern critics of caste, and particularly of Brahmin power. Born into the Mali, or gardener caste, a Shudra caste, and educated in a Scottish missionary high school, he became a prominent advocate for those he called *shudra-atishudra*, linking lower castes and Untouchables. For Phule, education was the primary means to counter the power of Brahmins over the impoverished majority, and state policies remained critical to this endeavor. Phule established a voluntary society, the Satyashodak Samaj (Truth-Seeking Society) in 1873, and along with his wife, Savitribai, founded schools for children from untouchable castes, as well as a home and orphanage for Brahmin widows and their illegitimate children. Phule also wrote extensively, both for a British and American audience and for Shudras and Untouchables themselves.[68] Although Phule's writings addressed colonial policies in more general terms than Ranade, they lavished detail on the conditions of existence of the socially and economically oppressed.

Phule also highlighted the deeply ingrained divisions within Indian society. In some sense, the core issue for Phule was the radical nonexistence of a unified social totality implied in the model of social economy. Where Ranade emphasized the role of the colonial state in fomenting discord within Indian society, and tended to depict Indian society itself as harmoniously integrating unequal groups into a unified whole,[69] Phule

---

[66] Ibid., 344. Such a vision fits with Foucault's depiction of the distinctive form of the modern state. See Foucault, "Governmentality."

[67] Chandra, "Introduction," *Ranade's Economic Writings*, xxiv*ff*, lvi.

[68] *Collected Works of Mahatma Jotirao Phule*, edited by Mahatma Jotirao Phule Death Centenary Central Committee (Bombay: Bombay Education Department, 1991). For discussion of Phule's writings, see O'Hanlon, *Caste, Conflict and Ideology*; see also Dhananjay Keer, *Mahatma Jotirao Phooley: Father of Our Social Revolution* (Bombay: Popular Prakashan, 1964).

[69] See, for example, M. G. Ranade, "The Central Provinces Land Revenue and Tenancy Bills," in *Ranade's Economic Writings*, 98–120, esp. 108–109. Notably, Ranade diverged

highlighted the role of the colonial state in exacerbating the Brahmin subjugation of the lower-caste poor majority. Thus, Phule opened his major 1883 tract, *The Cultivator's Whipcord (Shetkaryaca Asud)*, with his analysis of some of the causes of the woes of the "shudra farmers": "Because of an artificial and tyrannical religion, and because almost all the government departments are dominated by brahmans, and because the European workers are lazy, the shudra farmers are ill-treated by the brahman workers."[70] For Phule, the problem of the farmer's subjection to the moneylender was simply folded into his much broader subjection to the village Brahmin, who in many cases *was* the moneylender. Because of the farmer's ignorance and subjection to religion, the Brahmin was able to "loot" the farmer over and over through all manner of superstitious ceremonies and the expenses thereof.[71] Yet the British were also at fault: They taxed the farmer at oppressive rates and took over forest resources that had been common to the community, forcing the poor into factory labor while importing cheap British manufactures that undermined the artisans, driving weavers and others to "near starvation," surviving on "the piths of mangos."[72] The colonial government also burdened the farmer with new taxes and loans for canals that never helped him in his fields, for foreign military expeditions to enhance British glory, and to support their own extravagant lifestyle, saddling the farmer with debts and forcing him to mortgage his fields to the Brahmin moneylender.

Phule and Ranade in fact articulated similar critiques of the socially pernicious and fundamentally unjust nature of the colonial courts, both describing in detail the kinds of corruption and duplicity that shaped the judicial process. In Phule's account, the British courts were staffed by corrupt and caste-ist Brahmin clerks, lawyers, and judges, who did not hesitate to line their pockets at the farmer's expense, while failing entirely to deliver justice and disrespecting and demeaning the farmer in the process.[73] Meanwhile the British in the higher courts were lazy and

from this in his treatment of the condition of women and women's rights, as discussed in Chapter 4. Phule's major writings – "The Cultivator's Whipcord" ("Shetkaryacha Asud") and *Slavery (Gulamgiri)* – revolved around the oppression of the *shudra-atishudra* by Brahmins.

[70] Phule, "The Cultivator's Whipcord," in *Selected Writings of Jotirao Phule*, edited by G. P. Deshpande, translated by Aniket Jawaare, 113–189 (New Delhi: Leftword Books, 2002), p. 117.

[71] Ibid., esp. 120–130.

[72] Ibid., 132.

[73] Ibid., 134–135, 137, 138.

ignorant, "engrossed in a luxurious and a peaceful life," and allowed the Brahmin employees in the courts to continue to exploit the farmer. Indeed, this was part of a larger pattern in which the British handed over most of the real activities of government to the Brahmins and "spent all their time in the pursuit of various pleasures; expensive clothes, objects, horses, carriages and food," and then increased the taxes on the farmer to support their extravagant salaries and pensions.[74] As quoted in one of the epigraphs to this chapter, Phule bitterly satirized "Christian" governance: "While reassessing the ignorant farmers' lands every thirty years, the European workers, blindly worshipping our virtuous government, do not say 'Amen' until they have raised the taxes at least a little."[75] Phule was clearly highly attuned to the political theology of the colonial state, its apotheosizing of its own governance, and to the parallels between Brahmin and British sovereignty in their economic exploitation of the poor.

Phule also developed a detailed ethnographic approach to documenting the material and spiritual subjugation within Indian society, taking the household as the critical unit of analysis. Like the contemporary urban muckrakers of Victorian England and America, Phule narrated in relentless detail the living conditions of the rural farmer:

Beside it lies a heap of waste fodder, and in the remaining area sits a youngish woman, with her back to the house, arranging cow-pats. She is up to her knees in the dung, pounding it with her feet.... Here is a heap of pith thrown about, and there a heap of rotting onions. A stale stink rises from them. In the middle, an ancient woman is lying on a sheet, groaning.... The walls are covered with stains left from squishing bugs and insects on them, and fingers wiping off snot. In a small cabinet is the oil pot, tooth powder, a horn comb, a rickety mirror, and on a ledge three or four stone lamps are stacked for the night. An oil stain spreads from them onto the ground.[76]

The contours of this material existence – the extraordinary deprivation, economic compulsion, and degradation of the Shudra agriculturalist household that Phule depicted – formed the basis for an analysis of the social reproduction of poverty and a call for necessary state intervention to interrupt it. Such a role for the state would itself have to operate at the level of the household, transforming material conditions as well as the forms of subjectivity that they produced at this most foundational level. Phule envisioned this transformation of the habitus through a wholesale

---

[74] Ibid., 152.
[75] Ibid., 134.
[76] Ibid., 160. This is a brief excerpt of a much longer description, which extends over several pages.

project of education. This concern with the role of the family in structuring existing social relations of domination would also become a significant issue for colonial officials. Notably, however, the official debate would come to focus on the joint Hindu family form and Hindu laws of inheritance, rather than on broader social relations as the cause of poverty.

The Uneconomical Family as Object of Policy

Beginning in the 1880s, the colonial administration turned its attention to the effects of the joint Hindu family on agricultural productivity, or what it termed "uneconomical holdings" – the division and fragmentation of agricultural plots through successive partitions to the point where they were no longer large enough to be economically viable. This process was interpreted as the product of an increase in population, coupled with the joint Hindu family "system" of granting equal, partible shares to all lineal male family members, which left each generation with strikingly diminished shares. By the late nineteenth century, officials of all political persuasions viewed partitions of joint family property as the bane of rural society.

The goal of preventing partitions suggests something of a conservative trend against individual autonomous property holding, and some of the proponents of legislation to address this issue indeed saw themselves in this light. Yet the impetus for reform also emerged out of comparable English legislation at this time, which aimed not so much to preserve traditional patriarchal power, as to limit the physical partition of real property in the interests of preserving its market value.[77]

Debates in the vernacular press on the issue emerged as early as 1880, with an article in the elite and high-caste oriented Marathi-language Pune journal, *Shivaji*, calling for a law of primogeniture in India to counter the ill economic effects of the joint Hindu family. Rehearsing familiar colonial arguments, as well as those developed by Ranade at this time, the paper called on the government to address this vital issue for "the welfare of the community":

Under the present system idleness is encouraged, because all the members of a family depend upon the ancestral heritage, and never dream of applying

---

[77] See, for example, Parliamentary Papers, 1928, Cmd. 3132, "Report of the Royal Commission on Agriculture in India, chapter 5," cited in Neil Charlesworth, "The Origins of Fragmentation of Landholdings in British India: A Comparative Examination," in Peter Robb, ed., *Rural India* (London: Curzon Press, 1983): pp. 181–215.

themselves to opening out new channels of industry for the benefit of themselves and their children. Accumulation of capital for such purpose is therefore become an impossibility, and without capital there can be no enterprize [*sic*]. The nobility on account of their large interests at stake constitute the back-bone of the strength of a government; and that country, in which that strength is wanting, cannot be said to be well circumstanced.[78]

Anticipating the argument that such a change was "against the spirit of the ancient laws," the article countered that "it should be remembered that the British Government is not influenced by any such consideration of veneration for antiquity, when the advantages from a departure from the old course are patent, as for instance, witness the suppression of *sati*, infanticide, &c. The old must always make way for the new if the latter is decidedly more advantageous." Such an argument resonated strongly with the contemporary interests of rural elites (such as *vatandars*, as explored in the next section), simultaneously lauding the new while seeking to bolster the position of the rural "nobility."

In the mid-1880s, legislators began to pursue the possibility of amending the law of partition along the lines of the recently passed English Partition Act of 1868.[79] Draft legislation emerged as early as 1884, to mixed response.[80] In 1886, Henry Starling, a member of the Bombay Bar, again proposed a Government of India Act along such lines. The proposal, following the English legislation, aimed to enable individual family members seeking partition of the family property, or the courts called on to enact partitions of highly fragmented estates, to do so through the sale of the property and division of the proceeds. Again a draft bill was circulated and allowed to lapse.[81] In 1889, eminent Calcutta High Court lawyer, social reformer, and moderate nationalist Dr. Rashbehari Ghose reintroduced the legislation, submitting a revised draft bill.[82] Again a flurry of equivocal responses ensued: In the Bombay Presidency, several district judges supported the proposed measures, at least in principle, as a salutary response to the desperate problem of fragmentation of holdings,

---

[78] *Shivaji*, September 17, 1880, RNP, 10.

[79] 31 and 32 Vict., c. 40. MSA, JD 1889, 39/1203, p. 277.

[80] B. G. Tilak's English language *Mahratta*, also a paper of the high-caste Pune elite, criticized it as putting "the Brahmans and Rajputs ... to such an immense trouble and inconvenience that they will sooner like to give up their five acres of land than consent to submit to the Partition Act." *Mahratta*, February 3, 1884, RNP, 14.

[81] MSA, JD 1890, 36/451, pp. 165–176.

[82] MSA, JD 1889, 39/1203, pp. 263–288. The bill allowed for any family member who wanted to purchase the entire property to do so, and also provided for any family members wishing to continue to remain joint to continue to hold their portions of the property jointly, while the other portion would be sold.

and the advocate general as well as High Court Justice K. T. Telang also approved of it with some modifications.[83] Yet, the Bombay governor, Lord Reay, vociferously opposed the proposed legislation, as threatening the foundational nature and social role of "the Hindu family system":

Apart from the Hindu family system there is hardly an effective principle of coherence and conservatism at work in our rapidly changing native society. It is, under the operation of economic and moral causes, becoming chaotic, and the state of weltering confusion with which we are threatened can be combated or converted into a gradual and beneficial transition only by the power of historical institutions and the associations connected with them. Of these the family system is the most important and the most powerful. The individualism which is the central notion of modern English and European life is creeping in more and more even in India. This is inevitable. But being out of harmony with the general mass of native institutions, which have grown up on an entirely different basis from those of western countries, this individualism, unless the process is conducted and controlled with prescience and sagacity, cannot be established without infinite suffering and even moral degeneration.[84]

If this conservative opinion resonated strongly with those of West and Maine, in Reay's view the "excessive" subdivision of property was a problem that required a retrenchment that went even beyond the terms of Hindu texts and orthodox practice: "The unqualified right to claim a partition now recognized as vested in every male coparcener in this Presidency ought ... to be abolished. The partition ought not to be claimable against the will of a father or even an older brother or other head of a Hindu family except in circumstances where it can plainly be seen to be beneficial."[85] Yet as the governor's proposal suggests, the diversity of opinions on the partition legislation masked a shared conviction that producing social economy out of the uneconomical joint Hindu family depended on a powerful, consolidated, and individualized ownership, whether achieved through patriarchal power or marketization. In 1893, the government of India passed a Partition Act along the lines proposed by Dr. Rashbehari Ghose, which enabled joint property to be sold instead of divided when two thirds of the coparceners requested it. As a permissive

---

[83] MSA, JD 1890, 36/451, pp. 165–176. Many of the concerns regarding the bill paralleled those of the debates surrounding the Deccan Agriculturalists' Relief Act: that moneylenders holding a claim on a portion of a family's property could use the legislation to force the sale of a family's ancestral property or home. This possibility itself existed only as a result of the shift in the courts' jurisprudence that began to treat individual shares as alienable, as discussed in Chapter 3.

[84] Ibid., 165.

[85] Ibid., 166.

act only, however, its application remained limited, and the larger issue of fragmentation of holdings remained unresolved.

A quarter of a century later, in 1918, the director of the Agriculture Department, G. F. Keatinge, returned to the issue, drafting a proposed Economic Holdings Act, whose aim was "to prevent the excessive subdivision of agricultural holdings in the Presidency of Bombay." The bill proposed to enable persons to register their property as an "economic holding," and thereby render it impartible property, subject to the laws of primogeniture, and take it out of the operation of the personal laws of inheritance altogether, as had been suggested by the journal *Shivaji* nearly four decades before, and as something of an ironic reprise on Lord Reay's patriarchal vision. This bill likewise met with strong opposition, however, and failed in its early stages.

One of the major voices on this issue – and one of the few to critique the terms of debate – was economist, scholar, and preeminent Dalit leader B. R. Ambedkar. Although Ambedkar had worked with Keatinge in 1916 to pressure the government on the issue of fragmentation of holdings, he strongly criticized the way the debate came to be framed. The critical issue, Ambedkar argued, like earlier economic nationalists such as Ranade, was the extensive agricultural surplus population, a product of the lack of capital and hence of industrial development. Critiquing the colonial depiction of Indian culture – and specifically the laws of the joint Hindu family – as responsible for the fragmentation of holdings, he argued,

This enormous pressure [of the agricultural population] is the chief cause of the subdivision of the land and not the law of inheritance. The law of inheritance is invoked because it is profitable [for the colonial state to do so]. Farming is the only occupation and to get a small piece of land is better than to have none.... People cultivate the small piece not because their standard of living is low as Mr. Jevons seems to think but because it is the only profitable thing for them to do at present. If they had something more profitable to do they would never prefer the small piece.[86]

Although Ambedkar's critique seems to have been largely ignored by the colonial administration, it offered, like Phule's critique of more than three decades before, a structural analysis of the problem of rural poverty, in

[86] B. R. Ambedkar, "Small Holdings in India and Their Remedies," in *Dr. Babasaheb Ambedkar, Writings and Speeches, Vol. 1*, edited by Vasant Moon, 455–479 (Bombay: Government of Maharashtra, Education Department, 1979), pp. 471ff. Also cited in V. D. Nagar and K. P. Nagar, *Economic Thought and Policy of Dr. Ambedkar* (New Delhi: Segment Books, 1992), p. 42.

which the significance of the laws of inheritance emerged as a result rather than the cause of rural poverty. From this perspective, the colonial emphasis on the joint Hindu family could be understood as at once creating new openings for state intervention and also as obscuring the responsibility of the colonial state and of colonial capitalism in producing rural poverty. Nonetheless, the existing terms of debate remained resilient. The dilemma of seemingly inexorable progress to uneconomical holdings through the operation of the Hindu law of partition in fact reemerged in the postcolonial debates on the Hindu Succession Act in the 1950s, when the question of producing social economy took on a new valence.[87]

For the colonial state, the question of the causes, implications, and solutions of widespread rural poverty and indebtedness took shape through the ambiguous goals of remaking existing modes of compulsion. Such efforts sought to utilize both juridical and economic means to inculcate new structures and sentiments of social obligation. These efforts abjured social shaming and violence, but heightened the operation of impersonal modes of compulsion and deepened the reach of both state and economic forces. The goal of producing autonomy therefore intrinsically brought in its train a variety of new modes of state power and new imaginings of personhood and of social life. The ambiguities this involved emerged with particular salience in the treatment of hereditary offices.

PART II: FEUDAL PROPERTY IN COLONIAL SOCIETY: REGULATING HEREDITARY OFFICES

The colonial effort to regulate hereditary offices, or *vatan*, like its treatment of rural indebtedness, was centrally concerned with the question of how the dictates of political economy played out in Indian society. It was also similarly concerned with the existence and potential transformation of a prior system of value and social power. Yet, the explicit social aims of *vatan* policy in the late nineteenth century were generally quite limited. Despite occasional official visions of a wholesale transformation of Indian society, the general rhetoric of colonial policy regarding *vatan* during this era was to attempt to reform and redefine the role of these hereditary offices in government, while preserving the social relations of which they were a part. These efforts proved both successful and unsuccessful.

---

[87] See Rochona Majumdar, *Marriage and Modernity: Family Values in Colonial Bengal* (Durham, NC: Duke University Press, 2009), chapter 6.

Ultimately, they led to the disappearance of *vatan* as a property form, but the social relations and forms of material and symbolic value that *vatan* entailed were both preserved and transformed.

From early colonial officials down to recent scholars, a narrative of inevitable decline and loss so poignantly expressed in Ravinder Kumar's phrase, "the twilight of the watandars," has told the story of the transformation of *vatan* from a primary structure of rural dominance to a subordinate and ultimately humiliating position of employment.[88] Equally crucial in this narrative was the transformation in the role of *vatan* in the symbolics of status: from a person's connection to a *vatan* both embodying and signaling, or serving as the "outward and visible sign" (in the words of one government resolution) of his broader social status and rural power, it increasingly came to operate merely as an index of wealth or reputation.[89] Indeed, as this section will discuss, by the last decades of the century, elites who held *vatans* now preferred to pursue wealth and status through the new professions in the cities.

In fundamental ways, however, this scholarly narrative has remained within the terms of resistance posed both by *vatandars* themselves and by colonial officials; that is, a rhetoric of traditional patriarchal loss.[90] This

---

[88] Kumar, *Western India*, chapter 4, esp. 150. See also R. D. Choksey, *Economic History of the Bombay Deccan and Karnatak (1818–1868)* (Puné: Oriental Watchman Publishing House, 1945); Kotani, *Western India in Historical Transition*.

[89] Government Resolution No. 6141, October 12, 1877, MSA, RD 1877, 210/793, pp. 153–154.

[90] The question of patriarchal power remained one of the major frameworks in which *vatandars* as well as colonial officials debated and resisted colonial policies. For some of the extensive history of the treatment of women as *vatandars*, see, for example, MSA, RD 1875, 37 Part II/676, pp. 13–668 (pp. 317–326); MSA, RD 1882, 245/1203, pp. 503–545. For ongoing colonial discussion and often acrimonious debate on this issue, involving numerous officials at a variety of levels, see MSA, RD 1838, 4 (864)/166, pp. 125–127; MSA, RD 1883, 15/1279, pp. 7–8, 13–15, 25; MSA, RD 1885, 349/506, pp. 310–425; MSA, RD 1885, 350/342, p. 41; MSA, RD 1886, 311/519, p. 123; MSA, RD 1888, 7/270, p. 363. For cases that followed involving widows' and daughters' claims, see MSA, RD 1874, 142/1510, pp. 129–170; MSA, RD 1893, 96/1082, pp. 173–192; and MSA, RD 1898, 63/129, pp. 83–122; MSA, RD 1891 226/1591, pp. 27–29. For further alterations and reassessments see MSA, RD 1900, 272/1166, pp. 73–74; MSA, LD 1922, 3/226, pp. 299 348; as well as the following court cases: *Bhikaji v. Secretary of State* (1925) ILR 49 Bom 554; *Malgauda Paragauda Patil v. Babaji Dattu Bhakare* (1912) ILR 37 Bom 107; *Hanmant Ramchandra Kulkarni v. Secretary of State* (1929) ILR 54 Bom 125; *Sundrabai v. Hanmant* (1931) ILR 56 Bom 298; *Fakirgowda Basangowda Patil v. Dyamawa* (1932) ILR 57 Bom 488. For debates on the issue in the contemporary Marathi and bilingual press, see *Mahratta*, August 16, 1885, *Dñyanprakash*, September 20, 1885, both in OIOR, *Reports on Native Papers* (1885).

language eventually provided an affective narrative for the *vatandars'* own ultimate devaluation and supersession of this property form. As in the words of the *vatandars* of Nasik District reported by one of the British sub-collectors, they "might as well not be watandars for all the benefit they got from their position."[91] Missing from this declension narrative, however, is any sense of the ways in which *vatandars* marshaled old forms of dominance to situate themselves within new forms of social power.[92] The history of *vatan* in this era involved not only the incomplete and uneven supersession of one form of value, but also the potential for transposing the social capital of *vatan*, enabling it to operate within a new framework.

As discussed in Chapter 1, *vatan* was a hereditary claim to perform a particular kind of labor and to receive certain payments and perquisites, binding socially differentiated persons to specific forms of labor and social status. It occupied a central place in colonial administration because tax collection and maintenance of records – issues of primary importance to the colonial state – were historically accomplished by those who held the *vatan* for each of these tasks. As a form of property held collectively by male coparceners, however, *vatan* had also always been connected to the affairs of families. During this era, colonial policy centered on the familial nature of *vatan* holding. It attempted at once to rationalize the performance of *vatan* service and privatize the distribution of *vatan* property by limiting familial claims, and yet it also aimed to preserve existing social economies of status and worth in which familial politics played a critical role, for example, in the enhanced marriageability of daughters associated with *vatandar* status.[93] At the same time, the intrinsic centrality of the family to *vatan* holding provided an idiom for a variety of largely elite public campaigns and responses to colonial *vatan* policy. Ultimately, state policy and the actions of *vatandars* coalesced to preserve the social relations of differentiation and domination that *vatan* entailed, even as the modalities of these social relations were largely transformed.

[91] MSA, RD 1874, 36/541, p. 59.
[92] Perlin, "Of White Whale and Countrymen."
[93] MSA, RD 1876, 43/Part I; Comp. 112/Part II, pp. 102–103; MSA, RD 1877, 210/793, pp. 61–65; Resolution No. 6141, Oct. 12, 1877, in MSA, RD 1877, 210/793, pp. 153–154. For some sense of the transformations in the market in brides and grooms at this time, see MSA, RD 1913, Comp. 1070, Part I, pp. 149–150. For recent discussions of the emergence of a modern marriage market and connections to the expansion of dowry, see Majumdar, *Marriage and Modernity*; Ranjana Sheel, *The Political Economy of Dowry: Institutionalization and Expansion in North India* (Delhi: Manohar Press, 1999).

Redefining Ownership, Redefining Family

Chapter 1 detailed changes in *vatan* as a property form from the establishment of colonial rule to the early 1860s. This chapter takes the story to the early twentieth century, when the elite village *vatan* of *kulkarni* (village accountant) was superseded and abolished. During this half-century, legislation focused on elite village officers. The most significant legislation of this era was the Bombay Hereditary Offices Act of 1874 (Act III of 1874), frequently referred to as the Watan Act. This act was depicted as preserving existing rights of *vatandars*, and it was clearly framed to garner the support of elite village *vatandars*, who were wary of any encroachment on their claims, as well as to assuage a central government committed to a rhetoric of preserving tradition.[94] In contrast to the treatment of district officers a decade before, the Vatan Act did not seek to sever the connection of these *vatans* to the state, nor to challenge the hereditary performance of village administration. Yet in effect, despite its conservative rhetoric, the Vatan Act aimed not to restore an earlier legitimacy, but to create more efficient office holding by limiting both the number of *vatan* officiators and the number of co-sharers (frequently in the dozens) who laid claim to its payments and benefits, and by privatizing (but not eradicating) its more complicated and objectionable forms of social relations.

The act proceeded by narrowing the meaning and claims of family in relation to this form of property, as well as the way this property form linked social relations to political power. It attempted to regulate the performance of service and make it more efficient by curtailing the practice of rotating service among all the sharers in the *vatan*. This was to be achieved by restricting the claim to perform the *vatan* service to those who were now termed "representative *vatandars*," whose name would be recorded as sole bearer of this right in the government register.[95] It also established that, in so far as possible, "representative *vatandar*" status was to go to the "head of the family," defined as the eldest male, and to pass through the lineage of eldest males.[96] In other words, in ways that officials would

---

[94] MSA, RD, 1874, 36/541, p. 130.

[95] This may be viewed as following earlier administration that developed the language of "registered *vatandar*" and "officiating *vatandar*," as in Act XI of 1843, discussed in Chapter 1.

[96] The Bombay government's narrative justification for the 1874 Watan Act explained that the earlier Act XI of 1843, which had also aimed to restrict the practice of rotation, had ultimately had the opposite effect, especially following the institution of cash payments

later draw on to address the uneconomical family in general, the act concerned itself with the fragmentation of property and perquisites, and the effects this had on economy and governance. Beyond these provisions, it also reconfirmed a preexisting prohibition on alienating *vatan* property from the *vatandar* family, which dated back to Elphinstone's Regulations of 1827. The terms of this legislation thus restricted the mobility both of *vatan* property and of *vatan* service, while they also strengthened what in most cases had been a rather weak logic of primogeniture. Additionally, in the case of the subaltern Mahar *vatan*, the act also confirmed the rights of villagers to extract customary and degrading forms of labor from the Mahar, defining such relations of domination and degradation as merely private or social, similarly to the treatment of the "useful and useless village servants" discussed in Chapter 1.[97]

As the benefits of *vatandar* status became tied more tightly to performing the service, or "officiating" the *vatan*, family members avidly sought this denomination for themselves. Although the new category of "representative *vatandar*" posed the eldest male merely as first among equals, in practice it worked to restrict *vatandar* status and its benefits to a single male and his line, eradicating the unlimited parsing of the *vatan* into shares. The legislation thus had the effect of limiting the social authority and status that flowed from a family's connection to a *vatan* to those segments of a family that could claim "representative *vatandar*" status.[98] Such trends were further exacerbated by an amendment to the Watan Act in 1886 (Act V of 1886), which effectively eliminated women's claims to *vatandar* status entirely by "postponing" all females in the line of heirs to any potential male heir. Following the failure of male heirs, the *vatan* would escheat to the state.[99]

---

in the early 1850s. The major reason for this proliferation of service by rotation, however, which remained missing from the state's own analysis, was that the 1843 legislation aimed to restrict the benefits and perquisites of *vatandar* status to those performing the *vatandar* service, thus rendering the performance of service crucial in a way it had never been before. See Bombay Act No. III of 1874, Appendix A.

[97] The Mahar *vatan* is discussed in detail in Chapter 5.

[98] For resistance to this legislation, both from *vatandars* and from collectors and sub-collectors, again framed simultaneously in terms of the dictates of political economy and the legitimacy of tradition, see Letter from A. C. Trevor, First Assistant Collector of Nasik, to H. Erskine, Collector of Nasik, No. 26 of 1874, MSA, RD 1874, 36/541, pp. 48–9. Similar opinions were expressed by Mr. Charles, another Nasik sub-collector at p. 59.

[99] Cited in MSA, RD 1888, 7/270, p. 363. For official debates about women's potential to serve as *vatandars* following this act, see MSA, RD 1891 226/1591, pp. 27–29; MSA, RD 1900 272/1166, pp. 73–74; MSA, LD 1922, 3/226, pp. 299–348. *Sitabai v. Secretary of State* (1925) ILR 49 Bom 554.

The new administrative treatment of *vatans* produced a flurry of claims; it also began to transform the value and social operation of this form of property.[100] This process itself involved something of a narrowing, if not a trend toward individualization, of wealth and status, making the *vatandar* more recognizable as a kind of private owner, tied to his own direct lineage, and little beholden to the claims of his brothers. Moreover, although still unable to permanently alienate or transact with the *vatan*, *vatandars* now maintained a more direct, transparent, and autonomous relationship to it; *vatan* could increasingly be conceptualized as direct payment for the performance of service – long a goal of colonial policy – with service itself leeched of much of its earlier sociopolitical power.

The Mobility of Social Capital

These colonial policy changes provoked shifts in the social meanings of *vatandar* status, as well as arguments that drew on the rhetoric of a vast social transformation to attempt to preserve "traditional" society intact. Nonetheless, *vatandar* families were often able to use both the existing and the changing nature of *vatan* to launch themselves into newly emergent positions of privilege. Such local social processes effectively took shape in a liberal register, recasting claims to natural hereditary relations of social dominance as matters of individual family striving, personal propensities, connections, and luck. This idiom obscured persistent forms of social domination and instead limited questions of justice and rights to the context of competing familial claims.

This process of transforming social capital emerged most prominently in colonial policy regarding the Brahmin office of village accountant, or *kulkarni vatan*. By the turn of the twentieth century, there was widespread official conviction in the desirability of abolishing the office of *kulkarni*. As the commissioner of the Central Division expressed, he personally "wish[ed] it were practicable, with a stroke of the pen, to abolish kulkarnis altogether, and replace them with an organized service of better paid, better disciplined, and more efficient stipendiary accountants."[101] Ironically,

---

[100] Among the plethora of claims, see the particularly notable examples at MSA, RD 1883, 259/891, pp. 309–327; MSA, RD 1880, 83/549, pp. 569–629; and the suggestive petition of Bapoo wullud Sunkrajee at MSA, RD 1874, 138/938, pp. 357ff.

[101] MSA, RD 1913, Comp. 1070, Pt. I, pp. 193–194. This opinion was actually toward the moderate end of the spectrum. For more extreme examples, see the opinions of the Collectors of Sholapur and of Satara, at ibid., pp. 200–201. Such opinions were not unchallenged, however. See, for example, the reports of the Collectors of Nasik and Ahmednagar at MSA, RD 1895, 294/549, pp. 93–98.

however, in the first years of the twentieth century, the proposals to reform and overhaul the *kulkarni* system actually aimed not to replace *kulkarnis*, but instead returned to earlier models of attempting to convert the *vatan* into an efficient civil service, seeking to extend their term of service to a life term (or to age fifty-five), to increase their remuneration, and to try to encourage representative *vatandars* to serve in person.[102]

It appears that by the early twentieth century, representative *kulkarni vatandars* rarely themselves conducted the work of their office. Although *kulkarnis* still commanded respect within the village because of the service component of their *vatan*, and although they still valued their claims to *vatan* service, this sentiment did not extend to respect for the actual performance of service, but only to the claim to appoint a deputy to perform the service in their place.[103] This involved not a shift, but rather the expansion of, an earlier feudal mode previously only available to the most elite *vatandars*, to demur from performing the actual labor of service. At the same time, however, those who no longer served in person had begun to pursue other opportunities elsewhere. It was now widely accepted that members of *vatandar* families who had the education and ambition left the village for better opportunities in government service, and village *kulkarni*-ships were perceived as low-paying jobs "without prospects."[104] Thus, a letter from the *Times of India*, dated November 2, 1904, concluded,

Lastly, there lies the question of prospects. A kulkarni who has taken the trouble to pass the 6th standard and thereby earns his Rs. 12 a month in the village, should be able to look forward to better employment. If not, he is in danger of experiencing the same despondency which the more intelligent kulkarni at present feels. Why should he not, after a course of good service in the village, be eligible for a clerkship in the taluka office, whether as account karkun, barnishi karkun, or otherwise? Why, in other words, should not the village accountancy and some of the appointments in the Mamlatdar's office be made interchangeable?[105]

This opinion was echoed in a letter in B. G. Tilak's vernacular paper, *Kesari*, of January 17, 1905, stating that "even peons in Government service get higher pay than the kulkarnis, and have further the prospects of

[102] Ibid., 180–202.

[103] Ibid. Other notable details that emerge from this correspondence include the fact that in cases where there were still lands attached to the *vatan*, those lands were almost always already paying nearly the full assessment, if not the full assessment, on the land as *judi* (quitrent). Ibid., 193–194.

[104] Ibid., 249.

[105] Ibid., 281–282.

promotion and pension open to them, while the kulkarnis are permanently debarred from aspiring to these privileges though they may have put in 25 or 30 years' service without making the slightest default."[106] Both writers thus sought a form of *kulkarni*-ship that was defined by its full integration with the rest of the colonial bureaucracy: a hereditary office that nonetheless offered "prospects" for personal advancement. From the perspective of the liberal binary of hereditary status versus merit, the irony of such proposals is apparent. Yet considering *vatan* as a mode of social power, it is clear that in the ancien régime, *vatan* holding had been a definitive mode of familial advancement.[107] In this context, what these proposals aimed to do was to connect *vatans* with the new modes of social distinction and advancement that had increasingly replaced the earlier structures of which *vatan* was a part. In other words, these proposals aimed to preserve the supple value of *vatans* and to ensure the continued dominance of the old *vatandars* within the new dispensation. The latter article also suggested the particular caste prick of the *kulkarnis'* position, complaining that "the Kulkarnis in this or any other district are mostly Brahmins, while the chief authority in the village, viz., the Patil, is a Kunbi, a Muhammadan, or even a Mahar, and draws a much higher salary without sharing any responsibility. Government can tolerate even an illiterate Patil, while woe be to the Brahmin Kulkarni who commits even the slightest default."[108]

By 1913 the shift in official discussions from reforming *kulkarni vatans* to replacing *kulkarnis* appears to have been complete. At this time, the government circulated proposals that aimed to commute these *vatans* in a similar manner to the treatment of district officers in the 1860s.[109] In contrast to the situation of the district officers, however, in this case, the duties performed by *kulkarnis* were still critical to revenue collection and village administration. In fact, *kulkarnis* had been trained to take on new duties involved with the colonial government's land surveys and revenue assessment, which had not previously formed a part of the *kulkarnis'* work. In this context, these efforts to abolish *kulkarni vatans* also included provisions to replace *kulkarnis* with "stipendiary clerks," or

---

[106] Cited in MSA, RD 1913, Comp. 1070, Pt. I, pp. 249, 281–282.

[107] Perlin, "Of White Whale."

[108] Cited in MSA, RD 1913, Comp. 1070, Pt. I, pp. 281–282.

[109] The *kulkarnis* would be required to purchase exemption from performing the service (at a rate of eleven annas in the rupee), and would be allowed to continue to hold the remaining five annas as their *vatan*. Alternate proposals drew on the example of the extinction of cash allowances of useless village servants, also from the 1860s, as discussed in Chapter 1.

talatis, expanding on a system that had long been present in the northern districts of Gujarat, where village *kulkarnis* were few.

James McNeill, acting collector of Poona, drafted one of the main proposals for replacing *kulkarnis* with *talatis*. According to McNeill's report, as presented in one of the epigraphs to this chapter,

> The system of distributing work according to ancient hereditary rights of service with practically no regard to the capacities of the workers, the nature of the work, or the adequacy of the remuneration can tend only to inefficiency. These ancient rights now conflict with the rights of the public to have the public service efficiently administered through a well-selected, properly-trained, and adequately-paid subordinate staff.... The hereditary rights of privileges of individuals must give way to the needs of the public.[110]

McNeill's focus on efficiency as a matter of "public interest" thus sought to link the interests of society with those of the colonial state. Recasting property as private – a matter of the privileges of individuals – would form a crucial step in protecting the needs of this public.

Although in 1914, the *kulkarnis* in the Central and Southern Divisions organized themselves and bombarded Viceroy Lord Hardinge with petitions urging government to protect their "ancient hereditary rights,"[111] reports filed that same year by the revenue commissioner of the Central Division suggest that in many cases, *kulkarnis* fearing the direction of government policy, were petitioning for the commutation of their *vatans*.[112] In most parts of the Bombay Presidency, the government effectively commuted the service portion of *kulkarni vatans* during the period of 1913 to 1915.[113] Nonetheless, a late ironic twist of this history can be seen in the case of those perhaps "despondent" *kulkarnis* still performing the *vatan* service in the village. According to a 1915 report by R. E. Enthoven on commutation in the Central Districts, the process of appointing *talatis* to replace *kulkarnis* was then nearly 75 percent complete, the *talatis*, in nearly all cases, being the ex-*kulkarnis*.[114]

---

[110] MSA, RD 1913, Comp. 1070, Pt. I, p. 383.

[111] MSA, RD 1914, Comp. 1070, includes hundreds of standard typed petitions signed and submitted by *kulkarnis* from across these districts (although especially from Southern Districts of Belgaum, Bijapur, and Dharwar) compiled in several volumes; see, for example, Part V, pp. 3–16 for two versions of these petitions.

[112] MSA, RD 1914, Comp. 1070 Pt. I, pp. 207–211.

[113] See discussions in MSA, LD 1914, 16/145, pp. 123–134; 16/156, pp. 135–156; 16/301, pp. 205–208; LD 1915, 1/101, pp. 157–176. Petitions in MSA, RD 1916, Comp. 1070, Pt. II at pp. 17, 79ff. suggest that at least some *kulkarnis* who had petitioned for commutation did not realize it would lead to giving up their right to serve.

[114] MSA, LD 1915, 1/101, p. 170. A final coda actually played itself out in the late 1920s, in the context of the politicization of *vatans* by the non-Brahmin and Depressed Classes

The story of *vatan*, which will be completed in Chapter 5, suggests both the resilience of this structure of social relations, and its eventual marginalization in the name of the interests of state and the public good. The general transformation of elite hereditary offices into salaried employment and private property involved a recalibration of the symbolic economies of which it was a part, restructuring – although not necessarily transforming – the flows of social and economic capital.

CONCLUSION

The colonial attempt to produce social economy during the late nineteenth century, as a problem of wealth, security, productivity, and moral governance, continually provoked engagement with the failure or unreality of abstract human universality, autonomy, and equality. The weakness, oppression, and misery of the governed, as well as their commitments to uneconomical forms of property and governance, called forth divergent and ambivalent colonial responses. Despite the contemporary strength of arguments for leaving such social conditions untouched by the colonial state, colonial policies did focus on these issues, albeit in narrow and uneven ways, attempting at the most ambitious level to produce new forms of obligation, a new vernacular theory of economic and social value, and new bureaucratic forms of governance that depersonalized political power.

The policies that ensued did not so much aspire to decrease inequality – indeed, those formulated in relation to *vatan* as well as in relation to the partition of agricultural holdings sought to curtail what was perceived as the uneconomical equality among brothers. Nor did they unambiguously seek to supersede existing formal and informal modes of coercion. Rather, in India as in Britain, they linked matters of governance and the nature of legal subjecthood inextricably to the question of societal "systems" of inequality and coercion. Diverse Indian reformers took up this issue, seeking to counter the existing economic and social weaknesses within rural society through active state policy. Phule in particular also emphasized how formal and informal structures of power, and economic and noneconomic modes of coercion intertwined in everyday life. Colonial officials debated whether the state should seek to transform

---

Movements. A large group of *kulkarnis* filed suits, which went in appeal to the High Court, complaining that they had agreed to commutation of their *vatans* under pressure and duress, and requesting that their *vatans* be restored to them. The claims were rejected by the court. See LD 1927, Vol. B 13/64 Comp. 151, pp. 147–986.

these societal modes of coercion, neglect them, operate symbiotically with them, or put them into the service of the state, but the significance of the social to the state became inescapable.

In this context, an idiom of preservation underwrote ambivalent transformations. In relation to debt, the state legally reconceptualized personal bonds as depersonalized social obligations without materially transforming them. In relation to *vatan*, colonial policy effectively superseded elite village offices, but did so by transposing the relations of domination of which they were a part into new modalities of social power. In both cases, the shift that began to emerge in the 1860s may be understood as a set of attempts to fashion the legal boundaries and ethical claims of a new domain of private life, at once continuing the process of recasting as private a set of property relations that had previously structured the state (in the case of *vatan* and *inam*), instilling a sense of impersonal financial obligation in the debtor, and, as will become clear in Chapter 3, limiting the burdensome reach of the obligations of family. Indeed, shadowing much of these debates was the question of the family – specifically, the role of the joint Hindu family in impeding a more effective social economy. Beginning in the 1860s, the nature and claims of the joint Hindu family became a subject of increasing controversy. Conceived at once as the very foundation of society and as a domain of crushing encumbrance and oppression, redefining its boundaries and claims was to become a primary outcome of the operation of colonial law.

PART II

THE POLITICS OF PERSONAL LAW

3

Hindu Law as a Regime of Rights

The last decades of the nineteenth century and the early decades of the twentieth were marked by a quiet consolidation of what might be termed a modern "secular" Hindu law. Hindu law assumed a modern secular form not in the sense that it became separate from matters relating to religion, nor in the sense that it became a rationalized system per se, but in the sense that formally it came to operate through the structures of liberal legalism – procedural uniformity, formal equality, and the like – and more importantly, that substantively its jurisprudence came to turn on the problem of equality. Such jurisprudence did not necessarily seek to produce equality, but it implicitly or explicitly framed other logics – religious dictate, custom, societal norms, natural law – in relation to the *question* of equality. Integral to this process, Hindu law became primarily concerned with rights, rather than with a variety of ritual forms, statuses and significations, questions of proper comportment, modalities and hierarchies of honor, and the like. Thus, rather than a separation of Hindu law from the arenas of secular law and administration that were explored in Chapters 1 and 2, the jurisprudence of Hindu law overlapped to a significant extent with those policy efforts. That is, Hindu law relentlessly operated through and referenced the "higher power" of the modern liberal state, and it came to embed within itself the problems of colonial liberal governance.[1]

The problematic of equality or equalization that came to pervade Hindu law took shape first in a reconceptualization of property as a form

---

[1] Agrama, "Secularism, Sovereignty, Indeterminacy"; Agamben, *Homo Sacer*; Hent de Vries and Lawrence E. Sullivan, eds., *Political Theologies: Public Religions in a Post-Secular World* (New York: Fordham University Press, 2006).

of value. At the legal level, if never in social life (in India or the West), objects were increasingly stripped of their multiple registers of value and signification to become fundamentally commensurable exchange values.[2] Such equation itself relied on the fundamental commonality and exchangeability of owners, and in the case of owners, buying, selling, and holding property were increasingly conceptualized as founded in certain shared competencies: the cognitive and legal capacities that might be termed self-possession.[3] In this sense, the secularization of property involved not so much a separation of property from personhood, but a resignification of the connection between the two, as both came to revolve almost exclusively around questions of exchange value: the potential economic commensurability of objects and the potential legal commensurability of persons. In the operation of colonial Hindu law, caste Hindu men (especially sons, brothers, and husbands) became increasingly autonomous, interchangeable owners and full legal subjects whose abstract capacity for ownership was itself signaled by the exchangeability of property forms.

Indeed, it is not an exaggeration to suggest that this era may be termed the era of emancipation of caste Hindu sons. This historical evaluation encompasses at once the changing legal treatment of sons in relation to fathers, a new definition of the jointness of the joint Hindu family, and an emergent legal understanding of the universal mobility and exchangeability of property. It is perhaps unsurprising that many of the major cases that chart this transition involved the great merchant, banking, and industrialist families of Bombay.[4]

Yet if colonial Hindu law, as a law of property, became infused with a model of innate universal male mental and bodily capacities, replacing the hierarchical differentiation of bodies along multiple axes, a concept of innate embodiment remained crucial to this new theorization of capacities and rights.[5] This ongoing emphasis on the significance of birth and

---

[2] For early efforts to theorize modalities of resisting the logic of commoditization, see Annette Weiner, *Inalienable Possessions: The Paradox of Keeping-While-Giving* (Berkeley: University of California Press, 1992); Margaret Radin, *Reinterpreting Property* (Chicago: University of Chicago Press, 1993). From the perspective of colonial histories, and offering an implicit critique of Weiner, see Nicholas Thomas, *Entangled Objects: Exchange, Material Culture and Colonialism in the Pacific* (Cambridge, MA: Harvard University Press, 1991).

[3] Carole Pateman, "Self-Ownership and Property in the Person: Democratization and a Tale of Two Concepts," *Journal of Political Philosophy* 10, 1 (2002): 20–53.

[4] Mytheli Sreenivas, "Conjugality and Capital: Gender, Families and Property under Colonial Law in India," *Journal of Asian Studies* 63, 4 (Nov. 2004): 937–960.

[5] Scott, *Only Paradoxes to Offer*; Mehta, *Liberalism and Empire*.

heredity drew both from preexisting Indian theories of the meaningful differences of bodies, and from liberalism itself, which simultaneously posited human universality and preserved ideas of innate differential embodiment and capacities, particularly through categories of gender, race, and ability.[6] In relation to property, the legal recognition of inheritance confirmed the ongoing legal centrality of differences of birth. Indeed, in the English context, the significance of inheritance was elevated to a political principle in the very model of the "Rights of Englishmen."[7] The formation of a modern secular Hindu law would likewise remain entangled in this dilemma.

These contrary pulls between human universality and bodily difference were reflected in the highly uneven jurisprudence of the joint Hindu family in this era, in which various efforts at commensuration or compensation for family members excluded from a share in the family property (widows, daughters, illegitimate or disabled sons, and the like), were paralleled by rulings that sought to reinforce the distinctions among bodies and rights.[8] This complex modality took shape in a general asymptotic expansion and equalization of property rights within the family, which nonetheless accompanied the valorization of differential rights, especially for women, as appropriate to the family in general, and as in accordance with the dictates of Hindu law.[9] This uneven pattern emerged with particular force in relation to the rights of inheritance and maintenance of elite Hindu widows, who by the late nineteenth century had long been established as both embodying and signifying the extremity of social abjection and the need for external amelioration. This treatment of women's property claims, and indeed the relentless questioning of women's (and especially high-caste widows') property rights that characterized this era reflected a concern not merely with women's material existence and constraints, but

---

[6] Ibid.

[7] As Hannah Arendt argued, the Burkean notion of political rights as itself an inheritance, as the hereditary "Rights of Englishmen," in contrast to the French model of abstract universal "Rights of Man," in some sense rendered race-thinking the intellectual core of English political rights. Hannah Arendt, "The 'Rights of Englishmen' vs. The Rights of Men," in *The Origins of Totalitarianism*. See also Mehta, *Liberalism and Empire*.

[8] Scott, *Only Paradoxes to Offer*; Wendy Brown, *States of Injury: Power and Freedom in Late Modernity* (Princeton, NJ: Princeton University Press, 1995). For a different analysis of the effects of the distinction between substantive and procedural law, see Jonathan K. Ocko and David Gilmartin, "State, Sovereignty and the People: A Comparison of the Rule of Law in China and India," *Journal of Asian Studies* 68, 1 (Feb. 2009): 55–133.

[9] For such dynamics in postcolonial contexts, see Kapur and Cossman, *Subversive Sites*; Povinelli, *Cunning of Recognition*.

with the state's valuation of women as persons; that is, with how women, as a universal category, were defined as subjects within the law.[10]

PART I: FROM THE UNECONOMICAL FAMILY TO THE PRODUCTION OF ABSTRACT SUBJECTS

The issues of social economy discussed in Chapter 2 both implicitly and explicitly raised critical questions concerning the joint Hindu family. This was foremost because of the juridical model of the joint Hindu family itself. The colonial state recognized broad regional distinctions in familial patterns, which reflected and perhaps rigidified the prevailing authority of different textual traditions: In the northeastern regions of Bengal and Assam, the twelfth-century commentary by Jimutavahana, known as the *Dayabhaga*, formed the dominant textual authority, while in most of the remainder of the subcontinent the dominant text was the late-eleventh-century *Mitakshara* by Vijñaneshwara.[11] Both of these texts emerged as part of the commentarial tradition on the classical *Dharmashastra* work of Yajñavalkya, known as the *Yajñavalkyasmriti*, which dated to the Gupta dynasty of the third to fifth century C.E. The slightly later *Dayabhaga* offered a critique of the widespread *Mitakshara* tradition. Both works, particularly as they were taken up under the British, focused on the inheritance of property and on the rights and duties of family members. In addition, both systems were based on the principle of *sapinda*-ship, linking lineal males who shared in the same corporeal essence to the duty of providing offerings to male ancestors and to the right of inheritance.[12] Both texts envisioned a "joint" family in which all lineal males lived and ate together and had a potential claim to any familial property. According to the *Dayabhaga*, however, the male head of the family held any such family property personally, and was entitled to transact with it at will during his lifetime. After his death, this property

---

[10] Agnes, *Law and Gender Inequality*; Kapur and Cossman, *Subversive Sites*; Menon, *Recovering Subversion*; Nair, *Women and Law*; Sarkar "A Pre-History of Rights"; Rajan, *Scandal of the State*; Sinha, *Specters of Mother India*.

[11] Other customary systems were also followed in some places, most notably the matrilineal Marumakkathayam and Aliyasantana systems in practice on the Malabar Coast. In western India, the *Vyavahara Mayukha* by Nilakantha was also a prominent authority, particularly in Gujarat.

[12] The two systems nonetheless diverged in the weight accorded to the theory of shared corporeal substance (*sapinda*-ship): the *Dayabhaga* supported the claims of all those eligible to provide such offerings, while the *Mitakshara* emphasized the degree of corporeal relatedness.

would be distributed in equal shares among his legitimate sons and his widow. In contrast, under the principles established in the *Mitakshara*, which prevailed in most of the subcontinent, all lineal male members of the household were considered joint holders – in British legal language, "coparceners" – of a notional share in any family property from birth. Jointness under the *Mitakshara* thus referenced a form of collective ownership among all male members of the family. Wives, widows, unmarried daughters, disabled sons, and other dependents were entitled to maintenance out of this joint property, but they were not entitled to a share. A sonless widow in a previously partitioned family could inherit her husband's share, although the nature of this right formed a subject of major contention within colonial jurisprudence, as will be seen.

Within this framework, and confirmed by the colonial courts, virtually all property was assumed to be joint family property. As discussed in Chapter 2, for many colonial officials such a system of property holding posed significant impediments to the goals of social economy. It also became constraining to some men within the mercantile and professional classes most effectively integrated into the colonial economy.[13] British and Indian critiques came to center around several aspects of this family form. Given the British focus on the power to transact with the object (and specifically on the right of alienation) as the defining mark of property holding, one of the earliest and most prominent colonial concerns revolved around the limitations on transactions with family property. Although the head of the family might alienate or transact with the family property in times of need, ordinarily, individual male family members could not transact with their shares, and indeed, individual shares were never calculated except on the break up, or partition, of the family, which started new joint families. Moreover, central to this family form was the principle that any property acquired through the use or benefit of joint family property itself became joint family property. Although the category of "self-acquired" property, as personal property separate from joint family property, long existed both in Sanskrit textual commentaries and in practice, it was evidently quite narrow in application. For many colonial officials, this created stark impediments to entrepreneurial initiative: Individuals within the family had no incentive to labor or to personal

---

[13] This is congruent with Sreenivas, "Conjugality and Capital," and *Wives, Widows and Concubines: The Conjugal Family Ideal in Colonial India* (Bloomington: Indiana University Press, 2008), and somewhat at odds with Ritu Birla, *Stages of Capital: Law, Culture and Market Governance in Late Colonial India* (Durham, NC: Duke University Press, 2009).

striving because all that they gained became part of the joint property, and at the same time, this joint stock was regularly depleted and rendered increasingly "uneconomical" through the partition of the property among brothers with each passing generation. Further, along with this weighty union of interest, both according to textual dictates and social practice, sons inherited their father's debts, even if they did not inherit any property from him.[14]

In this sense, relations of birth and nurturance bound sons to the family: Their future acquisitions became the family's future acquisitions; the family's debts became their debts. In this conceptualization, the joint Hindu family itself operated through the metaphor of debt, with sons endlessly tied to its claims.[15] This model was enforced by the early colonial courts. As one major case from the initial years of British rule established, the possible use of a family horse or slave girls worked to tie all a man's future earnings to the coparcenary.[16] At the same time, although largely ignored in the legislative debates regarding agricultural indebtedness discussed in Chapter 2, the social structures of indebtedness inherently involved relations of family because financial debt was inherited. In this mutual imbrication of debt and the family, what began to emerge in the first half of the century, and became even more forceful in later decades, was a conceptualization of the bonds of the joint Hindu family as an impediment both to social economy and to masculine autonomy.

During the 1830s and 1840s, the question of one family member's power to mortgage or recover his personal share of undivided joint property came repeatedly before the courts, as creditors sought to enforce their claims. The legal question at issue in these cases fundamentally concerned the separability and alienability of joint family property: Could a member of a joint family transact with his share of the family property while it remained undivided, and in fact unspecified? During these decades, the courts repeatedly ruled that he could not.[17] On the one hand, this seemed to limit property transactions. On the other hand, however, it suggested that for any mortgage or debt, the whole of the family property was liable

---

[14] Derrett, *Religion, Law and the State*, 113–114.
[15] Ibid. This is also explicit in the textual tradition.
[16] MSA, JD, 1821–1823, 10/10, pp. 302–303. For the history of such "domestic" slavery, see Indrani Chatterjee, *Gender, Slavery and Law*, and Indrani Chatterjee and Richard M. Eaton, eds., *Slavery and South Asian History* (Bloomington: Indiana University Press, 2006).
[17] MSA, JD 1836, 5/358, pp. 114–148; *Dewarkur Josee v. Naroo Keshoo Goreh* (1837) Bom Sel. SDA Rep. 1820–1840, pp. 190–192; MSA, JD 1847, 11/1274, Comp. 17, pp. 48–156.

for repayment. Both the Sadr Diwani Adalat and the Court of the Agent for Sardars[18] upheld this collective liability as a means of enhancing the security of creditors.[19]

The centrality of the joint family form to the interests of creditors emerged most powerfully in the relations between father and son, however, since both textual authorities and customary practice confirmed that a son inherited his father's debts. In 1839, a ruling by the Sadr Diwani Adalat limited this liability in a case where a father was still living and had allowed his son to separate from the family. In 1861, the court extended this ruling, but it did so based on a view of the inchoate nature of a son's claim to joint family property while his father was alive, the court holding that "a son's contingent interest in undivided Ancestral Property is not of such a nature as to be regarded as a Debt, nor such as to make this Property 'his property' and so capable of attachment."[20] In other words, it was precisely because the nature of the son's share in joint property was undefined, and his right to partition during his father's lifetime (against his father's will) uncertain, that such property could not be considered liable for his father's debts. In this context, any clear determination of the son's right would have produced the result of binding him more tightly to the debts of his father.

Along these lines, the son's liability after the death of his father presented a clearer, and hence less rosy, picture for the son. Thus, an 1847 decision by the Sadr Diwani Adalat confirmed that "the Hindoo Law binds a son to pay the debts of his deceased father even if he have [sic] not inherited property from him."[21] This principle was modified only in 1866, with the passing of the Hindu Heirs Relief Act (Bombay Act VII of 1866), which aimed to bring the Bombay *mofussil* into line with the general practice that was now being observed in the other presidencies and in the city of Bombay, by limiting the son's liability to the amount of any ancestral property he inherited.[22]

---

[18] Sardar was an honorary title accorded to leading families; the British continued and expanded the use of such ranks and titles (e.g., creating Sardars of the First, Second, and Third Class), as a strategy for enhancing their support among the old ruling elite. Among the most important perquisites attached to the title, a continuation of precolonial privileges, was immunity from certain forms of judicial process. This translated within the British system as immunity from regular process in the civil courts. Civil disputes were thus handled by the specially appointed Agent for Sardars.

[19] For a prominent example, see MSA, JD, 1833, 2/267, pp. 193–196, 264–265.

[20] *Moolchund Bhaeechund v. Dhurmlal Deepalal* (1861) Bom Sel. SDA Rep., Vol. VIII, 9–11.

[21] *Hurbujee Raojee v. Hurgovind Trikumdass* (1847) Sel. SDA Rep., 1840–1848, 76.

[22] Moreover, even this legislation, although the product of efforts by some officials since at least the early 1850s, faced considerable opposition framed at once in the now familiar

The passage of the Bombay Hindu Heirs Relief Act in 1866 paralleled and expanded a trend in the High Court, beginning in the 1860s, of enhancing the individual claims of family members against each other and solidifying individual control over self-acquired property, particularly to the benefit of sons (or younger brothers). In contrast to the decisions of the 1830s and 1840s, which had repeatedly limited the expression of separate interests within the family, the High Court now readily established that a member of an undivided family had the power to mortgage his share of joint property without the consent of his coparceners.[23] In other words, the court began treating joint, undivided property as composed of separable and alienable claims.[24] From this juncture, while the court continued to secure the bonds of joint family in order to protect the security of creditors, it also sought to increase the independence of family members in relation to each other in order to promote market transactions. As in the efforts to rationalize and privatize *vatan* discussed in Chapters 1 and 2, this process of individualizing the notion of "shares" in joint family property and making them increasingly separable and available for exchange lay the groundwork for the trend toward secularizing property and personhood, in that it lessened the distinctions among property forms, and partially unyoked property from the attributes of differential personhood, thereby positing the qualities of all owners as fundamentally shared.

Two cases from this era involving major banking and industrialist families chart some of the terms of this transformation. In 1861, Ramchandra Dada Naik filed a case against his father in the Bombay Supreme Court that told a story of patriarchal persecution and filial reason, in which an eldest son who criticized his father's irrational business practices found himself hounded and excluded from the family estate.[25] In this suit, the ruling of the court involved two related issues: the right

---

linked idioms of political economy and religious tradition. MSA, JD 1851, 12/518, pp. 52–3. Nonetheless, reports in the aftermath of the Deccan Riots discussed in Chapter 2 suggested that a considerable amount of peasant debt was in fact ancestral debt, which remained a liability on inherited land tenures. *Report of the Committee on the Riots in Poona and Ahmednagar, 1875* (Bombay: Government Central Press, 1976), pp. 38–39.

[23] *Gundo Mahadev v. Rambhat bin Bhaubhat* (1863) 1 Bom HCR 39. See also *Tukaram v. Ramchandra* (1869) 6 Bom HCR 247, and *Vasudev Bhat v. Venkatesh Sambhav* (1873) 10 Bom HCR 139.

[24] *Gundo Mahadev v. Rambhat bin Bhaubhat* (1863) 1 Bom HCR 39. Also *Damodhar Vithal Khare v. Damodhar Hari Soman* (1863) 1 Bom HCR 182; *Tukaram v. Ramchandra* (1869) 6 Bom HCR 247; and *Vasudev Bhat v. Venkatesh Sambhav* (1873) 10 Bom HCR 139.

[25] *Ramchandra Dada Naik v. Dada Mahadev Naik* (1861) 1 Bom HCR, Appendix, lxxvi.

of a son to call for partition of the family property while his father was still living, and the different forms of ownership that different forms of property entailed, most importantly, whether movable and immovable property entailed different kinds of claims. Ultimately, it was this latter question that decided the suit.

Ramchandra and his father, Dada Naik, were members of a wealthy banking and money-lending family (*shroff*), who operated a family business in the town of Shapur, in the princely state of Sangli, with branches in Bombay and other places. The business had belonged to Ramchandra's grandfather, Mahadev, and on the latter's death in 1847, Dada had inherited it jointly with eight other male family members, including Dada's elder brother, Harba, and Dada's three sons, Ramchandra and his brothers Lakshuman and Keshav. Dada assumed management of the business and the estate because Harba, although elder, was mute and considered unable to run the business. Disputes quickly arose within the family about Dada's management, however, and by 1857, Dada's elder brother Harba as well as his nephews had all separated from the family, leaving Dada and his sons alone as the joint family carrying on the ancestral business and holding the remainder of the ancestral estate.

Soon Ramchandra, the eldest of Dada's sons, found himself in a similar position to these other relatives: quarreling with his father over the latter's unconventional business practices, while his father resisted any efforts to rationalize or otherwise interfere with the business. In particular, Ramchandra claimed that his father staunchly refused to keep the kind of regular and detailed accounts that were typically used by *shroff*, and that he would not allow Ramchandra and his brothers access to the one book that he did keep, the *bode khata* (main register), even though the three brothers worked in the family business as clerks, or *mehtas*.[26]

By June 1858, Ramchandra's relationship with his father had so deteriorated that his father tried to get the local police authority, the Mamlatdar, to evict Ramchandra from the family house and shop, claiming that he was divulging the family's business secrets. Following several further serious disputes, including Dada's attempt to have Ramchandra imprisoned for robbery, Ramchandra was expelled from the family home and business, although allowed to remain in a separate family residence.[27] Ramchandra's 1861 suit against his father and two brothers was his

---

[26] Ibid. From the one-sided nature of the narrative, it is highly likely that this account was itself drawn from the plaint Ramchandra submitted in filing the suit.

[27] For details of these disputes, see ibid.

response to this circumstance, and it aimed to enable him to take his share of the property and permanently separate from the family, against his father's will. Ramchandra also claimed that an important incentive for taking his share immediately, rather than waiting until his father's death, was that his father was in the meantime making exorbitant gifts from the ancestral property to his brothers, his sister, and his sister's husband, in order to diminish the total value of the ancestral estate and thus defraud Ramchandra of his proper share.[28] The estate included some immovable property,[29] but extensive movable property in the form of cash, jewels, furniture, and the like, as well as the banking business itself, in which Ramchandra and his two brothers had participated with their father.

Within colonial Hindu law, the right of a male family member to partition the joint family property and claim his share was undisputed, and indeed was central to the very definition of joint family. Yet the question of whether a son had the power to call for partition of the family property during his father's lifetime had been a subject of legal uncertainty and contention for decades.[30] Ramchandra's case came before Chief Justice Sausse, who was appointed the first chief justice of the new High Court, established by legislative act within months of Ramchandra filing his suit in 1861. In his deliberation on the case, Chief Justice Sausse attempted to skirt the troublesome question of whether a son had the right to call for partition during his father's lifetime and against his will, by instead emphasizing that joint family property took different forms, and that these entailed their own respective forms of ownership. In particular, the chief justice focused on the Hindu textual distinction between movable and immovable property to argue that "the right to compulsory partition, if it exist at all, does not extend to moveable property ..." and that "the highest authorities recognised in Hindu law hold that as between a father and his sons in the distribution of paternal or other ancestral estate the father takes the moveable property absolutely, or subject only to certain conditions, none of which have been broken upon the facts appearing on this record."[31]

---

[28] Ibid. Subsequent disputes among the brothers of the family were fought in 1876 and in 1880 over the multifarious efforts of Dada Naik to disinherit Ramchandra.

[29] These were primarily in the form of houses in the princely state of Sangli, which was outside of British jurisdiction.

[30] See *Moolchund Bhaeechund v. Dhurmlal Deepalal* (1861) Bom Sel. SDA Rep. Vol. VIII, 9–11. Indeed the High Court considered the point incompletely established even in the Nathubhai case in 1886, discussed later in this section.

[31] *Ramchandra Dada Naik v. Dada Mahadev Naik* (1861) 1 Bom HCR, Appendix, lxxvi.

The court recognized this distinction between movable and immovable property as a shared feature of British and Brahminical traditions and of local customary practice, and such widespread recognition meant that colonial officials at every level treated immovable property as involving different rights and claims from movable property. Nevertheless, in the context of the expansion of commerce and heightened commodification of land, this at one time unquestioned distinction between movable and immovable property now raised fundamental questions about the nature of ownership. How was ownership of money different from ownership of land, or ownership of jewels different from ownership of a house? This was a critical issue animating seventeenth- and eighteenth-century British legal and political theory, and it was central to colonial adjudication of local property claims.[32]

The sources in the Hindu authorities for the distinction between movable and immovable coparcenary property comprised a couple of brief passages from the primary textual authorities in the region, which suggested that although a man's sons and grandsons each had a claim equal to his own in ancestral *immovable* property, he himself had independent control over ancestral *movable* property. The specific passages were translated as follows:

Therefore, it is a settled point, that property in the paternal or ancestral estate is by birth, [although] the father have independent power in the disposal of effects other than immoveables, for indispensable acts of duty and for purposes prescribed by text of law, as gifts through affection, support of the family, relief from distress, and so forth.[33]

The father is master of all gems, pearls, and corals; but neither the father nor the grand-father is so of the whole immoveable estate.[34]

These passages suggested that joint movable property was fundamentally different from joint immovable property: that a man might have absolute control, or failing that, absolute control during his lifetime, over joint movable property, even as his power over immovables was severely circumscribed. This possibility suggested serious consequences for wealthy banking and merchant families, who held most of their property in movables, such as the family of Ramchandra and his father, Dada Naik.

---

[32] Pocock, "Mobility of Property"; Pincus, "Neither Machiavellian Moment."

[33] *Mitakshara*, chapter I, section I, par. 27, cited in *Lakshman Dada Naik v. Ramchandra Dada Naik and Ramchandra Dada Naik v. Lakshman Dada Naik* (1876) ILR 1 Bom 561 at p. 566.

[34] *Mayukha*, chapter IV, section I, para. 5, cited in ibid., 567.

Chief Justice Sausse's judgment in what became known in judicial
circles as "the Dada Naik case" held that during his lifetime Dada Naik
could dispose of his joint movable property, which was the bulk of his
property, according to his own pleasure. This judgment bolstered the
authority of the father, but it also simultaneously enhanced the mobility
and alienability of movable family property by implying that a father
could, during his lifetime, give, sell, or otherwise transact such property,
regardless of the sons' claims as coparceners in the family estate.[35] In
retrospect, it is the seemingly divergent or mixed implications of this ruling that perhaps mark it as the beginning of the end of an era. For it
shored up the patriarchal power of fathers by drawing on a common
distinction between types of property, but in order to confirm (if not
expand) the mobility of movable property. In the decades that followed,
it was this mobility, and ultimately the fundamental exchangeability of
both movable and immovable property, that came to form the new common sense.[36] And alongside this extended principle of exchangeability
emerged a new dispensation in favor of sons.

The 1886 case of *Jugmohandas Mangaldas v. Sir Mangaldas
Nathubhoy*[37] demonstrated the distance the court traveled in the decades
after Ramchandra Naik brought his original suit in 1861. Although the
court resisted a judgment that would have directly overturned Chief
Justice Sausse's ruling in the Dada Naik case, the decision nonetheless
turned the presumptions of that case on their head and created a new and
more powerful precedent, abandoning the Dada Naik case to the rank of
dusty anachronism.

The circumstances of this later case were in many ways parallel to
the Dada Naik case. Jugmohandas was the youngest (rather than
the eldest) son of the prominent businessman and public figure Sir

---

[35] That this power was restricted to the father's lifetime was confirmed by the second suit,
fought among the Naik brothers after their father's death, which disputed the power
of the father to bequeath virtually the entire ancestral estate to one son, so as to disinherit the disobedient son, Ramchandra. The court ruled that such a bequest was invalid.
See *Lakshman Dada Naik v. Ramchandra Dada Naik and Ramchandra Dada Naik v.
Lakshman Dada Naik* (1876) ILR 1 Bom 561.

[36] Nonetheless, fundamental procedural distinctions between movable and immovable
property continued to be applied without question – for example, the statute of limitations during which a suit could be brought for the recovery of property wrongfully held
laid out numerous distinctions among property forms and rights, ranging from a matter
of months to sixty years. For immovable property, the standard period was twelve years,
for movable property, three years.

[37] *Jugmohandas Mangaldas v. Sir Mangaldas Nathubhoy* (1886) ILR 10 Bom 528.

Mangaldas Nathubhai, who held extensive properties, both ancestral and self-acquired, movable and immovable. Due to disagreements within the family, however, Jugmohandas had left the family house upon attaining majority in 1880. He had applied to his father for an allowance for maintenance out of the family property, but his father had refused, except under conditions Jugmohandas would not accept. He then brought a suit for partition of the ancestral estate, including movable and immovable property in his father's hands, and failing that, for maintenance out of the estate during his father's lifetime.[38]

The case came before Justice Scott, who, like Chief Justice Sausse, skirted the question of the rights of sons to partition during their father's lifetime. Although he ultimately found in favor of such right, his opinion focused instead on the relative power or position of fathers and sons and on the distinction between movable and immovable property. Reviewing the textual authorities, as well as the Dada Naik case and other precedents, Scott concluded that the textual authorities consistently emphasized the equal claims of sons and fathers in ancestral property both movable and immovable, particularly within the *Mayukha*, which was the primary authority for Gujaratis such as the Nathubhais.[39] This slight but notable distinction between the *Mayukha* and the *Mitakshara* on the issue of movable property ultimately provided the justice with a way to distinguish this case from the Dada Naik case, which had involved parties from the Southern Maratha Country, for whom the *Mitakshara* was considered the primary authority. Yet, even beyond this regional distinction, Justice Scott noted that for those governed by the *Mitakshara* as well, a recent decision by the Privy Council[40] had "defined the relations of fathers and sons in a joint family in a manner which reduces the position of the father, so far as the joint property is concerned, to that of manager, pure and simple. There is not a shadow of the *patria potestas*[41] left. This

---

[38] The complex nature of the properties involved in the suit produced lengthy and protracted deliberations by the court. Extensive self-acquired properties belonging to Mangaldas's ancestors had passed to him by will, and it was a matter of dispute whether some of his business ventures were acquired through ancestral property or through self-exertion. Moreover, this was also one of the few cases in which a caste custom was set up to defeat a claim to inheritance, as discussed in Chapter 4.

[39] This feature of the *Mayukha* resonated with the prominence of commercial communities in Gujarat.

[40] *Suraj Bunsi Koer v. Sheo Proshad Singh* (6 MIA, 88 at p. 100).

[41] Absolute power of the father, as defined in Roman law and applied to the Indian context by Henry Maine in *Ancient Law*.

decision undoubtedly is in favour of the son's right to divide against the father's will."[42] And the Justice went on to quote the Privy Council:

> The rights of a co-parcener in an undivided Hindu family governed by the law of the Mitakshara, which consists of a father and his sons, do not differ from those of the co-parceners in a like family, which consists of undivided brethren, except so far as they are affected by the peculiar obligation of paying their father's debts which the Hindu law imposes upon sons; and the fact that the father is in all cases naturally, and, in the case of infant sons, necessarily, the manager of the joint family estate.[43]

Noting that virtually none of the case law recognized the distinction between movable and immovable property in partitions, the justice concluded that such a distinction was not admissible in those areas governed by the *Mayukha*. This decision therefore homogenized movable and immovable joint property, while it also worked to expand the autonomy of the son in relation to his father.

The Dada Naik and Nathubhai cases trace a process of redefining the legal relationships that joint family entailed. Alongside the Nathubhai case, other decisions in the 1880s began to work to redefine the limits of jointness itself. Thus, in 1884, the court reinforced the legal presumption that all Hindu families were joint, but it also circumscribed the claims to jointness that it would uphold.[44] Distinguishing sharply between the moral and the legal claims of poor dependent relatives, the court ruled that support of such relatives neither implied nor established a legal relationship of joint family:

> The presumption of Hindu law is that every family is joint, and that all property possessed by the family is joint. A member of an undivided family may, however, acquire separate property, but the burden of proof lies on him to prove the independent character of the acquisition. The essence of his exclusive title is that the separate property was acquired by his sole agency without employing what is common to the family.
>
> If the property is separate the presumption operates no longer, and each member is separate owner of what he possesses. Even in the case of a separate family blood relationship within certain degrees imposes a moral duty, though not a legal duty, towards dependent relatives. The support on a liberal scale of poor relatives and even payment of their marriage expenses are not in themselves without evidence proof of a joint family.[45]

[42] *Jugmohandas Mangaldas v. Sir Mangaldas Nathubhoy* (1886) ILR 10 Bom 528 at pp. 548–549.
[43] Ibid.
[44] *Moolji Lilla v. Gokuldas Vulla* (1883) ILR 8 Bom 154.
[45] Ibid.

This distinction between moral and legal claims enabled the court to clarify the limits of joint family relationships it would enforce, while it also served to expand the autonomy of sons and brothers.

Moreover, beginning in the 1880s, the decisions of the High Court also began to expand the definition of self-acquired property so that property acquired through the new colonial professions, such as the occupation of lawyer or civil servant, could be more readily classed as self-acquired. This process occurred by treating the use of family property to gain education or training as inconsequential for the property later acquired through those professions. As long as the training was not advanced and specialized in nature, the court began to treat the financial obligations incurred by being raised, fed, and educated by one's family as moral rather than legal claims. This new conceptualization was adopted at the all-India level (and expanded to include scientific and technical education) with the enactment of the Hindu Gains of Learning Act in 1930 (Act XXX of 1930);[46] however, the Bombay High Court had long been treating much of such property as self-acquired.[47]

Something of the apotheosis of this process can be seen in a 1937 High Court case in which Chief Justice Beaumont reversed the previously prevailing colonial legal assumptions about joint family and joint property: "The law, I think, is clearly established that from the existence of a joint family it is not to be presumed that there is any joint family property. There is no presumption that property which belongs to a member of a joint family is joint family property."[48] Although the law had long established the first of these statements,[49] in relation to the second, it was precisely the opposite principle – that all Hindu families are presumed to be joint and their property presumed to be joint family property – that had structured colonial adjudication throughout the nineteenth century and was explicitly enunciated even in the mid-1880s.[50] These changing legal principles operated not to place sons outside of the family (although they may have facilitated partitions), but rather to adjust the law more centrally around their claims within the family. The burdens and attachments

---

[46] See discussions in Sreenivas, *Wives, Widows and Concubines*; Eleanor Newbigin, "A Post-Colonial Patriarchy? Representing Family in the Indian Nation-State," *Modern Asian Studies* 44, 1 (2010): 121–144.

[47] See *Luximan Narayan v. Jamnabai* (1882) ILR 6 Bom 225.

[48] *Babubhai Girdharlal v. Girdharlal Hargovandas* (1937) ILR 61 Bom 708.

[49] John Dawson Mayne, *A Treatise on Hindu Law and Usage* (Madras: Higginbotham & Co., 1878), pp. 223–236.

[50] *Moolji Lilla v. Gokuldas Vulla* (1883) ILR 8 Bom 154.

of family that figured so prominently in the minds of officials and of an emergent class of Indians were thus increasingly replaced by new forms of autonomy and of social and economic capital that the family could provide for caste Hindu sons.

PART II: THE CONUNDRUMS OF INCOMMENSURABILITY

This emergent logic in the treatment of sons as owners and legal subjects also shaped the treatment of dependents. Particularly in the context of property claims by elite caste Hindu women, colonial legal personnel likewise largely saw themselves as applying Hindu laws and principles, and yet a new framework of interpretation shaped their treatment of women as owners.[51] This jurisprudence both produced "women" as a universal category, designifying existing distinctions of caste, wealth, and status, while it also defined women as particular (not universal) holders with limited capacities and rights in comparison to men.[52] Moreover, and in contrast to the treatment of male property holding, in cases involving women's property claims, colonial law retained the multiple distinctions of property and ownership encompassed under the Brahminical textual category of *stridhan*, literally, "women's wealth."[53] In this jurisprudence,

---

[51] The discussion that follows focuses on widows, but the treatment of daughters' claims is likewise significant. The courts recognized that in western India daughters came earlier in the line of heirs and were accorded greater powers of ownership than in other regions. Daughters inherited ancestral property only in the case of a separated male who had no lineal heirs for three generations and no widow, but such daughters inherited prior to separated male heirs and more distant male kin, and took such property as an absolute estate. Notably, in the 1880s, this came to be cast as taking the property "as though male," a gendered normativization of property holding that was powerfully critiqued by Justice K. T. Telang in *Manilal Rewadat v. Bai Rewa* (1892) ILR 17 Bom 753 at p. 765. Moreover, from the turn of the century, the High Court seems to have moved to restrict the nature of daughters' (as well as sisters') inheritance and property holding, bringing it more in line with the jurisprudence in other regions. See, for example, *Krishnanath Narayan v. Atmaram Narayan* (1891) ILR 15 Bom 543; *Krishnarao Ramchandra v. Benabai* (1895) ILR 20 Bom 571; *Haridas Narayandas Bhatia v. Devkuvarbai Bhratar Mulji* (1926) ILR 50 Bom 443. See also cases of *Bai Mamubai v. Dossa Morarji* (1890) ILR 15 Bom 443; *Javerbai v. Kablibai* (1890) ILR 15 Bom 326; *Bhaskar Purshotam v. Sarasvatibai* (1892) ILR 17 Bom 486; *Anandrao Vinayak v. The Administrator General of Bombay* (1895) ILR 20 Bom 45; *Muktabai v. Antaji* (1899) ILR 23 Bom 39; *Bhau bin Abaji Gurav v. Raghunath Krishnagurav* (1905) ILR 30 Bom 229; *Jinnappa Mahadevappa Kundachi v. Chimmava* (1934) ILR 59 Bom 459. See discussion in Sturman, "Family Values," Chapter 7.

[52] Sturman, "Family Values"; Sinha, *Specters of Mother India.*

[53] The question of what constituted *stridhan* was a matter of major debate both among Brahminical commentators and among the colonial judiciary. P. V. Kane, *History of*

the colonial courts and administration mainly followed Nilakantha's *Vyvahara Mayukha*, otherwise recognized as the primary authority only for Gujarat, which established differential forms of ownership and patterns of succession for gifts a woman acquired at marriage, gifts made at other times, gifts from her husband, inheritance from her father, inheritance from her mother, and property acquired by other means.[54] These multiple distinctions of *stridhan* as applied by the colonial courts thus created a system of adjudication that was based on numerous differentiations, all of which were placed within the foundational colonial distinction between men and women as property holders. Thus, although the High Court and administration moved broadly in this era to privatize and rationalize certain forms of property and ownership, such as *vatan* or the Hindu coparcenary itself, this trend did not extend to the treatment of *stridhan*. In the adjudication of women's property claims, the differentiations among objects of property; timings, modes, and sources of acquisition; and types of ownership continued to preoccupy the courts, even as they also introduced their own particularisms, namely the "widow's estate" – a concept drawn from English jurisprudence, deriving from a common European legal fiction in which married women were subsumed under the legal person of their husbands.[55]

The colonial courts and administration applied the concept of the "widow's estate," as an exceptional estate that a widow inherited from her husband, to cases in which the woman's husband had separated from his brothers during his lifetime and had no lineal male heirs. According to the *Mitakshara*, in cases where the husband lived jointly with his brothers at the time of his death or had surviving sons or grandsons, the husband's inchoate share would simply be absorbed by the coparcenary, increasing the (also inchoate) shares of the surviving male family members. In such a situation, a widow had no claim to her husband's share whatsoever, but she did have a legitimate claim to maintenance out of the joint family property.

Dharmashastra, vol. 3 (Pune: Bhandarkar Oriental Research Institute, 1946); Raymond West and Johann Georg Bühler, *A Digest of the Hindu Law of Inheritance and Partition, From the Replies of the Sastris in the Several Courts of the Bombay Presidency, with Introductions, Notes, and an Appendix*, 2nd ed. (Bombay: Education Society's Press, 1878), p. 100.

[54] West and Bühler, *Digest of Hindu Law*, pp. 64–65, 224–227.

[55] Shanley, *Feminism, Marriage and the Law*. Social reformist nationalist lawyers would point this out with great satisfaction in the context of the debates on the Hindu Women's Right to Property Bill in the 1930s, as discussed in Chapter 5.

In the case of a widow of a man who had separated from his brothers and had no living sons or grandsons, the concept of the widow's estate was applied to define her position as heir. Initially, the concept of the widow's estate defined the widow as a tenant for life, a temporary placeholder, until her death and the "reversion" of the property to the husband's heirs.[56] As the concept of the widow's estate was applied to colonial Hindu jurisprudence, its signature element quickly became the prohibition on the widow alienating the property to the detriment of the interests of the husband's "reversioners." Whereas in the context of fathers and sons, the courts treated the power to alienate property as the essence of autonomy and of ownership, it was the absence of this power that defined the widow's lack. Yet notwithstanding the widespread colonial definition of the widow's estate as the quintessential form of non-autonomous property holding, the precise terms of this estate shifted considerably during the late nineteenth and early twentieth centuries, eventually holding a position approaching – but never achieving – equivalence to adult men.

In contrast to the rights of widows as heirs, a widow's or abandoned wife's right to maintenance raised intractable issues that derived from the uncertain nature of a right based in dependence. The jurisprudence of maintenance claims in this era remained shifting and inconsistent, tending at once toward confirming the widow's right to maintenance, while limiting the encumbrance she could impose on the property of others. Eventually, suits by a wife for maintenance became linked to a subject of widespread controversy in this era – provisions for the restitution of conjugal rights. Their related conceptual grounds – the wife's dependency and the husband's rights in her person as defining elements of the marriage relation – were consolidated and enforced by the colonial state through a convergence of colonial Hindu and English law.

Widows as Heirs

Although colonial records from the earliest days of British rule included regular demands by widows to succeed to their husbands' property against relatives who were obstructing their claims,[57] one of the earliest major

---

[56] *Pranjivandas Tulsidas v. Devkuvarbai* (1859) 1 Bom HCR 130.
[57] See, for example, MSA, Pune, Records of Early British Rule, Papers for Further Research, Rumal No. 46, Document no. 20279, "Return of Civil Suits Filed & Decided upon within the Collectorate of Ahmednagar, by the First Assistant from 20th Oct. 1818 to 31st April 1819," Nos. 67, 216, 111, 145. See also MSA, JD 1828, 18/165 and 19/166. As in

judicial attempts to define the nature of a widow's inheritance occurred only in 1859, in the case of *Pranjivandas Tulsidas v. Devkuvarbai.*[58] Chief Justice Sausse (who a couple years later would decide the Dada Naik case in strikingly resonant terms), established the widow "as having uncontrolled power over the moveable estate, but as having nothing more than a life-use in the immoveable estate." In Sausse's words, "In regard to immoveable property her estate is in the nature of that of a tenant for life."[59] This decision formed a major precedent that remained largely unchallenged until the rulings of Justice West in the mid-1880s.

In 1883, Justice West argued that the classical and customary restrictions on a widow's alienation of her deceased husband's property were integral to a system in which *all* alienation of family property was restricted, and that it was thus inappropriate to retain the restrictions on widows' ownership while expanding the powers of ownership by men.[60] Noting that "the Smriti passage in the Mayukha [cited to show that a Hindu wife has no authority to alienate immovable property given to her by her husband] had reference probably to a stage of progress in which the severance of an estate from the family was still looked on as impossible, or, at least, as sacrilegious," he concluded that "as the general power of disposal of property has become recognized by the modern law, it seems impossible to say that it is to be subjected to restrictions when exercised in favor of a widow which were provided for an entirely different state of things."[61]

Justice West developed these logics in other directions in 1886, in what became an important precedent known as Bhagirthibai's case, where he further asserted that any restrictions on a widows' inheritance were contrary to the Brahminical traditions of commentary and argumentation, as

---

partition cases, many of the cases elaborating widows' claims came not from the widows themselves, but from a widow's creditors, or the creditors of her in-laws. *Bhaeeshunker Nurbheram v. Baee Ruttun* (1860) Bom SDA Rep. Vol. VIII, 106; *Treebhowan Khooshal v. Lulloo Soorchund* (1861) Bom SDA Rep. Vol. VIII, 198.

[58] *Pranjivandas Tulsidas v. Devkuvarbai* (1859) 1 Bom HCR 130 (Late Supreme Court, Equity Side). See also explicatory note found in *Gangabai v. Thavar Mulla* (1863) 1 Bom HCR 71 at p. 76.

[59] *Pranjivandas Tulsidas v. Devkuvarbai* (1859) 1 Bom HCR 130 at pp. 131–133. This opinion also exemplifies some of the ways that the court utilized and recast the opinions of the Hindu law officers or court *shastris*.

[60] *Ghelabhai Mulchand v. Bai Mancha* (1883) ILR 7 Bom 491. See also *Damodhar Madhowji v. Purmanandas Jeewandas; Purmanandas Jeevandas v. Damodhar Madhowji* (1883) ILR 7 Bom 155. This decision was confirmed by Justice Ranade in 1895 in *Motilal Lalubhai v. Ratilal Mahipatram* (1895) ILR 21 Bom 170.

[61] *Ghelabhai Mulchand v. Bai Mancha* (1883) ILR 7 Bom 491 at p. 493.

well as to accepted practice in western India.[62] Nevertheless, he ultimately hedged conditions around such statements to retain limitations on a widow's power of alienation.[63] This side-by-side expansion and limitation of the rights of women as owners offers some sense not only of West's ambivalence regarding women's claims, but of the broader dilemma of attempting to produce something approaching commensuration while retaining and valorizing women's dependence.[64] This jurisprudence forcefully highlighted the significance of property in indexing women's legal subjecthood.

Moreover, even these limited attempts to mitigate the legal disability of Hindu widows were muted by other highly restrictive interpretations of such widows' legal claims. These interpretations emerged in the late 1880s and shaped prominent decisions well into the twentieth century, particularly in the new legal terrain of wills or testamentary bequests. Such legal instruments had no presence in Hindu textual authorities and little in practice until the eighteenth century.[65] By the early nineteenth century, the validity of Hindu testamentary dispositions of separate or self-acquired property was accepted by the Bengal courts, but in Madras and Bombay, the validity of Hindu wills remained in question through the 1860s. The passage of the Hindu Wills Act in 1870 (Act XXI of 1870) formalized such instruments for those residing or bequeathing property located in the presidency towns of Bombay, Madras, and the lower provinces of Bengal. Both before and after the Hindu Wills Act, any bequest that altered the pattern of regular succession, or that the testator could not have validly made during his lifetime, was considered invalid. Thus, a testator could only dispose by will of self-acquired property; he could

---

[62] See *Bhagirthibai v. Kahnujirav* (1886) ILR 11 Bom 285 at p. 298. Bhagirthibai's case was also an important one for defining daughters' rights of inheritance.

[63] See the caveats introduced at ibid., pp. 298, 309.

[64] See, for example, West's treatment of the proposal to abolish provisions for restitution of conjugal rights, discussed in Padma Anagol, *The Emergence of Feminism in India, 1850–1920* (Burlington, VT: Ashgate, 2006), p. 200, and in the next subsection.

[65] By the eighteenth century, wealthy Hindus had begun to make wills with some regularity, drawing primarily on British forms. Wills also formed an integral part of Muslim textual dictates and elite practice, although restricted to one-third of the property. For those it affected, the Hindu Wills Act (Act XXI of 1870) generally applied the contemporary English testamentary law. It rendered a nuncupative (oral) will void (although they remained valid in the *mofussil*) and required those claiming under a will to apply for grant of probate (legal certification of the validity of a will). The terms of this act were largely extended to the *mofussil* in the 1880s. G. S. Henderson, *The Law of Testamentary Devise as Administered in India, or the Laws Relating to Wills in India*, Tagore Law Lectures, 1887 (Calcutta: Thacker, Spink & Co., 1889), pp. 5ff.

dispose of separate property (e.g., his share of ancestral property taken in partition) by will only if he had no lineal heirs.[66]

Yet the very emergence of wills reflected the expansion of new meanings of property and the desire to dispose it outside the established terms of the joint Hindu family. As a new legal instrument for the mobility of property, wills became a key terrain in which the rights of widows and their nature as property holders was defined. In 1887, the High Court ruled that wills bequeathing estates to Hindu widows should be read in the most limited sense.[67] In 1893, the court extended this dictate to gifts as well.[68] Another 1893 case overturned an earlier precedent and held that a widow further had no power to bequeath movable property inherited from her husband, and that such property descended at her death to her husband's heirs.[69] Following these precedents, a series of cases in the late 1890s consistently read in the most limited sense the widow's estate taken by her husband's will. For example, the 1896 case of *Lallu v. Jagmohan*[70] involved the property of Jamnadas Natha, who died in 1876 leaving a will to the following effect: "When I die, my wife named Suraj is owner of that property. And my wife has powers to do in the same way as I have absolute powers to do when I am present, and in case of my wife's death, my daughter Mahalaxmi is owner of the said property after that (death)." In this case, as in many others, the court held that despite the language conferring absolute powers on the widow, the provision in favor of the daughter on the widow's death operated to limit the bequest to Suraj to a widow's estate.[71]

Beginning at the turn of the twentieth century, such decisions limiting the widow's powers came to operate side by side with decisions that explicitly shifted the terms in which the widow's estate was understood, incorporating aspects of Justice West's formulations that expanded the widow's powers while retaining (as he did) the limitations on alienation of property. This uneven process characterized the remainder of the colonial era, representing at times divergent judicial efforts to position the

---

[66] Mahendra Chandra Majumdar, *The Hindu Wills Act (Act XXI of 1870), with Which Is Incorporated the Probate and Administration Act, with Elaborate Notes and Commentaries* (Calcutta: Sanyal & Co., 1904). See also MSA, JD 1881, 32/1411; MSA, JD 1882, 33/71, pp. 25–214.

[67] *Lakshmibai v. Hirabai* (1886) ILR 11 Bom 69.

[68] *Annaji Dattatraya v. Chadrabai* (1892) ILR 17 Bom 503.

[69] *Gadadhar Bhat v. Chandrabhagabai* (1892) ILR 17 Bom 690. The ruling that was overturned was *Damodar Madhowji v. Purmanandas Jeewandas* (1883) ILR 7 Bom 155.

[70] *Lallu v. Jagmohan* (1896) ILR 22 Bom 409.

[71] See also *Mithibai v. Meherbai* (1921) ILR 46 Bom 162.

widow more firmly within her husband's family, to enhance her status and even at times her partial autonomy therein, and also to retain the model and structures of "guardianship" in its modern form.[72] Thus, in a major shift from the early formulation of Justice Sausse, in an 1897 case from Nasik district, the High Court held that while the estate willed by a husband to a widow was a widow's estate, "still she is its full owner."[73] In 1921, a Privy Council ruling confirmed that earlier decisions had held that "under the Hindu law, as interpreted up to the present in the case of immoveable property given or devised by a husband to his wife, the wife has no power to alienate, unless the power of alienation is conferred upon her in express terms."[74] Yet Lord Buckmaster noted that the Privy Council had in a recent ruling[75] established that they considered such rulings "no longer sound."[76] Thus, he continued, in the present case, "if a Hindu testator in making a disposition in favour of his widow uses words conferring absolute ownership, she enjoys all the rights of an owner, including that of alienation, although those rights are not conferred by express and additional words, unless the circumstances or the context are sufficient to show that absolute ownership was not intended."[77]

The underlying change in the meaning of the "widow's estate" can be seen in what the High Court considered "beyond question" by the late 1930s. In the 1937 case of *Mohanlal Khubchand v. Jagjivan Anandram,*[78] Justice Rangnekar expounded,

It is well established by authorities, which cannot now be disputed, that a Hindu widow is not a tenant-for-life, but is the owner of the property inherited by her from the husband, subject to certain restrictions on alienation and subject to its devolving upon the next heir of her husband upon her death. The whole estate is for the time vested in her and she represents it completely.... In *Janaki Ammal v. Narayanasami Aiyer*[79] their Lordships of the Privy Council observed... : "Her (widow's) right is of the nature of a right of property: her position is that of an owner:" and they stated that so long as she is alive, no one has any vested interest in the succession. Apart from legal necessity, a Hindu widow can alienate immoveable property with the consent of the next reversioner, or for certain religious or charitable purposes. Under the Mayukha she can dispose of moveable

[72] *Panachand Chhotalal v. Manoharlal Nandlal* (1917) ILR 42 Bom 136.
[73] *Anandibai v. Rajaram Chintaman Pethe* (1897) ILR 22 Bom 984 at pp. 985–6.
[74] *Bhaidas Shivdas v. Bai Gulab* (1921) ILR 46 Bom 153 (Privy Council).
[75] *Surajname v. Rabi Nath* (1903) 25 All. 355.
[76] *Bhaidas Shivdas v. Bai Gulab* (1921) ILR 46 Bom 153 at p. 159.
[77] Ibid., 159–160.
[78] *Mohanlal Khubchand v. Jagjivan Anandram* (1937) ILR 62 Bom 292.
[79] *Janaki Ammal v. Narayanasami Aiyer* (1916) LR 43 IA 207, s.c. 39 Mad 634.

property by act *inter vivos*. An alienation of immoveable property by her without any legal necessity is valid and passes her life interest to the alienee. These principles are too well settled to require any authority to be cited.[80]

This description of the widow's estate in fact resembled nothing more than a jerry-rigged version of the way in which the courts had at one point been accustomed to portraying the joint property of an adult man. What had changed in the meanwhile, however, was men's relationship to property within the family and the extent to which a man's ownership now implied absolute, individual, and separate control over property, defined by his power of alienation. The shifting meaning of the widow's estate thus ultimately redefined the nature of the widow's ownership of property; that is, her *capacity* as heir to her husband's property came to approach and approximate (if never to achieve) that of male heirs. As this asymptotic movement suggests, the problem of the widow as property owner came to be conceptualized almost exclusively and relentlessly as a problem of commensuration.

Wives and Widows as Dependents

In contrast to the distinctive forms of ownership for widows as occasional heirs, women's more general claims to maintenance within the family reflected their condition of exclusion from the coparcenary. Maintenance claims within colonial Hindu law extended far beyond widows and wives: mentally and physically disabled sons, illegitimate sons, unmarried daughters, the insane, as well as those suffering from incurable diseases such as leprosy were all treated as subject to guardianship and entitled to maintenance. Scholars have argued that such claims to maintenance had historically constituted a valuable right,[81] as well as one that was central to structures of rural power through the eighteenth century.[82] These works suggest that the claim to maintenance had long been treated as marking the subject's exclusion from full claims to family property (except in the case of the temporary dependence of minor sons), even though it was also recognized as a valuable claim. The right to maintenance, as a

---

[80] Ibid., 297. Parenthetical comments in original.
[81] J. D. M. Derrett, "Adoption in Hindu Law," and "Inheritance by, from and through Illegitimates at Hindu Law," in *Essays in Classical and Modern Hindu Law*, vol. 3 Anglo-Hindu Legal Problems (Leiden: E. J. Brill, 1977): 24–84; 182–219.
[82] Chatterjee, *Unfamiliar Relations*; Indrani Chatterjee and Sumit Guha, "Slave-Queen, Waif-Prince: Slavery and Social Capital in Eighteenth-Century India," *Indian Economic and Social History Review* 36, 2 (1999): 165–186.

right grounded in bodily difference that had structured precolonial family and property relations, took on new meanings in the colonial context. In India, as in the West, as property ownership came to reflect legal capacity, autonomy, and individual rights, the claim to maintenance now defined its holder as lacking in full legal status.[83] At the same time, the rights associated with dependence that maintenance entailed also raised questions for the colonial state concerning the governance of social life – that is, both pragmatically and ethically, what kind of support need it mandate for those dependent on others for their very sustenance?

Notably, it was particularly in relation to women's claims that the question of the rights and entitlements of non-abstract subjects became fraught with difficulty, as signaled by the high degree of instability in this jurisprudence from the 1860s through the first decades of the twentieth century, and beyond. In contrast, the limited rights and capacities of people with illnesses or physical disabilities, as well as of illegitimate children, were enforced by the state with little question. Thus, in 1877, a series of rulings in the Bombay High Court confirmed that in accordance with the prescriptions of Hindu law, leprosy and congenital blindness acted as a bar to inheritance.[84] People who suffered these afflictions were entitled to maintenance, the court ruled, but not to ownership. Such rulings continued until well into the twentieth century.[85] Leprosy and congenital blindness remained formal grounds for disqualification from inheritance until the passing of the Hindu Inheritance (Removal of Disabilities) Act in 1928 (Act XII of 1928). In a parallel manner, well into the twentieth century, the court not only confirmed the limited claims of illegitimate children, but also enforced caste-based differences in these rights with little question, confirming that the rights of illegitimate sons of high-caste Hindus were different from those of illegitimate sons of Shudras. Illegitimate sons of high caste (*dwija*, or twice-born castes) could only claim maintenance from their fathers, and were excluded from coparcenary claims, while illegitimate sons of Shudras could claim half the share of a legitimate son or daughter inheriting from his or her father, unless their mother was of high

[83] Nancy Fraser and Linda Gordon, "A Genealogy of Dependency: Tracing a Keyword of the U.S. Welfare State," *Signs* 19, 2 (1994): 309–336.

[84] *Murarji Gokuldas. v. Parvatibai* (1877) ILR 1 Bom 177; *Ananta v. Ramabai* (1877) ILR 1 Bom 554; *Umabai v. Bhavu Padmanji* (1877) ILR 1 Bom 557. In the first and third cases, involving blindness, the suits actually turned on the question of whether noncongenital blindness acted as a bar to inheritance. The court ruled that it did not, based on the distinction between congenital and noncongenital blindness.

[85] See, for example, *Mancharam Bhiku Patil v. Dattu* (1919) *Dundappa Basappa Yedal v. Bhimawa* (1920) ILR 44 Bom 166; ILR 45 Bom 557.

caste, in which case, they had no claim whatsoever. This was a distinction that reflected and facilitated high-caste male sexual access to lower-caste women, and that denigrated lower-caste men in their lack of control over "their" women, while it retained high-caste male property within their own caste lineages. This distinction became a subject of non-Brahmin agitation in the 1920s, with non-Brahmin and Dalit activists calling on the British government to end the preferential treatment of the high castes.[86]

In the context of wives' and widows' claims to maintenance, however, from the middle of the nineteenth century the courts' rulings were highly uneven and complex. Ultimately, the High Court defined maintenance as a right grounded in the relations of family or marriage itself, a right that existed in counterdistinction to contractual rights.[87] The layered valorization of incommensurability that emerged in this jurisprudence – casting it at once as culturally authentic to Hindu society and as intrinsic to the universal nature of marriage – produced complex significations of such rights and of the persons who bore them.

Two legal judgments in a case that was filed in the early 1860s involving an elite Hindu widow's right to maintenance highlighted the foundational question that structured maintenance cases in the courts: whether widows were essentially objects of charity whose claims were fundamentally moral rather than legal, and if not, then what kind of treatment could the law demand from those who were in any case not moved by the ethical or affective claims of such figures?[88] This question highlighted the dilemmas entailed in setting in motion either the coercive or the disciplinary mechanisms of the state, particularly in a context where the state sought to minimize its own liabilities. Throughout this era, then, the courts' rulings remained highly ambiguous and uneven. In the first opinion, written by the district judge of Satara, R. F. Mactier, confirming the award of bare maintenance to one of the widows of a wealthy figure of very high status in the region,

I think the award a fair one. By the strict Hindu law, a widow childless is only entitled to what will mess her, and to no more, and though a large allowance has

[86] See demands in the newspaper *Vibhakar*, RNP, April 21, 1922, 445–446.
[87] As other feminist scholars have argued, maintenance inherently formed a legal right based in dependence, reflecting the incomplete legal subjecthood of the wife or widow within marriage. Agnes, *Law and Gender Inequality* and "Maintenance for Women: Rhetoric of Equality," *Economic and Political Weekly* 27, 41 (Oct. 10, 1992): 2233–2235; Kapur and Cossman, *Subversive Sites*; Fraser and Gordon, "A Genealogy of Dependency."
[88] Dipesh Chakrabarty, "The Subject of Law and the Subject of Narratives," in *Habitations of Modernity: Essays in the Wake of Subaltern Studies* (Chicago: University of Chicago Press, 2002), pp. 101–114; Chakravarti, *Rewriting History*.

been, and is often, made for persons of a high family, yet this is not the strict law, but merely the opinion of the authorities making the order: therefore, if the present plaintiff coming into court seeks the assistance of the law, she can only have what the law gives, and no more. In the present case the plaintiff quotes what others get as maintenance, or rather as allowance; this, I think, we have nothing now to do with.... She claims to live where she pleases: this I do not think she can do, for, as she is living on enforced charity, she must not be held to have a choice in the matter: she wishes to have money, to keep a certain amount of state; but properly a Hindu widow has nothing to do with this: she ought to have relinquished all connection with the outer world, and ought to live strictly as a Hindu widow, in seclusion; and the law, as she appeals to it, can give her no more than is necessary for this. The allowance decreed by the lower court appears to be quite sufficient for this, and the plaintiff must remember that, as she is only an object of charity now, she cannot dictate terms, but ought to have what she gets, and be thankful for it, and, as I think the Principal Sadr Amin's award was fully enough, she must rest content with this.[89]

This starkly punitive decision was in fact overturned by the Sadr Diwani Adalat in 1864, with Justices Newton and Janardhan confirming that "a widow has by Hindu law a legal right to maintenance, and the amount should be determined on a consideration not merely of her absolute necessities, but also of the circumstances of her family."[90] Quoting early colonial official and ethnographer Sir Thomas Strange, they ruled that maintenance "must be proportioned to the condition of the party who is to receive it, and the circumstances of those who are to provide it."[91]

As these two opinions underscore, there were strongly divergent views of a widow's legitimate claims and of the courts' role in securing them. Several early High Court decisions offered an expansive view of the widow's claims as inherent in her position and activated by her condition of need. In 1863, the High Court held that a widow was entitled to maintenance from her in-laws, even if she had shared in her husband's estate and maintained herself independently for many years.[92] Further, in 1873, the first Indian to sit as a permanent justice on the Bombay High Court, Justice Sir Nanabhai Haridas, held that a widow was entitled to such maintenance, "quite independent of any property acquired by her father-in-law from his deceased son as well as of any ancestral property in which such son had a joint interest with him. She is entitled *whenever she is in need*."[93] Such decisions, like the provision for inheritance of

[89] *Sakvarbai v. Bhavanji Raje Ghatge Zanjarrav Deshmukh* (1864) 1 Bom 197.
[90] Ibid., 198–199.
[91] Ibid.
[92] *Bai Lakshmi v. Lakhmidas Gopaldas* (1863) 1 Bom 13.
[93] *Udaram Sitaram v. Sonkabai* (1873) 10 Bom HCR 483 at p. 486. Emphasis in original.

debts, construed the obligation to provide maintenance as integral to the relationship of the widow to her conjugal family – that is, as intrinsic to the legal status of family – regardless of the existence of property.

Yet, in a manner parallel to the treatment of hereditary debt, beginning in the late 1870s, several decisions limited the widow's claims by conceptualizing them as a claim merely on any property held by her deceased husband. In 1878, after reviewing all the precedents and textual authorities, the court ruled that a widow's in-laws were only responsible for her maintenance if they had been living jointly with her husband during his lifetime, and if they were holding property from him.[94] This opinion was confirmed in an 1883 case in which the court held that a widow could not claim maintenance out of her father-in-law's estate if his property was entirely self-acquired, even though she and her children were admittedly destitute.[95] These decisions placed the claim to maintenance on quite different footing, construing it as a widow's limited interest in her husband's property, rather than as a broad claim to familial support inherent to her relationship to her conjugal family.

This shift accompanied and deepened a long-term trend of limiting the circle of those encumbered with the widow's claims, a trend that had initially emerged as an interest in preserving the claims of creditors as prior to the operation of a widow's claims.[96] In 1899, the court further confirmed that a widow's claims to maintenance were solely on her *conjugal* family's property, and that she had only a moral and not a legal claim against her natal relatives.[97] This ruling functioned to place widows more firmly within their conjugal families, even as their claims within their conjugal families were themselves being narrowed.[98]

Moreover, while the courts consistently recognized the principle of a widow or abandoned wife's right to maintenance, the actual measure of such rights remained unspecified. Central to this issue was the question of the widow's appropriate wants and needs, and the unresolvable problem

---

[94] *Savitribai v. Luximibai* (1878) ILR 2 Bom 573; *Kalo Nilkanth v. Lakshmibai* (1878) ILR 2 Bom 637. This was a debate within the Sanskrit textual tradition as well, but took on particular valence in the modern context.

[95] *Kalu v. Kashibai* (1882) ILR 7 Bom 127; also *Yamunabai v. Manubai* ILR (1899) 23 Bom 394.

[96] *Bhugwunt v. Goozabaee* (1860) 8 Bom HCR 120; *Lakshman v. Satyabhamabai* (1877) ILR 2 Bom 494; *Parvati v. Kisansing* (1882) ILR 6 Bom 567; *Dalsukhram v. Lallubhai* (1883) ILR 7 Bom 282; *Manilal v. Bai Tara* (1892) ILR 17 Bom 398.

[97] *Bai Mangal v. Bai Rukhmini* (1898) ILR 23 Bom 291.

[98] See also explicit discussion of this issue in *Udaram Sitaram v. Sonkabai* (1873) 10 Bom HCR 483.

of the rights and entitlements of an object of charity. The problematic needs of the widow's body, her perceived disposability and unproductive consumption of the wealth of others, formed the basis for a right that the law itself defined in unstable terms, underscoring the precariousness of the claims of a legal subject defined by her dependence.[99]

The cases that put the most pressure on this right based in dependence were those that involved a widow's or a wife's claim to separate maintenance (to live apart from her in-laws), and cases as to whether a woman forfeited her right to maintenance by her unchastity.[100] In an important 1878 ruling that involved both of these questions, Chief Justice Sir Michael Westropp[101] framed the issue as fundamentally a question of the nature of marriage and the rights that it entailed. In the case of *Sidlingapa v. Sidava*, an appeal from a case from Dharwad District, Sidava had originally sued her husband Sidlingapa for separate maintenance, claiming that he had recently turned her and her two children out of the house. In the appeal, Sidlingapa claimed that his wife had in fact eloped some fourteen years previously with another man, that she had had two children by illegitimate intercourse, and that he had divorced her some twelve years previously as a result of their discord. It also appeared from the evidence before the subordinate judge in the original suit that Sidava had at some point ten or twelve years previously torn off her *tali* (marriage ornament)

---

[99] For an acute example of the instability of this right, see the reflections of Justice Beaman in *Karbasappa v. Kallava* (1918) ILR 43 Bom 66 at p. 68, and from a different angle, *Gurushiddappa v. Parwatewwa* (1936) ILR 61 Bom 113. While judges at times sought to secure generous provision for widows and wives, these efforts were framed in terms of her pitiable abjection and the discretionary role of the judge himself in mitigating her plight. These public enactments of compassion underscore the ways in which the ethical vision of human incommensurability formed an integral part of liberal legalism. *Udaram Sitaram v. Sonkabai* (1873) 10 Bom HCR 483; *Karbasappa v. Kallava* (1918) ILR 43 Bom 66. Alternately, judges occasionally emphasized these women's moral but not legal claims, and the possibilities of justice outside the law, ironically positing the affective realm of the family that had produced the legal claim as an ethical supplement to the limited rights provided by law. *Bai Mangal v. Bai Rukhmini* (1898) ILR 23 Bom 291; *Gurushiddappa v. Parwatewwa* (1936) ILR 61 Bom 113.

[100] Such cases were conceptually connected as a woman living separately inherently suggesting the possibility for sexual lapse. *Chandrabhagabai v. Kashinath Vithal* (1866) 2 Bom HCR 323; *Timmappa Bhat v. Parmeshriamma* (1868) 5 Bom HCR 130; *Udaram Sitaram v. Sonkabai* (1873) 10 Bom HCR 483; *Girianna Murkunki Naik vs. Honama* (1890) 15 Bom 236. The right to maintenance was typically construed as dependent on her chastity: *Rango v. Yamunabai* (1878) ILR 3 Bom 44, and *Kasturbai v. Shivatiram* (1879) ILR 3 Bom 372; although the court at times ruled otherwise: *Honamma v. Timmanabhat* (1877) ILR 1 Bom 559; *Valu v. Ganga* (1882) ILR 7 Bom 84.

[101] He also would rule the following year on the question of a daughter's unchastity disqualifying her from inheritance: *Advyapa v. Rudrava* (1879) ILR 4 Bom 104.

and returned it to her husband, and that since that time she had been residing with her parents.[102]

Although the subordinate judge had initially decreed in favor of the husband, the district judge, N. Daniell, had reversed the decree and awarded Sidava maintenance. The logic of his decision, however, relied on the ongoing claim that her husband still had on her person. The district judge had concluded that the circumstances of the case (the breaking of the *tali*, the living apart from her husband, the illegitimate children) "did not relieve her of her conjugal duties or position, or amount to a sufficient ground for a divorce, as the defendant might legally have compelled her to return to him, and that no proof had been given of an alleged caste custom of divorce by mutual consent."[103] In other words, all of her actions only constituted misbehavior within an ongoing marriage relationship that her husband could have chosen to enforce against her at any time.

While refusing Sidava's claim to separate maintenance, Justice Westropp's opinion in this case came to focus on the assertion of Sidlingapa's legal counsel that the claim to maintenance was a contractual claim. In answer to the question of whether marriage could be conceptualized as a contractual agreement (and thus maintenance itself a contractual right, which Sidava had violated or voided by her actions), Westropp looked to another recent suit, the highly publicized English divorce case of *Mordaunt v. Mordaunt*, and quoted approvingly the opinion in that case, written by Lord Penzance, who had apparently struggled with the same question that Westropp now faced. In the words of Lord Penzance:

But, is it true that marriage is an ordinary contract? Surely, it is something more. I may be excused if I dwell on this matter, because I conceive it lies at the very root of the question in discussion. Marriage is an institution. It confers a *status* on the parties to it, and upon the children that issue from it. Though entered into by individuals, it has a public character. It is the basis upon which the framework of civilized society is built, and, as such, is subject in all countries to general laws which dictate and control its obligations and incidents, independently of the volition of those who enter upon it.[104]

That the words of Lord Penzance in a contemporary English case resonated so strongly to a High Court justice in colonial Bombay deciding a

---

[102] *Sidlingapa v. Sidava* (1878) ILR 2 Bom 624.

[103] Ibid., p. 626. This was Chief Justice Westropp's analysis of the district judge's decision, and not a direct quote from that decision itself.

[104] *Mordaunt v. Mordaunt* LR 2 Pro. and Div. 103 at p. 126, cited in *Sidlingapa v. Sidava* (1878) ILR 2 Bom 624.

case involving Hindu marriage, speaks to the broad circulation of a shared
debate on marriage across the colonial world in the late nineteenth century,
as discussed in Chapter 4. At the same time, this recent English precedent
formed the basis for reframing the question of the rights that marriage
entailed. From this position, Justice Westropp argued that marriage and
the family produced rights grounded in status, rather than contract:[105]

> We should take too narrow a view of the nature of maintenance, if we were to
> limit it to the case of husband and wife. In numerous instances maintenance is
> recoverable, in which there is not the most remote connexion [*sic*] with contract:
> *e.g.*, where a Hindu, personally disqualified from inheritance by congenital blind-
> ness, or deafness, or dumbness, or insanity, or idiotcy [*sic*], or sanious leprosy, or
> illegitimacy, is entitled to be maintained out of the family estate.... The proper
> view seems to us to be to regard maintenance in its general aspect, as a liability
> created by the Hindu law in respect of the jural relations of the Hindu family....
> The liability of the husband to maintain his wife is an obligation arising out of the
> *status* of marriage amongst Hindus, expressly imposed by law.[106]

In other words, marriage created a socio-legal status, as well as atten-
dant duties and rights enforceable in the courts – including the right to
maintenance – which derived from a person's dependency and connection to his or her family or protector. The chief justice went on to argue
that the same also held true in England and "other Christian countries,"
where marriage also "creates a special *status* from which, and not, except
mediately, from the volition of the parties, spring the rights and duties
of married people as such."[107] Westropp's judgment thus established a
crucial principle: that a wife's right to maintenance was a noncontractual
right – a right that established its holder not as an abstract universal subject, but rather as a concrete, embodied subject whose rights arose from
the status created by her marriage.

Further, in the face of several conflicting decisions on the right to maintenance of an unchaste wife or widow, in the early twentieth century, the
High Court attempted to resolve the question by affirming the right to
maintenance of widows "only briefly unchaste"[108] and to unchaste widows "who become chaste."[109] In the words of the court:

> The general rule to be gathered from the texts is that a Hindu wife cannot be
> absolutely abandoned by her husband. If she is living an unchaste life, he is bound

---

[105] *Sidlingapa v. Sidava* (1878) ILR 2 Bom 624. See also *Narbadabai v. Mahadeo Narayan*
(1880) ILR 5 Bom 99.
[106] Ibid., 628.
[107] Ibid.
[108] *Parami v. Mahadevi* (1909) ILR 34 Bom 278.
[109] *Bhikubai v. Hariba* (1924) ILR 49 Bom 459.

to keep her in the house under restraint and provide her with food and raiment just sufficient to support life; she is not entitled to any other right. If, however, she repents, returns to purity and performs expiatory rites, she becomes entitled to all conjugal and social rights, unless her adultery was with a man of a lower caste, in which case, after expiation, she can claim no more than bare maintenance and residence.[110]

This impossibility of the wife's absolute abandonment thus reinvoked the powerful linkage between sexuality and caste hierarchies. It also posited a wife's right to maintenance as a legal provision for her ongoing abjection that entirely mooted her claim to or in her own person. As Justice Sir Nanabhai Haridas had argued to quite different ends in 1873, the right to maintenance was, "in truth, inalienable."[111] This later conceptualization of maintenance as a right to abject life underscores the unstable and ultimately potentially dehumanizing nature of such a right, in which the needs of the widow's body perpetuated her living separation from social and familial life. At the same time, it also reconfirmed the state's refusal of liability for such abject figures: The family, rather than the state, would remain exclusively responsible for such support.

A very different grounding for this "inalienable right" emerged at this time in the criminal law, however. Section 316 of the 1861 Code of Criminal Procedure established that the failure of a husband to maintain his dependent wife (and children) constituted a penal offence.[112] The code framed the issue as one of public interest in preventing the wife's destitution and eventual public charge, coming under the provisions for "desertion and willful neglect," rather than as an ethical question shaped either by Hindu or by Christian conceptions of marital duty. In this sense, the criminal provisions for a wife's maintenance took the form of confirming as a private obligation what would otherwise have been a burden on the state. Such a legal provision thus represented an expression of state interest in delimiting the entitlements of humanity as strictly private rights. As such, it may also be understood as another facet of the importance of cultivating social economy, as discussed in Chapter 2.

This expansion of the avenues for a wife to claim maintenance – one particularly useful for subaltern women, given the greater speed and lower cost of criminal suits – was, however, accompanied by the elaboration of new means to defeat such claims. By the 1890s, it became

---

[110] *Parami v. Mahadevi* (1909) ILR 34 Bom 278.
[111] *Udaram Sitaram v. Sonkabai* (1873) 10 Bom HCR 483.
[112] This provision was carried over in Section 488 of the revised Code of Criminal Procedure, 1882 and 1898.

standard practice to use the legal provision for restitution of conjugal rights mandating a wife to live with her husband as a primary means to defeat a wife's claim to maintenance.[113] Restitution of conjugal rights was a form of legal action that derived from British law. It was first deployed in cases involving Muslim personal law as well as Parsi matrimonial cases in the middle of the nineteenth century. Within a few decades, it was applied in cases involving Hindu law, although the validity of such usage within personal law remained in question.[114] Subaltern women had also heavily used the provisions to establish claims to residence and maintenance, as Padma Anagol has shown.[115] The masculine use of such provisions against unwilling wives became notorious in the mid-1880s, however, as major public outcry and debate swirled around what became known as the Rakhmabai case.[116] In that case, Rakhmabai, who had been married as a child to Dadaji, refused to consummate the marriage or to live with her husband after attaining majority. Dadaji eventually sued for restitution of conjugal rights, thereby raising the specter of court-ordered marital rape on the one hand, or of the delegitimation of the widespread and religiously sanctioned practice of arranged child marriage on the other.[117] Justice Pinney decided the original case

---

[113] *Purshotamdas Maneklal v. Bai Mani* (1896) 21 Bom 610.

[114] Anagol, *Emergence of Feminism*, 183–187, 192–194; Sudhir Chandra, *Enslaved Daughters: Colonialism, Law and Women's Rights* (Delhi: Oxford University Press, 1998); Chakravarti, *Rewriting History*.

[115] Anagol, *Emergence of Feminism*, 183–187, 192–194.

[116] *Dadaji Bhikaji v. Rukhmabai* (1886) ILR 9 Bom 529. For discussion of such transnational debates as political events see Sinha, *Specters of Mother India*. For the contemporary debates in the press, including letters and pamphlets by Rakhmabai and Dadaji themselves see *Bombay Gazette*, September 22, 24, 28, and 30, 1885 (includes extracts from other newspapers); *Indian Spectator* (English, Bombay) RNP, September 28, 1885, 6–7; *Dnyan Prakash* (Anglo-Marathi, Pune) RNP, October 1, 1885, 7; for the appeal, see *Bombay Gazette*, March 19, 1886; *Subodh Patrika* (Anglo-Marathi, Bombay) RNP, April 4, 1886, 16; *Native Opinion* (Anglo-Marathi, Bombay) RNP, April 11, 1886, 6; *Bombay Samachar* (Gujarati, Bombay) RNP, March 7, 1887, 12; *Indian Spectator* (English, Bombay) RNP, March 13, 1887, 7–8; *Dnyanodaya* (Anglo-Marathi, Bombay) RNP, March 17, 1887, 7–8; *JameJamshed* (Gujarati, Bombay) RNP, March 16, 1887, 7–8; *Indu Prakash* (Anglo-Marathi, Bombay) RNP, April 5, 1886, 15–16 and August 2, 1886, 12–13; Dadaji Bhikaji, "An Exposition of Some of the Facts of the Case of Dadaji v. Rakhmabai," *Advocate of India*, 1887, and "Rukhmabai's Reply to Dadajee's Exposition," reprinted from the *Bombay Gazette*, June 29, 1887, in OIOR Law Tracts, 1851–1887, 5319.111.28, nos. 11 and 12, pp. 1–12.

[117] This case has formed a major subject of scholarly interest and analysis. See Chandra, *Enslaved Daughters*; Chakravarti, *Rewriting History*; Meera Kosambi, "Gender Reform and Competing State Controls over Women: The Rakhmabai Case (1884–1888)," *Contributions to Indian Sociology*, n.s. 29, 1–2 (1995): 265–290, and "Girl-Brides and

in Rakhmabai's favor, but his decision was reversed by Justice Farran in appeal. Rakhmabai had publicly stated her decision to go to prison rather than abide by the decree, but the case was eventually settled by an agreement in which Rakhmabai paid Dadaji Rs. 2,000 out of her considerable inherited property in exchange for his agreement not to enforce the decree.[118]

In the aftermath of this case, the provisions for imprisonment associated with violation of a restitution decree were eventually revoked,[119] but only after considerable legal debate, in which Justice West (among others) prominently and staunchly argued for the importance of retaining such provisions as essential features of customary law, which could not be substantially altered "without great risk of disintegration of the indigenous family system and of the whole scheme of society that rests upon it."[120] Further, according to West, the wifely disobedience which such provisions held in check was also inauthentic: In West's view, a Hindu wife "cannot sincerely embrace the [Western] creed of freedom, equality and wedlock of souls, and at the same time remain sincerely a Hindu."[121] Although West had earlier argued in the context of widows' inheritance that historical change was integral to custom and must be reflected in the law, he nonetheless viewed the inequality of husband and wife as integral to the nature of Hindu (but not Christian) marriage as such.[122]

Moreover, even after this abolition of imprisonment, as a judge commented several decades later, the provisions for restitution continued to "serve a really useful purpose": defeating a wife's claim to separate maintenance. The reasoning underlying these cases was that a wife was entitled to a decree for separate maintenance only when her husband had been proven guilty of desertion or willful neglect. Hence, if a husband could demonstrate that he had sought to compel his wife to live with him, and she had resisted his attempts, she had no legal standing to demand

Socio-Legal Change: Age of Consent Bill (1891) Controversy," *Economic and Political Weekly* 26, 31–32 (August 3–10, 1991): 1857–1868.

[118] Both parties viewed the property issue involved in this case as central. See Bhikaji, "Exposition of Some of the Facts, and "Rukhmabai's Reply." Also Chakravarti, *Rewriting History*, 161–162.

[119] Order XXI, Rule 33 of the Code of Civil Procedure (1908) gave the courts discretion on the enforcement of a decree for restitution by imprisonment.

[120] Minute by Justice Raymond West, dated August 5, 1887, on the Proposed Amendment of Section 260 of the Code of Civil Procedure, 1882, MSA, JD, 1888, 4/235, quoted in Anagol, *Emergence of Feminism*, 200.

[121] Ibid., 201. Bracketed comments added.

[122] West's views on custom, law, and social change are discussed further in Chapter 4.

separate maintenance. From the 1890s until the late 1920s, the standard reasoning of the High Court was that a wife's right to maintenance derived from her husband's refusal to live with her.[123] In 1920, the court explicitly acknowledged and legitimated this use of suits for restitution of conjugal rights.[124] In Chief Justice Macleod's words, "The days are past when a wife was considered as a mere slave or chattel of the husband."[125] Yet, as Justice Heaton further elaborated,

> The decree for restitution of conjugal rights accompanied by a direction that the decree shall not be executed by imprisonment [of the wife] is not a nullity. It is a declaration that the marital obligation of living with her husband rests on the wife, and it protects the husband against any proceedings for maintenance which the wife may institute under section 488 of the Criminal Procedure Code. Such a decree, therefore, does serve a really useful purpose.[126]

This legal sanction for using a decree for restitution of conjugal rights to defeat a wife's claim to maintenance was questioned and rejected only in 1926.[127] At the same time, the broader framework of maintenance claims, as a right grounded in the dependence that is integral to relations of marriage or family, and a right moreover that is contingent on the wife's or widow's chastity (in the case of separate maintenance), was reconfirmed in the postcolonial reform of Hindu law as enshrined in the 1956 Hindu Adoptions and Maintenance Act, and this logic has remained in place up to the present.[128]

Adoption and the Widow's Will: Toward a Reformist Hindu Law

In the decades surrounding the turn of the twentieth century, the question of widows' legal agency took on new salience in a body of cases involving widows and adoption. In these cases, a modern orientation to questions of the widow's consciousness, motivations, and intent gave way to competing modern arguments concerning her intrinsic rights and capacities.

---

[123] *In re: Gulabdas Bhaidas* (1891) ILR 16 Bom 269; *Purshotamdas v. Bai Mani* (1896) 21 Bom 610; In re: Bulakidas (1898) ILR 23 Bom 485. This last case also cited earlier cases to this effect: *Lulpotee Moonomy v. Tikha Moodoi* (1870) 13 Cal WR 52 Criminal Rulings, and *In re: Kalidas Mansukram* (1878) Criminal Revision No. 119 of 1878.

[124] *Bai Parwati v. Ghanchi Mansukh Jetha* (1920) ILR 44 Bom 972 at p. 974.

[125] Ibid., 975–976.

[126] Ibid., 976–977. Bracketed comments added.

[127] *Bai Jivi v. Narsingh* (1926) ILR 51 Bom 329 at p. 336. The reporting of such linked suits in the colonial Bombay High Court seems to end with this case.

[128] Sec. 18, Hindu Adoptions and Maintenance Act (Act 78 of 1956); Sec. 25, Hindu Marriage Act (Act 25 of 1955); Kapur and Cossman, *Subversive Sites*, 140.

This shift occurred through the efforts of major Hindu social reformist justices on the High Court, M. G. Ranade and N. G. Chandavarkar, who took up and refashioned an earlier colonial bifurcation of adoption into secular and religious components, thereby making an explicit claim on behalf of a secular Hindu law – a law that applied to Hindus as a demographic (and affective) unity, but that enforced rights and relationships in their secular significance.

The colonial administration had long treated adoption as a subject of contention. The precolonial practice of formal adoption in western India had construed adoption as a ritual act, like marriage, that transformed the social status and relationships of the parties. Formal adoption effectively created a son and heir to the family line and family property where none existed.[129] Except in certain matrilineal communities such as temple-dancer (*devadasi* or *murali*) and courtesan communities, only sons could be formally adopted and only parents who did not have living direct lineal male heirs could adopt. While formal adoption was just one of a range of practices for including various dependents within the circle of kin, it remained completely separate from fostering orphans. Orphans were regularly integrated into families, but they could not be formally adopted because the ritual transfer of the child in adoption required the presence of one of his parents, thereby ensuring that his lineage and status were known.

From the beginning of colonial rule, the British approached adoption, and especially adoption by a widow, with suspicion, perhaps not least because of their own kinship culture: In Britain, claims of blood were so central to notions of kinship – and particularly to inheritance claims – that adoption was not legally recognized until 1926. It was perhaps because of this suspicion that in the early nineteenth century the British initially separated adoption into secular and religious components, in which the courts ruled adoptions valid for the spiritual purposes of providing an heir to perform funeral obsequies and the like, but invalid for the transmission of property.[130] The most notorious British engagement with Indian adoption practices was the infamous mid-nineteenth-century "doctrine of lapse" instituted by Governor-General Lord Dalhousie, in which the British refused Indian kings and local lords permission to

---

[129] For further discussion of adoption and other modes of incorporation into kinship units in the precolonial era, see Chatterjee and Guha, "Slave-Queen, Waif-Prince"; Derrett, "Adoption in Hindu Law."

[130] *Sewram Moreshwar Pettae v. [illegible], widow of Moro Mahadarow Pettae* (1830) MSA, RD 1831, 26/354, pp. 96–97; see also Regulations of 1825 in ibid., 125–126.

adopt, and then used the failure of male heir to claim that those lands and kingdoms thereby "lapsed" to the British colonial state. To this policy of annexation was later attributed one of the causes of discontent leading to the Revolt of 1857.

By the late nineteenth century, however, the colonial administration had long, if reluctantly, accepted the legitimacy of adoption, and in western India the courts treated widows as entitled to adopt even without the express permission of their husbands or in-laws. Such adoption had crucial implications for a widow. In cases where the husband had been part of a joint family at the time of his death, it created an heir entitled to the husband's share of family property who would be likely to support her. In cases where the husband had separated from the joint family, however, it immediately divested the widow of any property she had inherited from her husband and vested it in her adopted son. Thus, in addition to suits by family members whose expectations of inheritance were foiled by an adoption, the courts were rife with disputes between widows and their adopted sons, as widows regretted their earlier actions. These cases produced a variety of lines of thought on the question of the widow's legal agency.[131]

At the turn of the century, this concern with the widow's agency – depicted alternately as incomplete competence or as excessive and perverse control – emerged in a brief series of cases that revolved around the question of the adopting widow's motives. The question of motives reframed in new ways the earlier colonial concern with the ritual efficacy of adoption. The fundamental question at issue in these cases was whether an adoption was invalid if it could be proved that it was not motivated by spiritual concerns. This questioning of the widow's motives formed a departure both from the Brahminical textual commentaries, which focused primarily on the inherent qualities and ritual states of the parties and on the correct performance of ritual acts, and from colonial personal law up to this point, which applied Hindu or Muslim law essentially demographically and virtually without reference to belief.[132]

---

[131] For one complex and highly evocative case, see *Ravji Vinayakrav v. Lakshmibai Shankarsett* (1887) ILR 11 Bom 381. Also *Kuverji v. Babai* (1886) ILR 19 Bom 374; *Shivabasava v. Sangappa* (1904) ILR 29 Bom 1 (Privy Council).

[132] This concern with motivations did not necessarily imply a question of individual internal states. Thus, in an 1877 dispute among *kolis*, the lawyer for the widow who contested an adoption argued that *kolis*, as "tribals," were not motivated by the spiritual concerns of Hindus, and therefore they could not adopt. The judge in this case rejected this argumentation, but without challenging the putative link between caste and spiritual character. Rather, he argued that *kolis* had the right to adopt, even though their

The question of motivations or intent, raised largely in relation to elite widows at the end of the century, concerned the internal states that produced particular actions, and it brought together a modern theological concern with belief and a legal question concerning the nature of will.[133] From the cases that came before the High Court at this time, it appears that judges in the lower courts had begun to reject adoptions as invalid where it had been demonstrated that the widow had adopted a son on payment of money by the child's birth parents, or out of the desire to prevent property from falling into the hands of other claimants. In a series of cases responding to these lower court rulings, the High Court developed several legal grounds for rejecting this logic. In the first of such cases, Chief Justice Farran deprecated the legal consideration of motives altogether, contending,

It must be at once manifest that, if the view of the District Judge is correct, the Court in every case of disputed adoption may be led into abstruse ethical discussions as to the motives which induce a Hindu widow to adopt, and the validity or invalidity of such an adoption will depend upon a consideration, not of facts, but of the feelings, which actuate the Hindu female mind at the time of adoption – feelings, which, even if truthful, she would herself probably be unable to define.... The problem is a difficult one for a Court of justice to solve. The task would seem better fitted for a Court of conscience.[134]

Several additional High Court cases decided that same year by Justices Parsons and Ranade followed Justice Farran's position, but also moved into somewhat original terrain: These cases began to articulate a view of adoption as an act of secular liberal legal agency. In the first case, Ranade concluded that "the exercise of a valid power by a properly authorized person cannot be held to be capricious or malicious in law solely because it defeated the expectations of others."[135] This ruling was followed by another case heard by the Full Bench, where the court aimed to put to rest the question of the widow's motives altogether. After considering all the cases that might have formed legal precedents, Justice Parsons argued that if a widow had not been expressly prohibited from adopting by her husband, then it "follow[s] necessarily that she is left free and unfettered

caste evidently lacked in spiritual motivation. *Bhala Nahana v. Parbhu Hari* (1877) ILR 2 Bom 67.

[133] This question of will had actually been bracketed within nineteenth-century British reformulations of the law of contract. See Gordley, *Modern Contract Doctrine*.

[134] *Mahableshvar Fondba v. Durgabai* (1896) ILR 22 Bom 199 at p. 202.

[135] *Bhimawa v. Sangawa* (1896) ILR 22 Bom 206 at p. 207. Ranade's opinion in this case nonetheless also suggests something of his grappling with conflicting logics.

to exercise her own choice in the matter.... Whenever the widow has this power to adopt, any enquiry into her motives must be irrelevant, for her action is that of a person who does what she has the right to do."[136] In similar terms, Justice Ranade argued that the widow's "freedom of choice" in the "exercise of this right" allowed "little scope for an investigation of [her] motives."[137] Ranade extended this logic even further in another case that year in which he characterized adoption explicitly as "a secular act," distinct from "purely religious acts and observances."[138] In this sense, the High Court Justices did not abandon the question of intent, but rather reframed it in narrow legal terms as purely a question of the intent to adopt by a person with the legal right and capacity to do so.

This depiction of adoption was further solidified a decade later in an opinion by Justice N. G. Chandavarkar, who, like Ranade, was a major Hindu social reformer and moderate nationalist of the day. In a 1909 decision, Chandavarkar wrote:

It is now more or less an exploded theory that a Hindu who has no son born to him adopts merely for his spiritual benefit and that secular objects either do not enter into the act or that they enter incidentally. Whatever the spiritual theory which originally gave rise to adoption in Hindu society, its motives and effects are at least as secular as they are spiritual; and an adoption is made as much, if not more for the purpose of having an heir and continuing the family as for spiritual ends.[139]

Justice Chandavarkar thus insisted on an ethnographic orientation toward adoption, viewing it as a cultural strategy that reflected multiple considerations of personal and familial interest. Furthermore, like Ranade, he opened this terrain by making adoption at once a Hindu and a secular act, a right, a matter of free choice.[140]

---

[136] *Ramchandra Bhagavan v. Mulji Nanabhai* (1896) ILR 22 Bom 558 at p. 566.

[137] Ibid., 567–568.

[138] *Lakshmibai v. Ramchandra* (1896) ILR 22 Bom 590 at p. 595. As in *Bhimawa v. Sangawa* (1896) ILR 22 Bom 206, this opinion is also marked by contradictory logics regarding the potential legal force of ritual status.

[139] *Anandi v. Hari Suba Pai* (1909) ILR 33 Bom 404 at p. 410.

[140] In the 1920s and 1930s the High Court (as well as other presidency High Courts and the Privy Council) returned to an acknowledgment of the spiritual purposes of adoption, and indeed to the distinction between the spiritual and material aspects of adoption. These rulings all concerned the question of whether adoption by a widow divested property that had already vested in her husband's heirs. The reassertion of the spiritual purposes of adoption thus enabled the courts to confirm the widow's legal agency to adopt (regardless of the consent of her husband's heirs) in the Privy Council rulings in *Bhimabai v. Gurunathgouda Khandappagouda* (1932) ILR 57 Bom 157 and *Vijaysingji Chhatrasangji v. Shivsangji Bhimsangji* (1935) ILR 59 Bom 360, but then eventually

CONCLUSION

During the last decades of the nineteenth century, the conundrums of liberalism pervaded colonial Hindu law. Although little discussed at the time or since, this took shape first and foremost in the legal reconceptualization of caste Hindu men as autonomous and interchangeable owners of similarly exchangeable property forms. Integral to this process was a resignification of the capacity for property ownership as an index of legal subjecthood, categorizing persons as either full or incomplete legal subjects. In this process, objects of property became integral to a new symbolic economy that revolved around questions of equality, equivalence, and commensuration, and female family members (and others) became newly incommensurable subjects – an unstable position that took shape in a combination of asymptotic rights, legal erasure, and the valorization of their incommensurability. These questions of commensurability in turn became the grounds for an explicit Hindu reformist engagement with the potentialities of a secular Hindu law that centered on rights, equity, and historical change. Yet the question of how this law would relate to existing custom and to the existing significations of bodies and birth remained highly unresolved. This question would be taken up further both by state agencies and by Indian reformers and nationalists, as they grappled with the ethical terrain of the law and the morality of social life.

to reestablish that such adoptions did not have the effect of divesting heirs of property that had already vested in them in favor of the adopted son. Notably, Justice Rangnekar dissented from this latter opinion in *Balu Sakharam Powar v. Lahoo Sambhaji Tetgura* (1936) ILR 61 Bom 508. The issue remained an unsettled one. *Ishwar Dadu Patil v. Gajabai* (1925) ILR 50 Bom 468; *Bala Anna Gurav v. Akubai* (1926) ILR 50 Bom 722; *Sitabai v. Govindrao Ramrao Deshmukh* (1926) ILR 51 Bom 217; *Bhimabai v. Gurunathgouda Khandappagouda* (1932) ILR 57 Bom 157; *Vijaysingji Chhatrasangji v. Shivsangji Bhimsangji* (1935) ILR 59 Bom 360; *Dhondi Dnyanoo Sinde v. Rama Bala Sinde* (1935) 60 Bom 82; *Shankar Vinayak Nigade v. Ramrao Sahebrao Nigade* (1935) ILR 60 Bom 89; *Umabai v. Nani* (1935) ILR 60 Bom 102; *Balu Sakharam Powar v. Lahoo Sambhaji Tetgura* (1936) ILR 61 Bom 508. A decision by the Privy Council in an appeal from the Patna High Court proved a crucial precedent: *Amarendra Mansigh v. Sanatan Singh* (1933) 12 Pat. 642.

4

Custom and Human Value
in the Debates on Hindu Marriage

The British Empire in India ... governs, not indeed on the principle that no religion is true, but distinctly on the principle that no native religion is true.

    – James Fitzjames Stephen, *Liberty, Equality, Fraternity*, 1873

To say that usage is the rule, does not necessarily limit us to that sole sense of the word "usage" which shuts out all amelioration. The practices of an abandoned class are, no doubt, a usage in the sense of a tolerably uniform series of acts; but they do not, therefore, spring from a consciousness of compulsion; rather from mere habit, imitation and ignorance, of which, indeed we have evidence in this case. Such usage is not a law, for over it presides the higher usage of the community at large from whose approval it must have derived any conceivable original validity, and in opposition to which it cannot subsist.

    – Justice Raymond West, *Mathura Naikin v. Esu Naikin*, 1880

When one sees how men who had grown grey in the denunciation of these evils, turned round immediately a suggestion was made for practical action, and join the orthodox majority in their praise of the existing arrangements, the Political Rishi's warning about the defects of the Hindu character seem to be more than justified. There appears to be no ground for hope, under such circumstance, of seeing any genuine reform movement springing up from within the heart of the nation, unless that heart is regenerated, not by cold calculations of utility, but by a cleansing fire of a religious revival.

    – M. G. Ranade, 1885[1]

---

[1] M. G. Ranade, "Introduction," in *A Collection Containing the Proceedings Which Led to the Passage of Act XV of 1856*, edited by Pandit Narayan Keshav Vaidya (Bombay: Mazagaon Printing Press, 1885), p. iv. The "Political Rishi" was the name signed by an

The last few decades of the nineteenth century were marked by a broad reengagement with the authority of custom, shaping debates that traversed the legal arena and the colonial and vernacular public spheres. Although the question of custom in this era emerged in a variety of contexts – ranging from the customary relationship between landlord and tenant to the customary nature of caste regulations[2] – no issue was more critical to these debates than the customs of Hindu marriage.[3] This charged atmosphere of debate concerning Hindu marriage in part reflected a broad politicization of marriage across the metropolitan and colonial world in the nineteenth century.[4] In India, however, this heightened political salience of marriage was additionally layered with colonial significations. British commentators across the political spectrum had long denigrated Hindu marriage (or a variety of practices connected to Hindu marriage that the colonial power identified as distinct social ills: *sati*, child marriage, enforced widowhood, and female infanticide most notably), as the touchstone of an oppressive and degenerate civilization.[5]

---

anonymous writer of a series of articles in the *Indu Prakash*. N. G. Chandavarkar later revealed that he was the author of the pieces. Although he was also the editor of the journal at the time, he sought to bring special attention to these issues through the intrigue surrounding the anonymous articles.

[2] Neeladri Bhattacharya, "Remaking Custom: The Discourse and Practice of Colonial Codification," in *Tradition, Dissent, Ideology: Essays in Honour of Romila Thapar*, edited by R. Champakalakshmi and S. Gopal (Delhi: Oxford University Press, 1996), pp. 20–51; Dirks, *Castes of Mind*.

[3] The scholarship on this issue is extensive. For critical early delineations of the issues at stake, see Uma Chakravarti, "Whatever Happened to the Vedic Dasi? Orientalism, Nationalism, and a Script for the Past," in Sangari and Vaid, eds., *Recasting Women*, 27–87; Mani, *Contentious Tradition*; and Chatterjee, "Nationalist Resolution." See also Sarkar, "Rhetoric against Age of Consent: Resisting Colonial Reason and the Death of a Child-Wife," *Economic and Political Weekly* 28, 36 (Sept. 4, 1993): 1869–1878, and "Pre-History of Rights"; Chakravarti, *Rewriting History*; Chakrabarti, *Provincializing Europe*, 117–148; G. Arunima, *There Comes Papa: Colonialism and the Transformation of Matriliny in Kerala, Malabar c. 1850–1940* (New Delhi: Orient Longman, 2003); Pravena Kodoth, "Courting Legitimacy or Delegitimizing Custom? Sexuality, Sambandham, and Marriage Reform in Late Nineteenth-Century Malabar," *Modern Asian Studies* 35, 2 (May 2001): 349–384.

[4] Mary Poovey, *Uneven Developments: The Ideological Work of Gender in Mid-Victorian England* (Chicago: University of Chicago Press, 1988), Shanley, *Feminism, Marriage and the Law*; Ann Laura Stoler and Frederick Cooper, eds. *Tensions of Empire: Colonial Cultures in a Bourgeois World* (Berkeley: University of California Press, 1987); Julia Ann Clancy-Smith and Frances Gouda, *Domesticating the Empire: Race, Gender, and Family Life in French and Dutch Colonialism* (Charlottesville: University Press of Virginia, 1998).

[5] Some of the ironies of the concomitant view of English women's high socio-legal status emerge forcefully in Poovey, *Uneven Developments*, and in Shanley, *Feminism, Marriage and the Law*.

By the late nineteenth century, for both supporters and critics of existing practices – Indians and Britons – the customs of marriage formed the grounds for a highly politicized fashioning of intimate life, linked at once to the material and symbolic reproduction of society and to questions of colonial governance. As in this chapter's epigraphs, colonial judges, lawmakers, and reformers raised fundamental questions concerning the customs of marriage and their proper ethical and legal force.

Recent scholarship on the colonial state and on anti-colonial nationalism has emphasized both a late-nineteenth-century official "turn to custom" and the rise of a powerful populist Hindu revivalism that mobilized in the name of custom or tradition.[6] Despite the importance of this scholarship, it sits rather uneasily both with the evident emphasis on legal codification and institutionalization that characterized this era, as many of the same scholars recognize, and with recent feminist scholarship on the colonial treatment of Hindu marriage, which has emphasized not a rule by custom but rather the marginalization of subaltern customs and the homogenization of the elite marriage form.[7]

Yet rather than assessing whether the colonial state ruled by custom or marginalized custom, this chapter suggests that it was the continued *questioning* of the authority and significance of custom in this era that produced critical new forms of knowledge, power, and investment. This process did have the effect of marginalizing custom in important ways, but of greater significance, it rendered debates on custom a key terrain for the extension of state power and for new forms of individual and community self-fashioning. In this sense, Hindu marriage customs became the grounds for new modes of state power in which the state positioned itself as both a transcendent ethical power and an immanent social force. Moreover, addressing the customs of Hindu marriage became critical to both legal and social reformist projects of humanization that centered on the social significance of female bodies.[8] In the legal arena, these projects came to focus on ensuring that marriage remained irreducible to contractual social relations, while in the elite Hindu reformist public sphere, such projects took shape as an effort to recast valorized customs premised

---

[6] Washbrook, "Law, State and Agrarian Society"; Dirks, *Castes of Mind*; Mantena, *Alibis of Empire*; Sartori, *Bengal in Global Concept History*; Gooptu, *Politics of the Urban Poor*.

[7] Chakravarti, *Rewriting History*; Kodoth, "Courting Legitimacy"; Sen, "Offences against Marriage."

[8] Samera Esmeir, "At Once Human and Not Human: Gender, Law, and Becoming in Colonial Egypt," *Gender & History* 23, 2 (Aug. 2011): 235–249.

on notions of female inauspiciousness and impurity as social ills that dehumanized women and girls and perpetuated their bodily and psychic suffering. The work of humanization thus involved separate but interconnected processes of distinguishing women from property and limiting the commodification of marriage in the case of state regulation, while in the case of Hindu reformers, it involved according women new human value, grounded in the secularization and universalization of the female body.

PART I: MARRIAGE AND THE MORALITY OF EXCHANGE

Colonial Ethnography and Hindu Law

In 1878, eminent justice of the Calcutta High Court Sir Gooroodass Banerjee opened his Tagore Law Lectures on "The Hindu Law of Marriage and Stridhan" with a brief discussion of the nature and sources of Hindu law, and of the origins and forms of marriage. On the latter subject, he drew on contemporary European historical sociology and ethnography to emphasize at once the diversity of cultural practices regarding marriage, and its evolutionary and functionalist development.[9] Adopting the historicist approach of Henry Maine, he argued that "to understand social institutions properly, you must know, not only what they are, but also what they have been. They do not stand isolated from the past, and are often unintelligible without a knowledge of the past."[10] Following the theory and methodology of Herbert Spencer, he argued that the "laws and legends of ancient societies" and the "present condition of savage people" suggested that the institution of marriage had emerged out of a primitive promiscuity: "By the law of the survival of the fittest in the struggle for existence, groups having definite sexual relations would evolve out of groups with prevailing promiscuity."[11] This explained the emergence of monogamous marriage as well as the highly valorized, sacramental nature of Hindu marriage.

---

[9] These colonial reflections thus drew on and formed part of a broader nineteenth-century discourse on custom, marriage, the family, and political forms. See Rosalind Coward, *Patriarchal Precedents: Sexuality and Social Relations* (London: Routledge & Kegan Paul, 1983). For a discussion of how a new generation of young men from the matrilineal Nair community used contemporary European kinship theories to mobilize state intervention to transform their community customs, see G. Arunima, *There Comes Papa*.

[10] Sir Gooroodass Banerjee, *The Hindu Law of Marriage and Stridhan*, (Calcutta: Thacker, Spink & Co., 1879), pp. 21–22.

[11] Ibid., 22–24. He also drew on M'Lennan's *Primitive Marriage* (1865) and on John Lubbock's *Origin of Civilization* (1870) in this disquisition.

For Banerjee, the project of detailing the Hindu law of marriage and *stridhan* (women's property) was of interest both for the field of comparative ethnography and for an understanding of the current legal treatment of these social relations. If Banerjee followed contemporary European fascination with the origins of marriage and the rise of civilization, this necessitated at once an attentiveness to the diversity of custom and a theorization of the rationality both internal and external thereto: Customs emerged out of the local conditions of life, but also followed a universal evolutionary logic. Attending to such logics also ultimately involved the deduction of abstract "inner principles" or theories that explained existing custom even when it could not explain itself, and that enabled its systemization.[12]

Custom as the foundation of colonial law was explicitly established in the Punjab following its conquest in 1848; it also became a widely influential principle after the publication of Sir Henry Maine's *Ancient Law* in 1861. It received judicial recognition in the major 1868 Privy Council ruling in *Collector of Madura v. Mootoo Ramalinga Sathupathy*[13] that, "under the Hindu system of law clear proof of usage will outweigh the written text." And the Privy Council further clarified the legal foundation for custom in an 1872 ruling[14] to the effect that "it is of the essence of special usages, modifying the ordinary law of succession, that they should be ancient and invariable," and that they "should be established to be so by clear and unambiguous evidence."[15] In Bombay Presidency, this renewed emphasis on custom confirmed the earlier principles established by Mountstuart Elphinstone's Regulations of 1827, but in this later context, custom was also newly problematized.

Following intellectually in the wake of Maine, several major texts on Hindu law emphasizing the centrality of custom were published in succeeding decades: Raymond West and Georg Bühler's *Digest of Hindu Law* published in 1868, which treated the replies of the Shastris in the Bombay Presidency Sadr courts as an expression of the living tradition of popularly revered Brahminical commentary; John Dawson Mayne's

---

[12] The colonial treatment of custom thus embedded and jostled together multiple theories of reason, as Neeladri Bhattacharya has compellingly argued. Bhattacharya, "Remaking Custom."

[13] *Collector of Madura v. Mootoo Ramalinga Sathupathy* (1868) 12 MIA 397 at p. 435.

[14] *Ramalakshmi Ammal v. Sivanantha* (1872) 14 MIA 570. Appeal of *Sivanananja Perumal v. Muttu Ramalinga* (1866) 3 Mad. HCR 75 *Ramalakshmi Ammal v. Sivanantha* (1872) 14 MIA 570.

[15] Sripati Roy, *Custom and Customary Law in British India*. Tagore Law Lectures, 1908 (Calcutta: Hare Press, 1911), p. 25.

influential 1878 *Treatise on Hindu Law and Usage*; Sir Gooroodass Banerjee's *Hindu Law of Marriage and Stridhan*, published the following year; Sripati Roy's 1911 *Customs and Customary Law in British India*; and major Dharmashastra scholar P. V. Kane's later work, *Hindu Customs and Modern Law*, published in 1947, among others. Integral to many of these works was the idea that the textual tradition itself derived from custom and in fact confirmed the legitimacy thereof. J. D. Mayne took these principles even further to argue that the Brahminical textual tradition derived out of the early Aryan interaction with the non-Aryan peoples they encountered in the subcontinent, and reflected the Brahminical integration, formalization, and transformation of non-Aryan customs that did not conflict with their own:

My view is, that Hindu law is based on immemorial customs, which existed prior to and independent of Brahmanism. That when the Aryans penetrated into India they found there a number of usages either the same as, or not wholly unlike, their own. That they accepted these, with or without modifications, rejecting only those which were incapable of being assimilated, such as polyandry, incestuous marriages, and the like. That the latter lived on a merely local life, while the former became incorporated among the customs of the ruling race.... That the religious element subsequently grew up, and entwined itself with legal conceptions, and then distorted them in three ways. First, by attributing a pious purpose to acts of a purely secular nature. Secondly, by clogging those acts with rules and restrictions, suitable to the assumed pious purpose. And, thirdly, by gradually altering the customs themselves, so as to further the special objects of religion or policy favoured by Brahmanism.[16]

Mayne thus reversed the standard analysis of subaltern adoption of elite norms, identifying instead a Brahminical absorption of existing local practices and eventual appending of spiritual elements as a superstructural edifice. From this position, he emphasized that the logic of local customs frequently differed from the Brahminical law, such that even when they appeared superficially similar, the latter should not be applied to the former. Although the local customs "have been largely altered and supplanted by that [Brahminical] law":[17]

we should be prepared to find that rules, such as rules of inheritance, adoption, and the like, may have been accepted from the Brahmans by classes of persons who never accepted the principles or motives from which these rules originally spring; and therefore, ... we should not rashly infer that a usage which leads to necessary developments, when practiced by Brahmans, will lead to the same

[16] John Dawson Mayne, *A Treatise on Hindu Law and Usage*, 4.
[17] Ibid., 10.

developments when practiced by alien races. It will not do so, unless they have adopted the principle as well as the practice.[18]

Mayne's theory thus emphasized both the mutual interaction between custom and text, and the plurality of law (or incomplete hegemony of Brahminical law) actually in operation in "Hindu" society. This required both the European and the Brahmin judge to be attentive to the variant rationalities that might underlie practices outwardly similar to the Brahminical law.

Implicit in this account, as in that of other European ethnographers and sociologists of the "historical" school, including Henry Maine, was a notion at once of the historical depth and of the historical mutability of custom. Antiquity was central to the very definition of custom. As Sripati Roy stated, "Custom, therefore, may be defined to be a rule of conduct uniformly governing a community from time immemorial."[19] It was this antiquity that distinguished custom from mere usages (which might also have legal validity) but which, although a "uniform practice among a people or class," might be of quite recent adoption.[20] Yet Roy also acknowledged that custom must in addition be a thing of continual growth and change: "Even in these days of codes and statutes, there is still growing up *pari pasu* a body of unwritten laws, or, customs and usages, in every sphere of human activity, which commands all the reverence and obedience of a king-made law."[21] This depiction of the living nature of the unwritten law, as continually emerging out of the material conditions and consciousness of the people, involved a model of organic, holistic, and consensual uniform practice within the community, howsoever defined. Such practice, in this view, came into existence and was preserved through the internal principles underlying the life of the community itself.

Roy summarized the colonial jurisprudence on the requisites to establish that a custom had the force of law as follows: "It should be *ancient* and *invariable, continuous* and *uniform, reasonable* and *not immoral, certain* and *definite, compulsory* and *consistent*."[22] Yet if he acknowledged that at times customs had been granted the force of law without meeting all of these requirements, the burden of proving a community (or caste) custom

---

[18] Ibid., 10.
[19] Roy, *Custom and Customary Law*, 5.
[20] Ibid., 6.
[21] Ibid., 6.
[22] Ibid., 24.

lay prominently before the eyes of some colonial judges. Thus, in the case of *Jugmohandas Mangaldas v. Sir Mangaldas Nathubhoy*,[23] discussed in Chapter 3, Justice Scott reflected on the inherent difficulties in satisfying the terms set out by the Privy Council ruling, that any such usage should be, "ancient and invariable" and "should be established to be so by clear and unambiguous evidence."[24] This standard, Scott recognized, was effectively producing a juridical homogenization and Brahminization of the law: "As long as the establishment of a custom is made dependant on its proof by instances, very few customs will ever be proved. Instances will be met by instances. The cost and delay of sifting the good from the bad will always be greater than the parties will face or the Court permit; and almost every custom will fail for apparent want of uniformity. The obvious result will be the continually widening influence of the Brahminical law."[25] Scott went on to argue that even a vote by a caste assembly would not yield "the truth," pointing to the ways in which the legal questioning of custom became the subject of caste mobilizations, which, from official perspectives, muddied the very issues at stake.[26] The politicized nature of caste thus inherently had the potential to undermine the legal integrity of custom.

Yet if Scott was concerned with the effect of the courts in marginalizing custom, legal scholars also foregrounded the critical role the High Court had to play in recognizing the authentic mutability of custom.[27] This view at once of the inevitability of change and of its progressive character implied an important role for the judge. As West argued in the 1880 case of *Mathura Naikin v. Esu Naikin* (quoted in the second epigraph to this chapter), decisions must, "in truth, be founded on an appreciation of the legal consciousness of the community; but where that consciousness is unsettled and fluctuating, its nobler may properly be chosen in preference to its baser elements as those which are to predominate."[28]

---

[23] *Jugmohandas Mangaldas v. Sir Mangaldas Nathubhoy* (1886) ILR 10 Bom 528.

[24] *Ramlakshmi Ammal v. Sivanantha*, 7 Mad HCR 250 at p. 254.

[25] *Jugmohandas Mangaldas v. Sir Mangaldas Nathubhoy* (1886) ILR 10 Bom 528 at pp. 543–544.

[26] Ibid. Notably, this problem was recognized by Arthur Steele during the first decade of colonial rule in his classic, *Summary of the Law and Custom of Hindoo Castes, within the Dekhun Provinces Subject to the Presidency of Bombay, Chiefly Affecting Civil Suits* (Bombay: Courier Press, 1827), as pointed out in Banerjee, *Hindu Law of Marriage and Stridhan*, 13.

[27] *Ghelabhai Mulchand v. Bai Mancha* (1883) ILR 7 Bom 491 at p. 493. See also *Damodhar Madhowji v. Purmanandas Jeewandas; Purmanandas Jeevandas v. Damodhar Madhowji* (1883) ILR 7 Bom 155. This decision was confirmed in Ranade's 1895 decision in the case of *Motilal Lalubhai v. Ratilal Mahipatram* (1895) ILR 21 Bom 170.

[28] *Mathura Naikin v. Esu Naikin* (1880) ILR 4 Bom 545 at p. 553.

The case of *Mathura Naikin v. Esu Naikin* involved the practice of adoption of daughters among *naikins,* in British parlance "prostitutes" or "dancing girls," who typically followed their adoptive mother's profession and inherited her property. West's ruling against the legitimacy of any such custom was grounded in a model of the stadial development of legal and moral consciousness, in which customs could and would be abandoned when the community attained to a higher level of progress. What Justice West sought to nullify in this case was the claim that *naikins* formed a community with its own particular customs of adoption, joint family, and inheritance through the female line that both derived and diverged from the customs of the broader Hindu caste community, but nevertheless had the force of law. In West's words,

> The naikin class, like other classes, would fain adopt rules favouring the organization of the class, as such, and furthering its proper end. To such an organization the law which regards the end as baneful, can lend no aid. A mere practice has in itself no binding force; and the Courts formulating the decision of society must refuse to allow to the naikins a legislative power which as individuals they cannot possess.[29]

In fact, West argued, "There is, indeed, no definite class of the kind, united in the expression and observance of a common corporate will, although individual looseness of behaviour may be as common as ever."[30] In this, West refused to admit the naikins' claim to constitute a community as such for whom particular customs could stand.[31]

West's refusal of naikins' claim to "give special laws to themselves"[32] highlighted a fundamental tension in the legal treatment of custom – between a view of custom as the foundation of law in general, as in

---

[29] *Mathura Naikin v. Esu Naikin* (1880) ILR 4 Bom 545 at pp. 570–571.

[30] Ibid., 555.

[31] This opinion did not remain uncontested. In a case nearly a decade later concerning the inheritance of a temple endowment by an adopted temple dancer (*devadasi*), the High Court held that "the existence in India of dancing girls in connection with Hindu temples is according to the ancient established usage, and the Court would not be justified in refusing to recognize existing endowments in connection with such an institution." Further, in a more direct refutation of Justice West's ruling, it continued, "This Court would, in our opinion, be taking far too much upon itself to say that it is so 'opposed to the legal consciousness' of the community at the present day as to justify the Court in refusing to recognize existing endowments in connection with such an institution." *Tara Naikin v. Nana Lakshman* (1889) 14 Bom 90 at pp. 90, 93. This legal recognition may have reflected the court's greater reticence to intervene in property connected to religious endowments. In contrast, the *naikins* who were the subject of West's 1880 ruling had no connection to religious institutions. This conjecture seems to be supported by the Madras case of *Kamalam v. Sadagopa Sami* 1 Mad 356 (1878), discussed in Roy, *Customs and Customary Law,* 565.

[32] *Mathura Naikin v. Esu Naikin* (1880) ILR 4 Bom 545 at p. 556.

the English common law or in Elphinstone's model for governing the Bombay Presidency, and the standard legal treatment of custom as community practice that contravened (or lacked support in) the dominant, written law. In subscribing to the former view of custom, West advanced the notion of custom as integral to a dominant community consciousness, in which subaltern practices would have little legal or ethical claim.

The category of immoral custom that West relied upon and developed in this ruling was acknowledged in all the contemporary treatises on custom, and indeed many, such as Sripati Roy, pointed to the Brahminical textual foundation for this category. Roy opened his discussion of "Illegal and Immoral Customs" with a quote from Manu: "A king who knows the revealed law must inquire into the particular laws of classes, the laws or usages of districts, the customs of traders and the rules of certain families, and establish their peculiar laws, if *they be not repugnant* to the law of God."[33] Yet this framework underscored the unstable legal grounding of custom in general, since, as Sir Gooroodass Banerjee pointed out, "The truth is, that custom, from its very nature, must be inconsistent with the general rule of law."[34] The question of what made a custom that by definition involved a departure from the law or textual authorities of the overarching community into an immoral and illegal act thus rested on the determination of a sovereign power – that is, custom was inherently located within, and at the sufferance of, the will of the sovereign.[35] In this light, despite Roy's eloquent brief for the constant, living operation of custom and usage that effectively (within the sphere of social life) had the force of law, what his lectures in fact detailed were the specific customs that that had received positive juridical recognition by the colonial state.[36] Although in a few places he questioned the colonial judicial treatment of a given practice, the work was in essence an exposition of the existing positive law of custom, as established by judicial precedent.

The same may be said of the other works. While some scholars, such as Banerjee and Kane, gave significant weight to the Dharmashastra tradition,

---

[33] Roy, *Customs and Customary Law*, 556. Emphasis in original.
[34] Banerjee, *Hindu Law of Marriage and Stridhan*, 230.
[35] The theory of law as the "command of the sovereign," most closely associated with early-nineteenth century legal positivism of Utilitarian John Austin, was cited in all these texts for its view of custom as positive law, but typically the content of this idea was ignored or dismissed in favor of a claim regarding the intrinsic authority of custom. John Austin, *Lectures on Jurisprudence, or the Philosophy of Positive Law*, Vol. II, 4th ed. (London: J. Murray, 1873). For a recent argument on sovereign power in colonial India, drawing on the work of Schmitt and Agamben, see Hussain, *Jurisprudence of Emergency*.
[36] Roy, *Customs and Customary Law*, 38.

they all eventually turned to the decisions of the High Courts and Privy Council to delineate the diverse content of the term "Hindu customs." In this sense, while the official attentiveness toward custom sought to recognize existing social practice as the foundation of law in a vision of seamless connectivity between law and society, it was, nevertheless, the state, not society, that determined whether a custom would have legal force. As such, the morality of custom would inevitably be determined according to norms and principles external to it, and moreover, the legitimacy of multiple ethical norms within a given society became increasingly difficult to sustain.

One question that was seemingly not asked in these legal writings on custom was what made a custom immoral. The answer was not straightforward.[37] Rather than reflecting a direct expression of Victorian British or Brahminical values (or some combination of the two), it was customs related to marriage and sexuality that seemed to render women subjects or objects of exchange that came to be designated immoral customs. The designation as "immoral" involved a reconceptualization of the ethical relations of marriage as properly exceeding (if not repudiating) relations of interest, selfish calculation, and commodification. Marriage customs and sexual relations that appeared overly contractual were thus delegitimized by the High Court for their failure to adequately resemble marriage as such. In this concern with the commodification of women, sexuality, or the marriage relation, the state sought to curtail what it identified as their susceptibility to becoming objects of barter and exchange.

Marriage Custom in Colonial Jurisprudence

In the Bombay Presidency, the legitimacy of custom as a source of law had primarily framed *early* marriage cases, prior to the reorganization of the courts.[38] In contrast, starting in the mid-1860s, cases that had previously been decided in the language of the legitimacy of custom and caste practice (claims that were still made by defendants), were now determined based on the questionable "policy" of affording such practices legal recognition. In cases that drew upon both civil and criminal provisions, the High Court now defined various subaltern-caste marriage practices as immoral customs. This problematization of caste customs thus formed the basis for an extension of state power in relation to caste

---

[37] For example, a variety of practices that suggested some degree of impropriety both in the textual authorities and in contemporary British culture were allowed to stand: cross-cousin marriage, adoption of a daughter's or a sister's son, levirate, and the like.

[38] See Sturman, "Family Values," chapters 3 and 4.

authorities, framed in the rhetoric of "public policy." "Public policy" linked the interests of state with the public good, underscoring the state interest in regulating a social practice – marriage – that it viewed as foundational to society itself. The marginalization of caste authority thus not only involved the expansion of colonial state power but a new framing of society and its relation to the state.

These trends were connected to the contemporary process of removing marriage from ecclesiastical control in England, marked by the Marriage Act of 1836, which for the first time permitted civil marriage, and by the 1857 Matrimonial Causes Act, which removed divorce from the jurisdiction of ecclesiastical courts. This English process of secularizing marriage thus occurred as an expansion of state jurisdiction at the expense of the church. In England as in India, the state's claim to regulate marriage "in the interests of public policy" linked state interest in the emergent domains of social and intimate life with an absorption of transcendent or theological power. In India, although marriage remained firmly within the jurisdiction of colonial personal law, the courts now began to conceptualize it in terms of the binary of sacrament and contract, quite consistently defining the morality of Hindu marriage in terms of its noncontractual character. As such, the emphasis on marriage as a sacrament that exceeded contractual relations was itself saturated and defined by liberal contract ideology.[39] Likewise, contractual logics frequently pervaded every aspect of the framing of these cases. Indeed, the imagining of the morality of marriage was multifarious and complex: While marriage was properly irreducible to contract, it ideally was also based in the mutual consent between bride and groom; that is, in the properly contractual nature of the agreement. At the same time, the insistence on the transcendent nature of marriage – its irreducibility to contract – also indexed the transcendent nature of the state, which now claimed for itself the power to define moral and immoral social relations through the operation of its law.

Problematizing the Contractual Character of Marriage

In the efforts to establish the permanence and inviolability of marriage, colonial criminal law played a prominent role. Sections 494 and 497 of

---

[39] For a recent example of the ongoing power of this binary see Monmayee Basu, *Hindu Women and Marriage Law: From Sacrament to Contract* (Delhi: Oxford University Press, 2001).

the 1861 Indian Penal Code (IPC) defined bigamy and adultery as penal offenses.[40] Since many lower castes had regularly allowed couples to separate and both parties to remarry, the provisions against adultery and bigamy, which denied the possibility of legal separation or divorce and remarriage, put the legal status of such marriages into question.[41] Notably, women were exempt from the provisions against adultery, as the IPC defined adultery as a crime committed by the paramour against the husband, while the provisions against bigamy applied only to women, as Hindu and Muslim men were considered legally entitled to polygamy.[42] Women's remarriages were now recast by the courts in the language of immoral contract.

The question of terminability of marriage emerged in the ensuing years in a series of reported cases that concerned what the court construed as a system of marriage as a voluntary contract, made or broken through simple payments, at will. The volume of such cases reached their greatest concentration in the 1880s, with additional important cases reported well into the twentieth century. These cases received considerable legal attention at the time, and have garnered scholarly attention in recent years.[43]

[40] This code was a revised version of the Indian Penal Code originally drafted in 1837 by Utilitarian liberal Thomas Babington Macaulay. It did not attempt to integrate Indian customary or religious law, but derived from British legal norms.

[41] Adultery (*badkarma, sinalki*) had been considered an offense against the precolonial regional state in the eighteenth century. From the records of the Pune Kotwal analyzed by N. K. Wagle, these cases appear to have been punished exclusively by fines imposed on both parties. Caste punishments, which presumably also accompanied many of these fines, are not mentioned in this record. Wagle, "Women in the Kotwal's Papers," 15–60. In contrast, V. S. Kadam, drawing on the records of the Peshwa Daftar, presents a considerably grimmer picture of women imprisoned, enslaved, and occasionally mutilated for such sexual lapses. Kadam, "The Institution of Marriage," 341–370. It is possible that the divergence in their accounts is a product of the difference between the everyday functioning of the local police and the extraordinary and highly normativizing decisions by the Peshwa rulers themselves.

[42] See lengthy discussion at MSA, JD 1861, 3/72. Macaulay's 1837 draft version of the Penal Code had likewise excluded all provision for punishment of adultery because Macaulay considered adultery a "private wrong." Moreover, he argued that the code should not buttress marriages in India since they were based in a legal inequality – the husband was allowed to engage in polygamy while the wife was punished for infidelity. See Singha, *Despotism of Law*, 164–165.

[43] These cases were widely cited as judicial precedents and referenced in all the texts on custom discussed in the first subsection of this chapter. For more recent discussions, see J. D. M. Derrett, "Divorce by Caste Custom," in *Essays in Classical and Modern Hindu Law, Vol. IV: Current Problems and the Legacy of the Past* (Leiden: E. J. Brill, 1978), pp. 95–104; Agnes, *Law and Gender Inequality*, 18–26; Chakravarti, *Rewriting History*, 134–138; Anagol, *Emergence of Feminism*. Anagol has viewed these cases primarily through the lens of female agency against male oppression, highlighting the convergence

The first of such cases, which became a precedent for many later decisions, was the 1864 case of *Reg. v. Karsan Goja* and *Reg. v. Bai Rupa*, in which Karsan Goja was accused of having sexual intercourse with Bai Rupa, and Bai Rupa was accused of contracting a *natra*, or secondary marriage, with Karsan Goja during the lifetime of her husband.[44] In their appeal before the High Court, both of the accused claimed that in their caste of Talabda Kolis, women were customarily allowed to divorce their husbands and to contract a *natra*, as had happened in this case, with or without the previous consent of the husband or of the caste.[45] In rejecting this defense, the High Court held that "such a caste custom as that set up, even if proved to exist, is invalid, as being entirely opposed to the spirit of the Hindu Law."[46]

This logic was extended in the 1876 case of *Reg. v. Sambhu Raghu*, in which the court explicitly refuted the authority of castes, "to declare

of British and Indian patriarchies. Anagol, *Emergence of Feminism*, 120–121. Anagol's study is exemplary in bringing to light a wealth of Marathi-language sources, and especially materials written by women. Nonetheless, her argument that the extraordinary politicization of marriage and the so-called women's question in the nineteenth century was due to a reactionary response of Indian men to the agency of Indian women of all castes and classes, who were taking advantage of the openings provided by the colonial state to resist their bondage under indigenous patriarchy, fundamentally obscures the nature and operation of colonial state power, not least in the very formation of "women" as a universal category. Anagol points intriguingly to the emergence of the term *stri-jati*, literally "woman-caste," in late-nineteenth-century feminist writings, but this new political conceptualization of the collectivity or community of women linked by their birth as such remains underexamined in her work. Anagol, 90–91, 214–215. See further discussion of this in note 121. In contrast, and more persuasively, scholars such as Uma Chakravarti and Samita Sen have interpreted this jurisprudence as a key terrain of struggle between caste authorities and state authority, in which the state increasingly usurped the power of castes to regulate marriage relations and to define the morality thereof. Their work suggests that these cases marginalized subaltern marriage customs, integrating these communities into the norms of higher castes by extending valorized patriarchal norms from which they had previously been excluded. Chakravarti, *Rewriting History*, 129–138; Sen, "Offences against Marriage." Such reforms thus ironically had the potential to raise the status of the subaltern communities involved; they also enhanced the power of a new upwardly mobile elite within these castes at the expense of earlier caste authorities. For similar processes in Malabar, see Arunima, *There Comes Papa*; Kodoth, "Courting Legitimacy."

[44] *Reg. v. Karsan Goja* and *Reg. v. Bai Rupa* (1864) 2 Bom HCR 124.

[45] Kolis denominated various groups in Gujarat, the Deccan, and the Konkan that functioned at the margins of caste Hindu communities and ritual practices. Labeled as "tribals" within colonial ethnography, they were nevertheless increasingly drawn under the purview of caste Hinduism. In this context, the court's decision forms part of that larger process, not only privileging textual dictate over custom, but extending the application of Brahminical textual prescription to communities that had previously existed outside of it.

[46] *Reg. v. Karsan Goja* and *Reg. v. Bai Rupa* (1864) 2 Bom HCR 124 at p. 130.

a marriage void or to give permission to a woman to remarry."⁴⁷ This
judgment recast what had earlier been treated as a question of custom as
instead a matter of jurisdiction: The state would determine the legitimacy
of a marriage, in the interests of public policy.⁴⁸ Nonetheless, contractual
elements pervaded every stage of this case.

The case involved a woman named Narbada of the Teli (oil-presser)
caste of Khandesh, who discovered her husband had leprosy. She decided
to remarry, sending her husband notice that he was "either to send a cer-
tificate of his cure, or to consent to her remarriage." Her husband dictated
a letter and replied by post "that he was too ill to come; that Narbada
was to bring her ornaments to Shirpur, [returning the gifts he had given
her at the time of the marriage, thereby ending his marital claims] and
that if a few were broken it was no matter." A few months after this,
Narbada had a caste meeting convened to decide whether she should be
allowed to remarry. The meeting, by a unanimous decision, declared her
first marriage void and authorized her to marry again. Narbada therefore
remarried. Her first husband then brought a complaint to the colonial
authorities, stating that he had not agreed to her remarriage and had not
been repaid for his marriage expenses. Narbada was convicted of bigamy
and sentenced to two months' simple imprisonment. The question at issue
in this case was as to the guilt of Sambhu Raghu, who had performed the
second marriage ceremony. Critical to the session judge's deliberation in
the original case had been the question of the will of the husband; that
is, whether the caste had such authority, "in the absence of a *sod chitti* or
pharkhut [deed of release]" from the husband, releasing his wife from the
marriage.⁴⁹ The issue of divorce *against the husband's will* would become
an integral feature of the compilation of the case in all-India legal digests
and treatises such as those discussed in the first subsection of this chapter.
Yet it is not clear that the court would have viewed a divorce by mutual

---

⁴⁷ *Reg. v. Sambhu Raghu* (1876) ILR 1 Bom 347 at p. 352.
⁴⁸ Indeed, this issue had been directly addressed in the original decision by the assistant ses-
sions judge, and was favorably quoted in the High Court opinion: "Whether a *Panchayat*
[council for dispute resolution] ... could be regarded as a Court at all, has not been def-
initely ruled. From the illustration adverted to above, it seems as if it could not, on the
maxim '*Espressio unius est exclusio alterius.*' Whether it could be regarded as a Court
of competent jurisdiction to declare a marriage void, seems, from the case of *Reg v.
Manohar* and the cases cited in the note to it, still more questionable." *Reg. v. Sambhu
Raghu* (1876) ILR 1 Bom 347 at pp. 349–350. Bracketed comments added. For further
example of this kind of ambiguous relationship to custom, see *Empress v. Umi* (1882)
ILR 6 Bom 126.
⁴⁹ *Reg. v. Sambhu Raghu* (1876) ILR 1 Bom 347. Bracketed comments added.

consent with greater favor. As Sir Gooroodass Banerjee noted, the English law at this time, as embodied in the 1869 Divorce Act, treated the consent of both parties as collusion, and hence as grounds for rejecting an application for divorce.[50] Judicial debates regarding the "policy" of a custom of divorce and remarriage thus turned, on the one hand, on views of the contractual rights of husbands, and on the other hand, on critiques of marriage forms that might be construed as immoral contracts or immoral insofar as they were reducible to contracts.

Cases concerning the terminability of marriage and legitimacy of remarriage, which were prosecuted under the bigamy statutes, reached their greatest concentration in the 1880s, at which time they were also the subject of extensive public debate in the vernacular and English language press as well.[51] As Hindu marriage became a matter of public debate, it worked in a quite material sense to consolidate linguistically segmented and stratified vernacular and colonial public spheres. In Marathi, Gujarati, and English, as well as in bilingual English-vernacular journals, writers and editors made use of the technologies of print capitalism and sought to produce a variety of new reformist, conservative, and female publics. Reformers focused on what contemporary British feminists called the "sexual double standard": that women were convicted of bigamy while men were free to enter into other liaisons, and to marry more than one wife.[52] In contrast, conservatives argued that female immorality was becoming increasingly widespread, and that harsh punishments were required to prevent a groundswell of women from abandoning their husbands to contract secret second marriages.[53] In these wide-ranging

---

[50] Banerjee, *Hindu Law of Marriage and Stridhan*, 180. See Sec. 13, Act IV of 1869. Notably, however, the Madras High Court ruled in 1894 that a caste custom of divorce and remarriage by mutual agreement, on repayment of the party's original marriage expenses was valid. *Sankaralingam Chetti v. Subban Chetti* ILR 17 Mad 479.

[51] See *Bai Vijli v. Nansanagar* (1885) ILR 10 Bom 152, as well as the extensive debates and exhortations in the vernacular press, such as in the *Din Bandhu* (Friend of the Downtrodden) OIOR, RNP, week of July 29, 1882, 7–8; week of August 19, 1882, 5–6; week of July 9, 1887, 16; in the *Maharashtra Mitra* (Friend of Maharashtra), RNP, week of April 18, 1886, 16; in the *Subodh Patrika* (Paper of Plain Words/Good Advice) RNP, week of August 12, 1882, 5–6; and in the *Bombay Chronicle*, RNP, week of July 22, 1882, 8.

[52] See the Gujarati *Jame Jamshad*, RNP, August 5, 1884, week of August 9, 1884, 5; the Anglo-Marathi *Subodh Patrika*, RNP, week of August 12, 1882, 5–6; and the Anglo-Gujarati *Bombay Chronicle*, RNP, July 16, 1882, week of 22nd July 1882. For nineteenth-century British feminists' articulation of this issue, see Judith Walkowitz, *Prostitution and Victorian Society: Women, Class and the State* (Cambridge: Cambridge University Press, 1980), as well as Shanley, *Feminism, Marriage and the Law*.

[53] *Din Bandhu*, RNP, July 23, 1882, week of July 29, 1882, 7–8; ibid., week of August 19, 1882, 5–6.

debates, the centrality of family arrangements to the societal order and to the state was rendered explicit and contentious.[54]

After the late 1880s, there was a lapse in reported cases on this issue in the High Court, as well as in vernacular newspaper critiques for some twenty-five years. When the issue reemerged in the second decade of the twentieth century, it was in the context of a civil suit from Ahmedabad concerning an asserted caste custom allowing dissolution of marriage on payment of a fee.[55] The court's ruling in this case again explicitly opposed the interests of morality and the state to those of caste authority, and again revolved around the question of the legitimacy of a contractual model of marriage. The case, which did not involve assertions of adultery or bigamy, but merely the possibility of dissolving a marriage, involved a husband and his minor wife of the Pakhali caste, the latter represented by her father. They had been married some thirteen years previously, but presumably subsequent to their marriage, the caste had split into two factions, with the parties in opposing factions, and the bride had never gone to live with her husband.[56]

When her husband sued for restitution of conjugal rights, her father filed a countersuit for dissolution of the marriage, contending that

> marriage in parties' caste was a simple contract subject to a condition sanctioned by custom; that it may be put an end to at the wish of the wife subject to a payment of money; that according to the resolution of the caste a husband was bound to divorce a wife on offer of Rs. 94 to caste Patel by the wife's side; that an amount of Rs. 28 out of this was to be paid to the husband; that the fixed amount of Rs. 94 was offered to the leaders of the faction to which defendant belonged; that the amount was not accepted.[57]

In the original suit, the subordinate judge found "that the custom in the caste of giving divorces was proved and that it could be acted upon according to law."[58] He therefore ruled in favor of the wife in her suit for

---

[54] For a similar argument regarding the effects of the age of consent debates in colonial Bengal, see Sarkar, "Pre-History of Rights."

[55] This is the last reported case found in the Bombay Indian Law Reports through the 1930s asserting a special caste practice in order to legitimate a dissolution of a marriage.

[56] This use of a suit for restitution of conjugal rights conforms to Uma Chakravarti's analysis that such suits may have formed a crucial part of nineteenth-century strategies by competing caste fractions (modernizing and wealthy versus "traditional" and poor) to shape power and authority within the changing caste. See her discussion of the Rakhmabai case in these terms in Chakravarti, *Rewriting History*, 134–138, 151–164. See also Anupama Rao, "Introduction," in *Gender and Caste*, edited by Anupama Rao, 1–47 (New Delhi: Kali for Women, 2003) and *The Caste Question*.

[57] *Keshav Hargovan v. Bai Gandi* (1915) ILR 39 Bom 538 at p. 539.

[58] Ibid., 540.

dissolution of the marriage, a decision that was confirmed on appeal to the District Court. On the husband's further appeal to the High Court, however, the justices questioned the legal basis for such a custom. In the opinion written by Chief Justice Sir Basil Scott, he reflected that

> the custom pleaded is … a custom by which the marriage tie can be dissolved by either husband or wife against the wish of the divorced party, and for no reason but out of mere caprice, the sole condition attached being the payment of a sum of money fixed by the caste. That sum admittedly is liable to alteration from time to time at the will of the caste: Rs. 55 today, it may be Rs. 5 tomorrow. We need only say that in our opinion it is impossible for the Court to recognise any custom as this; it is opposed to public policy as it goes far to substitute promiscuity of intercourse for the marriage relation, and is, we think, equally repugnant to Hindu Law, which regards the marriage tie as so sacred that the possibility of divorce on the best of grounds is permitted only as a reluctant concession. The requirement of the payment of a sum of money, on which the learned District Judge relies, seems to us to be immaterial, and we can see no substantial distinction between the recognition of this custom and the declaration that the tie of marriage does not exist among Hindus of the Pakhali caste.[59]

Chief Justice Scott's view of the problem with such a caste custom thus revolved precisely around the way that it posited marriage as dissolvable at will by either party "out of mere caprice" upon payment of a fee.[60] The fee suggested, as the defense in fact explicitly claimed, that marriage could be configured as a simple contractual agreement, made and broken at will. In refusing to sustain such a view of marriage, the High Court countered with the ethical and jurisdictional claims of the state.

The Problem of the Bride as Property

This state concern with defining marriage as an agreement that transcended contract and material exchange emerged forcefully in a series of cases spanning the last decades of the nineteenth century, involving what was called in English law "marriage brokerage" or "marriage brocage": receiving payment in exchange for arranging a marriage between two parties. Because it suggested that financial interests superseded an interest in the well-being of the spouses, marriage brokerage was treated as

---

[59] Ibid., 543. Chief Justice Scott also cited *Reg. v. Sambhu Raghu* (1876) ILR 1 Bom 347, as well as *Reg. v. Karsan Goja* and *Reg. v. Bai Rupa* (1864) 2 Bom HCR 124 in his opinion.
[60] This determination resonates strongly with the late-nineteenth-century determination of the Nair custom of *sambandham* as "not marriage." See Arunima, *There Comes Papa*; Kodoth, "Courting Legitimacy."

an immoral and invalid contractual arrangement, and one that the courts would not enforce. Yet, it seemed virtually indistinguishable from the regular practice of arranged marriage in India, which typically involved transactions of money and goods to the benefit of at least one set of parents, and often involved reliance on intermediaries.[61] Beginning in the 1880s, the British critique of marriage brokerage became linked to a Brahminical textual and customary denigration of bride-price or bride-wealth marriage. This form of marriage was usually practiced in subaltern communities, and was characterized by the gift of goods and money from the groom's family to the family of the bride. Such marriages, known in the Brahminical textual tradition as "demonic," or Asura, marriages[62] (a term that was adopted by the courts), increasingly came to be considered by the colonial courts as "nothing more than the purchase of a wife from her father by the husband."[63] In contrast, in the textually "approved" dowry form of marriage, Brahma marriage, both goods and money, as well as the bride herself, were transferred to the groom's family in an elite model of the extraordinary gift.[64] Although such dowry marriages were privileged within Hindu textual traditions and contemporary practice as the preferred, elite form of marriage, in the colonial context, the distinction between dowry as "gift" of a bride and bride-price or bride-wealth as "sale" of a bride took on new valences. Despite the shared emphasis on the bride as an object of value in both marriage forms, the distinction between the two forms was treated as a distinction between crass material interest and noble affect, as though gifts were removed from the logic of commodity exchange.[65]

---

[61] For the changing role of marriage brokers in the nineteenth century (with a focus on Bengal) see Majumdar, *Marriage and Modernity*.

[62] This term itself referenced the mythical Brahminical conquest of lower orders, which became prominent in Shudra self-narratives of the origins of their degraded status.

[63] *Pitamber Ratansi v. Jagjivan Hansraj* (1884) ILR 13 Bom 131; *Dholidas Ishvar v. Fulchand Chhagan* (1897) ILR 22 Bom 661 at p. 664.

[64] For now-classical historic anthropological discussions of dowry see M. N. Srinivas, *Some Reflections on Dowry*, J. P. Naik Memorial Lecture, 1983 (Delhi: Oxford University Press, 1984); Jack Goody and S. J. Tambiah, *Bridewealth and Dowry*, Cambridge Papers in Social Anthropology, no. 7 (Cambridge: Cambridge University Press, 1973). More recently see Agarwal, *Field of One's Own*; Lucy Carroll, "Daughter's Right of Inheritance in India: A Perspective on the Problem of Dowry," *Modern Asian Studies* 25, 4 (1991): 791–809; Ranjana Sheel, *The Political Economy of Dowry: Institutionalization and Expansion in North India* (Delhi: Manohar Press, 1999); Srimati Basu, ed., *Dowry and Inheritance* (New Delhi: Kali for Women, 2005); Majumdar, *Marriage and Modernity*; Veena Talwar Oldenburg, *Dowry Murder: The Imperial Origins of a Cultural Crime* (New York: Oxford University Press, 2002).

[65] See the now widely accepted critiques of the early anthropological theory of the gift imagined as an economy prior and oppositional to economies based on capitalist exchange,

The slippage between Asura marriage and sale of a child became evident in a series of cases starting in the 1880s. A decision by High Court Justice Sir John Scott in 1884 laid out the terms of debate. The case involved an agreement made by Jagjivan Hansraj, the eldest of three brothers whose mother had been excommunicated from the Lovana caste for marrying a man of a different caste. In 1864, Jagjivan entered into an agreement with one of the leaders of the Lovana caste, Pitamber Ratansi, to arrange for the three brothers to be readmitted into the caste and married to girls of their caste. Jagjivan agreed to pay Rs. 5,000 to Pitamber, to be turned into brass vessels and utensils for use by the caste, after the third brother's marriage. The third brother was finally married in 1880, and when the debt had not been fully repaid some two years later, Pitamber filed the suit for payment of the outstanding debt, some Rs. 3,149. In evaluating this suit, one of the central issues of concern to Justice Scott was whether the agreement constituted a form of marriage brokerage, and whether such an agreement could be enforced by law.[66] Scott proceeded by analogy with English law, reflecting that, "In England such a contract would not be enforced in law.... It would be held to be contrary to public policy and public interest as having a tendency to cause matrimony to be contracted as a mere matter of bargain and sale."[67] Pitamber's lawyers, Kirkpatrick and Dhairyawan, countered such analogy with a pointed critique of the false neutrality of colonial "public policy," arguing that "the basis of marriage and all the usages connected with it in India are wholly different to those in England. The 'public policy' to which the English cases refer, is the public policy which aims at maintaining the English social system.... [Yet] English public policy is not necessarily public policy everywhere. The English doctrine as to marriage brocage would be altogether out of place in India."[68] Ultimately, however, Justice Scott dismissed their analysis. Moving back and forth between Asura marriage, defined explicitly as marriage by purchase, and marriage brokerage, he

---

most prominently that developed in Marcel Mauss, *The Gift: Forms and Functions of Exchange in Archaic Societies*, translated by Ian Cunnison (Glencoe, IL: Free Press, 1954). For example, Thomas, *Entangled Objects*.

[66] *Pitamber Ratansi v. Jagjivan Hansraj* (1884) Ind. Dec. NS 7 Bom 88 (corresponding to ILR 13 Bom 131) appended to 13 Bom 126, Pauper Petition, No. 20 of 1,888. One of the interesting aspects of this case is that it called on the colonial state to adjudicate caste regulations, shuttling between contract theory on the one hand, and the regulation of caste associations on the other. The jurisdiction of the court over this type of case does not seem to have been questioned, however.

[67] Ibid., 91.

[68] Ibid., 90.

argued staunchly against what he viewed as a further commodification of Indian marriage:

> The asura form of marriage, which is legal among the lower castes, is, no doubt, nothing more than the purchase of a wife from her father by the husband. As long as the custom of infant marriages is maintained, mutual affection and choice cannot be the basis of marriage. But I do not think it follows that the English rule can have no *raison d'etre* in India. Although custom and local law in this country may be defective in the matter of marriage, that is no reason why an additional evil should be engrafted upon them. I had no proof given me that "marriage brocage" is an established usage in India.... I think it is immoral and against public policy, even in the present state of matrimonial relations in India.[69]

Justice Scott thus articulated an overarching moral claim of the state to refuse to enforce this or any agreement that smacked of marriage by sale. Nevertheless, a striking feature of this judgment is the vision of marriage it promoted as properly a matter of "mutual affection and choice," of agency, volition, and consent of the marrying parties; in other words, of marriage as a kind of contract between husband and wife. Thus a vision of the ethicality of contractual relations – based in mutuality and consent – merged with an aspiration of transcending within marriage the crass, interested nature of contractual relations.[70]

In 1909, an important High Court decision in a case from Pune decided by Justices Chandavarkar and Heaton articulated principles for judicial determinations of the marriage form, and placed Asura marriages on a new footing:[71]

> Under Hindu Law, where the paternal or maternal relation of a girl, who is given in marriage, receive money consideration for it, the substance of the transaction makes it not a gift but a sale of the girl. The money received is what is called "bride-price." That is the essential element of the *Asura* form. The fact that the rites prescribed for *Brahma* form are gone through cannot take it out of that category, if there was a pecuniary benefit to the giver of the girl. The taint of the *Asura* form lies in the gratuity paid to the giver of the bride for his benefit, not in anything paid to her.

> Unless rebutted by evidence, the prima facie presumption no doubt is that every marriage under the Hindu Law is according to the *Brahma* form.[72]

---

[69] Ibid., 91–92.

[70] For another case in which the conceptualization of bride-price as an immoral contract became even more explicit, see *Dulari v. Vallabdas Pragji* (1888) Ind. Dec. NS 7 Bom 84 (corresponding to ILR 13 Bom 126); also *Mulji Thakersey v. Gomti and Kastur* (1887) ILR 11 Bom 412; *Rambhat v. Timmayya* (1892) ILR 16 Bom 673.

[71] *Chunilal Prashankar v. Surajram Haribhai; Bhogilal Valabhram v. Surajram Haribhai* (1909) ILR 33 Bom 433.

[72] Ibid. at p. 437.

This decision had two striking effects. First, it established that the basis of Asura marriage was the transaction of bride-price, and that such exchange rendered a marriage Asura, even if the marriage ceremonies that were performed were for a Brahma marriage. In so doing, the decision focused the legal critique of Asura marriage exclusively on the mode of exchange that it entailed.[73] Second, it simultaneously established the legal presumption that all marriages were Brahma marriages, thereby placing the burden of proof on those claiming that an Asura marriage had occurred.[74] In some sense, this presumption that all marriages were "approved" can be read as a sort of benefit of the doubt: All marriages were to be treated as conforming to the moral standards of the Brahminical elite. Given Chandavarkar's renowned reformist leanings, it is likely he intended this decision to recast practices that marked elite and subordinate social status so that elite practice was now promoted as normative, rather than exclusive. Nonetheless, the language of "taint" in the justices' opinion suggests that Asura marriages were now not just "unapproved," but morally and legally dubious. To what extent could a practice be morally unapproved and still legally acceptable?[75] In contrast to the distinction between moral and legal claims operationalized in the jurisprudence on inheritance and maintenance discussed in Chapter 3, which enabled the court to establish the limits of rights, here the question of morality intrinsically drew state scrutiny and intervention.

A High Court decision a few years later suggests the degree of legal marginalization of Asura marriages that this entailed: Asura marriage became literally unintelligible as such.[76] In this case, a *Koli* woman had divorced her husband and remarried, after her future husband paid a sum of money to her parents to secure her divorce. After her death, a dispute

---

[73] Given the longstanding textual tradition concerned with modes of marital exchange, the emphasis on exchange here may be understood as tracking a shift from a noncapitalist form and meaning of commodity exchange to a capitalist one. See Dipesh Chakrabarty, "Two Histories of Capital," in *Provincializing Europe: Postcolonial Thought and Historical Difference* (Princeton, NJ: Princeton University Press, 2000), pp. 47–71.

[74] See also the discussion of this case in Sheel, *Political Economy of Dowry*, 73–74.

[75] Notably, in the context of Muslim law, the court did not have a problem enforcing triple *talaq* divorces (*at-talaqu'l-ba'in; talalaqu'l-bid'a*), even though such divorces were considered in Hanafi law in similar terms, as valid but disapproved. See Faiz B. Tyabji, *Principles of Muhammadan Law*, 4th ed. (Calcutta: Butterworth & Co., 1919), pp. 213–219; Asaf A. A. Fyzee, *Outlines of Muhammadan Law*, 2nd ed. (London: Oxford University Press, 1955), pp. 126–131.

[76] *Hira v. Hansji Pema* (1912) 37 Bom 299. See also *Jagannath Raghunath v. Narayan Shethe* (1910) ILR 34 Bom 553, also decided by Justices Chandavarkar and Heaton, in which they held that "even among Sudras, the law assumes marriage to have been in one of the approved forms."

arose between her half-sister and her husband concerning who was the rightful heir to the property she had inherited from her father before her death. This depended on the form of her marriage: If the marriage were Asura, her heirs would be her closest relatives in her father's family; if not, her husband would be her heir. When the case came before the High Court, Justice Batchelor reconfirmed that the essence of Asura marriage was "that a bride-price should be paid to the father or other relative who gives away the bride in consideration for the marriage."[77] Yet he added, "Admittedly, re-marriage between parties of the Koli caste is valid, and there is nothing before us to suggest that the people of that caste regard it with any social censure or disapproval."[78] He thus concluded that "a marriage between a man and a divorced woman belonging to the Koli caste is not to be regarded as being an unapproved form of marriage under Hindu Law."[79] Batchelor's logic appears to have been that since the marriage was not disapproved within the community, it was therefore not Asura. This decision reaffirmed the validity of the custom of divorce and remarriage among Kolis, but it did so by denying that they practiced Asura marriage. The legal recognition of caste custom in this case thus rested upon a misrecognition of bride-price marriage.

In this jurisprudence on bride-price marriage, as in that concerning customs of divorce and remarriage for women, the focus on the appropriately sacramental character of marriage took a particular form – that is, on marriage as exceeding relations of interest and exchange. The court rejected customs that seemed too much like contracts – the sale of a daughter, or the dissolution of marriage upon payment of a fee. At the same time, a view of the morality of marriage as grounded in contract also emerged in key ways – as in the deprecation of marriage not based in mutual affection and consent. This widespread framing of marriage in terms of the morality of its sacramental and/or contractual character thus reflected the profound discursive saturation of liberal contract ideology. It also in effect undermined the legitimation of marriage practices based on their customary character. If marriage customs were to be admitted by the courts, it would not be because of their practice from time immemorial, but because of their proper relationship to (and distinction from) contract. From the perspective of the colonial state, the commodification of marriage – its treatment as a matter of barter and sale – posed a

---

[77] *Hira v. Hansji Pema* (1912) 37 Bom. 299.
[78] Ibid., 302.
[79] Ibid., 295.

problem of women's humanity, where women's exchange value as commodities undermined or negated their humanity. This humanity would now be created as a legal status by the state, but in ways that nevertheless highlighted women's ongoing vulnerabilities as non-abstract subjects of rights and as bodies especially prone to commoditization.

In retrospect, one issue is notable for its absence in this jurisprudence: the expansion of dowry. In a perhaps unusual confluence of legal and social norms, the jurisprudence that sought to replace bride-price with dowry in fact operated alongside a general social trend to the same effect. Historians have concluded, based on colonial census evidence as well as caste publications, that by the early twentieth century, a large majority of communities that had previously practiced bride-price marriage were now practicing dowry marriage. This was treated at the time as a measure of social progress, implying a shift away from the commodification and "sale" of girls, as well as an increase in claims to higher social status by lower caste communities. In western India, while the commodification and expansion of dowry demands formed a subject of concern and critique within contemporary caste associations and occasionally in the wider press, as well as in early feminist writings, it was bride-price rather than dowry that was identified as the major social ill.[80] Thus, unlike in Bengal and in northern India, where extended critiques of the new form of dowry as a commodification of marriage emerged as early as the 1870s, in western India as late as 1891, M. G. Ranade, while acknowledging dowry as "an evil," nonetheless viewed it as a lesser problem than bride-price, and one to be addressed gradually, through internal reform in due course.[81] Likewise, although there are occasional references to dowry in colonial administrative and judicial records, there was virtually no official comment thereon.[82]

Scholars have emphasized this shift from bride-price to dowry as a measure of the modern commodification of marriage – reflecting a context in which wealth had become indexical of status rather than the reverse, and a measure not of the noncommodification of daughters, but of their

---

[80] For the contemporary feminist critique of dowry, or *hunda*, see Anagol, *Emergence of Feminism*, 91–95. For critiques in the broader press, see, for example *Hitechhu* (Anglo-Gujarati, Ahmedabad) RNP, February 16, 1882, 6–7. Jotirao Phule also addressed the issue in "The Cultivator's Whipcord."

[81] M. G. Ranade, "Fifth Social Conference – Nagpur: The Practice of Exacting Money for Gift of Girls in Marriage," in *Miscellaneous Writings of the Late Honourable Mr. Justice M. G. Ranade*, published by Mrs. Ramabai Ranade, with an Introduction by D. E. Wacha (Bombay: Manoranjan Press, 1915), pp. 105–108.

[82] Such critiques were folded into critiques of "marriage expenses," however, which formed a major object of colonial and reformist attention, as discussed in Chapter 2.

devaluation, as several critics argued at the time.[83] Indeed, both dowry and bride-price became enmeshed in the problematics of a commoditized valuation of girls. This concern with commoditization as a form of dehumanization or human devaluation posed the dual problem of the susceptibility of the human body to economic valuation and exchange, and of the incommensurability of women and girls as abstract subjects. The colonial jurisprudence on marriage custom both raised and sought to resolve this problem of the bride's humanity.

PART II: PRODUCING HUMAN VALUE: LIBERAL HINDU REFORMIST DISCOURSES

Perhaps ironically, both the operation of the colonial courts and British and Indian debates on Hindu marriage customs worked to delegitimize the authority of custom as such. Yet the debates on Hindu marriage customs, and particularly the intellectual labor of reformers, nonetheless reinvested custom with new significance, working to transform it into a newly imagined social foundation for law, at once constituting a "Hindu society" and the Hindu law proper thereto. Although these reformers undermined the legitimacy of custom, they nonetheless largely confirmed the critical relationship between law and societal norms, carving out a crucial role for themselves in transforming the deadweight of custom into meaningful ethical practice that would ultimately form the basis for a new juridical regime and its new object – Hindu society.

In focusing on the plight of Hindu women and girls, Hindu male elite reformist campaigns involved a labor of self-transformation, calling forth a new attentiveness to and compassion for female suffering.[84] Their agitation particularly against practices of temple dedication (often described at the time as a system of religious prostitution), child marriage, and enforced widowhood involved efforts to evacuate bodies and ritual practices of forms of stigma and defilement, shifting the emotional signification of bodies to a new problematic of the suffering of the weak, and reframing the terms of debate as a matter of legal rights and protections.

---

[83] Majumdar, *Marriage and Modernity*, 57–69; Tambiah, *Dowry and Brideprice*; Oldenburg, *Dowry Murder*; Sheel, *Political Economy of Dowry*.

[84] In an important analysis, Dipesh Chakrabarty has argued that the campaign to ameliorate the condition of high-caste Hindu widows in Bengal involved a project of nationalist elite self-fashioning, but he does not connect these efforts to a broader attempt to refashion the relationship between society and the state. Chakrabarty, "Domestic Cruelty and the Birth of the Subject" in *Provincializing Europe*, 117–148.

In each of these cases, the reformist campaign to end the practice confronted a custom with religious validation (if not mandate) that was also integral to broader social hierarchies. These campaigns thus involved a reimagining of the social order in which reformers came to view deeply valorized practices even of the dominant community as grounded in the coercion and bodily pain of women and girls.[85] The vulnerabilities of women and girls thus produced an opening both for legal intervention and for a reformist fashioning of a new morality and intimate life.

In this context, the reformist projects were not directed at female emancipation per se, but rather at a broader process of establishing women's humanity as a project of societal remoralization. This societal remoralization would be achieved in part by extending marriage (in its new form) to women such as high-caste widows and low-caste dedicated women whom they simultaneously viewed as objects of pity and as a societal danger. The reformed society they sought would thus be more rather than less structured by marriage. It also stopped far short of undermining caste. Yet despite the limited terms of their more specific aims, the reformist critiques of the rule of custom returned to the question of women's humanization not as a problem of their susceptibility to commoditization but as a problem of the oversignification of female bodies as sites of inauspiciousness and ritual defilement, and their undersignification as sites of human suffering.

The Evils of Temple Dedication

Efforts to eradicate temple dedication emerged at the turn of the twentieth century from a variety of quarters – from Christian missionaries, elite Indian social reformers, and reformers within communities that traditionally practiced dedication. In western India, these campaigns targeted the practice of dedicating girls to the god Khandoba at Jejuri; such dedicated women and girls were known as *muralis*.[86] This practice existed

---

[85] Sarkar, "Rhetoric against Age of Consent," 1869–1878, and "A Pre-History of Rights"; also Sreenivas, *Wives, Widows and Concubines.*

[86] The term *devadasi*, literally "servant" or "slave" of the god, was eventually applied generally to all temple-dedicated women, although several different types of dedicated women existed, especially in south India. The practice of dedicating girls as *muralis* was most prevalent in the Kannada-speaking districts of the Southern Maratha Country, especially Sholapur and Dharwad. There were significant differences between the more elite women who served in the major south Indian temples, historically with strong connection to regional kings and the rituals of kingship, and who typically were trained in specialized dance traditions and often were explicitly supported by temple endowments (*inam*), and the women who became *muralis*, who were typically of lower-caste status, often received little or no specialized training, and often had no particular connection to temples.

mostly among members of the Mang, Mahar, and *kunbi* communities, as
well as various itinerant communities. Mangs and Mahars formed two
of the major Untouchable castes in the region, while *kunbis* formed a
broad class of agriculturalists, who in this era often associated themselves with Maratha identity.[87] Some families regularly dedicated at least
one member; others made an exceptional vow to dedicate a child, typically if the child survived a life-threatening illness. While boys as well as
girls were dedicated, dedicated males, or *vaghyas*, who may have largely
supported themselves through religious mendicancy, did not become an
object of obloquy. The ceremony of dedication for girls, however, which
involved their ritual marriage to the god, permanently excluded *muralis*
from human marriage, and customarily required them to provide sexual
services to men as part of their service to the god. Although dedicated
women often supported themselves through a variety of forms of sexual
patronage, as well as through land grants associated with temples (*inam*),
and through other forms of inheritance, the sexual availability and vulnerability of *muralis* became major objects of social critique at this time.

The reformers had different visions and aims, they generally
shared the view that the dedication of girls was both an evil done to the
girls themselves, consigning them in childhood to a lifetime of prostitution,
and one productive of broader social ills – of sexual and social hygiene,
and the degradation of lower castes. The latter issue foregrounded the
ways in which access to the sexuality of lower-caste women, and especially high-caste male access thereto, was critical to the very designation
of lower castes as such.[88] Lower-caste activists as well as high-caste social
reformers thus viewed the eradication of temple dedication as integral to
enhancing the status and respectability of these castes.

The elite reform and missionary campaigns against temple dedication
emerged in a broader context of mobilization that had been occurring for
several decades against various forms of sexual patronage and what were
now viewed as "incomplete" marriage forms.[89] This context had shaped

---

[87] Deshpande, "Caste as Maratha"; O'Hanlon, *Caste, Conflict and Ideology*; Rao, *The Caste Question*.

[88] Kalpana Kannabiran and Vasanth Kannabiran, "Caste and Gender: Understanding Dynamics of Power and Violence," in *De-Eroticizing Assault: Essays on Modesty, Honour and Power* (Calcutta: Stree, 2002), pp. 55–67; Kodoth, "Courting Legitimacy"; Rao, *The Caste Question*.

[89] Arunima, *There Comes Papa*; Kodoth, "Courting Legitimacy." For Calcutta see Sumanta Banerjee, *The Parlour and the Streets: Elite and Popular Culture in Nineteenth-Century Calcutta* (Calcutta: Seagull Books, 1989), and *Under the Raj: Prostitution in Colonial Bengal* (New York: Monthly Press Books, 1998); for northern India, see Charu Gupta,

contemporary judicial engagements with the question of custom within these various communities, such as Justice West's 1880 ruling in the case of *Mathura Naikin v. Esu Naikin*, discussed in the first subsection of this chapter. Morally disapprobatory references to the practice of dedication are scattered through the colonial archives from the mid-nineteenth century, and as early as 1869 the High Court ruled that the dedication of a girl by performance of the Shej ceremony was a violation of Section 372 of the Indian Penal Code, prohibiting the disposal of minors with the intent or likelihood of prostitution.[90] Yet despite these occasional references, temple dedication came under sustained scrutiny only beginning in the late 1890s.[91] In the last years of the century, it was publicized in scandal-mongering missionary writings, and Christian missionaries along with elite Indian reformers launched a new association, the Society for the Protection of Children, in part to address this social evil.[92] These reformers framed their efforts largely through the twin lenses of social

Sexuality, Obscenity and Community: Women, Muslims and the Hindu Public in Colonial India (New York: Palgrave, 2002); Veena Talwar Oldenburg, "Lifestyle as Resistance: The Case of the Courtesans of Lucknow," in *Contesting Power*, edited by Douglas Haynes and Gyan Prakash (Berkeley: University of California Press, 1991), pp. 23–61. Bombay publicists played an active role in these efforts, publishing articles from the late 1870s through the mid-1880s calling for the removal of prostitutes from respectable areas and giving their support to police actions that did so: *Kaside Mumbai* (Gujarati), RNP, May 4, 1881, 7; *Subodh Patrika* (Anglo-Marathi, Bombay) RNP, May 18, 1884, 16; *Poona Vaibhav* (Marathi) RNP, June 7, 1885, 15; *Induprakash* (Anglo-Marathi, Bombay) RNP, June 7, 1886, 8; *Bombay Samachar* (Gujarati) RNP, March 31, 1887, 11–12. Some reformist papers did critique those who sought to segregate the daughters of prostitutes from respectable girls in government schools, and sought more stringent enforcement of the provisions of the IPC regarding trafficking: *Malwan Samachar* (Marathi, Vingorla) RNP, Sept. 23, 1878, 7–8. In sum, these efforts sought at once to segregate the social canker represented by the prostitute and to save vulnerable girl children from violation, degeneracy, and a lifetime of prostitution by recuperating them for marriage.

[90] *Reg. v. Jaili Bhavin,* (1869) 6 Bom HCR 60; *Re: Padmavati* (1870) 5 Bom HCR 415.

[91] The *Kaira Vartaman* newspaper of Oct. 5, 1881, also called for an end to the practice of dedicating both boys and girls, as producing a population of beggars and prostitutes. This article was unusual both in its equal concern for the dedication of boys, and in that, as the *Vartaman* was a Gujarati paper from Kheda, it was rather at a remove from the practice, since most dedications involved Marathi- and Kannada-speaking families in the southern districts of the presidency. RNP, Oct. 5, 1881, 12.

[92] *Missionary Review of the World,* edited by Rev. Arthur T. Pierson, Vol. XII New Series (XXII Old Series), Jan.–Dec. 1899 (New York: Funk & Wagnalls Co., 1899), p. 75. One of the earliest extended critiques specifically directed at Muralis is Mrs. Marcus Fuller, *Wrongs of Indian Womanhood* (Edinburgh: Oliphant & Ferrier, 1900), pp. 100–111. This book also references a meeting by the Christian Women Workers' Union in Bombay the previous year to launch a campaign to rescue minor girls at risk of dedication. N. G. Chandavarkar seems to have been connected to the Society for the Protection of Children from at least the early years of the twentieth century.

hygiene and the protection of girl children. As such, they approached the question of caste and community custom not as primarily a matter of the denigration of lower castes, which formed the core of internal community critiques, but as an infraction of voluntarism and consent, with the specter of a girl's lifelong sexual violation and exploitation as a result of her parents' actions or as a result of her birth to a *murali*. The *murali's* ineffaceable bodily status and the occupational vulnerabilities that this entailed thus formed the basis for a liberal critique of the compulsions of caste, in which the consignment of a girl child to a future of sexual exploitation demonstrated the barbarity and perversity of contemporary social relations that denied the possibility of individual choice.

Former newspaper publicist, eminent social reformer, pleader, and from 1901 High Court justice, N. G. Chandavarkar took a prominent role in this association and wrote on its behalf. His close colleague, social reformer and Orientalist scholar, R. G. Bhandarkar, likewise played a significant role in the movement. By October 1905, Bhandarkar had submitted a petition to the government calling for special legislation on the subject.[93] In response, the Bombay government issued a call for opinions on the need for such special legislation. It also gathered statistics and solicited opinions regarding dedication in the various districts of the Deccan and Southern Maratha Country. District officials and other local elites overwhelmingly condemned the practice, but remained uneven in their support of government measures to suppress the custom, which at any rate would not touch prostitution as a whole. Many argued (as the government itself ultimately concluded) that the existing provisions were satisfactory, but required more stringent enforcement.[94] This official initiative in turn generated considerable debate in both the English and the Marathi press, which largely supported government suppression of the practice, but raised a number of doubts, particularly concerning the use of police action to prevent dedication, the removal of children from their parents' custody, and the ultimate effectiveness of any such measures. Many argued that education of the "poor and ignorant classes" was the only means to put an end to the practice. And both newspapers and Indian district officials expressed sympathy for parents who dedicated their daughters out of ignorance.[95] Some argued that the institution was not itself immoral, but

[93] The Memorial, dated October 26, 1905, was signed by numerous leading figures, particularly from the Marathi region of the presidency. MSA, JD 1906, 140/1113, pp. 281–285.

[94] MSA, JD 1907, 143/2078, pp. 368–378.

[95] See especially opinion of G. K. Gokhale, MSA, JD 1909, 155/1559, pp. 183–184.

that women could not support themselves on their earnings from temples and could not control their passions, hence they turned to prostitution.[96] Others held no stock in "revolutionizing human nature by legislation."[97] Finally, a letter by the editor of the journal *Vrittasar* to the assistant collector in Wai Taluka, Satara District, noted the strangeness of the proposal, and its futile violation of the laws of political economy:

A curious feature of the proposal that strikes me is that the principal and real offender is let off quite with immunity. Mothers and temple authorities are to be made the accessories of the offence and the customer in whose interest the commodity is created is not intended to be made punishable. It is these persons who take a principal share in leading these girls into a bad life. This is all the world over and no country is free from this pestilence in one form or another. As long as there is a demand in the market producers of articles will not be slow in satisfying it. This is the rule of political economy.[98]

This attentiveness to the critical issue of consumption was unusual in this context, although perhaps not in the broader context of Victorian feminist critiques of prostitution. It also highlighted the contemporary tension between theorizing the commoditization and exploitation of sexual labor and theorizing the production of the sexualized body itself as commodity.

Ultimately, the government concluded that special legislation was unnecessary, but in 1909, it promulgated a special statement to publicize that such cases would be prosecuted under Section 372 of the Indian Penal Code.[99] Ironically, this treatment of dedication, which de-exoticized the practice by making it essentially a form of sexual trafficking, largely ignored the questions of custom or religion that lay at the heart of both elite and subaltern reformist campaigns: The problem of belief in or attachment to the practice remained outside the purview of the law. The Society for the Protection of Children monitored prosecutions under the existing section and repeatedly sought more stringent sentences and more robust legislation to facilitate these efforts, although with little success until the early 1930s, when the Bombay Legislature passed the Bombay Devadasi Protection Act (Bombay Act X of 1934).[100]

---

[96] Opinion of Deputy Collector, Ahmednagar, in MSA, JD 1907, 143/2078, p. 365.

[97] Opinion of B. R. Bomanji, Collector, Bijapur, in ibid., 377–378.

[98] Ibid., 370–371.

[99] Resolution No. 3866 of July 8, 1909, MSA JD 1909 155/1559, pp. 187–188.

[100] MSA, JD 1910 216/687; MSA, JD 1913, 715, Parts I and II. For the broader anti-*devadasi* movement, see S. Anandhi "Women's Question in the Dravidian Movement," *Social Scientist* 19, 5–6 (May–June 1991): 12–41, and "Representing Devadasis: *Dasigal Mosavalai* as a Radical Text," *Economic and Political Weekly* 26, 11–12 Annual Number

These efforts intersected with the treatment of dedication in contemporary jurisprudence. The issue of inheritance practices connected to dedication had come before the colonial administration as early as the mid-nineteenth century, as part of the state regulation of hereditary offices, or *vatan*, discussed in Chapters 1 and 2. Colonial authorities had found that in districts where dedication was common, low-caste communities with connections to the hereditary offices of Mahar and Talwar allowed dedicated daughters to inherit the *vatan* and pass it on to their sons, thereby preserving the *vatan* in the family in the case of failure of lineal male heirs. In response to official concerns that this state recognition was encouraging immoral practices, the government refused to recognize such inheritance to *vatans* in 1858; this was modified in 1874 for the Southern Maratha districts by allowing the illegitimate sons of dedicated women to retain the *vatan*, while preserving the earlier prohibition of such holding by dedicated women themselves.[101] This regulation was limited to hereditary offices, however, and did not affect other property forms. The 1907 case of *Tara v. Krishna*, an appeal to the Bombay High Court from Sholapur District, brought legal scrutiny to dedicated women's customary property claims in the context of general private property. Justice Chandavarkar ruled on the case.

The case involved an inheritance dispute among sisters, pitting two sisters who were regularly married (and the husband of one of them) against a third sister, Tara, who had been dedicated to the god Khandoba by her father, Hari Shinde, who himself had been a *vaghya*.[102] The question at issue in the suit was whether Tara was entitled to inherit her father's property in preference to her two married sisters, in accordance with community custom that drew notionally on the Shastric injunction

---

(March 1991): 739–746; Amrit Srinivasan, "Reform and Revival: The Devadasi and Her Dance," *Economic and Political Weekly* 20, 44 (Nov. 2, 1985): 1869–1876; Janaki Nair, "The Devadasi, Dharma and the State," *Economic and Political Weekly* 29, 50 (Dec. 10, 1994): 3157–3167; Kalpana Kannabiran, "Judiciary, Social Reform and Debate on 'Religious Prostitution' in India," *Economic and Political Weekly* 30, 43 (Oct. 28, 1995): WS59–WS-69; also Geraldine Forbes, *Women in Modern India* (Cambridge: Cambridge University Press, 1996), pp. 103–120, 185–186.

[101] This was sanctioned particularly for Dharwad, where the practice of dedication was most extensive, but it was apparently adopted in other districts as well. MSA, JD 1909 155/1559, pp. 37–48.

[102] *Tara v. Krishna* (1907) ILR 31 Bom 495. Notably, the sister whose husband claimed the land denied her husband's claim, but asserted instead that all three sisters were entitled to share equally in the property. The other sister argued that because Tara was "by profession a prostitute" she was not the heir to her father, and that the two married sisters were exclusively entitled to the property.

that an unmarried daughter inherits from her father in preference to a married one. In the original case, the subordinate judge of Pandharpur, C. R. Karkare, ruled in favor of Tara, arguing:

> The defendants have cited no authorities for holding that a *Murali* is disqualified from inheriting the property of her parents. *Muralis* and *Vaghyas* do not relinquish their worldly affairs. They own property. In fact they lead their lives just like other people. I, therefore, hold that a *Murali* can inherit, just like other women.... Plaintiff admits that she follows the profession of a prostitute. She has admittedly got children from prostitution. But there is no doubt at all that under the Hindu Law prevailing in the Bombay Presidency, a daughter is not excluded from inheritance by her unchastity or incontinence.[103]

Tara's sister Krishna appealed the case to the Sholapur District Court. The district judge, F. X. DeSouza, altered the decree in the original suit, ruling that the reason for the preference in Hindu Law for an unmarried daughter was to ensure adequate provision for such a daughter's marriage, and since Tara was admittedly "incapable of contracting a legal marriage," he concluded that "the reason for the rule not subsisting the rule itself has no force."[104] He therefore directed the division of the property equally among all three sisters.

Tara appealed the case to the High Court. Here, her lawyer G. K. Dandekar argued that the Shastras did not mention the practice of dedicating girls as *muralis*, and that the colonial compendia of local customs showed that according to the custom of the caste, a *murali* and her son would inherit any property left by her father. He also argued that the Shastric injunction as to the preference for unmarried daughters was based not strictly on providing for the daughter's marriage, but on the obligation to financially support unmarried daughters, an obligation that was transferred to a daughter's husband if and when she married.

Justice Chandavarkar's ruling in this case largely ignored these arguments, however. Instead, he offered an exegesis of the Sanskrit corpus that critically distinguished Tara's legal status both from that of unmarried daughters, which formed the basis for her preferential claim to inheritance, and from that of married daughters, with whom the district judge had ruled her entitled to inherit equally. In Justice Chandavarkar's words,

> According to [the principal Hindu law-givers], the *status* of a *kanya* stands conspicuously distinguished from the *status* of a prostitute who is designated a

---

[103] *Tara v. Krishna* (1907) ILR 31 Bom 495 at p. 497; citing ILR 4 Bom 104.
[104] Ibid., 498.

sadharan stri (literally, a common woman).... That is, a *kanya* (maiden) is one who is fit, according to the *shastras*, to be given in marriage in conformity with the prescribed rites, to one man, whereas a *sadharan stri* (prostitute) is a woman, who cast herself away from all parental and other control and guardianship and the injunctions of the *shastras*, and, being a woman accessible to all men (*sarva purusha sadharanataya*), she has become ineligible for marriage.[105]

Chandavarkar's categorization of female statuses and rights thus used Shastric injunction to universalize the female body along an axis of sexual exposure. Rather than the distinction of female bodies according to caste, in this framework all female bodies could be assessed according to the single question of sexual access. In his words,

When the Hindu law says that a maiden who has become a prostitute shall cease to be a maiden, and shall not be regarded as a married woman either, it means that she loses her *status* as a maiden, and acquires a new *status* – that of a *sadharan stri*, not that of a married woman.... It involves a mere change of *status* just as much as if the *kanya* had ceased to be a maiden after marriage and become a wedded woman.[106]

Drawing on this logic, his ruling also went further. Although the sisters had not challenged Tara's equal sharing in the property, Chandavarkar made clear that such a ruling should not stand. Arguing that the district judge's decision had effectively and inexplicably given Tara, whom he characterized as "a prostitute," the status of a married woman, and hence an equal claim to her father's property, he concluded that in fact she should have no claim at all as long as her married sisters (and their heirs) existed in the line of heirs: "Under these circumstances, the only place which such a daughter can take as heir in the line of daughters is in the absence of the unmarried or the married."[107] Thus, as in the justice's similar treatment of Asura marriage in the last section, denying legal recognition to customary practices that signaled and marked low-caste status would form the basis for redeeming those castes.[108]

---

[105] *Tara v. Krishna* (1907) ILR 31 Bom 495 at pp. 505–506. Parenthetical comments in original. J. D. M. Derrett questioned whether Chandavarkar didn't go too far in his elaboration of a Shastric argument in this case, in *Religion, Law and the State in India*, 304, fn. 3.

[106] *Tara v. Krishna* (1907) ILR 31 Bom 495 at p. 511.

[107] Ibid.

[108] Chandavarkar explicitly made caste central to his reformist efforts, playing a role in the founding of the Depressed Classes Mission Society in 1906, serving as its president for a number of years, and fighting against caste and caste discrimination in the National Social Conference, the Bombay Social Conference (founded in 1903), and in the Indian National Congress. N. G. Chandavarkar, *A Wrestling Soul: Story of a Life*

This aim emerges even more clearly in Justice Chandavarkar's involvement in the official administrative debates on temple dedication that were occurring at this time. In 1908, the year after ruling on Tara's case, his was one of few voices emphasizing the importance of excluding illegitimate sons of dedicated women from inheriting in the case of hereditary government offices, as a means of improving the social status of the communities that practiced dedication. In response to a proposed government resolution to establish such a policy, he argued, "In my opinion, such a law will discourage the custom [of temple dedication] and strengthen the hands of those who have been educating public opinion among Shudras on this question about the marriage of Hindu girls to gods. It will particularly strengthen the hands of the enlightened portion of the Shudra community who have been trying to elevate the *status* of the community as to bring up its moral sense to the level of that of the classes regarded as higher by the Hindu hierarchy."[109] Legal de-recognition of dedication would thus form the handmaiden to lower-caste social uplift.

In contrast to these elite efforts, the internal anti-dedication campaign from within communities that practiced dedication was one of several contemporary movements in south and southwest India against "incomplete" marriage forms, such as among the Nairs of Malabar (Sambandham), and against other forms of concubinage and temple dedication (broadly categorized as *devadasi* dedication).[110] As such, it formed part of a broader context of lower-caste masculine political assertion, marked by efforts to establish more effective regulation of

---

of Sir Narayan G. Chandavarkar (Bombay: Popular Book Depot, 1955), pp. 99–102. Ambedkar discusses Chandavarkar's role in the Depressed Classes Mission and in the 1917 passage of the Congress Resolution on the Depressed Classes in *What Congress and Gandhi Have Done to the Untouchables* (Bombay: Thacker & Co., 1945), pp. 14–18.

[109] Letter from Justice N. G. Chandavarkar to Mr. H. O. Quin, Acting Secretary to Government, Judicial Dept., Bombay, Nov. 18, 1908, in MSA, JD 1909 155/1559, pp. 85 and 87. Notably, Chandavarkar offered as legal precedent for such a measure the example that the colonial government had previously intervened in the Hindu law of inheritance regarding such hereditary offices by excluding women altogether from the right of inheritance thereto. This exclusion of women from hereditary office holding was established by Sec. 2 Act V of 1886, referenced in Chapter 2.

[110] Sambandham entailed a nonpermanent alliance by Nair women with younger sons in Namboodiri Brahmin families. The extent to which the establishment, termination, and initiation of new alliances was a matter of the woman's choice has been a subject of scholarly dispute, but these connections also fit into the pattern of high-caste male sexual access to women from subordinate communities, especially in areas where the Nairs were tenants on Namboodiri lands. Arunima, *There Comes Papa*; Kodoth, "Courting Legitimacy."

women's sexuality within the community as well as more regular marriage forms, with the goal of placing the community on a new footing and claiming for themselves their "rightful" masculine authority within the family and over the sexuality of "their" women.[111] These campaigns from within dedicating communities attacked the practice both for the status to which it consigned the community, and for the internal degradation it produced.[112] Some dedicated women also participated in these campaigns, but perhaps with the exception of the later anti-*devadasi* campaign in south India, their critiques were to a considerable extent marginalized or turned to different ends.[113]

While the leaders of the subaltern movement did look to state involvement in the shape of criminalization, in contrast to the elite reformers, their primary focus was on breaking the attachment to custom, changing valorized meanings and practices within the community. As such, they shared much in common with what were perhaps the most prominent nineteenth-century Hindu reform movements, the elite movements to end child marriage and the enforced asceticism of elite child widows.

Child Marriage and Enforced Widowhood between Law and Social Reform

Child marriage and enforced widowhood were grounded in widely recognized interpretations of the Shastric literature, as well as in longstanding practice. Nearly universal among elite castes, child marriage also prevailed much more widely at this time, and ascetic widowhood was adopted by upwardly mobile communities as integral to their claims to higher social status.[114] Thus, while these practices shared with temple

---

[111] For example, the Malabar Marriage Commission of the early 1890s, which culminated in the Malabar Marriage Act of 1896, and the agitation against *devadasi* dedication, which eventually resulted in legislative actions such as the 1934 Bombay Protection of Devadasis Act and the 1947 Madras Devadasi (Prevention of Dedication) Act.

[112] For example, in 1906, an organization called the Naik Maratha Mandal, an organization aiming to raise *kunbi* community status, passed an internal regulation condemning dedication and encouraging parents to get all their children married, while allowing them "as a concession to ignorance and superstition," to dedicate a maximum of one girl, "with her consent," when she reached fifteen years of age. *Subodh Patrika*, June 10, 1906 in MSA, JD 1907, 143/2078, p. 291. Similarly, the emergent Dalit movement radically critiqued the practice for its effects on the honor of the community, and especially on masculine self-respect. See the discussion of the contemporary letters and editorials in the Pune monthly journal *Somavanshiya Mitra* launched by Dalit leader Shivram Janba Kamble, in Rao, *The Caste Question*, 63–67.

[113] Rao, *The Caste Question*, 63.

[114] Chakravarti, *Rewriting History*, 28, 52, 152–153.

dedication a connection to religious sentiment and to a broader structuring of the caste order, unlike dedication, they reflected the dominant ethos and vision of the foundation of a moral society. Nonetheless, by the middle of the nineteenth century, men from within this dominant elite began to subject these practices to new forms of scrutiny and critique. By the late 1830s and early 1840s, both issues appeared as matters for debate in the emergent public sphere of vernacular newspapers in western India.[115] By the 1880s, the issues had come to define the major planks of elite social reform, and the debate both for and against the practices congealed into somewhat predictable and well-rehearsed arguments and themes.[116] Civil and criminal cases in the courts at this time also incited and shaped the terms of debate: the Rakhmabai case in the context of child marriage;[117] the trial of the Brahmin widow Vijayaluxmee for infanticide in the context of enforced widowhood.[118]

[115] Essays on widow remarriage appeared in Bal Gangadhar Shastri Jambhekar's *Darpan* in 1837 and 1841. Meera Kosambi, "Life after Widowhood: Two Radical Reformist Options in Maharashtra," in *Intersections: Socio-Cultural Trends in Maharashtra*, edited by Meera Kosambi (Hyderabad: Orient Longman, 2000), pp. 92–117, 95. Essays on raising the age of marriage appeared in Bhau Mahajan's Marathi journal, *Prabhakar*, in the 1840s. Narendra K. Wagle, "Three Letters of Govind Babaji Joshi on Inter-Jati Marriage in Nineteenth Century Maharashtra," in *Writers, Editors and Reformers: Social and Political Transformations of Maharashtra, 1830–1930*, edited by Narendra K. Wagle (New Delhi: Manohar, 1999), pp. 200–217, 202.

[116] See replies in "Papers Relating to Infant Marriage and Enforced Widowhood in India," *Selections from the Records of the Government of India*, No. CCXXIII, Home Dept. Serial No. 3 (Calcutta: Superintendent of Government Printing, 1886). For some sense of the broader social field and response at this time, see *Bombay Samachar* (Gujarati, Bombay) RNP, March 5, 1886, 7; *Shetkaryancha Kaivari* (Anglo-Marathi, Bombay) RNP, March 5, 1886, 7–8; as well as the multiple accounts of a major public meeting of "the Maratha and Gujarati Hindus" against legislative interference in the matter of child marriage by the government, held in Madhav Bagh, Bombay, on September 5, 1886, under the chairmanship of renowned conservative barrister V. N. Mandlik, reported week of September 18, 1886, 12–15.

[117] For contemporary newspaper commentary on the Rakhmabai case, see discussion in Chapter 3.

[118] For contemporary newspaper commentary on the Vijayaluxmee case, see *Bombay Samachar* (Gujarati, Bombay) RNP, May 11, 1881, 8; *Indu Prakash* (Anglo-Marathi, Bombay) RNP, May 30, 1881, 3; *Subodh Patrika* (Anglo-Marathi, Bombay) RNP, May 29, 1881, 4–5; *Bombay Chronicle* (Anglo-Gujarati, Bombay) RNP, May 29, 1881, 7–8; *Rast Goftar* (Gujarati, Bombay) RNP, June 5, 1881, 5; *Yajdan Parast* (Gujarati, Bombay) RNP, June 26, 4–5. Tarabai Shinde was inspired to write her famed tract, *Stri-Purush Tulana* (A Comparison of Women and Men) in response to the cruel treatment of Vijayaluxmee. See Rosalind O'Hanlon, *A Comparison between Women and Men: Tarabai Shinde and the Critique of Gender Relations in Colonial India* (New York: Oxford University Press, 1994).

Both of these reformist movements have received extensive and important scholarly treatment.[119] This analysis departs from these works, however, in focusing on the way these movements were conceptualized at the
time as addressing the relationship between law and social life.

The debates on these issues were concatenated in the 1880s by Parsi
social reformer Behramji Malabari's 1884 *Notes on Infant Marriage and
Enforced Widowhood in India*, which were representations submitted to
the government seeking state action. The initial state response was to solicit
opinions on Malabari's representations and the proposals therein from a
wide range of elite men, both conservatives and reformers, throughout
India. Although the result of these inquiries was a state refusal to proceed
with any further action on either matter, the debate triggered by these
writings played out extensively in the solicited responses to Malabari's
writings and in the contemporary press. Many condemned Malabari's
portrayals as exaggerated and overdrawn, and as unwarranted interference by one outside of the affected community (since Malabari was
a Parsi) and ignorant of the real conditions therein. Many also deprecated Malabari's specific proposals: While Malabari explicitly rejected
legislation, he nonetheless called for punitive state measures that would
discourage child marriage, and for state intervention to aid and protect
high-caste widows who might seek to remarry.[120]

No woman's opinion was solicited in the state inquiries, but a number
of individual women and women's organization at the time participated in the debate and wrote publicly calling for legislation to raise
the age of consent, and excoriated orthodox men and women for their
maltreatment of high-caste widows.[121] Among the elite male responses

---

[119] Chandra, *Enslaved Daughters*; Chakravarti, *Rewriting History*; Kosambi, "Gender
Reform"; "Girl-Brides and Socio-Legal Change," 1857–1868; and "Life after
Widowhood"; O'Hanlon, "Issues of Widowhood: Gender and Resistance in Colonial
Western India" in *Contesting Power: Resistance and Everyday Social Relations in South
Asia*, edited by Douglas Jaynes and Gyan Prakash, 62–108 (Delhi: Oxford University
Press, 1991); Sarkar, "Pre-History of Rights." For the agitation in the late 1920s to raise
the legal age of marriage, which eventually culminated in the 1929 Child Marriage
(Restraint) Act, widely known as the Sarda Act, see Sinha, *Specters of Mother India*.

[120] "Papers Relating to Infant Marriage and Enforced Widowhood," 4, 6–7.

[121] See discussion in Anagol, *Emergence of Feminism*, 95–100, 209–218. It is notable that
the intrinsic authority of experience, which grounded many criticisms of Malabari, also
formed the platform for some of these feminist arguments in support of social change:
These women argued that men, who didn't know the pain and suffering that women
experienced, should not have the authority to legislate on it. *Induprakash*, December 8
and 22, 1890, cited in Anagol, *Emergence of Feminism*, 214. This appeal to a shared
female bodily experience of suffering offers an alternative framing of the universalization of female bodies seen earlier in Chandavarkar's ruling in the case of Tara Shinde.

that dominated the debate, enforced widowhood was widely perceived as the more intractable and problematic of the two issues. In the case of child marriage, in contrast to the contemporary situation in Bengal, in western India there was widespread support for Malabari's view that child marriage was socially debilitating and must inevitably change. Even proponents of child marriage largely refrained from supporting early consummation thereof. More contentious was the question of whether these practices should be subject to state regulation. The overwhelming response, even among reformers, was that state action was undesirable and likely to be counterproductive. Such change would of necessity be the work of reformers, or, as Ranade argued in frustration in the epigraph to this chapter, of a religious revival. Reformers thus claimed for themselves a leading role in the shepherding of society.

Those reformers who did support state action in the form of legislation adopted the language of utilitarianism and of state interest, emphasizing the necessarily coercive power of the state, and construing the age of marriage as a matter at once political, social, and economic, and hence of intrinsic state interest. Thus, High Court Government Pleader Shantaram Narayan, one of the most forceful advocates of state intervention, argued that "it is the duty of the State, and the State alone, to fix a reasonable standard of age for marriage. The question is as much political as it is social. All civilized Governments have so regarded it, and whoever knows anything of Hindu society may rest assured that it will not move in the matter, unless the lead is taken by the state."[122] Against those who resisted state intervention into religious matters, Narayan argued that the entire system of colonial Hindu law entailed such intervention:

Some people argue as if the State or Sirkar has not yet interfered with our social customs. What do we witness every day in our Courts of Justice? We have a Hindu Law, it is true, but is not that law involved in confusion, and is it not a fact that our Courts are expounding it as best they can, and bringing into vogue, in effect, new adaptations which Hindu lawyers of a bygone age would have probably stared at?

It also sheds some light on the significance of the neologism presented by Anagol that emerged in some feminist writings of this time – *stri-jati*: in conceptualizing women as a generic category, literally as a caste, this term linked an innate bodily form and the experience it entailed to an intrinsic collectivity. For two important analyses of the portrayal of the widow's plight, suffering, and also desire within the emergent genre of women's periodicals in south and north India, see Sreenivas, *Wives, Widows and Concubines*, 107–116, and Francesca Orsini, *The Hindi Public Sphere, 1920–1940: Language and Literature in the Age of Nationalism* (New Delhi: Oxford University Press, 2002), pp. 274–289.

[122] "Papers on Infant Marriage and Enforced Widowhood," 196.

The whole administration of the Hindu Law is, in fact, based upon a legal fiction, and it affords a signal example of the fact that our customs are already being regulated by judiciary interference of a sort.... Those, therefore, who think that there is no State interference now with our religious practices or social customs are either not aware of the real state of things or are ignoring it.[123]

In depicting colonial Hindu law as an entire edifice of state regulation, Narayan thus highlighted the ironies of a Hindu law that claimed a position of nonintervention while it placed the Hindu legal tradition within an entirely novel juridical frame.

M. G. Ranade also supported state intervention, although his writings in this context were more equivocal. In other contemporary writings directed primarily to a Western-educated Indian audience, he staunchly supported such intervention by the state, arguing that such a role formed an integral part of the state's legitimate functions:

Whenever there is a large amount of unredressed evil suffered by people who cannot adopt their own remedy, the State has a function to regulate and minimize the evil, if by so regulating it, the evil can be minimized better than by individual effort and without leading to other worse abuses. The State in its collective capacity represents the power, the wisdom, the mercy and charity, of its best citizens.... The regulation of marriageable age has in all countries, like the regulation of minority, or the fit age for contracts, been a part of its national jurisprudence, and it cannot be said with justice that this question lies out of its sphere. The same observation holds true of the condition of the widow rendered miserable in early life, and thrown helpless on the world.... [T]o the extent that the evil they suffer is remediable by man, it cannot be said that this remedy may not be considered by the State as fully within its proper function.[124]

Ranade thus articulated an argument for state intervention grounded at once in state interest and in the state's responsibility for – and unique efficacy in advancing – the welfare of its people. Yet in his response to Malabari's tracts addressed to the state, Ranade did not develop the full force of these arguments. He maintained that the age of marriage was properly regulated by the state,[125] yet he also argued that it was only when the state more properly represented the people – or at least the social and political vanguard thereof – that such intervention could be legitimate and effective: "The Legislative Councils, as at present constituted, cannot grapple effectively with these questions."[126] Ranade called

---

[123] Ibid.
[124] M. G. Ranade, "Introduction," in *A Collection Containing the Proceedings*, xiii–xiv.
[125] "Papers on Infant Marriage and Enforced Widowhood," 93.
[126] Ibid.

for the formation of a commission of elite Hindus who would assess the issues at stake and make recommendations to the government, but even this action was long rejected by the state as overly interventionary.[127] The colonial state ultimately reluctantly passed age of consent legislation in 1891 and eventually prohibited child marriage in 1929, in both cases at the behest of Indian reformers. Yet these laws effectively remained a dead letter. The questionable potential of law to change social norms likewise shaped approaches to the plight of the child widow.

Custom and Conscience in the Plight of the Child Widow

By the 1880s, resistance to enforced ascetic widowhood, especially for child widows, had a long history. In western India, evidence of individual resistance to the strictures of ascetic widowhood date to the eighteenth-century Peshwa era, typically involving fathers who sought to remarry daughters widowed in childhood, or to avoid their disfigurement.[128] Within a couple decades of the British conquest of the region, Brahmin reformers initiated public efforts directed at their own community to save child widows from lifelong ascetic widowhood and social ostracism by enabling them to remarry.[129] Christian converts as well as anti-caste activists such as Jotirao Phule also sought to alleviate the plight of high-caste widows through their writings and through the establishment of new charitable institutions.[130]

---

[127] With the passage of the Age of Consent Act of 1891, reformers succeeded in pushing a reluctant state to raise the age of consent for girls from ten to twelve, despite vociferous objections from the orthodox and from conservative cultural nationalists, most prominently B. G. Tilak in western India. This became possible only in the aftermath of the scandalous death of the ten-year-old Bengali girl Phulmonee from injuries sustained due to forced consummation by her husband. In this context, even some reformers who had eschewed any call for state action at the time of Malabari's publications a few years before now viewed strong state action as entirely necessary and appropriate. See, for example, N. G. Chandavarkar, "The British Government and Hindu Religious Customs," in *Speeches and Writings of Sir Narayan G. Chandavarkar* (Bombay: Manoranjak Grantha Prasarak Mandali, 1911), pp. 313–314.

[128] Kadam, "The Institution of Marriage," 356; Kosambi, "Life after Widowhood," 95. At least one of the major Brahmin communities of the region, the Deshastha Brahmins, did not regularly enforce tonsure of widows, and were disciplined by the Peshwa for this laxity. Kadam, "Institution of Marriage," 355–357. This custom was also referenced by Justice Ranade in *Lakshmibai v. Ramchandra* (1896) ILR 22 Bom 590 at p. 595.

[129] For details of these efforts from the late 1830s through the 1850s, see Kosambi, "Life after Widowhood," 95; Dhananjay Keer, *Mahatma Jotirao Phoolay: Father of the Indian Social Revolution* (Bombay: Popular Prakashan, 1974; reprint 1997), pp. 84–85.

[130] Ibid. See also Phule's response to Malabari's tracts in "Papers Relating to Infant Marriage and Enforced Widowhood," 47.

The efforts of such reformers, agitating alongside the renowned work of Ishwarchandra Vidyasagar and others in Bengal, encouraged government legislation on the issue to render permissive the remarriage of widows. The Hindu Widows Remarriage Act (Act XV of 1856), legalized widow remarriage, which was textually and customarily prohibited for high-caste women.[131] Following its passage, reformers in western India established a Society for the Promotion of Remarriage. They engaged in public debates with orthodox supporters of ascetic widowhood, they established institutions to support widows and their illegitimate children, and they engaged in more activist efforts to get widows married.[132] During the 1880s and into the 1890s, the issue was further sharpened through the circulation of Behramji Malabari's *Notes*. By the late nineteenth century, advocacy for widow remarriage became a central subject of reformist discourse, integral to virtually all the broader social reform associations, although the number of widow remarriages remained extraordinarily low throughout the century and beyond.[133]

[131] Although rarely discussed in the scholarly literature, this act was advanced at the time as a matter of religious conscience: that Brahmins and other high castes who interpreted the Shastric provisions differently, and thus held different beliefs regarding the prohibition on widow remarriage, were prevented from acting according to their conscience by state enforcement of the dominant interpretation. As such, its supporters developed a Protestant rhetoric of individual conscience and interpretive agency, which found support among the Legislative Council. Vaidya, ed., *A Collection Containing the Proceedings*. Moreover, the proponents of the legislation had attempted to defuse resistance to it by specifying that any property a widow inherited from her deceased husband would revert to the next heir on her remarriage – terms that had not necessarily been customary among the castes that regularly practiced widow remarriage. This discrepancy ultimately produced differences of interpretation in the High Courts, but in Bombay in particular, it led to a judicial narrowing of the customary property rights of lower-caste widows. The critical Bombay decision (reversing the court's earlier treatment of the issue in *Parekh Ranochor v. Bai Vakhat* [1886] ILR 11 Bom 119) was *Vithu v. Govinda* (1896) ILR 22 Bom 321. Notably, Justice Ranade was one of the authors of this decision. In contrast, in the mid-1880s Ranade had called for an amendment of the Hindu Widows Remarriage Act to enable such widows to retain their husband's property. Lucy Carroll, "Law, Custom, and Statutory Social Reform: The Hindu Widows' Remarriage Act of 1856," *Indian Economic and Social History Review* 20, 4 (1983): 363–388; Chakravarti, *Rewriting History*, 92, 132–133.

[132] Kosambi, "Life after Widowhood," 100; O'Hanlon, "Issues of Widowhood," 67, 82; Keer, "Mahatma Jotirao Phooley," 96; "Papers Relating to Infant Marriage and Enforced Widowhood," 148; *Jaganadarsh*, December 12, 1886, 10, OIOR, RNP, 1886.

[133] In 1893 at the Tenth Social Conference, Ranade cited statistics from the approximately sixty organizations that sent in reports, showing eight widow marriages in Bombay, twenty-five in Punjab, two in Madras, and one each in Bengal and Madras. The following year there were twenty-five such marriages reported in total. Ranade, *Miscellaneous Writings*, 176–177, 183. The 1881 Imperial Census, which included statistics on male and female widowhood for the first time, listed 1,424,739 widows and 443,917

Yet, as many responded to Malabari's appeal, beyond the legalization of remarriage, they saw little further scope for government action. The one potential state action that did garner considerable support in these papers was a prohibition on tonsure, especially of young women. The horrors of this practice were also evoked by widows themselves. In a series of (possibly coached) essays written by nine widows in the Poona Widows and Orphans Home and sent to Sir Herbert Risley in 1911, the writers returned again and again to the "torture" and "deformity" that this practice visited upon young widows.[134] The widespread heightened emotional response to this practice suggests something of the way that this disfigurement of the widow facilitated her dehumanization.[135] Abolishing tonsure thus formed a major initial step to her rehabilitation, one that would render more difficult the perpetration of everyday cruelties against her, by her own family as well as by strangers.

This question of how to change fundamental perceptions of the widow formed the core problem for the reformer, prompting extensive theorizing on the nature of custom, its connection to law, and the means of its transformation. M. G. Ranade and N. G. Chandavarkar, two of the towering figures in the movements for social reform of this era, both of whom also eventually served as High Court justices, became major voices in these efforts.[136] Notably, in these writings, the agency of law paled in significance. Societal change would form the basis for a future law.[137]

The reformist writings and speeches of both Ranade and Chandavarkar were primarily directed to the forging of dominant community norms, and

---

widowers for the Bombay Presidency, including 110 widows under 15 years of age for the Deccan. Cited in O'Hanlon, "Issues of Widowhood," 69–70.

[134] OIOR, MSS.Eur.D.356, pp. 1–29. These essays appear to be the result of coaching due to the extensive repetition of stories and themes. Two of the more suggestive essays are those by Radhabai Inamdar and Amba Bai Bapat.

[135] Some sense of this – as well as of the ways in which feminist writers sought to cultivate sympathy – can be seen in the writings of one woman who described in the feminist press the scene of a tonsure and breaking of the bangles of a thirteen-year-old widow, who was helplessly "mooing like a cow in distress." *'Gulabbai ani Shevantibai yancha bodhpar samvad* (Instructive Debates between Gulabbai and Shewatibai), *Arya Bhagini*, July 1891, 86–87, cited in Anagol, *Emergence of Feminism*, 95.

[136] Ranade was himself notorious for bowing to familial pressures on the issue of widow remarriage and marrying a previously unmarried child-bride instead of a widow after the death of his first wife. His efforts to produce real change in sentiment and belief were thus all the more weighty.

[137] See, for example, Ranade, "Address at Hislop College (December 1891) – Social Conference, Its Aims, and Methods," in *Miscellaneous Writings*, 113; Ranade, "True Tests of Social Progress," Address Delivered at the Seventh Social Congress at Lahore, 1893, *Miscellaneous Writings*, 137.

ın particular they sought to inculcate new structures of feeling, producing a recognition of the humanity and suffering of female family members.[138] Thus, in 1894, Ranade urged in a speech to the seventh annual meeting of the National Social Conference:

> Do I exaggerate in any way the character of this disorder in our system of family life? ... I appeal to every one of the many hundreds of the men before me, – I appeal to them most solemnly, – I ask them to lay their hands on their hearts, and stand up before this meeting and say, if any one can muster courage to say it, – that our family and social arrangements have not been out of joint for centuries together? Are we or are we not conscious that many of us, under the narcotic influence of custom and usage, too often violate the feelings of our common human nature and our sense of right and wrong, stunt the growth of our higher life, and embitter the existence of many of those who depend on us, our wives and children, our brothers and sons, our relatives and friends? Are we prepared to point out any single hour of the day when we do not unconsciously commit injustice of a sort by the side of which municipal injustice is nothing, when we do not unconsciously sanction iniquities by the side of which the most oppressant tyrant's rule is mercy itself? We resent the insult given by the oppressor. We protest against the unjust judge. Here however we are judge and jury and prosecutor and accused ourselves, and we are sometimes consciously and more often unconsciously committed to a course of conduct, which makes tyrants and slaves of us all and, sapping the strength of our resolution, drags us down to our fall – to be the laughing stock of the whole world. Till we set these matters right, it is almost hopeless to expect that we can have that manliness of character, that sense of our rights and responsibilities without which political and municipal freedom is hard to achieve and impossible to preserve.[139]

Although drawing on elements of the colonial justification for withholding political rights, as well as on a Protestant missionary rhetoric of internal change, this formulation also developed a new way of thinking about social and legal rights. In urging the necessity of a change of heart among men, Ranade conceptualized the family in ways that distinguished it both from the colonial critique of Indian society, and from the cultural nationalist position that constituted the family as the terrain of the uncolonized nation.[140] In Ranade's formulation, the family was envisioned as

---

[138] Dipesh Chakrabarty has brilliantly argued that in this reformist context the widow concatenated the figure of the modern subject, whose internal emotions and desires could now be newly imagined, and imagined as the paradigmatic example of the subordination of the individual to society. Chakrabarty, *Provincializing Europe*, 133. See also Sreenivas, *Wives, Widows and Concubines*, 107–116.

[139] Ranade, "True Tests of Social Progress," *Miscellaneous Writings*, 124.

[140] For the nationalist formation, see Chatterjee, "Nationalist Resolution"; Sarkar, "Pre-History." Ranade's longer formulation of which this is a part may nonetheless be

a zone of unfreedom that paralleled the tyrannies of colonial rule, and custom appeared as a morass that dulled men's senses and lulled them away from their own true sense of common humanity.[141] In this context, the domain of society would play a critical role in the cultivation of conscience. Conscience would be cultivated "through the fires of religious revival," or more mundanely in the sphere of civil society represented by the organizations for social reform. The family could scarcely serve as the cradle of Enlightenment.

Likewise, N. G. Chandavarkar, who was appointed to the High Court in 1901 on Ranade's retirement, berated those who would oppose the remarriage of child widows on similar terms:

Do you realize – will you not realize how God's curse has fallen upon us for being so cruel, so hard-hearted, and relentless to the suffering society has gone on inflicting on this poor creature of the child-widow? ... We find fault with Government when the famine-stricken starve; and yet we have not a word of indignation for our society which treats the child-widow as if she has no right to exist! It is the home in which all the active virtues that adorn private and public life should be not only taught but actively exercised.... But in our homes, if there are widowed girls, what are we taught. We are taught not to feel actively for their sufferings. We are ordained to be passive in our sympathy for them, to bear their condition with equanimity instead of raising our hands for the betterment of their widowed condition. Society has gone on without pity for the child-widow.[142]

Thus for Chandavarkar as well, the masculine cultivation of sympathy and forging of a new intimate – both premised on the transformation of family life – formed the critical means to changing the broader moral and political condition of society.

In contrast to cultural nationalists and to what Partha Chatterjee has identified as the "nationalist resolution of the women's question," both men emphasized the importance of internal change in this process. In Ranade's words:

It seems to many that it is the outward form which has to be changed, and if this change can be made, they think that all the difficulties in our way will vanish. If

distinguished from a long Western tradition of theorizing public and private, for example, Hannah Arendt's framing of the Greek notion of the private as domain of necessity versus public as domain of freedom, in Arendt, *Human Condition*, as well as from the contemporary Victorian ideology of separate spheres.

[141] Indeed, Ranade rejected entirely the separation of the social and the political that formed a critical plank of the cultural nationalists. See Ranade, "Bombay Social Conference – Satara, 1900," in *Miscellaneous Writings*, 230.

[142] Chandavarkar, "Marriage of Child-Widows" – Speech at the Indian Social Conference, Calcutta, 1901, in *Speeches and Writings*, 103–104.

we change our outward manners and customs, sit in a particular way or walk in a particular fashion, our work according to them is accomplished. I cannot but think that much of the prejudice against the reformers is due to this misunderstanding. It is not the outward form, but the inward form, the thought and the idea which determines the outward form, that has to be changed if real reformation is desired.[143]

Moreover, Ranade recast the problem of political dependence in classical liberal terms as a reflection of the real problem of internal moral dependence on custom rather than conscience.[144] For Ranade, unthinking fidelity to custom or past authorities was the very basis of dependence that extended from personal to political life, and that needed to be addressed in order to achieve political independence.[145]

For both justices, the necessary transformation could only be produced by active struggle. Chandavarkar thus regularly quoted Ranke, that "all progress is through conflict,"[146] and argued that "we must be prepared to suffer if we wish to succeed and make society purer and better,"[147] and that time itself is no agent of change, "it is men, not time, that are the moving springs of society."[148] Ranade similarly drew on the metaphor of the quintessential engine of progress, the railway, to underscore the limitations of passive change: "When one drifts into reform, he is not reformed, he remains exactly as he was. The fastest railway train does not give exercise to our body, if we do not ourselves move."[149] Yet Ranade also emphasized the inevitability of reform, and both men argued for a universal vision of justice and human nature. At the Bombay Social Conference at Satara in 1900, a year before his death, Ranade reflected, "Above all mere

[143] Ranade, "Eleventh Social Conference – Amraoti, 1897 – Revival and Reform," *Miscellaneous Writings*, 191–192. This formulation also seems to offer a contemporary riposte to the critiques of the Bengali Babu discussed in Sartori, *Bengal in Global Concept History*, chapter 3.

[144] M. G. Ranade, "Eleventh Social Conference – Amraoti, 1897: Revival and Reform," *Miscellaneous Writings*, 191–192.

[145] Ibid., 194. According to Ranade, it was men's own "self, heart, and head and soul" that needed to change. Ranade, "Address at Hislop College," in ibid., 112. Similarly, Chandavarkar repeatedly called for listening to the "still small voice within," Chandavarkar, "Hindu Reform, 1893: The Telang School and the Line of Least Resistance," *Speeches and Writings*, 29. Notably, Chandavarkar also emphasized the historical dynamism of the Shastric tradition itself. Chandavarkar, "Social Reform" – Lecture at Madras, 1896, in *Speeches and Writings*, 65.

[146] Chandavarkar, "Social Reform" – Lecture at Madras, 1896, *Speeches and Writings*, 30; "Social Reform" – Lecture at Mangalore, 1900, *Speeches and Writings*, 89.

[147] Ibid.

[148] Ibid., 69.

[149] Ranade, "Address at Hislop College," *Miscellaneous Writings*, 111–112.

ordinances and institutes stands the law eternal, of justice and equality, of pity and compassion, the suggestions of the conscience within and of nature without us. We can no more resist the stream of these influences as working for righteousness than we can roll back the tide."[150] Thus despite his frustration with men's weakness, Ranade's writings remained fundamentally optimistic about the ultimate inevitability of change grounded in the very universality of righteousness it espoused.

Reformers such as Ranade and Chandavarkar sought through this critical project of reform to produce a masculine self animated by an emotional and ethical life appropriate to a modern Hindu law. The cultivation of human sympathy would provide the basis for new social practice, for new ways of conceptualizing the value of persons – for example, in the context of child widows, replacing notions of ritual defilement and sentiments of loathing and disgust with those of pity and personal guilt. This masculine recognition of women's humanity would in turn enable their own (as well as women's) humanization. This was thus an attempt to transform or replace the emotional investment in the habitus of elite social life by creating a new emotional content focused on the disparity between the truth of human universality and the actual oppression and helplessness suffered by the weak. In Ranade's words, "The change which we should all seek is thus a change from constraint to freedom, from credulity to faith, from status to contract, from authority to reason, from unorganised to organised life, from bigotry to toleration, from blind fatalism to a sense of human dignity. This is what I understand by social evolution, both for individuals and societies in this country."[151] Ranade thus articulated not just the quintessential liberal vision of the transition from tradition to modernity, but a desire for an authentic continuity stretching from individual subjectivity to social and legal norms. Such a process would inevitably be universalizing, and unapologetically so.

These reformist efforts to create what might be termed a secular Hindu law, focused on rights, designifying ritual status, and defining the category "Hindu" as a sociological, legal, and political status, at once posited women's humanity and rendered it dependent upon new labors of social and legal recognition.[152] These efforts also clearly – if ironically – articulated

[150] M. G. Ranade, "The Bombay Social Conference – Satara, 1900," in ibid., 234. See also M. G. Ranade, "The Tenth Social Conference – Calcutta, 1896: A Brief Outline of the Work of the Year," in ibid., 179.

[151] M. G. Ranade, "Social Evolution: Speech at the Sixth National Social Conference, Allahabad, 1892," in ibid., 116–117.

[152] Esmeir, "At Once Human and Not Human."

with religious as well as secular nationalisms. Indeed, this work of reform was conceptualized as specifically Hindu, and in terms that at times drew upon a communal logic.[153] Yet it is of equal significance that those seeking to produce it aimed to create a new recognition of human value that would operate across and transform both law and social life. These efforts reflected the centrality to this nationalist imaginary of new masculine models of marriage in which human sentiment, grounded in the forging of a new intimate, would be yoked to a horizon of female commensuration to be pursued through the agency and principled action of reformist men. These reformers thus recast the significance of custom, grounding legitimacy not in usage from time immemorial but in intentional practice and in the dynamic potentialities of a remade "Hindu society" for forging an ethical polity. Reform would make possible an imagined future in which law could ethically derive from social life. As such, these reformers both appropriated and transformed the liberal ethics of the human that came to structure the colonial jurisprudence of Hindu law discussed in Chapter 3, turning the valorization of incommensurability within the family into a project of securing women's human value – and their own.

CONCLUSION

The late nineteenth century saw an intensification of state interest, scholarship, and public debate concerning the societal ramifications of existing forms of marriage and sexuality. The discourse on marriage customs set into motion a logic of the universal and particular in which the universality of marriage and its particular cultural forms tended to collapse into a state de-recognition of those customs that failed to adequately resemble (universal, that is, Christian) marriage as such. Moreover, operating in the wake of this expansive state power, contemporary ethnographic-juridical compendia on Hindu marriage customs came to largely follow the contours of contemporary jurisprudence that established which customs had the force of law.

---

[153] Thus, in an 1893 speech to one of the emerging centers of this Hindu nationalism, the Arya Samaj's Dayanand Anglo-Vedic College, Ranade urged, "We have outlived Buddhism.... We have outlived Mahomedan repression." Further, he claimed to speak "as a representative of no particular Samaj, but as a member of the great Hindu community which peoples this land and forms one-sixth of the human race." M. G. Ranade, "The Seventh Social Conference – Lahore, 28th December 1893: True Tests of Social Progress," *Miscellaneous Writings*, 126, 127. Notably, the tenor of his writings changed in the later 1890s toward emphasizing the unity and friendship of Hindus and Muslims, certainly in response to the powerfully expanding communalism of the era.

In the jurisprudence discussed in the Chapter 3, property rights became the basis for an articulation at once of abstract human universality or commensurability and for a valorization of human incommensurability and uniqueness represented especially by women and the family. In contrast, in the debates on Hindu marriage, both the state and liberal social reformers claimed an agentive role in the work of producing women's humanity out of what were now cast as dehumanizing social practices. In these efforts, the problem of female incommensurability took a different form – less as a problem of producing abstract subjecthood and rights, and instead as a problem of women's susceptibility to commodification on the one hand, and of their vulnerability to stigmatization on the other. Infusing society with the recognition of women's humanity would thus require a resignification of female bodies that removed them from the logics of exchange value while retaining their potential human equivalence, to be achieved through the ongoing labors of law and social reform. In the case of elite Hindu social reformers, these efforts sought to fashion a new Hindu society whose conformity with universal ethical norms would ground its claims to self-government and the force of law. By the early decades of the twentieth century, however, such emergent dominant nationalist formations began to produce a variety of new forms of political mobilization as Muslims, Dalits, as well as liberal feminists both critiqued and utilized the ongoing politico-legal salience of bodies and birth.

5

Law, Community, and Belonging

The early decades of the twentieth century saw several crucial shifts in the forms and strategies of Indian nationalism, moving definitively away from the earlier visions and tactics of liberal reformers and moderates such as Ranade and Chandavarkar. After more than a decade of internal struggle within the Indian National Congress, in the aftermath of the First World War the Congress was transformed from a bastion of the Western-educated, middle- and upper-middle-class elite into a mass movement that deployed public agitation and nonviolent direct action under the leadership of M. K. Gandhi. This transformation occurred alongside and in relationship to a broadening out of the political arena on a number of levels: the gradual consolidation of a discrete Hindu nationalist ideology, shared by some members of the Congress, as well as the rise and expansion of new forms of popular political action; the emergence of Muslim claims first to the status of political minority, and then to the status of an internal nation; and the articulation of new forms of anti-caste politics and eventually of claims to minority status, most notably.[1] Additionally, these decades saw the formation of all-India feminist organizations and women's wings of the major nationalist organizations (largely composed of elite women), as well as large-scale public participation by middle-class women in the nationalist campaigns led by Gandhi.[2] These various

---

[1] Faisal Devji, "The Minority as Political Form," in *From the Colonial to the Post-Colonial: India and Pakistan in Transition*, edited by Dipesh Chakrabarty, Rochona Majumdar, and Andrew Sartori (New Delhi: Oxford University Press, 2007), pp. 85–95; Gooptu, *The Politics of the Urban Poor*; Gupta, *Sexuality, Obscenity, Community*; Rao, *The Caste Question*.

[2] The Women's India Association was formed in 1917 and the All India Women's Conference in 1927. Both were founded through the combined labors of European and

political formations acutely reflected questions of political equality and representation within democracy, and centered on the implications of the status of demographic minority that were and are singular thereto.

Many historians have argued that by the early 1930s, a moment of political possibility had passed, particularly for anti-caste and feminist politics, and that the late 1930s constituted a further negative turning point in nationalist and communal politics.[3] By the mid-1930s, the refusal of both Gandhi and the Congress to imagine anything but the subsumption of minority and marginalized groups into a dominant secular Hindu nation collided with a colonial approach of offering extremely limited concessions to Congress demands, coupled with efforts to bolster the power of such competing minority interests as a means of weakening the Congress.[4]

This era was shaped by the Government of India Act of 1935, which laid out a new structure of central and provincial governance that allowed greater Indian representation and established a measure of provincial autonomy, although elections remained indirect, the franchise limited, and control of the key state structures remained in British hands. In 1937, the Congress, along with the Muslim League and numerous other parties, avidly contested provincial elections held under this act. These elections proved a major victory for the Congress, and a rout for the Muslim League.[5] They also bolstered a broader shift in the character of the Congress from a popular movement to a dominant political party, which nonetheless continued to claim to represent the Indian nation in its totality and heterogeneity. In the aftermath of these elections, Nehru took the Congress's success as a mandate for the party and rebuffed Muhammad Ali Jinnah's demands for inclusion of the League in ministerial appointments, pushing Jinnah to pursue a politics of incitement, instilling Muslim fear of Hindu domination in order to garner

Indian feminists, but Indian feminists quickly became the leading forces therein. Aparna Basu and Bharati Ray, *Women's Struggle: A History of the All India Women's Conference, 1927–1990* (New Delhi: Manohar, 1990); Forbes, *Women in Modern India*.

[3] Anandhi, "Women's Question"; V. Geetha, "Periyar, Women and an Ethic of Citizenship," in Rao, ed., *Gender and Caste*, 180–203; Sinha, *Specters of Mother India*; Rao, *The Caste Question*.

[4] D. A. Low, *Britain and Indian Nationalism, 1929–1942: The Imprint of Ambiguity* (Cambridge: Cambridge University Press, 1997).

[5] The Congress won a majority in six of the eleven provinces, and a plurality in an additional three. The Muslim League in contrast won less than 5 percent of the total Muslim vote, and did not win a majority of seats in any of the Muslim majority provinces. In the important province of Punjab, it won only a single seat, while the regional Unionist Party, representing primarily agricultural interests, was able to form a majority.

mass support among Muslims for the League. This highly fraught context formed a moment both of consolidation of new politics of community and of their material and symbolic positioning within the law.

This final chapter focuses on this late-1930s moment as one of political crystallization in which questions of the legal rights and recognition of communities came powerfully to the fore. The four historical episodes of late-1930s lawmaking examined in this chapter reflected this new political context and its break with the past. These episodes involved disparate sites of collective action, linked by their use of law and especially of property in forging and redefining community. If colonial policy to this point had sought to depoliticize and privatize property and to limit personal law to matters regarding the family, in this moment property became the basis for new forms of political mobilization and community identification. In their focus on property – and indeed on inheritance – these campaigns made use of the ways in which inheritance at once located persons socially and juridically according to their birth into communities and also materialized those social differences in politico-legal and economic inequalities. As such, this politics of community reflected and set in motion particular liberal dilemmas concerning political equality and representation, especially the ways in which the law would recognize the inheritances of birth. These politics were thus instantiations of rather than divergences from core liberal state dilemmas. Moreover, in contrast to earlier reformist efforts, these campaigns resolutely sought to utilize the force of law to represent and transform social life.

This chapter opens and closes with an examination of the formation and politicization of communities from below. In between it examines the constitution of dominant national Hindu and Muslim religious communities, focusing at once on the distinctive concerns that shaped legislation in each community and on the peculiar forms of state rationality that came to shape the treatment of both. In moving back and forth between these regional and national vantage points, it considers how local and regional politics became integral to the fashioning of national communities.

PART I: THE SHIFTING POLITICS OF BELONGING: DEFINING
COMMUNITY IN THE COLONIAL CONTEXT

The powerful consolidation of national religious communities in the interwar era relied on an understanding of community that represented a significant innovation from earlier meanings and concerns. The colonial history of the Khojas and the Kutchi Memons, two small, largely elite western Indian trading groups positioned at the margins of religious law, suggests how the concomitant expansion of colonial state power and emergence of a national Muslim community produced fundamental shifts in the actions, aims, self-perceptions, and self-definitions of members of these collectivities. For these groups, the inheritance rights of women had long formed a core subject of debate, definition, and fragmentation. Yet the intertwined meanings of women's inheritance and community fundamentally shifted from the mid-nineteenth century to the early twentieth. Tracing the history of these two groups, with a focus on the Khojas, shows how internal movements within these collectivities shifted from an early emphasis on using state institutions to recalibrate power and authority within the community, to a later goal of acquiring state recognition and definition.[6] Central to this later aim was an effort to bring the community firmly and completely under the jurisdiction of Muslim law, a goal that was finally achieved with the passing of the Shariat Act in 1937, discussed in detail in the next section of this chapter. Integral to these shifting politics and meanings of community was a change in the signification of women's inheritance rights, from a bald question of materially empowering or disempowering wealthy women within the community (coupled with a question of custom defining the particularity of the community), to a question of women's rights signaling the location or marginality of the community within a national and transnational community of Muslims. The process of clarifying the relationship of these groups to Hindu and to Muslim law by redefining the inheritance rights of "their" women, thus ultimately created for these two collectivities a new national political intelligibility as Muslims.[7]

The unusual legal trajectory of these groups began in October 1847, when the chief justice of the Supreme Court at Bombay, Sir Thomas Erskine Perry, wrote an opinion on two parallel cases that had been argued before him during the previous months. In what later became known as the *Kojahs and Memons' Case*,[8] Perry concluded that Khojas

---

[6] Although the two groups were consistently paired within colonial records, this text has focused on the Khojas because of the much stronger collection of sources available on them in comparison to the Kutchi Memons.

[7] This text follows Nandini Chatterjee's eloquent point that community is "a species of political argument, as well as a manipulative category of legal governance," in "English Law, Brahmo Marriage," fn. 77, p. 548.

[8] The Khoja case was two joined suits, *Hirbae v. Sonabae* and *Gungbae v. Sonabae*. The Memon case was *Rahimatbae v. Hadji Jussap*. The report of the case, cited as the *Kojahs and Memons' Case*, is found at Thomas Erskine Perry, *Cases Illustrative of Oriental Life, Decided in H. M. Supreme Court at Bombay* (London: S. Sweet, 1853; reprint, New Delhi: Asian Educational Services, 1988), p. 110.

and Kutchi Memons, who were primarily merchants and traders from
Gujarat and Kathiawad in western India, were Muslims who had converted from Hinduism several centuries before, and who followed
many of the customs of the broader, largely Hindu, social environment
of which they were a part. In particular, his decision established that
Khojas and Kutchi Memons practiced a custom relating to inheritance
that was "nearly analogous to the Hindu rule," and that such a custom
was valid and carried legal force. By the early 1860s, this decision had
come to be interpreted by the Bombay courts to the effect that Khojas
and Kutchi Memons were Muslims governed by Hindu laws of succession and inheritance.[9]

The custom at issue in these cases concerned a daughter's right to
inherit property from her father. Perry's decision established that among
Khojas and Kutchi Memons, daughters were customarily excluded from
the inheritance rights they would have had under Muslim law, where they
were entitled to half the share of a son. The Hindu law to which Perry
held their custom "analogous" excluded daughters entirely from the very
concept of the joint family as a property-holding unit. Perry's validation
of Khoja and Memon custom thus amounted to a decision in favor of the
property claims of distant male relatives over any claim of a daughter to
inherit from her father.[10]

Although Perry's decision had aimed to protect existing customary
practice among the Khojas and Memons, this decision was complicated
in a couple of respects. First, by establishing the legal principle that these
groups were governed, not by Shari'at, but by a custom that paralleled
Hindu inheritance practices, the case raised the fundamental question –
at once sociopolitical, legal, and religious – of whether these collectivities
could continue to observe such a custom and still be orthodox Muslims.
The question of the validity of such a non-Qur'anic practice had in fact
been argued before the chief justice in 1847, but from Perry's perspective,
the court was not bound to administer the Shari'at per se, but rather the
"laws and usages" of Muslims as they found them.[11] In Perry's words,

---

[9] *Gangabai v. Thavar Mulla* (1863) 1 Bom HCR 71. The full determination provided a
proviso for customs proven to the contrary, but placed the burden of proof on those
claiming a practice that diverged from *Hindu* (not Muslim) law.

[10] Carissa Hickling's impressive M.A. thesis, "Disinheriting Daughters: Applying Hindu
Laws of Inheritance to the Muslim Khoja Community of Bombay, 1847–1937,"
University of Manitoba, 1998, focuses on the question of the impact of this legal treat-
ment on daughters' and other female family members' claims.

[11] Perry, OC 110 at pp. 123–125.

the early British commitment to govern matters concerning religion and family according to the religion of the parties was framed "on political views, and without any reference to orthodoxy, or the purity of any religious belief."[12] Thus, in Perry's reading, colonial policy committed itself to upholding existing customs, even if such customs were at variance with textual orthodoxy, as had been explicitly established by Elphinstone's Regulations of 1827.

For members of such collectivities deemed divergent from normative practice, however, this legal designation of their hybrid or heterodox status did not operate as a simple statement of fact. It transformed self-perceptions, as well as the way the groups were perceived by various external observers. Perry's decision in the *Kojahs and Memons' Case* provided an opening for members of these groups to interrogate and debate what their practices were and should be.

Particularly among the Khojas, however, the legal case was also itself the product of a preexisting debate within the collectivity about proper practices that went back at least a generation.[13] From this perspective, Perry's decision operated in favor of a wealthy, reformist segment of the Khojas, and against the claim of their purported spiritual head, the hereditary Imam of the Ismaili Shi'as, the Aga Khan. Throughout the century that followed, opposing members of the collectivity repeatedly looked to colonial institutions to enforce their divergent claims. In this

---

[12] Ibid., 123.

[13] As discussed further in this section, the central issue revolved around the relationship of the community to the Ismaili Shi'a Imam, the Aga Khan. The Aga Khan had been based in Persia, but after his defeat in a rebellion against the Shah in 1840, he fled to Sindh, where he aided the British in their Afghanistan campaigns for several years, before arriving in Bombay in 1845. At the request of the colonial government, he moved to Calcutta for several years, returning to Bombay in 1848. While he was in Calcutta, he was represented in Bombay by his brother, Bawkar Khan, who also represented his interests in the 1847 Khoja cases decided by Perry, *Hirbae v. Sonabae* and *Gungbae v. Sonabai* (1847) Perry OC 110. The sudden presence of the Aga Khan in Bombay brought to a head tensions that had been simmering since at least 1820, particularly concerning his authority over the community and his claim to a percentage of the income of all Khojas (12.5 percent), which was resented particularly by the wealthiest Khojas, who came together in the Reform Party. This narrative on the history of the community, along with that in the next paragraph in the text, is drawn from Asghar Ali Engineer, *The Muslim Communities of Gujarat: An Exploratory Study of Bohras, Khojas and Memons* (Delhi: Ajanta Publications, 1989); Hickling, "Disinheriting Daughters"; Jim Masselos, "The Khojas: The Defining of Formal Membership Criteria during the Nineteenth Century," in *Caste and Social Stratification among Muslims in India*, edited by Imtiaz Ahmed (Delhi: Manohar, 1978): pp. 97–116; Amrita Shodhan, *A Question of Community: Religious Groups and Colonial Law* (Calcutta: Samya Press, 2001); Members of the Subcommittee of the Khoja Sunnat Summat, *An Account of The Khoja Sunnat Jamat*, Bombay (1969).

sense, the exceptional legal treatment of these communities as such was matched by their own intensive use of colonial law to determine community governance.

The term "reformist" is complicated here: Those who supported the winning side in this 1847 case, and who dubbed themselves the "Reform Party," sought to distance themselves from the group's "traditional" spiritual head, to establish English-language schools within the collectivity, and to link it more firmly to the broader, and primarily Sunni, collectivity of Muslims in India. Yet they were also the ones who supported retaining as customary or traditional the practice of excluding daughters from inheritance and restricting women property owners from transacting with their property. In contrast, it was the "traditional" leader, the Aga Khan, who sought to bring the group's practice more in line with orthodox Shi'a Islam, and to enhance the position of women within it.[14] Clearly the terms "reformist" and "traditionalist" could be used in a number of different ways in relation to these groups, and the dispute between the Aga Khan and those who resisted his authority, called the Barbhai, (literally "twelve brothers," after the twelve families who initially opposed him), involved a variety of positions that did not fit neatly into a single ideological pattern.[15] What the dispute, and ultimately the court case, involved, was a question about power and authority within the community, and about what defined membership in the community as such. These larger struggles came to center repeatedly and forcefully on women's property claims well into the 1880s, in part because both the Aga Khan and the Reform Party (or Barbhai) viewed women as strong and generous supporters of the Aga Khan. From the Reform Party perspective, then, undermining the position of the Aga Khan required, among other things, restricting the potential power and resources of women. At the same time, the focus on women's property claims represented a long-established means of marking community within the colonial legal order.

Throughout the middle decades of the nineteenth century, ongoing bids for power among the Khojas led to repeated engagements with the police and the courts.[16] These revolved around the question of access

---

[14] Ibid.

[15] Hickling, "Disinheriting Daughters," suggests that the Barbhai position, identifying themselves with Sunni Islam and at the same time calling for the legitimization of heterodox custom, reflected the fundamentally strategic or self-serving nature of their campaigns, which were more concerned with opposing the Aga Khan than with laying out a coherent position of their own.

[16] For a full discussion of these at-times violent clashes, and the ways in which they involved multiple segments of the colonial government, see Masselos, "The Khojas."

to Jamaat property, particularly the meeting hall, or *jamaatkhana*, the Mosque, and the graveyard.[17] This strife eventually led to another suit in 1866, which came before what was now the Bombay High Court and was decided by Justice Arnould in favor of the Aga Khan, holding that the latter was indeed the spiritual head of the Ismaili Shi'a community. This case, widely known as "the Aga Khan case,"[18] ultimately led to a schism in the group, with the Barbhai section breaking away to form a community of Sunni Khojas. This new community nonetheless retained its animosity toward the Aga Khan and his supporters, the Ismaili Shi'a Khojas.[19] Moreover, the Aga Khan's victory in this 1866 case did not alter the treatment of the group in inheritance and succession disputes; Perry's 1847 decision remained in effect. This meant that inheritance disputes among the Khojas continued to be adjudicated with reference to colonial Hindu law, despite the fact that the Aga Khan, who was now the legally recognized head of the community, had called for enforcing orthodox Shi'a practice. This disjuncture provided further occasions for partisan positioning, with the Aga Khan and the Reform Party waging themselves on opposite sides of each succession dispute that came before the High Court in an effort to undermine the power of the other.[20]

In this climate of ongoing struggle, the initial call for legislation to govern the community came not from members of the group itself, but from those in the colonial administration involved in adjudicating it. In 1875, the High Court ruled on the case of *Hirbai v. Gorbai*,[21] which occupied twenty-four sitting days, plus an additional four days on the appeal. This circumstance, a result of competing claims to customary inheritance between a widow and a mother (with the Aga Khan successfully supporting the mother), so underscored the difficulties involved in

---

[17] The Jamaat was the congregation of all Khoja adult men. This strife revolved around access to physical space as well as to specific ritual performances, and it should be considered in terms of the operation of caste regimes as well as other formulations of community, particularly since part of what was at stake was the excommunication of the Reform Party members, an action that subjected them to exclusions typical of caste excommunication.

[18] *The Advocate General* ex relatione *Daya Muhammad v. Muhammad Husen Huseni* (1867) Bom HCR 203. See also Asaf A. A. Fyzee, *Cases in the Muhammadan Law of India and Pakistan* (London: Oxford University Press, 1974).

[19] *An Account of the Khoja Sunnat Jamat* dates the establishment of their community to 1862.

[20] Notably, in these suits, the positions taken by both sides often ultimately showed little concern for conformity to Shari'at. The case of *Hirbai v. Gorbai* (1875) 12 Bom HCR 294, is a good example of this.

[21] *Hirbai v. Gorbai* (1875) 12 Bom HCR 294.

claims to community custom, that Chief Justice Westropp, in his appellate ruling, called on the government to form a legal commission with
the goal of drafting a law of inheritance and succession for the Khojas.[22]
The 1878 commission that resulted from this judicial behest was itself
from the beginning subject to the same partisan disputes, however. The
Aga Khan, who initially opposed the goal of legislation, was ultimately
represented on the commission by his son, Aga Ali Shah, the future Aga
Khan.[23] While the Aga Khan (I and II) sought through the commission
to ensure that the authority of this position and its claims to community property were protected, those associated with the former Reform
Party, now considered Sunni Khojas, sought to draft legislation precisely
with the goal of undermining the wealth, power, and authority of the
Aga Khan.[24] Ultimately, despite some effective compromises and multiple
draft proposals through the 1880s, the commission ended without con-
clusive results in the shape of legislation. After this legislative impasse, the
law governing Khojas for another half-century remained that developed
through the application and revision of judicial precedent, dating back to
Perry's 1847 decision.[25]

In this history of extended community struggle, spanning the middle
decades of the nineteenth century, the limitations of colonial political
space encouraged the parties to adopt the forms and modalities of colonial civil society – petitions, pamphlets, newspaper articles, public meet-
ings, and the like – and colonial institutions provided multiple venues for
jockeying over community claims. Yet appeals to the state formed part of

[22] Opinion of Chief Justice Sir Michael Westropp, confirming on appeal the judgment of
Justice Charles Sargent in *Hirbai v. Gorbai* (1875) 12 Bom HCR 294 at p. 322. The com-
mission was modeled on the Parsi Law Commission, which had led to the passing of the
Parsi Intestate Succession Act of 1865.

[23] Aga Ali Shah was Aga Khan for only a brief period: from his father's death in 1881 until
his own in 1885. The third Aga Khan, who held the position for a lengthy and critical
period, became actively involved in educational reform and also worked prominently
with Jinnah to advocate for separate electorates for Muslims.

[24] The primary matter of debate was again that of women's succession to property, with
the Reform Party attempting to postpone female heirs in the order of succession and
to limit their rights as owners. A secondary issue concerned the lapse of property when
there were no close heirs (heirs within four degrees of relatedness). Customarily such
property had lapsed to the Jamaat, whose property had been legally determined in the
Aga Khan case to belong to the Aga Khan. The Reform Party now called for such property to descend to the seventh degree of relatedness, or to be divided among male family
members, while the representatives of the colonial administration at least initially viewed
such property as properly lapsing to the Crown.

[25] A fundamental change in the application of the precedent law occurred in the 1910s,
with a series of High Court decisions by Justice Beaman, as discussed in this section.

a strategy directed at internal ends within the collectivity. Thus, it is significant that the call for legislation came initially not from the group itself, but from the colonial government, and moreover, that the Khojas who sat as representatives on the commission remained primarily concerned with defeating the claims of the opposing segment. In other words, neither party particularly pursued state legislation, and even as they became involved in legislative efforts, they remained focused on solidifying power and authority within the community.[26]

Beginning in the mid-1880s, however, these features would change, producing a crucial shift in the relationship between the Khojas and the state. Decades of appeals by their members to the state had created a situation in which disputes that once had been regularly settled within the Jamaat were now typically brought before the colonial courts.[27] This trend increasingly marginalized the Jamaat and correspondingly strengthened the state, as was certainly the intention of the reformists.[28] As a result of this gradual shift in power, by the 1880s state definition became the crucial target for all competitors who sought to establish themselves as protectors of the community.[29]

Central to this process was a shift in the meaning and reach of community itself. A product of the synergy of late-nineteenth-century colonial governance and of broad internal movements among Muslims in India and transnationally to reform their personal practice, community mobilization and reform among the Khojas and Kutchi Memons came

---

[26] Historians have explored this history as a key example either of nineteenth-century formulations of community membership, as in the work of Jim Masselos, or of colonial sociopolitical structurings, as Shodhan emphasizes.

[27] Frank Conlon, "The Khojas and the Courts: A Study of the Impact of British Justice in India upon the Social and Religious Life and Institutions of a Muslim Community," M.A. thesis (University of Minnesota, 1963), p. 42, also confirms this point. I am grateful to the author for providing me with a copy of this important unpublished work.

[28] The Sunni Khojas continued to operate through their own local Jamaats, but also sought increasing control over them through the election of Jamaat officials. Ibid., 37–38; also, *An Account of the Khoja Sunnat Jamat*. It is notable that in this treatment of the Jamaat, the High Court at once repeatedly bolstered the position of the Aga Khan and of the Ismaili Khoja Jamaat, even as it also reaffirmed the validity of custom within the Khojas and Memons (against the Aga Khan's claims) and explicitly lowered the bar for the burden of proof of an alleged community custom. This is in contrast to the court's treatment of subaltern caste custom discussed in Chapter 4. See Opinion of Chief Justice Westropp, *Hirbai v. Gorbai*, (1875) 12 Bom HCR 294 at pp. 321–322.

[29] Shodhan, *A Question of Community*, suggests a changing colonial treatment of "community" from a locus of political authority and contestation to a site of prepolitical, primordial attachments, a sort of reverse transition in colonial treatment from *gesellschaft* to *gemeinschaft*.

to acquire a different valence and an expanded horizon. In linking up with broader Muslim reform and revival movements, beginning in the 1880s powerful strands within the Khojas and Kutchi Memons (especially the latter) increasingly came to identify their legal treatment as Hindu as their primary problem, and they actively sought to establish both their own conformity to Muslim law and colonial recognition of their status as orthodox Muslims.[30] This history fits easily within existing scholarly narratives that emphasize the rigidification of religious identities and efforts to "purify" personal and community practice in the late nineteenth and early twentieth centuries.[31] Indeed this is, in part, a story of bringing these collectivities more firmly under the logic of religious identity.

Yet it is also a story of the shifting political meanings of community. With these movements, there was a crucial, if subtle, shift in the locus of debate, from a dispute about the nature of community membership to a concern with how the community was recognized within colonial law.[32] Thus, in 1884 another small subsection of Khojas, who had broken away from the Ismailis in the late 1870s to form the Ithn'Ashari Shi'a community, called for the Khoja Law Commission to exempt them from any legislation that diverged from Muslim law.[33] Then in 1885, members of the Kutchi Memon community sought for the first time to pass legislation that would bring them under Muslim law.[34] These actions reflected a shift in which the legal status of the community as such became critical to its claims in relation to the emergent national community of Muslims. For example, in a mass public meeting to address their legal and religious status held in Bombay on the April 12, 1884, the Kutchi Memons discussed and subsequently sent a memorial to Viceroy Earl Dufferin and to the *Times of India* for publication. The memorial, signed by Hajee Hashem Hajee Abdullah Nooranee and Hajee Tayeb Hajee Rahematullah, observed that

---

[30] MSA, JD (1884) 27/668, pp. 353–366; JD (1885) 25/436, pp. 19, 114–115, 281.

[31] Barbara Daly Metcalf, *Islamic Revival in British India: Deoband, 1860–1900* (Princeton, NJ: Princeton University Press, 1982); Kenneth Jones, *Arya Dharm: Hindu Consciousness in Nineteenth-Century Punjab* (Berkeley: University of California Press, 1976).

[32] See Masselos, "The Khojas" for an important early article tracing the first part of this history, the process of establishing community boundaries among the Khojas.

[33] MSA, JD (1884) 27/668, pp. 353–389. In response to this appeal, the draft legislation included a provision enabling those who desired to declare themselves subject to the Muslim law of succession beginning in 1885. MSA, JD (1885) 25/436.

[34] MSA, JD (1885) 26/1424. The Memons were Sunnis, whereas the Ismaili Khojas, as well as the Ithn'Ashari Khojas, were Shi'as (the Ismailis believing in seven revealed Imams, whereas the Ithn'Asharis believe in twelve).

"by the light of [Eastern and Western learning] your Petitioners feel that they are awakened to a new sense of duty not only towards themselves but towards their posterity and their religion ..." and that "these hardships [of the current legal treatment] are still more hard to bear in consequence of the religious convictions of your Petitioners that as true and orthodox Mussalmans they ought to govern themselves according to the law laid down in the Koran and the Muhammadan law-books, and that to consider the laws as laid down in the Koran as not divine or as not obligatory ... amounts to infidelity."[35] Such appeals reflected a new self-consciousness regarding their own earlier practices. It also reflected the compulsions of contemporary politics in which the claim to community at once served as a demand for internal autonomy and simultaneously required state recognition.

In this shift, the possibility of framing oneself first and foremost as Muslim rather than Khoja or Memon offered a different conceptualization and politics of community. This politicization of community operated on at least two levels: (1) subsuming local attachments and particular identifications to a broader, more homogenous Muslim identity, and (2) also reframing this broader community not as a terrain of everyday practice and debate, but as a jurisdictional entity that paralleled, mediated, and competed with the state. On the road to unexceptional Muslimness, the Khojas and the Kutchi Memons moved in both of these ways from one concept of community to another.

This new politics involved a dual address: at once to the community (in this case, both the communities of Khojas or Memons and the broader Muslim community), and to the colonial state. If officials within the colonial state sought to conceptualize the Jamaat, like other caste assemblies, as an Indian form of civil society, leading members of the various segments of the Khojas and Memons increasingly adopted a secularized language of rights and of legal subjecthood. In deploying this colonial modality (at least to some extent), however, community mobilization also increasingly sought to replace an emphasis on community particularity with broader claims on the state of a homogenous Hinduism and Islam. This homogenizing form of community, with its demographic model of representation, emphasized the compulsions of both birth and belief, as the layered ways in which people were newly

---

[35] MSA, JD (1885) 63/1170 (unpaginated), "Extract from the *Times of India* issue of 1st July, 1885" and "Petition of the Undersigned Members of the Cutchee Memon Muhammadan Community of the City of Bombay," dated May 29, 1885.

interpellated as political subjects. At the same time, it posited community as a form of compulsory jurisdiction.

While legislation to change the legal status of these communities was not successfully enacted until the 1920s and 1930s, in the 1910s, a set of extended Bombay High Court opinions written by Justice Beaman attempted to put these communities on a different legal footing. In the 1915 Khoja case of *Mahomed v. Datu Jaffer*,[36] and in a Kutchi Memon case two years later, *Advocate General of Bombay v. Jimbabai*,[37] Justice Beaman revisited the legal history of these two communities dating back to Perry's fateful 1847 decision, as an object lesson in the dangers of judicial precedent. In Beaman's view, Perry had never intended for the Khojas and Kutchi Memons to be treated as Hindu in matters of inheritance and succession, but only to recognize a single custom and to note, as an aside, that it was consonant with Hindu practice. Unfortunately, later judgments had disastrously misinterpreted and extended Perry's opinion, according to Beaman,[38] and the operation of judicial precedent rendered this false common knowledge increasingly difficult to resist, not least because members of these groups themselves came to take it for granted that they were governed by Hindu laws of inheritance and succession, and to make decisions concerning their property accordingly. Beaman, responding to the increasingly powerful movements of the day to bring these groups under Muslim law, viewed it as unconscionable that they had ever been subjected to anything else.[39] Moreover, for the justice, in matters of property, Hindu law was itself a travesty bordering on the offensive. Deploying what will by now be familiar rhetoric, Beaman excoriated the concept of joint ancestral property, and particularly what he referred to as the "doctrine of the nucleus," which tied all later earnings by family members to any benefit received from the nucleus of ancestral property. In Beaman's view, this worked against all notions of individual initiative and personal gain, rendering Hindus poorly suited for capitalism and the modern world.[40] That even beyond Hindus, Muslims should be saddled

---

[36] *Jan Mahomed v. Datu Jaffer* (1915) ILR 38 Bom 449.

[37] *Advocate General of Bombay v. Jimbabai* (1917) ILR 41 Bom 181.

[38] Beaman subjected to particular scorn the opinions of Justice Sausse in the Khoja case of *Gangabai v. Thavar Mulla* (1863) 1 Bom HCR 71, and of Justice Scott in the Kutchi Memon case of *Mahomed Sidick v. Haji Ahmed* (1886) ILR 10 Bom 1. Nor did he have particularly good things to say about Chief Justice Westropp's opinion in the Khoja case of *Shivji Hasam v. Datu Mavji Khoja* (1874) 12 Bom HCR 281. See Beaman's extended opinion in *Jan Mahomed v. Datu Jaffer* (1915) ILR 38 Bom 449.

[39] *Jan Mahomed v. Datu Jaffer* (1915) ILR 38 Bom 449 at pp. 459–461, 464.

[40] Ibid. See especially where the justice refers to "the nightmare of the Hindu law of the joint family hanging over all [the Khoja man's] business activities," 464; and "the most

with such a burden seemed to Beaman a violation of justice, equity, and good conscience in the extreme.

Beaman was sympathetic to the efforts within these groups, particularly strong among the Kutchi Memons, to pass legislation that would enable them to declare themselves subject to Muslim law. In the meantime, however, he was himself subject to the same principle of precedent as those justices before him. His solution was, first, to note that much of what had been treated as precedent was actually obiter dicta, not relevant to the actual legal issue before the judge in those cases.[41] After dismissing some of what he viewed as the most problematic rulings in this manner, the justice then confirmed that these communities were indeed subject to Hindu laws of inheritance and succession, but *as applied to self-acquired property*.[42] In other words, all of the limitations placed on joint property or ancestral property no longer applied, even to property that Khojas or Kutchi Memons themselves referred to as joint property. This, combined with the existing judicial principle that allowed members of these groups to bequeath their entire separate property by will, would enable them to distribute their property according to the dictates of Shari'at. Ironically, this solution was itself a violation of Shari'at, which limited the portion of property that a Muslim could bequeath by will to one-third. This irony was not lost on Beaman, nor on the witnesses in these cases who testified to this effect, but such was the limit of the possible until 1920 for Kutchi Memons, and 1937 for Khojas.[43]

In 1920, the passing of the Cutchi Memons Act (Act XLVI of 1920) gave members of this group the option of declaring themselves subject to Muslim laws of inheritance. This right was confirmed in the Cutchi Memon (Amendment) Act, Act XXXIV of 1923. Moreover, ongoing pressure in this direction from within the group led to the further Cutchi Memon Act (X of 1938), which declared that henceforth, and retroactively in the case of wills, all Kutchi Memons would be governed by Muslim law in matters of succession and inheritance.[44] By this time, both the

---

[41] *Jan Mahomed v. Datu Jaffer* (1915) ILR 38 Bom 449 at pp. 458–459.

[42] Ibid., 511.

[43] *Advocate General of Bombay v. Jimbabai* (1917) ILR 41 Bom 181 at pp. 206–214, 221–262.

[44] This legislation was necessary because the Shariat Act only applied to intestate succession and Kutchi Memons, like Khojas, had been allowed to bequeath their whole property by will. The combination provided a significant opportunity for evading the terms of Shari'at, should an individual have been so inclined.

dangerous and injurious of all the features of the Hindu law of the joint family, the doctrine of nucleus," 487; also pp. 486, 493, 505–506, 509. See Birla, *Stages of Capital*, for an extended discussion of such colonial views of the Indian family firm.

Khojas and the Kutchi Memons had successfully had themselves brought within the homogenizing dictates of Anglo-Mohammedan law through the 1937 Moslem Personal Law (Shariat) Application Act, which made it compulsory on them to follow the dictates of Shari'at rather than custom, on all issues concerning inheritance and succession other than adoption, wills, and legacies.[45] In so doing, they achieved a desired homogenization with a broader imagined Muslim community, but via expanding state regulation. Personal law became a key site of politicization and community formation precisely for the ways it brought social life into the field of vision of the state. Nevertheless, the Shariat Act which produced this outcome emerged from additional political compulsions.

PART II: THE USES OF THE STATE IN FORGING THE NATION: THE POLITICS OF HINDU AND MUSLIM PERSONAL LAW

The Moslem Personal Law (Shariat) Application Act (Act XXVI of 1937) was debated in the central Legislative Assembly and passed within six months of another piece of legislation applying to Hindus, the Hindu Women's Rights to Property Act (HWRPA) (Act XVIII of 1937). Both acts were framed as measures to enhance the property rights of women, and they were clearly considered in relation to each other, with assembly members at times commenting on the parallels between the two, or on the superior benefit for women provided by one personal law over the other.[46] Both also operated to consolidate national religious communities and to solidify the status of Hindu and Muslim law as parallel streams of law. The acts positioned women firmly within Hindu and Muslim communities with their separate systems of personal law, while in the form in which they were ultimately passed, their actual effects on women's property rights were quite narrow. As Archana Parashar has argued, the aims and effects of both pieces of legislation had not been to improve women's rights or move toward female equality, but rather to strengthen and unify the community as such.[47]

---

[45] In the case of adoption, wills, and legacies, a declaration submitting oneself and one's descendants to the Shari'at was rendered optional on parties.

[46] In particular, a couple of the Muslim members hailed the rights accorded by Shari'at not just to widows but to daughters, who were excluded from the Hindu legislation as it ultimately passed. See, for example, speech by Sir Muhammad Yakub in the debates on the Hindu Women's Rights to Property Bill, Legislative Assembly Debates, February 4, 1937, p. 513.

[47] Archana Parashar's important account does not draw out the distinctive contexts and aims of each, however. Archana Parashar, *Women and Family Law Reform in*

This conclusion is supported by the limited role major women's organizations played in this legislation. In the case of the Hindu act, the legislation was the latest in a series of efforts by liberal assembly members to enhance women's legal rights, especially property rights. These Hindu law bills were initially framed alongside broader efforts to alter the nature of the Hindu male coparcenary, further resignifying coparcenary property and expanding individual rights thereto, as discussed in Chapter 3.[48] In the early 1930s, in the wake of the passage of the Child Marriage Restraint Act, Har Bilas Sarda (the author of that act) introduced further legislation to establish the right of Hindu widows to a share of their husband's property, but this was soundly defeated in 1932.[49] The All India Women's Conference (AIWC) supported such legislation, and went further, calling for comprehensive legislation and the establishment of an "unofficial committee to investigate and reform Hindu law," in its totality as it affected women.[50] In 1934, the AIWC declared a Women's Legal Disabilities Day, at the instigation of Renuka Ray.[51] Yet in contrast to the active role both the AIWC and the Women's India Association had played in the agitation in favor of the Sarda Act, on this issue their voices seem to have had little impact, and their involvement in the context of the HWRPA and the Shariat Act remained quite limited, although the Shariat Bill claimed to have the support of Muslim women's organizations.[52] Moreover, the

---

India: Uniform Civil Code and Gender Equality (New Delhi: Sage Publications, 1992), pp. 77*ff*, 144–150.

[48] The 1928 Hindu Inheritance (Removal of Disabilities) Act (Act XII of 1928) removed the exclusions from inheritance of persons suffering from congenital disabilities or chronic disease (such as leprosy and congenital blindness). The 1930 Hindu Gains of Learning Act (Act XXX of 1930) rendered the use of family property for education irrelevant to later earnings based on that education. Such property would now be classed as self-acquired rather than ancestral property. In the midst of this legislation, the 1929 Law of Hindu Inheritance (Amendment) Act (Act II of 1929) introduced additional female relatives and relatives through the female line in the line of heirs, such as son's daughter, daughter's daughter, and sister and sister's son, except in Bombay where they were already so recognized. See discussions in Eleanor Newbigin, "A Post-Colonial Patriarchy?," and in Sreenivas, *Wives, Widows and Concubines*.

[49] Nair, *Women and Law*, 198.

[50] Ibid., 199.

[51] The day was fixed as November 24, 1934. Ray was a Congress member and was later appointed to the Legislative Assembly as the AIWC representative, where she would take part in the debates on the Hindu Code Bill in the 1940s. Basu and Ray, *Women's Struggle*, 63*ff*.

[52] The Statement of Objects and Reasons for the Shariat Act claimed that "Muslim women's organizations have condemned customary law as it adversely affects their rights and have demanded that the Muslim Personal Law (Shari'at) should be made applicable to them." Cited in Nair, *Women and Law*, 193.

contemporary liberal feminist critique of the social and legal discrimination against women as a matter exceeding the terms of particular personal laws – as indeed a matter of women's legal disability across all the systems of personal law – were largely ignored by the state.[53] These pieces of legislation were the product of other agencies and interests.

The acts reflected the atmosphere of heightened communal jockeying and efforts at nationalizing and consolidating religious communities, but in fact both bills were introduced by members who were marginal to the major national parties. G. V. Deshmukh, who introduced the Hindu Women's Rights to Property Bill, was one of several liberal assembly members (such as Har Bilas Sarda) who had introduced similar measures, none of whom were major figures in the Congress Party. Nor did Congress members play an avid role in support of the legislation. In contrast to this liberal orientation, the Shariat Bill was introduced by H. M. Abdulla, member from the Punjab, and was a product of campaigns by the orthodox association of 'ulama, the Jamiat-e-'Ulema in the Punjab and northwest India to eradicate the operation of custom in place of the Shari'at, as had been established by colonial law. These orthodox scholars did not support the Muslim League and would oppose the creation of Pakistan up until 1947, fearing it would impose a secular state on Muslims. Likewise, although Jinnah, as the leader of the Muslim League, would ultimately play a major role in ushering the Shariat Act through, many League members, including Jinnah, were initially tepid in their reception of it, and Jinnah's eventual efforts on behalf of the legislation must be understood in the context of the aftermath of the 1937 elections, when he desperately needed to secure support for the Muslim League in the Punjab (where the League had been trounced by the Unionist Party), and to establish its Muslim bona fides.

Moreover, in content as well, the external parallels between the two acts are in some respects deceiving. Although both were framed as measures that would expand women's rights, the Muslim legislation sought the enforcement of Shari'at and represented the concerns of the

---

[53] Parashar, who focuses on the later postcolonial Hindu Code Bill debates, argues that women's organizations played only a marginal role in this earlier legislation, and that the legislation primarily reflected the interests of the state. Parashar, *Women and Family Law*, 133–134. Nair criticizes Parashar for minimizing the agency of women's organizations in this legislation, but argues that they did not push harder for such legislation due to their own class status and a desire not to disturb the dominant position of their men. This argument is not entirely convincing, given the staunch critiques these women launched both at the time and later. Nair, *Women and Law*, 199–200.

conservative *'ulema*, while the Hindu legislation was promoted by liberal reformers and sought to alter the standard legal interpretation of the *Mitakshara*. Perhaps most significantly, however, the two acts reflected the distinctive problematics of Hindu and Muslim claims to the status of national community. In this context, Muslim politics centered on forging a unified national community grounded in Muslim identity, while Hindu efforts involved the rather different problem of inequality within Hinduism. These legislative acts thus reflected at once the forging of parallel, overarching national Hindu and Muslim communities, and the unique conundrums of each that came to the fore at this moment. This became apparent in the Legislative Assembly debates.

The Moslem Personal Law (Shariat) Application Act: Nationalization via the State

The original proponents of the Muslim legislation were primarily concerned with establishing the legal force of Shari'at, and their own role as interpreters thereof. When Jinnah abandoned his initial opposition to the bill and threw his support behind the legislation, however, these original goals were sidetracked by the divergent aims of the Muslim League, which sought through the legislation to further the League's efforts to define Muslims as a political community. From Jinnah's perspective, the legislation was critical to "the needs of the day," which he defined as legal uniformity and a clear jurisdictional claim over all persons classed as Muslim.[54] Although totalizing claims over their members from within the community were complicit with and supported by the modern colonial state, by the 1930s, the familiar assertion of the jurisdiction of religious community had a different valence for Jinnah and the Muslim League, now geared toward countering their treatment as a political minority by asserting their status as a nation parallel and

---

[54] Legislative Assembly Debates, September 16, 1937, p. 1832. Jinnah had also opposed an earlier version of the legislation and sought changes that would limit its potentially detrimental effects on the interests of north Indian landlords. See discussion in Nair, *Women and Law*, 193; also Parashar, *Women and Family Law*, 149–150. Part of this difference in the debates on the Hindu and Muslim Personal Law Acts may have reflected the fact that some of the controversies surrounding the application of Hindu law to diverse communities had been settled earlier, primarily in the 1860s and 1870s, when elite-caste Hindu norms were extended to a variety of non-elite communities, as discussed in Chapter 4. The exclusion from Hindu law sought by communities like the Khojas and Kutchi Memons may thus be viewed in one sense, and ironically, as the final stage in this process of creating a unified social body subject to Hindu law.

equivalent to a Hindu national community.[55] Moreover, the initial aims of those who introduced the legislation were further sidetracked by the state, which treated these new legislative efforts no differently from other elements of personal law – as a matter under the jurisdiction of its own courts, rather than as expanding the power of the *'ulema* or as removing Muslims from state jurisdiction.

This divergence in goals became starkly apparent in a related piece of legislation introduced two years later, the 1939 Muslim Women's Divorce Act, which had similarly been a product of *'ulema* efforts to prevent Muslim women from using apostasy from Islam as their only means of exit from a bad marriage (in accordance to the tenets of the Hanafi school of law, which was the main school followed in the subcontinent). One of the major Deoband scholars, Maulana Ashraf 'Ali Thanawi, had prepared a treatise drawing on the provisions of other schools, primarily the Maliki, to establish provisions for Muslim women to attain a divorce without apostasy, and the Muslim Women's Divorce Act effectively rendered apostasy no longer sufficient to dissolve her marriage.[56] While this legislative effort fit within contemporary communal concerns with demography and control over women's sexuality, it diverged significantly from the standard Deobandi position of carving out a space of Muslim life and governance divorced from the state.[57] Indeed, integral to the aims of the legislation's promoters was that only a Muslim judge should be able to grant such a divorce. When these terms were rejected by the colonial state, the *'ulema* sought to have the bill withdrawn, but Jinnah refused to do so. The trajectories of these two pieces of legislation on Muslim personal law thus highlight the divergent positions and aims among Muslim promoters of such legislation, as well as the contradictions involved in attempting to utilize the state machinery to produce a national community under Muslim – but not state – jurisdiction. Nonetheless, these diverse proponents of the Muslim legislation attempted to use the state in the service of constituting a national community, and positioned Shari'at as at once proxy for and competitor with the state.

---

[55] This was part of what was at stake in the language of Hindus and Muslims as "two nations" within India. See Ayesha Jalal, *The Sole Spokesman: Jinnah, the Muslim League, and the Demand for Pakistan* (Cambridge: Cambridge University Press, 1985); Devji, "Minority as Political Form."

[56] Fareeha Khan, "Traditionalist Approaches to Shari'ah Reform: Maulana Ashraf 'Ali Thanawi's Fatwa on Women's Right to Divorce," Ph.D. diss. (University of Michigan, 2008); also Parashar, *Women and Family Law*, 151–158.

[57] Metcalf, *Islamic Revival*.

Resistance to this legislation from among Muslim members of the Legislative Assembly centered precisely on its universalizing claims. Those who benefited from legal recognition of inheritance practices that diverged from Shari'at norms argued that Muslims followed different legal schools and principles, and that a singular law could not be applied uniformly to all Muslims. This effort to exclude reference to a singular Shari'at proved politically untenable, however.[58] More successful was an effort to limit the substantive reach of the legislation. This effort was supported both by Jinnah and by the imperial government, and it concerned the use of the word "law" in the first line of the original bill, which was as follows: "Notwithstanding any custom, usage, or law to the contrary, in all questions regarding succession, special property of females, marriage, dower … the rule of decision in cases where the parties are Muslims shall be the Moslem personal law (Shari'at)." The logic of including the word "law" alongside "custom" and "usage" in the first line derived from historical conditions in the Punjab, the home of H. M. Abdulla, who introduced the bill. In the Punjab and in several other contexts (such as for Khojas and Kutchi Memons), it was established law that custom superseded the textual dictates of Hinduism and Islam. It therefore appeared imperative to include the word "law" in order to effectively halt the operation of customs that denied daughters and widows inheritance rights, and to close off any loopholes to the application of Shari'at.

Yet by including the word "law," the bill opened the door for a far more expansive reading of Shari'at. That is, Shari'at covered most aspects of life, not just domestic relations. Would the law exempt Muslims involved in domestic suits from the terms of the adjectival law, such as the Registration Act, or of the Statute of Limitations, insofar as such legislation diverged from Shari'at? Or, cutting closer to the limits of the "domestic," was the age of majority subject to secular law or Shari'at? The original bill had included adoption, wills, gifts, and legacies in its purview, all of which had specific dictates in Shari'at, but these were excluded by the Select Committee and accordingly amended out of the legislation. What were the limits to which the Shari'at would extend? This was also the tenor of questions posed both by the government-appointed

[58] See the objections of Sir Muhammad Yamin Khan, who represented the region of Agra, especially the wealthy north Indian landlords, or *taluqdars*, who benefited from rules of succession that held their property to be impartible and to pass by primogeniture, rather than according to the shares specified by Shari'at. Legislative Assembly Debates, September 9, 1937, pp. 1430, 1434–1436, 1439, 1441–1443.

member R. F. Mudie, who proposed his own amendment to ensure the preservation of the adjectival law,[59] as well as by M. S. Aney, member from Berar, known for his Hindu nationalist leanings: "We must know whether this Bill is intended to exempt the Muslims from the operation of most of the general laws which govern Hindus and Muslims today and which are not of the nature of the personal law at all."[60] This question was thus explicitly about the extent to which Muslims would be subject to the myriad laws that had come to shape the rule of property beyond the framework of personal law, but it was also symbolically or expansively a question of whether Muslims would be subject to the general laws of the land, or would really come to be an internal nation, governed by its own laws.

Jinnah's response to this problem was to propose an amendment that simply removed the words "or law" from the bill, leaving the introductory phrase to read, "Notwithstanding any custom or usage to the contrary."[61] This involved both a pragmatic adjustment and a tactical maneuver that strengthened Jinnah's aim of creating a national Muslim community defined as such by law. The concerns of those such as H. M. Abdulla were eventually allayed by the addition of a further amendment that explicitly withdrew the legal status of custom. In the end, those who opposed Jinnah's amendment were those, primarily in provinces in north India, where custom that contravened Shari'at had not previously had the force of law. They now worried that this act in fact limited the application of Shari'at from what it had been before (e.g., not extending to adoption, wills, gifts, etc.). As Maulvi Muhammad Abdul Ghani, from Tirhut Division in Bihar, exclaimed,

> The Mover of the Bill as well as a few of my Muslim friends will excuse me to say that they will have the only consolation that they have got the Shariat Bill passed by this House and thus they can save their face before the Muslim community. I don't like to be a party to such a crippled measure which gives nothing but name.... The Mussalmans of India do not like to be so coerced as to accept a crippled measure like this which is unjustly going to be forced upon them through their representatives.[62]

---

[59] Legislative Assembly Debates, September 16, 1937, pp. 1835–1845. Mudie also supported other limitations to the legislation.

[60] Ibid., 1829.

[61] This amendment was supported by a majority of the Select Committee reporting on the original bill.

[62] Legislative Assembly Debates, September 16, 1937, p. 1854.

In raising the specter of the coercions of political representation, Ghani's critique of the bill's limitations highlighted the way the people were held hostage to the political theater of the law that undermined their forms of life even as it spoke in their name. Yet in the end, those who would abstain from the symbolic importance of voting for the bill were few, and the assembly's agreement to this amendment paved the way for the passage of the bill into law.

This successful limitation underscores that although several members of the Legislative Assembly had called for the application to Muslims of "the whole of Shari'at," in fact nobody sought the application of Shari'at in all aspects of life for which a Shari'at principle existed, but only in those matters deemed related to the family. As passed, the Shariat Act established that Muslims would be governed by Muslim personal law (Shariat) in matters of marriage, divorce, women's property, and inheritance, notwithstanding any custom or usage to the contrary. Agricultural property had to be excluded from its purview, since the Government of India Act of 1935 had rendered agricultural property a provincial subject, no longer under the jurisdiction of the central legislature.[63] Nor did it attempt to establish Shariat as the basis for other areas of civil law, such as contracts or debts, or for any aspect of criminal law.

Moreover, although delimiting the domestic was itself an issue of debate, the selective application of Shari'at to domestic matters meant that the legislation – and the mediating role of community – would inevitably operate unevenly: As the members of the Legislative Assembly themselves emphasized, the bill aimed first and foremost to enhance the property claims of women. The bill was presented as restoring to Muslims, and especially to Muslim women, the benefit of their own law, a law that inherently provided for the just and humane treatment of wives, widows, and daughters, of which they had been deprived due to the operation of customary laws. By its enactment, a widow would have a right to one-eighth of her deceased husband's property, while a daughter would have a right to half the share of a son. Thus, on the one hand, while the legislation sought to enhance women's property rights, it did not seek equality for women within the family. On the other hand, while the bill conceptualized religious law as restricted in its sphere of authority, it would play a crucial role for women far more than for men in defining

---

[63] For a discussion of the importance of agricultural property for substantive rights for women, see Agarwal, *A Field of One's Own.*

their legal status, their claims, and their relationship to the state. This involved its own ironies, since the initiators of this legislation (though not Jinnah) had originally promoted it precisely in the interests of removing Muslim women from colonial jurisdiction and the colonial courts and placing them under the more exclusive jurisdiction of the *'ulama*. This, despite its reinforcement of the linkage between women and community, the legislation would not do.

The Hindu Women's Rights to Property Act: The Problem of Democracy

The diverse Muslim supporters of the Shariat Act shared a concern with defining and redefining the jurisdiction of the religious community; this constituted a problem not only of reach, but of competition with the colonial state, with the community seeking to posit itself as a potential state or as a proxy state. In contrast, the Hindu Women's Rights to Property Act, which sought to alter by legislation the standard judicial interpretation of women's property rights under the *Mitakshara*, thereby aimed to align Hindu law with the broader ethical position claimed by a proleptic secular liberal nation-state. Its concerns were less with occupying the position of the state than with creating congruence between an imagined liberal democracy and its dominant ethico-religious law.

The provisions of G. V. Deshmukh's original Hindu Women's Rights to Property Bill had been expansive in the property rights they sought for Hindu women. In the Select Committee, however, these were considerably cut down. Whereas the original bill had aimed to provide inheritance rights for daughters as well as for widows, the provisions concerning daughters were ultimately excluded. Also cut from the final bill were provisions to grant a widow an absolute estate in the property she inherited from her husband. Moreover, as with the Shariat Act, the bill necessarily excluded agricultural property. In its final form, the act would simply establish that a Hindu widow governed by *Mitakshara* law, living in a joint, undivided family, who had previously had a right only to maintenance, now had the right to call for partition from the coparceners, and to claim a share in the family property (other than agricultural property) equal to that of a son. (Widows already had these rights under the *Dayabhaga* system that prevailed in Bengal and Assam.) Even this share she could not alienate without necessity, and any remaining property reverted on her death to her husband's heirs. As one of the Legislative

Assembly members commented, the bill had been cut down by fifteen and a half annas, and what was left was a mere one-half anna.[64]

In the context of this pared-down legislation, and given that it sought to grant different rights than what was established in the *Mitakshara*, the terms of debate focused on questions of cultural authenticity and cultural change. More centrally, however, the debate revolved around the potential equality of different family members and the problem of the widow's autonomy, in ways similar to those detailed in Chapter 3. Its supporters framed the legislation as both improving the deplorable condition of Hindu widows, and as returning to widows their original rights. Rather than presenting the legislation as instituting social change or reform, Deshmukh went out of his way to insist on the traditional, orthodox nature of his proposals. This long-standing reformist strategy also took on a particular nationalist twist in this context, however. In his narrative, true Hindu law and the true rights of Hindu widows had been abrogated by the colonial interpretation of Hindu law. The British had imported their own ideas about inheritance, as well as their own legal terms: survivorship, reversioner, limited estate – and these had been incorporated into what even Hindus now understood as Hindu laws, to the great detriment of Hindu women. At its limit, this argument led to a rhetorical strategy that attempted to usurp the position of its conservative political opponents. Thus, Deshmukh called for the establishment of pure Hindu law, and decried the "hybrid, or mongrel law" the "half-caste laws" that had come to be treated as Hindu law.[65] Likewise, he proudly advanced his status as a Brahmin "not only by birth but also by mentality,"[66] as a way of asserting his legitimate authority to debate the real nature of Hindu law.

Deshmukh's second strategy focused on the potential equivalence of women and men within the textual authorities. Thus, he commented several times that "Mitakshara does not make any difference between male and female heirs. All these distinctions are of subsequent growth."[67] Similarly, he argued that "there is not the least doubt ... that the old law givers gave the right of co-ownership to the wife."[68] Yet he asserted that

---

[64] There are sixteen annas to the rupee. This statement was actually made by one of the bill's opponents, Babu Baijnath Bajoria, representing the commercial community of Marwaris. Legislative Assembly Debates, February 4, 1937, 500.

[65] Ibid., 488.

[66] Ibid.

[67] Ibid., 492.

[68] Ibid., 493.

"from this position of co-ownership, she was degraded. It went to sub-ownership and then from sub-ownership she has been reduced to a state of maintenance and residence.... This is the law under which we live today, and yet we think that we are being governed by the Hindu law."[69]

What Deshmukh's bill ultimately intended to do was to make the widow a member of the hitherto male coparcenary. For supporters of this legislation, the morality of an originary female co-ownership and equality extended not just to the relationship between husband and wife, but also to that between widow and son, and between son and daughter.[70] In each case, the position of the woman or girl was asserted as equal and equivalent to – even substitutable for – a man or boy. As Husenbhai Abdullabhai Laljee questioned, "Why should two children of one father and one mother be treated separately?"[71] Yet, it was precisely the non-equivalence of different family members that opponents of the legislation took for granted, and that was ultimately enshrined in the act: The exclusions in the final bill demonstrated the refusal to equate daughters with sons, or the nature of a widow's rights of ownership with those of a husband or a son.

Opponents of the legislation, even in this limited form, focused on the autonomy (however partial) that it would bestow on the widow: the right to call for partition of the family property, the rights she would have to transact with the property during her lifetime, and the extent to which she could stand in the place of her deceased husband as heir to his share of joint family property.[72] Of these, the primary debate turned on the right to call for partition, which opponents aimed to further restrict to cases where a widow could prove maltreatment or dissension within the family. In support of these arguments, they pointed to the vulnerability and ignorance of widows, which rendered them subject to easy manipulation, whether by her own family relations or by outside schemers. Such a widow could be induced to call for partition of the family property, and then squander it away, losing it all to the interested parties who surrounded her. Indeed, these debates continually returned to implicit assumptions about the inadequacy and incapacity of the widow as a

[69] Ibid., 495.
[70] See also speeches by Sir Nripendra Sircar, N. M. Joshi, and Husenbhai Abdullabhai Laljee. Ibid., 485–515.
[71] Ibid., 514. Laljee was himself a member of one of the communities treated as Muslim subject to Hindu laws of inheritance.
[72] See the speeches throughout by Lalchand Navalrai and Babu Baijnath Bajoria, ibid., 485–515.

contracting subject, as was seen in Chapter 3, and her inevitable position as the instrument of another's will. Thus, Babu Baijnath Bajoria claimed that "generally, Hindu widows, after the death of their husbands, are in the hands of designing persons; they are generally under the thumb of her maternal relations like an uncle or brother rather than under the will of the other coparceners, and very often we have seen that even litigation is started at the instance of these maternal relations."[73] From a similar perspective, Lalchand Navalrai proposed an amendment to restrict a widow's right to call for partition to the case where she could prove the desire of at least one of the coparceners for partition. In other words, "She should not be able to enforce the partition against their will."[74] He explained, "I am not against the widow's interest. Now a family generally consists of members, say three or four sons of the deceased and some uncles. All of them could not be against the widow unless she has gone astray, and her conduct is not approved of by members of the family, in which case she does not deserve a share of the property."[75] As this quick jump from support for the widow's interest to justifying the widow's dispossession suggests, for Navalrai and Bajoria the vulnerability, ignorance, weakness, and lax morals of the widow – her fundamental lack of mental autonomy – made it simply unimaginable that the widow could stand in the place of her husband as coparcener. That such a possibility was actually quite literally unimagined became clear in a telling exchange between Navalrai and Sir Nripendra Sircar, a prominent supporter of the bill:

Navalrai: A provision that a widow shall have, on the death of her husband, in the joint family property, the same interest which her husband had is liable to be misconstrued to mean that she gets all the interest exclusively to herself; that is not the intention of the Select Committee.

Sircar: That is the intention.[76]

Ironically, Sircar's and Deshmukh's legislative victory may nonetheless obscure the extent to which this legislation ultimately reflected Navalrai's and Bajoria's arguments. That is, the success of this bill did not enshrine the principle of the equivalent value of family members into law. While it expanded the rights of widows under *Mitakshara* law, it also reinscribed within the family the principle of incommensurability.

---

[73] Ibid., 500. See also the scenario depicted by Lalchand Navalrai at ibid., 504.
[74] Ibid., 510.
[75] Ibid., 504.
[76] Legislative Assembly Debates, February 4 1937, 506.

In these debates, the problem of women's property rights within Hindu law posed the problem of women's legal inequality. In so doing, this emphasis positioned the majoritarian religious community and the transitional colonial-nationalist state as fundamentally parallel or congruent governing bodies, since in both cases the primary question concerned the implications of authorizing unequal rights and unequal forms of legal and political subjecthood.

This relationship was underscored in the aftermath of the passage of the HWRPA, when questions about the application of the law and further legal efforts to define and enhance women's rights led to the appointment of a committee under B. N. Rau to consider all questions of Hindu women's legal disabilities and potential legal remedies.[77] The Rau Committee's Report, submitted in June 1941 and drawing heavily on the labors of national women's organizations, went beyond its initial brief and called for codification of Hindu Law, as well as its "comprehensive, fundamental and substantial modification,"[78] as had been formulated and urged by the AIWC since 1934.[79] This led to the formation of a second Hindu Law Committee in 1944, which submitted a Draft Hindu Code Bill in 1947. Although such codification was ultimately postponed until after Independence, it highlighted the ways in which inequality within religious laws flowed inevitably into the problem of producing political equality in a democracy. In the context of Hindu law, the relationship between religious community and nation-state was posited less as a matter of competing jurisdictions than as a question of how to achieve congruence between the ethics of civic and religious life. Here the question of the legitimate and illegitimate inequalities that operated in the domain of social life, and how they would be recognized by law, became explicitly politicized.

PART III: BELONGING AS SUBJECTION: REDEFINING PERSONHOOD THROUGH PROPERTY

This issue of the religious community's inherent inequalities also lay at the core of B. R. Ambedkar's efforts to emancipate Dalits from Hindu religion and society. During the late 1920s and 1930s, Ambedkar initiated

---

[77] See discussion in Forbes, *Women in Modern India*, 112–118; Nair, *Women and Law*, 198–203. Also Basu, *Women's Struggle*, 62–64.
[78] Cited in Forbes, 117.
[79] Forbes, 113; Nair, 199.

multiple campaigns against existing caste practices, as he attempted to transform the social and legal position that Dalits would occupy in a future independent India. Alongside his more famous campaigns in this era for separate electorates for Untouchables and for their access to Hindu temples and village wells, Ambedkar sought to abolish by legislation the hereditary offices (*vatan*) that tied certain Untouchable castes to hereditary forms of stigmatized labor.[80]

What Ambedkar aimed to do through this proposed legislation in the Bombay Provincial Legislative Assembly was to recast these relationships based on hierarchy and stigma as contractual relationships that could be terminated by either party. Among other things, this proposal aimed to do away with the mediation of caste or village community, to be replaced by direct relations between abstract, unmarked subjects and the state, and by the private relations of individuals. In contrast to the legislative success of the two personal law bills discussed in the previous section, however, Ambedkar's bill met with strong resistance from the colonial government and was ultimately not brought before the Legislative Assembly. Indeed, one of the ironies of this episode was that ultimately the colonial state used the ideology of contract to reframe the stigma of untouchability, but did so by drawing on the inequities inherent within contract ideology, rather than on its promise of transparent and equal social relations.

Ambedkar had been interested in this issue for at least ten years: An earlier version of the bill, which he had introduced in 1927 to 1928, also met with extensive government resistance, and had to be withdrawn.[81] In the meantime, Ambedkar had launched a major social movement and was intensely involved in negotiations with the colonial government and with Gandhi and the Indian National Congress to redefine Dalits' social and legal position. Ambedkar's differences with Gandhi over the issue of untouchability are renowned. Reaching a climax in 1932 over the issue of separate electorates for Dalits, the fundamental disagreements between the two scarcely subsided. For Gandhi, eradicating the moral enormity of untouchability formed a crucial ethical project for caste Hindus, and one that was essential to their claims to national independence. For Ambedkar, with his focus on the material and symbolic

---

[80] Colonial policy regarding these hereditary offices is discussed in detail in Chapters 1 and 2.

[81] D. D. Gholap, the first nominated Depressed Classes representative to the Bombay Legislative Council, was the first to propose abolition of the Mahar *vatan*, in February 1923. See discussion in Rao, *The Caste Question*, 110–111.

degradation of Untouchables, Gandhi's offers of incorporation not only rang hollow, but also threatened to undermine the transformation of Untouchables from a class-in-itself to a class-for-itself. Yet despite the divergent visions of these two men, on the limited issue of the Mahar *vatan*, Gandhi's organization for the uplift of Untouchables, the Harijan Sevak Sangh (Untouchable Service Society), seems to have strongly supported Ambedkar's efforts.

Ambedkar's campaigns were pragmatic, but they also bore heavy symbolic weight. Himself a member of the Mahar community, his concern with this issue derived from the special socio-legal position that the community occupied within the colonial state. Mahars were holders of village-level *vatan*, but whereas most forms of *vatan* designated an elite status for their holders, the Mahar *vatan* was virtually alone in ascribing a servile and stigmatized status to its holders. In the words of V. N. Barve, president of the Maharashtra Provincial Harijan Sevak Sangh,

While the superior Vatan gives its holders authority and power and therefore a position of social dignity in the village, the Inferior Vatan, particularly the Mahar Vatan, subjects its holders to, what is in effect, forced and ill-paid labour and perpetuates the inferior status of the Mahar community. To use some what [*sic*] exaggerated language, while the superior Vatan makes the holders, the masters of the village, the inferior Vatan makes the holders, the slaves of the village.[82]

For Ambedkar, because in the instance of the Mahar *vatan* the practice of untouchability was effectively integrated into the colonial state, the issue could create an opening for addressing broader issues of Dalit social status. Moreover, a century of colonial administration of *vatan* had overwhelmingly, if not always consistently, moved toward superseding and abolishing these hereditary offices as a corrupt feudal remnant. As discussed in Chapter 2, during the 1910s, the Bombay government had worked to abolish one of the two remaining elite offices, the office of *kulkarni*, or village accountant. In this context, Ambedkar's efforts to similarly transform the Mahar *vatan* were pragmatic and plausible.

Ambedkar's bill aimed to do three things: first, to enable the holder of the *vatan*, or *vatandar*, to give up his liability for performing the government service should he choose to do so; second, to provide better security to ensure that those who continued to hold the *vatan* were properly paid for their labor; and third, to define the specific duties required of the *vatandar*. Thus, the bill did not aim to abolish the *vatan* outright, but

[82] MSA, RD, File No. 7420/33-I, pp. 145–147.

rather to give Mahar *vatandars* the power to end their compulsory hereditary connection to what was viewed as a degrading and defiling form of labor. For those who chose not to end this connection, it aimed to provide greater rights and security, redefining the *vatan* as a form of employment, involving set tasks to be performed for specified payment.[83]

Each of these legislative provisions met with sustained opposition on the part of the colonial government. Yet by far the most controversial of the bill's measures had to do with the way it enabled *vatandars* to end their *vatandar* status. The bill's provisions established that a *vatandar* could apply to the collector to be relieved of his liability for performing *vatan* service, and so cease to be a *vatandar*. It also, in accordance with earlier government policy in the case of elite *vatans*, enabled such persons to retain any land they held as payment for their *vatandar* service, provided they paid the full revenue assessment on it. This entitlement was a product of the history of *vatan*, in which state remuneration of *vatan* service (both elite and non-elite) had taken the form of an exemption from paying the full revenue assessment for a given parcel of land. As discussed in Chapters 1 and 2, when the colonial state sought to supersede the elite offices in the second half of the nineteenth century, it arranged a series of settlements with elite *vatandars*, whereby the *vatandars* would give up their claim to perform the *vatan* service, but would continue to retain their *vatan* lands on agreeing to pay a portion of the land's revenue assessment. These settlements formed the basis for Ambedkar's essentially similar proposal.

Ambedkar's proposed legislation needed to seem just and equitable in the eyes of the colonial state, but also beneficial enough to Mahar *vatandars* to encourage them to give up their *vatan*. For, the *vatan* simultaneously marked those who held it with hereditary stigma, and gave them an elevated status within the Mahar community. Some sense of the value of these *vatan* to their holders is suggested by the significant

---

[83] To ensure that Mahar *vatandars* were actually paid for their service, one clause of the bill enabled *vatandars* to transform what was traditionally a payment in kind into a money payment, and to apply to recover that payment from the collector. Another clause provided for the government to draw up a list of the required duties for the *vatandar*, so that he could potentially refuse to comply with additional demands. Furthermore, where Mahars were conventionally thought of as performing services both for the village community as a whole and for the government, the legislation provided for a distinction to be made between these two forms of service, and for the *vatandar* to refuse to perform their service to the village community by giving up that portion of their payment. This provision sought to provide protection to Mahars against oppression and exploitation by the village community. MSA, RD, File No. 7420/33-I, pp. 45–49.

contemporary records of disputed claims to *vatandar* Mahar status during this period.[84] The resistance of *vatandar* Mahars to the potential loss of their special status within the Mahar community was also a matter of note to Barve, who commented that "amongst the Mahar community, which is now greatly awakened by the efforts of its leaders, it is the Vatandar Mahars who are most orthodox and reactionary in their outlook and habits and are least amenable to any kind of reform."[85]

Barve's broader comments in support of Ambedkar's bill also suggest some of the complications in thinking about the nature of community as stigma and the means for removing such stigma. On the one hand, he reiterated more traditional narratives of community pollution, explaining the resistance to reform among *vatandar* Mahars as a product of their practice of eating carrion, which derived from their duty of removing and skinning dead cattle.[86] It was this practice, or the fact of being habituated and possibly attached to such practices, that made it difficult to institute change that would bring them into the shared sentiments of revulsion that united caste Hindus. On the other hand, Barve argued in the liberal registers of modernity and progress that "the [vatan] system is entirely unsuited to modern times, as the proposed aim of all progressive parties in the country is to afford equal opportunity of development to all irrespective of castes and creeds,"[87] and "the assignment of particular occupations and professions to particular castes or endogamous groups, has broken up for good."[88] Barve's side-by-side invocation of the inertial force of defiling customary practices and of a modernity that would inevitably and permanently dissolve the bonds of caste encapsulated some of the struggles to imagine the transformation of stigmatized community at the level of social life. Would the caste community continue to exist but without the stigma? Would the "castes and creeds" he referred to become a private matter, irrelevant to social relations? Would caste communities simply cease to exist? Such imagining of the social space of caste conjured both the magic of teleological transformations and the resilience of the social as supplement to law and politics. Barve's writing also gestured

[84] MSA, RD (1934) File No. 1793/33. Also RD (1916) Comp. 384, 38–39; RD (1922), File No. 4026; RD (1928) File No. 1627/28.

[85] MSA, RD, File No. 7420/33-I, p. 147.

[86] Ibid. See also Ambedkar's explanatory narratives in B. R. Ambedkar, *The Untouchables: Who Were They and Why They Became Untouchables* (New Delhi: Amrit Book Co., 1948); *Who Were the Shudras? How They Came to Be the Fourth Varna in Indo-Aryan Society* (Bombay: Thacker, 1946; reprint, Bombay: Thackers, 1970).

[87] Ibid., 149–151.

[88] Ibid., 151.

obliquely at the problem of agency in this transformation: The narrative of community defilement, whatever its problems, had the virtue of suggesting a means by which the community could transform its status. Yet where was the agency in modernity and progress? More pointedly, how would the mere "spirit of the times" change the ways in which caste Hindus viewed Untouchables and the ways Untouchables viewed themselves? In this problematic, the issue resonated with the problem of high-caste Hindu widows, as discussed in Chapter 4.

Ambedkar's pragmatic provisional response to these implicit questions of the potentiality and agency of social change was to seek such change through the law. In the Vatan Bill, he sought to frame Untouchability as a socio-legal problem. Such a process, however, required that identification of and with such communities be simultaneously foregrounded and expunged. Thus, the language of his bill turned on an ambiguity between imagining the *vatandar* as liberal contracting subject and viewing him as a member of a community defined by its stigma. If *vatan* had historically consisted of a form of property that also established a form of personhood and a mode of social relations, what Ambedkar's bill proposed was precisely to redefine property, and thereby also personhood and social relations. Where possible, then, the labor and social identity should be given up, and the property turned into private property owned by individuals; where impossible, the labor should be recast as a transparent contractual relationship, and the property a direct payment for service.[89]

Notably, the question of property was central to the official response to Ambedkar's bill as well, but in somewhat different terms: Government resistance focused primarily on the fiscal implications of such legislation. Thus, the commissioner of the Central Division, J. W. Smyth, urged that "the compulsory commutation of vatans involves Government in a heavy financial loss,"[90] while the collector of Dharwad noted that "the immediate and direct result of this Bill will be to throw a great financial burden on the provincial revenue." The Revenue Department secretary took up these arguments, asserting that "the replacement of vatandar village servants by stipendiary ones will ... cause very heavy expenditure from the general revenues."[91] This last comment, in suggesting the potential difficulty of finding replacement labor that would work for the same remuneration, also hinted at the effects of this legislation on broader social

---

[89] Ambedkar's arguments here strongly resonated with British Liberal/Utilitarian arguments for abolishing *vatan* in the early nineteenth century. See discussion in Chapter 1.

[90] Ibid., 76.

[91] Ibid., 82.

relations. Commissioner Smyth's objections to the legislation likewise extended to a critique of its effects on "the union and working of the village unit."[92] In his view, "If in addition to costing enormous sums of money the effect of Dr. Ambedkar's proposal is to break up the organization of the villages, as it inevitably would, his proposal stands condemned or at least must be regarded as too far in advance of the times."[93] In other words, coupled with the goal of limiting colonial state expenditure, of central concern to the commissioner was preserving intact precisely the social relations that Ambedkar's bill aimed to undermine.

Nonetheless, the question of equity in the treatment of Mahars compared with earlier government settlements with elite *vatandars* was not lost on the officials who debated the legislation. Therefore in one report, the question was raised "whether Govt. was not bound to allow the mahars to retain their lands after commuting their service since desai, deshpande, and kulkarnis [elite vatandars] have been allowed to retain their lands when commuting their services."[94] The replies to this question were unusually bald in their effort to find a legal justification to cover what was essentially a decision based in the self-interest of the state. In his initial reply, the revenue secretary suggested, "The first answer is, I think, that the mahar lands are assigned for service whereas the other lands are not."[95] This argument flew in the face of more than a century of state regulation of *vatan*, however, as was noted in a minute recorded the very next day, which acknowledged that "it may be said that in pre-British times the vatan lands of all such officers were assigned for service."[96] Given this shared characteristic of elite and non-elite *vatan*, this second minute proposed a somewhat different tack. It was here that the Revenue Department returned to the language of contract that Ambedkar himself had espoused: "The relation between the ruling power and the hereditary District and village officers and servants may be considered as a sort of contract," the official explained. "In the cases of Hereditary

---

[92] Ibid., 76.

[93] Ibid., 77. Smyth concluded his discussion of another provision of the bill noting, "The object of the amendment as stated by Dr. Ambedkar is to define more clearly who shall be liable for service to the community. His real intention however appears to be to prevent individuals or the community from exacting the customary service from the vatandars whose vatan is not *primarily* meant for rendering such services. This virtually means that in certain cases the community is to be deprived of a right which it has enjoyed for a very long period of time. This is obviously unfair and it may also lead to complications." Ibid., 79. Emphasis in original.

[94] Ibid., 87.

[95] Ibid.

[96] Ibid., 89.

District Officers and Kulkarnis Govt. themselves wanted to terminate the contract but the other party were still willing to continue the service. Some consideration was, therefore, necessary to induce the hereditary Distt. [*sic*] Officers and Kulkarnis to agree to give up their source of livelihood. In the case of mahars, the position is the reverse and there is no reason why Govt. should make any sacrifice."[97]

In returning to the language of contract, this official response in effect used Ambedkar's vision against itself. Whereas his legislation had aimed to weaken the ascriptive and stigmatized relations of untouchability by redefining the Mahar *vatan* as a transparent contractual relationship between the laborer and the state, this official response relied precisely on the contradictions inherent in the ideology of contract in order to preserve existing social relations intact. It was precisely the unequal position of the two contracting parties, and the power of the employer to dictate the terms, that established that "there is no reason why Govt. should make any sacrifice." Adopting the language of contract thus ultimately preserved the hierarchy, stigma, and differential personhood that characterized the Mahar *vatan*, but it recast those terms as simple relations of inequality and exploitation.[98] A similar problem had pervaded Ranade's and Chandavarkar's efforts to recast the meanings of female bodies as simply a matter of the suffering of the weak, ultimately layering liberal concerns with commensuration and bodily pain with persistent notions of abjection and defilement.

With the rejection of Ambedkar's bill, the Mahar *vatan* was not legally abolished for more than twenty years. Only in 1958, nearly a decade after the Indian Constitution abolished untouchability itself, was this specific form of stigmatized labor explicitly abolished.[99] However, in the interim, a coda to Ambedkar's legislative effort emerged in the months after his bill failed. This small-scale government action focused specifically on the exaction of labor without payment, a problem faced not only by Mahars, but by numerous Dalit groups.[100] In August 1937, after ongoing pressure

---

[97] Ibid., 92.

[98] This resonates with the problematic Marx posed in his early political analysis in "On the Jewish Question."

[99] Inferior Village Watan Abolition Act (1958). Ongoing official efforts to end these practices emerge in the *Report of the Commission for the Abolition of Customary and Hereditary Rights in Maharashtra* (Bombay: Department of Social Welfare, Culture Affairs, Sports and Tourism, 1980).

[100] These were officially classed as "Inferior Village Servants Useful to Government." There were other groups classed as "Inferior Village Servants Useful to the Community" and "Useless Village Servants." See discussion in Chapter 1.

from Ambedkar, the government issued a memo prohibiting government officials from accepting personal service (such as fetching water or washing clothes) without payment from those classed as "Inferior Village Servants," including both Mahars and other Dalit groups who provided services to the state.[101] Again in 1938, Ambedkar campaigned for a further executive order, this time both to reconfirm the prohibition on government officers from exacting personal services from members of these groups without payment, and to have the duties of these Dalit groups specified, so that they could refuse additional demands.[102] Despite continued resistance by the district commissioners,[103] these limited claims were accepted, although enacted by executive order, rather than by legislative act.[104]

This victory, whatever its limitations, did establish the principle that such labor was contractual, rather than a measure of the denigration of those who performed it. Moreover, it had the concomitant effect of parsing this labor into definite tasks and establishing that each instance a task was performed required remuneration. As such, it shifted these forms of labor into the logic of the wage, further embedding these groups within the logic of capital, even as the labor retained its ascriptive form. The Mahar and other castes were thus granted rights that operated at the community level, but that sought to provide a status beyond community, in which they might be wage laborers and contracting subjects, rather than Mahar or Jaglya, even as it was precisely as Mahar or Jaglya that they were subject to these forms of labor. Community formed the ground for asserting what was essentially a claim to transcend community.[105] These rights thus subjected caste persons to an ironically doubled position, at once as economically marginalized wage laborers and as members

---

[101] The full list specified in a later resolution, MSA, RD No. 7420/33, September 13, 1938, included Mahars, Dheds, Vethias, Bhangis, Madhavis, Ramoshis/Ravanias, Vartanias, Chaugulas, Naikwadis, Jaglyas, Talbades, Kolis, Sanadis/Walikars, Talwars, Kolkars, Ugranis, and Barkers. This later resolution refers to the August 1937 order, Government Circular Memorandum, Political and Reforms Department, No. 1581/34, August 25, 1937.

[102] MSA, RD (1938) File No. 7420/33-II.

[103] J. W. Smyth, commissioner of the Central Division, was again a staunch opponent to any attempt to limit the labor that government personnel could exact from Dalits.

[104] This was the later government resolution referred to above, RD, No. 7420/33, September 13, 1938.

[105] See Brown, *States of Injury*; Povinelli, *Cunning of Recognition*; Charles Taylor, "The Politics of Recognition," in *Multiculturalism: Examining the Politics of Recognition*, edited by Amy Gutmann (Princeton: Princeton University Press, 1994), pp. 25–73; Rao, *The Caste Question*.

of communities ascriptively subject to such labor. In this small-scale story, social relations dominated by the stigma of untouchability were partially recast, but nonetheless remained structured by inequality layered with denigration and humiliation.

CONCLUSION

By the late 1930s, the place of community in defining laws of the subject, which had served as colonial common sense for a century and a half, had acquired an amplified valence in the question of the political commensurability of persons as members of communities. At the same time, the model of community as the basis for political subjecthood had itself been modernized and transformed in the decades leading up to this moment. Political communities were now conceptualized as demographic entities with a jurisdictional relationship to their subjects, and equally as primordial entities, based in the layered compulsions of birth, culture, and belief.

These new politics of community took shape persistently around questions of state recognition, with campaigns seeking legal recognition even in cases where the ultimate goal was to stand in the place of the state, as in the case of the initial supporters of the Shariat Act. Despite their differences, these campaigns also shared a desire and a strategy of utilizing law to remake existing social practice and to redefine the status of the community in law and in social life.

At the same time, in mobilizing a rhetoric of belonging, these diverse politics also relied on a logic of the inherited properties of persons – on the particularities of embodiment as the basis for political subjecthood. It is therefore not surprising that property – that trigger of state presence and signifier of legal subjecthood – became a key strategic and symbolic terrain for politicizing forms of social differentiation and for staging diverse ethical claims to right practice, to sociopolitical inclusion, and to parallel or mediate the state.

In these politics of community, however, the question of women's political subjecthood operated differently from each of the other community claims. Most notably, although the colonial state and Western discourses deployed the category "women" as a universal category, none of the societal or the state actors construed women as a community as such, but rather as "belonging to" their various religious, caste, and local communities. Community was constituted through women's sexuality, through endogamy, kinship, and birth, thus rendering women internal to communities constituted by their men as political bodies. While, as Mrinalini Sinha has compellingly argued, liberal feminist organizations founded at the all-India level during the interwar period sought state recognition of women as a political collectivity, outside of the systems of personal law, the critical problem faced by this feminist politics was the impossibility of conceptualizing women, to paraphrase Ambedkar, as "a separate element," whose political interests were defined over-whelmingly by their status as women, rather than by the convergence of gender *with* religion, caste, and the like.[106] Nor, despite their efforts, did they succeed in positing women as transcending religious, caste, or village communities, existing in direct, unmediated relationship to the state.[107] Thus, unlike Dalits, who in this period staked claims grounded in their separation from Hindus, the question of women's rights and polit-ical status remained in crucial ways enfolded within personal law, with women positioned as belonging to and governed by communities, and as simultaneously critical and devalued subjects therein. Women's humanity, which had emerged so forcefully in the late-nineteenth-century debates on Hindu marriage, was recast in this context as simply a matter of the obstacles to legal rights.

Nonetheless the question of women's legal disability underscored the dual problem: most immediately and transparently, that securing politico-legal equality could itself only be achieved through broader societal transformation, but also that modern formations of the social retained and even amplified the meaningfulness of bodies and birth. The modes of community self-empowerment that characterized this era oper-ated within and utilized the conundrums of liberalism to politicize the connection between social life and the state, but they did not supersede the dilemma it posed concerning how social life should be embodied within the law. At the same time, the state's commitment to preserving women's legal disabilities through the systems of personal law indexed not only its recognition of communities as the key framework of modern political representation, but also a modern model of power as residing in "interest groups" defined by and available for mobilization through the meanings of birth.

---

[106] Sinha, *Specters of Mother India.*
[107] Ibid.; Rajan, *The Scandal of the State.*

Conclusion

The postcolonial context has if anything intensified the politics of social life embedded in the system of personal law. The dominant narrative of this history tells of an impasse between progressive efforts to achieve a secular egalitarian nation and their confrontation with political limits. In this narrative, while the 1949 Indian constitution established the goal of abolishing the multiple systems of religious law by enacting a uniform civil code, such an aim was enshrined only in the nonjusticiable Directive Principles, rather than in the Fundamental Rights. Moreover, in the aftermath of partition, and given the minoritarian status of Muslims in India, Muslim law was considered an inappropriate object of state reform. Efforts thus focused instead on the project of modernizing Hindu law. In the early 1950s, the postcolonial state returned to the project of reforming and codifying Hindu law begun in the previous decade.[1] B. R. Ambedkar, as the law minister of Nehru's cabinet and former chairman of the Drafting Committee of the Constitution, drafted the initial post-colonial Hindu Code Bill. This bill was introduced into Parliament in 1951, and it significantly expanded women's rights. Yet Ambedkar's and other nationalists' and feminists' aims of ending women's legal disabilities through such a project of codification and reform foundered upon the powerful patriarchal vision mobilized by conservative Hindu lawmakers.[2]

---

[1] This endeavor had its direct antecedents in the 1941 Rau Committee, and the formation of a second (1944) Hindu Law Committee, which produced a 1947 draft Hindu code, as discussed in Chapter 5.

[2] When Nehru and the Congress failed to make good their pledge to support the controversial bill, Ambedkar resigned from the cabinet. Following this stalemate, the single bill was broken down into several pieces of legislation, and the provisions to enhance women's legal equality were significantly watered down.

The piecemeal legislation that ultimately passed in the mid-1950s did expand the inheritance rights of daughters in the family property and established the right of divorce, but it retained the Hindu male coparcenary and its inequities and exclusions intact.[3] Moreover, in the decades since the passage of these acts, women and their families have in practice quite effectively ignored even those limited rights that the legislation established for women.[4] This legislation thus set in motion one of the most intractable struggles of postcolonial feminism and other liberatory struggles: that laws fail to significantly change society, and legal rights do not in effect produce social rights.

Such a narrative conveys something of the drama and pathos of this history. Yet it also relies upon an explanatory framework in which various patriarchal, caste/communal, and class interests thwart a progressive teleology.[5] While entrenched interests certainly have been operational in various ways, such an explanatory framework recapitulates the foundational liberal political economic model of the universal operation of rational self-interest, or the related sociological analysis of the behavior of "interest groups." Moreover, this narrative has typically imagined emancipation from these oppressive interests either through state de-recognition of oppressive religious laws, or through an agonistic ethical encounter between egalitarian and nonegalitarian segments of given religious communities. In other words, these models identify some form of secularization as the path toward an emancipatory political life. In contrast, this book has suggested that the system of personal law is itself the product of secular liberal visions and ideologies, most prominently in the inescapable question that it produces concerning the ethics of recognizing differential forms of personhood and rights.

The postcolonial Indian nation-state's claims to secularism have been subject to much scrutiny and critique, particularly for the ways it has established Hindus as unmarked abstract subjects, as well as for its multifaceted forms of institutional discrimination against non-Hindus. Yet

---

[3] These are: The Hindu Marriage Act, 1955; The Hindu Succession Act, 1956; The Hindu Minority and Guardianship Act, 1956; and The Hindu Adoptions and Maintenance Act, 1956. See Srimati Basu, "Personal and the Political: Indian Women and Inheritance Law," in *Religion and Personal Law in Secular India: A Call to Judgment*, edited by Gerald James Larson (Bloomington: Indiana University Press, 2001); Majumdar, *Marriage and Modernity*, chapter 6.

[4] Agarwal, *Field of One's Own*; Basu, *She Comes to Take*.

[5] Even recent scholars who offer sophisticated critiques of standard models of secularism or the modern state have relied upon this line of analysis. Newbigin, "A Post-Colonial Patriarchy?"; Chatterjee, "English Law, Brahmo Marriage."

the dilemma of the postcolonial state is not that it is inadequately secular, despite the ways that religion and religious discrimination pervade its institutions and personnel. State secularism has always signaled an entailment with (and not simply separation from) an arena of power and authority denominated as "religious," and state secularism has also intrinsically involved a vision in which forms of difference, and also inequality, will continue to operate within an arena of social life that subsists in ambiguous relation to the state. In this context, the dilemma of postcolonial Indian state secularism, like state secularism elsewhere, is that it involves a form of state power that at once highlights, problematizes, and reinscribes the inexorable political force of social life and the differential politico-legal value of persons that such social life produces. Secularism names a foundational but paradoxical model of the possibility of abstract equivalence among state subjects that depends upon and is ultimately undermined by their concrete incommensurability in social life. It also entails a model of social life as distinct and autonomous from the state but as dependent upon state recognition, and also a model of social life as inegalitarian but as moving developmentally toward egalitarianism.

This ambiguous legal position of social life is in fact embodied in the constitution. Indeed, alongside the project of codification embodied in the Hindu Law Acts, the constitution also provided for legal recognition of caste *panchayats* and informal collective institutions to regulate familial relationships.[6] This diffusion of legal authority particularly to local caste collectivities has countered and partially undermined the homogenizing force of the Hindu Law Acts, underscoring the diversity of views, practices, and interpretations *within* nationalized religious communities at every level.[7] Yet this form of legal recognition has only intensified the debate over what forms of personhood and citizenship should be embodied within the law. This question has become a salient and inescapable political dilemma of the postcolonial state.

This nationalist project of making the law adequate to the people has also unfolded alongside the expansive agency of the postcolonial developmentalist state. As Partha Chatterjee has argued, the democratic

---

[6] Gopika Solanki, "Adjudication in Religious Family Laws: Cultural Accommodation, Legal Pluralism, and Women's Rights in India," Ph.D. diss. (McGill University, 2007).

[7] As Solanki shows, however, this diffusion of legal authority did not by any means involve the replacement or irrelevance of state forms and norms – on the contrary, informal authorities often adopted the external features of state legality, and arrangements worked out in these institutions took shape "in the shadow of the law" – that is, with an eye to the forms of redress available through formal legal channels. Ibid.

impulse of the postcolonial state was rapidly overtaken by an agenda of poverty eradication and social welfare that engaged not with a public or publics, but with populations, viewed as objects of governance.[8] As this book has shown, this postcolonial governmentality had its origins in the colonial state. Indeed, while independence constituted a genuine historical break, the Indian nation-state's dual use of law and governmentality as modes of governance has represented a significant continuity with the colonial state.

Chatterjee notes regarding the Western European and American contexts, "The activities of governmentality required multiple, cross-cutting and shifting classifications of the population as the targets of multiple policies, producing a necessarily heterogeneous construct of the social."[9] According to Chatterjee, drawing on the work of Nicholas Dirks, in India the colonial state produced this heterogeneous social of governmentality through its governance of community, in the profusion of castes, tribes, religions, regions, and the like. Yet the high colonial mode of governance in India is not fully encapsulated in Dirks's model of the "ethnographic state." While colonial governmentality involved efforts to govern populations in their heterogeneity, it also entailed efforts to instill universal morality and economic rationality in their members. Rather than seeing an exclusively ethnographic form of governmentality, we might do better to recognize the ways in which colonial governmentality was likewise saturated with the logics, modes of reasoning, and prevailing assumptions of political economy, even as it also promulgated a colonial logic of community.

If in the colonial context marriage and inheritance seemingly exemplified the resilience of premodern, traditional, or non-liberal thought and practice both at the level of the colonial state and among its Indian subjects, this book has argued instead that the colonial treatment of these issues formed an integral part of liberal state practice, although this took shape in several ways. It is perhaps easiest to identify this feature in processes that fit into a narrative, however incomplete, of secularizing property and personhood, such as in efforts to privatize inheritance by rendering it a matter of social rather than political claims, and in attempts to disencumber male coparceners from the burdens of inheritance, as well as in efforts to reconceptualize marriage as inextricable from the bodily and mental vulnerability and suffering of women and girls. Perhaps most

---

[8] Chatterjee, *Politics of the Governed*.
[9] Ibid., 36.

prominently, the colonial jurisprudence of Hindu law produced that law as fundamentally a regime of rights, eschewing questions of ritual status and ritual performance, ceremonial perquisites, spiritual states, and the like. Yet such instances of the ways in which the premises and paradoxes of liberalism came to pervade the jurisprudence of Hindu law form only one strand of the story.

At least two additional patterns reflect this complex history of colonial liberalism. The first is the significance of the family as a domain beyond the putative politico-legal equality of (masculine) subjects. If liberal political thought posited the possibility of abstract universal economic and political subjecthood, it also involved a recognition of humanity precisely in the incommensurable uniqueness of persons within social and intimate life. Such an ethics of incommensurability, centered most powerfully on the family, must be distinguished from the liberal concern with the cultivation of sentiment or the capacity for human empathy, which addressed the suffering of persons in their abstract universality.[10] In contrast, this ethics of incommensurability was grounded precisely in a recognition of the unique relationships, affective dimensions, and personal meanings generated by particular, irreplaceable persons. This liberal vision of the ethics of human incommensurability undergirded the juridical treatment of marriage and inheritance, with the ongoing meaningfulness it accorded to the differences of birth and embodiment.

The second pattern involves the ways in which the family became a privileged site of colonial governmentality. In defining the rights and incidents of inheritance, family property, marriage, guardianship, adoption, and the like, the colonial state rendered them integral to its work of governing society. At the same time, it also extended its intimate involvement in the family well beyond the systems of personal law through administrative as well as legislative and judicial techniques, such as revenue assessment (tax collection), the adjudication of petty debts, rural property legislation, and so forth. The family and its component parts were thus constituted as such and brought into a direct relationship to the state, even as this relationship was also structured by the system of personal law.

The system of personal law involved a peculiarly colonial juridicization of birth: Birth immediately located persons within the matrices

---

[10] As such, this book seeks to distinguish this strand of liberalism from the nonetheless stunning accounts provided by Rao, *The Caste Question*, and by Chakrabarty, *Provincializing Europe*.

of communities understood at once as legal-jurisdictional entities and as sites of affective-political commitment. Personal law also naturalized birth as the generative producer and reproducer of communities. Sexuality in this context became not a key node for the development of new forms of knowledge/biopower (e.g., in the human sciences of biology, medicine, and race), as Foucault suggested in the Western European context, but a key node for the simultaneous naturalization and juridicization of community as the framework for the political recognition of humanity.

The politics produced by colonial governmentality thus rendered the concrete corporeality of persons inescapable. Such a politics of community grounded in the meaningfulness of birth was located in and generated by the sexual and reproductive bodies of women. In this context, this book has highlighted not only the liberal conundrum that women were conceptualized as incommensurable and incomplete politico-legal subjects, but also the way that the colonial state made use of the meaningfulness of women's bodies in producing naturalized communities as the building blocks of society. This inescapably concrete meaningfulness of bodies and birth has long formed the basis for differential politico-legal rights and the denial of social recognition – that is, for the refusal to accord to women (as well as to Muslims and Dalits) the political and social integuments of humanity. The politics of the present have in no sense superseded this terrain. Yet they also hold out the potentiality of resignifying birth and refashioning the power of social life.

Select Bibliography

Archival Sources

Maharashtra State Archives, Mumbai
  Bombay Gazette, Selections (1880–1939)
  Home (Judicial) Department (1920–1937)
  Judicial Department (1860–1920)
  Legislative Department (1914–1927)
  Records of Select Cases of the *Sadr Diwani Adalat* (1820–1862)
  Reports on Native Papers (1868–1878; 1888–1920)
  Revenue Department (1818–1937)

Maharashtra State Archives, Pune

Deccan Commissioner's Files, Selected Papers
Early British Rule, Selected Papers
Inam Commissioner's Files, Selected Papers

Mumbai High Court

Bombay High Court Reports (1862–1875) (published)
Files of selected cases (1862–1937)
Indian Law Reports, Bombay Series (1875–1910) (published)
Selected Justices' Notebooks (1878–1907)

National Archives, Delhi

Home (Judicial) Department (1915–1938)
Legislative Assembly Debates, (1936–1937)

British Library (Oriental and India Office Records), London

European Manuscripts (Selected)
Indian Law Reports, Bombay Series (1910–1940) (published)
Legislative Assembly Debates (Selected, 1915–1937; 1955–6)
Pamphlet series (Selections in Marathi, Urdu, and English) (1860–1920)
Reports on Native Papers (1876–1887; 1920–1937)
Selections from the Records of the Government of Bombay (Selected Series)

Selected Published Government Reports (by date)

Indian Law Commission. *Report of the Law Commissioners on the Judicial System of India.* Commissioners: A. Amos, C. H. Cameron, F. Millett, D. Elliott, H. Borrodaile. OIOR, 1842.

Goldsmid, H. E., G. Wingate, and D. Davidson. "Measurement and Classification Rules of the Deccan Gujarat, Konkan and Kanara Surveys." *Selections from the Records of the Bombay Government Papers of the Joint Report of 1847,* No. DXXXII, n.s., Reprint, Nagpur: Government Press, 1975, p. 11.

Goodine, R. N. *Report on the Deccan Village Communities (Selections from the Records of the Bombay Government, No. IV)—With Special Reference to the Claims of the Village Officers in the Ahmednugger Collectorate to "Purbhara Huks," or Remuneration from their villages, independent of what they receive from Government.* Bombay: Education Society's Press, 1852.

"Adoptions Under the Peshwas." *Selections from the Records of the Bombay Government,* No. XXVIII, N.S. 1856.

Prinsep, H. T. *The Code of Criminal Procedure [Act XXV of 1861, and Act VIII of 1869] and Other Laws and Rules of Practice, Relating to Procedure in the Criminal Courts of British India. With notes, containing the opinions delivered by all the superior local courts.* Calcutta: Thacker, Spink & Co., 1869.

Stephen, James Fitzjames. "Minute on the Administration of Justice in British India." *Selections from the Records of the Government of India,* Home Dept. No. LXXXIX, Calcutta, 1872.

Etheridge, A. T. *Narrative of the Bombay Inam Commission and Supplementary Settlements.* Selections from the Records of the Bombay Government, n.s., no. 132. Poona: Deccan Herald Press, 1873.

Cooke, H. R. "Repression of Female Infanticide in the Bombay Presidency." *Selections from the Records of the Government of India,* Home Dept. No. CXLVII, N.S., 1875.

Report of the Committee on the Riots in Poona and Ahmednagar, 1875 with Appendices. 3 Vols. Bombay: Government Central Press, 1876.

"Correspondence Regarding the Law of Land Sale." *Selections from the Records of the Government of India,* Home Department, No. CLV, 1879.

Government of Bombay. *Gazetteer of the Bombay Presidency, Poona District.* Vol. 18, Parts 1–3. Bombay: Government Central Press, 1885. Reprint, Pune: Government Photozincographic Press, 1992.

"Papers relating to Infant Marriage and Enforced Widowhood in India." *Selections from the Records of the Government of India,* No. CCXXIII,

Home Deptartment. Serial No. 3. Calcutta: Superintendent of Government Printing, 1886.

"Papers relating to the Deccan Agriculturists' Relief Act, during the years 1875–94, Vol. II." *Selections from the Records of the Government of India*, Home Department. No. 342. Home Department Serial No. 20. Calcutta: Superintendent of Government Printing, 1897.

"Papers relating to Marriages and Marriage Registration from 1865." *Selections from the Records of the Government of India*, No. 437A, 1908.

Oral Evidence Tendered to the Hindu Law Committee, 1945. Madras: Superintendent Government Press, 1947.

Written Statements Submitted to the Hindu Law Committee, 1945. 2 Volumes. Madras: Superintendent Government Press, 1947.

Report of the Hindu Law Committee. New Delhi: Manager Government of India Press, 1947.

Report of the Commission for the Abolition of Customary and Hereditary Rights in Maharashtra. Bombay: Department of Social Welfare, Culture Affairs, Sports and Tourism, 1980.

Other Primary Sources

Ambedkar, B. R. *What Congress and Gandhi Have Done to the Untouchables.* Bombay: Thacker & Co., 1945.

    Who Were the Shudras? How They Came to Be the Fourth Varna in Indo-Aryan Society. 1946. Reprint, Bombay: Thackers, 1970.

    The Untouchables: Who Were They and Why They Became Untouchables. New Delhi: Amrit Book Co., 1948.

    "Small Holdings in India and Their Remedies." In *Dr. Babasaheb Ambedkar, Writings and Speeches, Vol. 1*, edited by Vasant Moon, 455–479. Bombay: Government of Maharashtra, Education Department, 1979.

Austin, John. *Lectures on Jurisprudence, or the Philosophy of Positive Law*, Vol. II. 4th ed. London: J. Murray, 1873.

Baden-Powell, B. H. *The Land Systems of British India: Being a Manual of the Land-Tenures and of the Systems of Land-Revenue Administration Prevalent in the Several Provinces, Vol. III.* Oxford: Clarendon Press, 1892.

    A Short Account of the Land Revenue and Its Administration; with a Sketch of the Land Tenures. Oxford: Clarendon Press, 1894.

Banerjee, Sir Gooroodass. *The Hindu Law of Marriage and Stridhan.* Calcutta: Thacker, Spink & Co., 1879.

Bernier, François. *Travels in the Mogul Empire, A.D. 1656–1668.* Translated and annotated by Archibald Constable. 2nd ed., revised by Vincent A. Smith. Delhi: Low Price Publications, 1989.

Bhikaji, Dadaji. "An Exposition of Some of the Facts of the Case of Dadaji v. Rakhmabai." *Advocate of India*, 1887. Reprinted from the *Bombay Gazette*, June 29, 1887. In OIOR Law Tracts, 1851–1887. 5319.111.28, nos. 11 and 12.

Birdwell, C. E. A. "Conditions for Admission to the Legal Profession throughout the British Empire, Part II." *Journal of the Society of Comparative Legislation*, n.s., 13, 1 (1912): 130–131.

Birdwood, H. M., and H. J. Parsons. *The Acts of the Legislature in Force in the Presidency of Bombay, Edited, with Occasional Notes, Cross-References, and an Index, Vol. VIII, 1878–1880.* Bombay: Education Society's Press, 1881.

Blackstone, William. *Commentaries on the Laws of England.* 4 vols. Oxford: Clarendon Press, 1765–1769. Reprint, from the 21st London edition, with notes by G. Sweet, and notes by John L. Wendell. New York: Harper & Bros., 1859.

Chandavarkar, G. L. *A Wrestling Soul: Story of the Life of Sir Narayan Chandavarkar.* Bombay: Popular Book Depot, 1955.

Chandavarkar, N. G. *Speeches and Writings of Sir Narayan G. Chandavarkar.* Bombay: Manoranjak Grantha Prasarak Mandali, 1911.

Chaplin, William. *Report Exhibiting a View of the Fiscal and Judicial System of Administration Introduced into the Conquered Territories above the Ghauts, under the Authority of the Commissioner in the Dekhan.* Orig., Bombay: Courier Press, 1824. Reprint, Bombay Government Press, 1838.

Chintamani, C. Yajñeswara. *Indian Social Reform, In Four Parts: Being a Collection of Essays, Addresses, Speeches, &c. with an Appendix.* Madras: Thompson & Co., 1901.

Clarke, Richard, ed. *The Regulations of the Government of Bombay in Force at the End of 1850; to Which Are Added, The Acts of the Government of India, in Force in That Presidency.* London: J. & H. Cox, 1851.

Colebrooke, H. T. *Treatise on Obligations and Contracts, Part I.* London: Black, Kingsbury, Parbury & Allen, 1818.

———. Translator. *Dayabhaga and Mitakshara, Two Treatises on the Hindu Law of Inheritance,* by Jimutavahana and Vijñaneshwara. Calcutta: B. Banerjee, 1883. Reprint, Delhi: Parimal Publications, 1984.

Cowell, Herbert. *The Hindu Law: Being a Treatise on the Law Administered Exclusively to Hindus by the British Courts in India.* Calcutta: Thacker, Spink & Co., 1870.

———. *The History and Constitution of the Courts and Legislative Authorities in India.* 6th rev. ed. Calcutta: Thacker, Spink & Co., 1936.

Elphinstone, Mountstuart. *Report on the Territories Conquered from the Paishwa.* Calcutta: A. G. Balfour, Government Gazette Press, 1821. Reprinted as *Territories Conquered from the Paishwa, A Report,* with introduction by J. C. Srivastava. Delhi: Oriental Publishers, 1973.

Engels, Frederick. *The Origin of the Family, Private Property, and the State.* New York: International Publishers, 1942.

Enthoven, R. E. *The Tribes and Castes of Bombay.* 3 vols. 1st ed. 1922. Reprint, Delhi: Low Price Publications, 1997.

Fuller, Mrs. Marcus. *Wrongs of Indian Womanhood.* Edinburgh: Oliphant & Ferrier, 1900.

Furdoonjee, Nowrozjee. *On the Civil Administration of the Bombay Presidency.* London: John Chapman, 1853.

Gidumal, Dayaram. *The Status of Women in India, or A Handbook for Hindu Social Reformers.* Bombay: Fort Printing Press, 1889.

Goldstucker, Theodor. *On the Deficiencies in the Present Administration of Hindu Law in India, Being a Paper Read at the Meeting of the East India Association on the 8th of June, 1870.* London: Trubner & Co., 1871.

Gupte, K. S. *The Bombay Land Revenue Code, 1879, as Amended Up to Date with Explanatory and Critical Notes, Exhaustive Commentary, Summary of Land Revenue Rules, Government Resolution, Orders, High Court Rulings, B. R. T. Decisions, etc.* Pune: Western India Law Printing Press, 1962.

Hegel, G. W. F. *Elements of the Philosophy of Right.* Cambridge Texts in the History of Political Thought. Cambridge: Cambridge University Press, 1991 (orig. 1820).

Henderson, Gilbert S. *Testamentary Succession and Administration of Intestate Estates in India, Being a Commentary on the Indian Succession Act (X of 1865), The Hindu Wills Act (XXI of 1870), The Probate and Administration Act (V of 1881), and All Other Acts Bearing upon the Subject, with Notes and Cross-References, and a General Index.* 3rd ed. by Alex Kinney. Calcutta: Thacker, Spink & Co., 1909.

Hobbes, Thomas. *Leviathan.* Cambridge Texts in the History of Political Thought. Edited by Richard Tuck. Cambridge: Cambridge University Press, 1996 (orig. 1651).

Ilbert, Sir Courtenay. "Indian Codification." *The Law Quarterly Review* 5, 20 (Oct. 1889): 347–369.

"Sir James Stephen as a Legislator." *The Law Quarterly Review* 10 (July 1894): 222–227.

"Application of European Law to Natives of India." *Journal of the Society of Comparative Legislation* 1 (1896–1897): 212–226.

"Common Law and Statute Law." *Journal of the Society of Comparative Legislation,* n.s. 1, 3 (Dec. 1899): 407–416.

The Government of India: Being a Digest of the Statute Law Relating Thereto, with Historical Introduction and Explanatory Matter. 3rd ed. Oxford: Clarendon Press, 1915. Reprint, Delhi: Neeraj Publishing House, 1984.

Indian Official. *Judicial System of British India, Considered with Especial Reference to the Training of Anglo-Indian Judges.* London: Pelham Richardson, 1852.

Janardhan, Rukhmabai. "Rukhmabai's Reply to Dadajee's Exposition." Reprinted from the *Bombay Gazette,* June 29, 1887. OIOR Law Tracts, 1851–1887. 5319.111.28, nos. 11 and 12.

Kane, P. V. *History of Dharmashastra.* Vol. 3. Pune: Bhandarkar Oriental Research Institute, 1946.

Hindu Customs and Modern Law. Bombay: University of Bombay Press, 1950.

Kikani, L. T. *Caste in Courts, or Rights and Powers of Castes in Social and Religious Matters as Recognized by Indian Courts.* Rajkot: Ganatra Printing Works, 1912.

Locke, John. "The Second Treatise of Government." In *Two Treatises of Government.* Edited by Peter Laslett, 265–428. Cambridge Texts in the History of Political Thought. Cambridge: Cambridge University Press, 1988 (orig. 1689).

Maine, Henry Sumner. *Ancient Law: Its Connection with the Early History of Society and Its Relation to Modern Ideas.* 1st American (2nd London) ed. New York: Scribner, Armstrong & Co., 1872.

Village Communities in the East and West: Six Lectures Delivered at Oxford. 3rd and enlarged ed. New York: Henry Holt & Co., 1889.

Marx, Karl. "On the Jewish Question." In *The Marx-Engels Reader.* 2nd ed. Edited by Richard Tucker, 26–52. New York: W. W. Norton & Co., 1978 (orig. 1844).

Mayne, John Dawson. *A Treatise on Hindu Law and Usage.* Madras: Higginbotham & Co., 1878.

Missionary Review of the World. Edited by Rev. Arthur T. Pierson. Vol. XII, New Series (XXII, Old Series), Jan.–Dec. 1899. New York: Funk & Wagnalls Co., 1899.

Mill, James. *The History of British India, Vol. I.* 1817. Reprint of 2nd ed., London: Baldwin, Gradock & Joy, 1920. New Delhi: Associated Publishing House, 1982.

Millett, Henry, and Frederick Clarke. *The Law and Practice of Insolvency in India, Being Victoria 11 and 12 Cap. 21, with Notes and Rules and Orders of the High Courts of Calcutta, Madras, and Bombay.* Calcutta: Thacker, Spink & Co., 1873.

Mitra, Ram Charan. *The Law of Joint Property and Partition in British India.* Tagore Law Lectures, 1895–1896. Calcutta: Thacker, Spink & Co., 1897.

Mitter, Sir Brojendra. *Indian Judges: Biographical and Critical Sketches.* Madras: G. A. Natesan & Co., 1932.

Molesworth, J. T. *A Dictionary, Marathi and English.* 2nd ed. Assisted by George Candy and Thomas Candy. 1857. Reprint, New Delhi: Asian Educational Services, 1989.

Morley, William. *The Administration of Hindu Law in British India, Comprising an Account of the Laws Peculiar to India.* 1858. Reprint, New Delhi: Metropolitan Book Co., 1976.

Mulla, Dinshah Fardunji. *Jurisdiction of Courts in Matters Relating to the Rights and Powers of Castes.* Bombay: Caxton Printing Works, 1901.

Naoroji, Dadabhai. *Poverty of India.* London: Vincent Brooks, Day & Son, 1878.

Nathubhai, Tribhovandas Mangaldas. *Hindu Caste, Law and Custom.* Bombay: Times of India Press, 1903.

Norton, John Bruce, and Mootoosawmy Iyer. *A Selection of Leading Cases on the Hindu Law of Inheritance.* Parts I and II. Edited by William Scharlieb. Madras: C. D'Cruiz, 1870.

Pandia, Nayansukhlal Harilal. *The Law of Castes: Being a Reprint after Careful Revision of Contributions Made to the Bombay Law Reporter and the Allahabad Law Journal.* Bombay: Shri Kalika Printing Press, for K. Ramrao & Co., 1914.

Perry, Thomas Erskine. *Cases Illustrative of Oriental Life, Decided in H. M. Supreme Court at Bombay.* London: S. Sweet, 1853. Reprint, New Delhi: Asian Educational Services, 1988.

Phule, Jotirao. *Slavery: In the Civilized British Government, under Cloak of Brahminism.* Bombay: Government of Maharashtra Education Department, 1991.

"The Cultivator's Whipcord." Translated by Aniket Jaaware. In *The Selected Writings of Jotirao Phule*, edited, annotations, and introduction by G. P. Deshpande, 113–189. New Delhi: LeftWord Books, 2002.

Platts, John T. *A Dictionary of Urdu, Classical Hindi and English*. 4th printing. London: Crosby Lockwood and Son, 1911. Reprint, Lahore: Sang-E-Meel Publications, 1994.

Pollock, Frederick. *The Law of Torts: A Treatise on the Principles of Obligations Arising from Civil Wrongs in the Common Law, to Which Is Added the Draft of a Code of Civil Wrongs, Prepared for the Government of India*. 2nd ed. London: Stevens & Sons, 1890.

Ranade, M. G. Introduction in *A Collection Containing the Proceedings Which Led to the Passage of Act XV of 1856*. Edited by Pandit Narayan Keshav Vaidya. Bombay: Mazagaon Printing Press, 1885.

—— *Essays on Indian Economics: A Collection of Essays and Speeches*. Bombay: Thacker & Co., 1898.

—— *Religious and Social Reform: A Collection of Essays and Speeches*. Collected and compiled by M. B. Kolasker. Bombay: Gopal Narayen & Co., 1902.

—— *Miscellaneous Writings of the Late Honourable Mr. Justice M. G. Ranade*. Published by Mrs. Ramabai Ranade, with an introduction by D. E. Wacha. Bombay: Manoranjan Press, 1915.

—— *Ranade's Economic Writings*. Edited by Bipan Chandra. New Delhi: Gian Publishing House, 1990.

Ranade, Ramabai. *Himself: The Autobiography of a Hindu Lady*. Translated and adapted by Katherine Van Akin Gates. New York: Longmans, Green & Co., 1938.

Rogers, Alexander. *The Land Revenue of Bombay: A History of Its Administration, Rise and Progress*. 2 vols. 1892. Reprint, Delhi: Low Price Publications, 1993.

Roy, Sripati. *Customs and Customary Law in British India*. Tagore Law Lectures, 1908. Calcutta: Hare Press, 1911.

Sapru, Sir Tej Bahadur. *Encyclopaedia of the General Acts and Codes of India*. Calcutta: Butterworth & Co., 1935.

Schmitt, Carl. *Political Theology: Four Chapters on the Concept of Sovereignty*. Translated by George Schwab. Cambridge, MA: MIT Press, 1985 (orig. 1922).

—— *The Concept of the Political*. Translated, introduction, and notes by George Schwab. Chicago: University of Chicago Press, 1996 (orig. 1927).

Smith, Adam. *An Inquiry into the Nature and Causes of the Wealth of Nations*. 1776. Reprint, the Modern Library edition. Edited, with an introduction and notes by Edwin Cannan, introduction by Max Lerner. New York: Random House, 1937.

Sorabji, Cornelia. The Law of Women's Property in India in Relation to Her Social Position. OIOR, Eur. MSS/F 165, no. 117, 1893.

Steele, Arthur. *Summary of the Law and Custom of Hindoo Castes, within the Dekhun Provinces Subject to the Presidency of Bombay, Chiefly Affecting Civil Suits*. Bombay: Courier Press, 1827.

Stephen, James Fitzjames. "Codification in England and India." *The Fortnightly Review* 17 (1872): 644–672.

"Minute on the Administration of Justice in British India." In *Selections from the Records of the Government of India*, No. LXXXIX. Calcutta: Home Secretariat Press, 1872.

"Legislation under Lord Mayo." In *The Life of the Earl of Mayo, Fourth Viceroy of India*, Vol. II. 2nd ed. Edited by W. W. Hunter, 143–226. London: Smith, Elder & Co., 1876.

History of the Criminal Law of England. 3 vols. London: Macmillan, 1883.

Liberty, Equality, Fraternity. 2nd ed. 1874. Reprint, Cambridge: Cambridge University Press, 1967.

Strange, Thomas. *Hindu Law, Principally with Reference to Such Portions of It as Concern the Administration of Justice, in the King's Courts, in India*. 2 vols. London: Parbury Allen, 1830.

Sykes, W. H. *Land Tenures of the Dekkan*. London: James Moyes, 1835.

Special Report on the Statistics of the Four Collectorates of the Dukhun, under the British Government. London: Richard & John E. Taylor, 1838.

Administration of Civil Justice in British India, for a Period of Four Years, Chiefly from 1845–1848, Both Inclusive. OIOR, Law Tracts, etc. 1851–1887, Tract No. 4.

Tek Chand, Bakhshi and Harbans Lal Sarin, eds. *The Law of Legal Practitioners in British India, Being an Exhaustive, Up-to-Date, and Critical Commentary on the Legal Practitioners' Act (XVIII of 1879), as Amended Up-to-Date....* Calcutta: Eastern Law House, 1935.

Telang, Kashinath Trimbak. *Telang's Legislative Council Speeches, with Sir Raymond West's Essay on His Life*. Edited with notes by D. W. Pilgamker. Bombay: Indian Printing Press, 1895.

Selected Writings and Speeches. Bombay: K. R. Mitra Manoranjan Press for the Gaud Saraswat Brahmin Mandal Mitra, 1916.

Trevelyan, Sir Ernest John. *Hindu Law, as Administered in British India*. Calcutta: Thacker, Spink & Co., 1912.

The Constitution and Jurisdiction of Courts of Civil Justice in British India. Calcutta: Thacker, Spink & Co., 1923.

Tyabji, Faiz B. *Principles of Muhammadan Law*. 4th ed. Calcutta: Butterworth & Co., 1919.

Vaidya, Pandit Narayan Keshav, ed. *A Collection Containing the Proceedings Which Led to the Passing of Act XV of 1856*. Bombay: Mazagaon Printing Press, 1885.

Vijñanesvara. *Yajñavalkya Smriti with the Commentary of Vijñanesvara Called the Mitakshara and Notes from the Gloss of Balambhatta. Book One, The Achara Adhyaya*. Translated by Srisa Chandra Vidyrnava. Allahabad: The Panini Office, 1918.

Wacha, Sir D. E. *Shells from the Sands of Bombay: Being My Recollections and Reminiscences, 1860–1875*. Bombay: K. T. Anklesaria, The Indian Newspaper Co., 1920.

West, Sir Raymond. *Acts and Regulations of the Legislature in Force in the Presidency of Bombay, from 1827 to 1866*, Vol. II. 2nd ed. Bombay: Education Society's Press, 1860–1863.

The Land and the Law in India: An Elementary Inquiry and Some Practical Suggestions. Bombay: Education Society's Press, 1873.

West, Sir Raymond, and Johann Georg Bühler, eds. *A Digest of the Hindu Law of Inheritance and Partition, from the Replies of the Sastris in the Several Courts of the Bombay Presidency, with Introductions, Notes, and an Appendix.* 2nd ed. Bombay: Education Society's Press, 1878.

Secondary Sources

Abrams, Philip. "Notes on the Difficulty of Studying the State." *Journal of Historical Sociology* 1, 1 (March 1988): 59–89.

Agamben, Giorgio. *Homo Sacer: Sovereign Power and Bare Life.* Translated by Daniel Heller-Roazen. Stanford, CA: Stanford University Press, 1998.

Agarwal, Bina. *A Field of One's Own: Gender and Land Rights in South Asia.* Cambridge: Cambridge University Press, 1994.

Agnes, Flavia. "Maintenance for Women: Rhetoric of Equality." *Economic and Political Weekly* 27, 41 (Oct. 10, 1992): 2233–2235.

Law and Gender Inequality: The Politics of Women's Rights in India. New Delhi: Oxford University Press, 1999.

Agrama, Hussein Ali. "Secularism, Sovereignty, Indeterminacy: Is Egypt a Religious or a Secular State?" *Comparative Studies in Society and History* 52, 3 (2010): 495–523.

Ambirajan, S. *Classical Political Economy and British Policy in India.* Cambridge: Cambridge University Press, 1978.

Amin, Shahid. *Event, Metaphor, Memory: Chauri Chaura, 1922–1992.* Berkeley: University of California Press, 1995.

Anagol, Padma. *The Emergence of Feminism in India, 1850–1920.* Burlington, VT: Ashgate, 2006.

Anandhi, S. "Representing Devadasis: *Dasigal Mosavalai* as a Radical Text." *Economic and Political Weekly* 26, 11–12 Annual Number (March 1991): 739–746.

"Women's Question in the Dravidian Movement, 1925–1948." *Social Scientist* 19, 5–6 (May–June 1991): 24–41.

Anderson, Michael R., and Sumit Guha, eds. *Changing Concepts of Rights and Justice in South Asia.* Delhi: Oxford University Press, 1998.

Arendt, Hannah. *The Origins of Totalitarianism.* 2nd enlarged ed. New York: Meridian Books, 1958.

The Human Condition. 2nd ed. Chicago: University of Chicago Press, 1998.

Armitage, David. *The Ideological Origins of the British Empire.* Ideas in Context, vol. 59. Cambridge: Cambridge University Press, 2000.

Arnold, David. *Colonizing the Body: State Medicine and Epidemic Disease in Nineteenth-Century India.* Berkeley: University of California Press, 1993.

Arthurs, H. W. *"Without the Law": Administrative Justice and Legal Pluralism in Nineteenth-Century England.* Toronto: University of Toronto Press, 1985.

Arunima, G. "Multiple Meanings: Changing Conceptions of Matrilineal Kinship in Nineteenth- and Twentieth-Century Malabar." *Indian Economic and Social History Review* 33, 3 (1996): 283–307.

There Comes Papa: Colonialism and the Transformation of Matriliny in Kerala, Malabar c. 1850–1940. New Delhi: Orient Longman, 2003.

Asad, Talal. *Genealogies of Religion: Discipline and Reasons of Power in Christianity and Islam.* Baltimore: Johns Hopkins University Press, 1993.

"Comments on Conversion." In *Conversion to Modernities: The Globalization of Christianity,* edited by Peter van der Veer, 263–274. New York: Routledge, 1996.

Formations of the Secular: Christianity, Islam, Modernity. Stanford, CA: Stanford University Press, 2003.

"Trying to Understand French Secularism." In *Political Theologies,* edited by Hent de Vries and Lawrence Eugene Sullivan, 494–526. New York: Fordham University Press, 2006.

Attwood, D. W., M. Israel, and N. K. Wagle, eds. *City, Countryside and Society in Maharashtra.* Toronto: University of Toronto Press, 1988.

Baird, Robert D., ed. *Religion and Law in Independent India.* 2nd ed. New Delhi: Ajay Kumar Jain for Manohar Publishers, 2005.

Balibar, Etienne. *Masses, Classes, Ideas: Studies on Politics and Philosophy before and after Marx.* New York: Routledge, 1994.

Ballhatchet, Kenneth. *Social Policy and Social Change in Western India, 1817–1830.* London: Oxford University Press, 1957.

Banerjee, Sumanta. *The Parlour and the Streets: Elite and Popular Culture in Nineteenth-Century Calcutta.* Calcutta: Seagull Books, 1989.

Under the Raj: Prostitution in Colonial Bengal. New York: Monthly Press Books, 1998.

Barrier, N. G., ed. *The Census in British India.* Delhi: Manohar, 1981.

Basu, Aparna, and Bharati Ray. *Women's Struggle: A History of the All India Women's Conference, 1927–1990.* New Delhi: Manohar, 1990.

Basu, Monmayee. *Hindu Women and Marriage Law: From Sacrament to Contract.* Delhi: Oxford University Press, 2001.

Basu, Srimati. *She Comes to Take Her Rights: Indian Women, Property, and Propriety.* Albany: State University of New York Press, 1999.

"The Personal and the Political: Indian Women and Inheritance Law." In *Religion and Personal Law in Secular India: A Call to Judgment,* edited by Gerald James Larson, 163–182. Bloomington: Indiana University Press, 2001.

ed. *Dowry and Inheritance.* New Delhi: Kali for Women, 2005.

Bayly, C. A. *Rulers, Townsmen and Bazaars: North Indian Society in the Age of British Expansion, 1770–1870.* Cambridge: Cambridge University Press, 1983.

"Maine and Change in Nineteenth-Century India." In *The Victorian Achievement of Sir Henry Maine: A Centennial Reappraisal,* edited by Alan Diamond, 389–397. Cambridge: Cambridge University Press, 1991.

Empire and Information: Intelligence Gathering and Social Communication in India, 1780–1870. Cambridge: Cambridge University Press, 1996.

Bellamy, Richard, ed. *Victorian Liberalism: Nineteenth-Century Political Thought and Practice.* London: Routledge, 1990.

Benjamin, Walter. *Reflections: Essays, Aphorisms, Autobiographical Writings.* Translated by Edmund Jephcott. New York: Harcourt, Brace, Jovanovich, 1978.

Benton, Lauren. *Law and Colonial Cultures: Legal Regimes and World History, 1400–1900.* Cambridge: Cambridge University Press, 2002.

Bhabha, Homi. *The Location of Culture*. London: Routledge, 1994.

Bhargava, Rajeev, ed. *Secularism and Its Critics*. Delhi: Oxford University Press, 1998.

Bhattacharya, Neeladri. "Colonial State and Agrarian Society." In *The Making of Agrarian Policy in British India, 1770–1900*, edited by Burton Stein, 113–149. Delhi: Oxford University Press, 1992.

"Remaking Custom: The Discourse and Practice of Colonial Codification." In *Tradition, Dissent, Ideology: Essays in Honour of Romila Thapar*, edited by R. Champakalakshmi and S. Gopal, 20–54. Delhi: Oxford University Press, 1996.

Bhattacharyya, Harasankar. *Zamindars and Patnidars: Study of Subinfeudation under Permanent Settlement*. Burdwan: University of Burdwan, 1985.

Birla, Ritu. *Stages of Capital: Law, Culture and Market Governance in Late Colonial India*. Durham, NC: Duke University Press, 2009.

Birmingham, Peg. *Hannah Arendt and Human Rights: The Predicament of Common Responsibility*. Bloomington, IN: Indiana University Press, 2006.

Bourdieu, Pierre. *Outline of a Theory of Practice*. Translated by Richard Nice. Cambridge: Cambridge University Press, 1977.

"The Force of Law: Toward a Sociology of the Juridical Field." Translated by Richard Terdiman. *Hastings Law Journal* 38 (1987): 805–853.

Bowen, John. *Islam, Law and Equality in Indonesia: An Anthropology of Public Reasoning*. Cambridge: Cambridge University Press, 2003.

Brewer, John. *The Sinews of Power: War, Money and the English State, 1688–1783*. New York: Alfred A. Knopf, 1989.

Brown, Wendy. *States of Injury: Power and Freedom in Late Modernity*. Princeton, NJ: Princeton University Press, 1995.

Burton, Antoinette. *Burdens of History: British Feminists, Indian Women and Imperial Culture, 1865–1915*. Chapel Hill: University of North Carolina Press, 1994.

Carroll, Lucy. "Law, Custom and Statutory Social Reform: The Hindu Widows' Remarriage Act of 1856." *Indian Economic and Social History Review* 20, 4 (1983): 363–388.

"The Ithna Ashari Law of Intestate Succession: An Introduction to Shia Law Applicable in South Asia." *Modern Asian Studies* 19, 1 (1985): 85–124.

"Daughter's Right of Inheritance in India: A Perspective on the Problem of Dowry." *Modern Asian Studies* 25, 4 (1991): 791–809.

Catanach, I. J. *Rural Credit in Western India, 1875–1930: Rural Credit and the Co-operative Movement in the Bombay Presidency*. Berkeley: University of California Press, 1970.

Chakrabarty, Dipesh. *Provincializing Europe: Postcolonial Thought and Historical Difference*. Princeton, NJ: Princeton University Press, 2000.

Habitations of Modernity: Essays in the Wake of Subaltern Studies. Chicago: University of Chicago Press, 2002.

Chakravarti, Uma. "Whatever Happened to the Vedic Dasi: Orientalism, Nationalism, and a Script for the Past." In *Recasting Women: Essays in Indian Colonial History*, edited by Kumkum Sangari and Sudesh Vaid, 27–87. New Brunswick, NJ: Rutgers University Press, 1990.

"Wifehood, Widowhood and Adultery: Female Sexuality, Surveillance and the State in Eighteenth-Century Maharashtra." *Contributions to Indian Sociology*, n.s., 29, 1–2 (1995): 3–21.

Rewriting History: The Life and Times of Pandita Ramabai. Delhi: Kali for Women Press, 1998.

Chandavarkar, Rajnarayan. *The Origins of Industrial Capitalism in India: Business Strategies and the Working Classes in Bombay, 1900–1940.* Cambridge: Cambridge University Press, 1994.

Imperial Power and Popular Politics: Class, Resistance and the State in India, 1850–1950. Cambridge: Cambridge University Press, 1998.

Chandra, Sudhir. *Enslaved Daughters: Colonialism, Law and Women's Rights.* Delhi: Oxford University Press, 1998.

Chanock, Martin. *Law, Custom, and Social Order: The Colonial Experience in Malawi and Zambia.* Cambridge: Cambridge University Press, 1985.

Charlesworth, Neil. "The Myth of the Deccan Riots of 1875," *Modern Asian Studies* 6, 4 (Oct. 1972): 401–421.

"Rich Peasants and Poor Peasants in Late-Nineteenth Century Maharashtra." In *The Imperial Impact: Studies in the Economic History of Africa and India*, edited by Clive Dewey and A. G. Hopkins. London: Athlone Press for the Institute of Commonwealth Studies, 1978.

"The Russian Stratification Debate and India." *Modern Asian Studies* 13, 1 (1979): 61–95.

"The Origins of Fragmentation of Landholdings in British India: A Comparative Examination." In *Rural India*, edited by Peter Robb, 181–215. London: Curzon Press, 1983.

Peasants and Imperial Rule: Agriculture and Agrarian Society in the Bombay Presidency, 1850–1935. Cambridge: Cambridge University Press, 1985.

Chatterjee, Indrani. *Gender, Slavery and Law in Colonial India.* New Delhi: Oxford University Press, 1999.

ed. *Unfamiliar Relations: Family and History in South Asia.* New Brunswick, NJ: Rutgers University Press, 2004.

Chatterjee, Indrani, and Richard M. Eaton, eds. *Slavery and South Asian History.* Bloomington: Indiana University Press, 2006.

Chatterjee, Indrani, and Sumit Guha. "Slave-Queen, Waif-Prince: Slavery and Social Capital in Eighteenth-Century India." *Indian Economic and Social History Review* 36, 2 (1999): 165–186.

Chatterjee, Nandini. "English Law, Brahmo Marriage, and the Problem of Religious Difference: Civil Marriage Laws in Britain and India." *Comparative Studies in Society and History* 52, 3 (2010): 524–552.

Chatterjee, Partha. "The Nationalist Resolution of the 'Women's Question'.'" In *Recasting Women: Essays in Indian Colonial History, edited by Kumkum Sangari and Sudesh Vaid*, 233–253. New Brunswick, NJ: Rutgers University Press, 1990.

Nationalist Thought and the Colonial World: A Derivative Discourse. London: Zed Books, 1986. Reprint, Minneapolis: University of Minnesota Press, 1993.

The Nation and Its Fragments: Colonial and Post-Colonial Histories. Princeton, NJ: Princeton University Press, 1993.

The Politics of the Governed: Reflections on Popular Politics in Most of the World. New York: Columbia University Press, 2004.

Choksey, R. D. *Economic History of the Bombay Deccan and Karnatak (1818–1868).* Pune: Oriental Watchman Publishing House, 1945.

Chowdhry, Prem. *The Veiled Women: Shifting Gender Equations in Rural Haryana, 1880–1990.* Delhi: Oxford University Press, 1994.

"Contesting Claims and Counter-Claims: Questions of the Inheritance and Sexuality of Widows in a Colonial State." *Contributions to Indian Sociology,* n.s., 29, 1–2 (1995): 65–82.

Christelow, Allan. *Muslim Law Courts and the French Colonial State in Algeria.* Princeton, NJ: Princeton University Press, 1985.

Clancy-Smith, Julia Ann, and Frances Gouda. *Domesticating the Empire: Race, Gender, and Family Life in French and Dutch Colonialism.* Charlottesville: University Press of Virginia, 1998.

Cohn, Bernard S. "Representing Authority in Victorian India." In *The Invention of Tradition,* edited by Eric Hobsbawm and Terence Ranger, 165–209. Cambridge: Cambridge University Press, 1983.

An Anthropologist among the Historians and Other Essays. Delhi: Oxford University Press, 1987.

Colonialism and Its Forms of Knowledge: The British in India. Princeton, NJ: Princeton University Press, 1996.

Comaroff, Jean, and John Comaroff, eds. "Introduction." In *Law and Disorder in the Postcolony,* 1–56. Chicago: University of Chicago Press, 2006.

Coronil, Fernando. *The Magical State: Nature, Money, and Modernity in Venezuela.* Chicago: University of Chicago Press, 1997.

Coward, Rosalind. *Patriarchal Precedents: Sexuality and Social Relations.* London: Routledge & Kegan Paul, 1983.

Coyajee, J. C. "Ranade's Work as an Economist." *Indian Journal of Economics* 22, 3 (Jan. 1942): 307–330.

Das, Veena. "Secularism and the Argument from Nature." In *Powers of the Secular Modern: Talal Asad and His Interlocutors,* edited by David Scott and Charles Hirschkind, 93–112. Stanford, CA: Stanford University Press, 2006.

Dasgupta, Ajit. *A History of Indian Economic Thought.* London: Routledge, 1993.

Datta, Bhabatosh. "The Background of Ranade's Economics." *Indian Journal of Economics* 22, 3 (1942): 261–275.

D'Cruze, Shani, and Anupama Rao, eds. "Violence and the Vulnerabilities of Gender." In *Violence, Vulnerability and Embodiment: Gender and History,* 1–18. Oxford: Blackwell, 2005.

de Vries, Hent and Lawrence E. Sullivan, eds. *Political Theologies: Public Religions in a Post-Secular World.* New York: Fordham University Press, 2006.

Derrett, J. D. M. *Introduction to Modern Hindu Law.* London: Oxford University Press, 1963.

Essays in Classical and Modern Hindu Law. 4 vols. Leiden: E. J. Brill, 1976–1978.

Religion, Law and the State in India. London: Faber & Faber, 1968. Reprint, Delhi: Oxford University Press, 1999.

Derrida, Jacques. "The Force of Law: The 'Mystical Foundation of Authority.'" In *Acts of Religion*, edited by Gil Anidjar, 228–298. New York: Routledge, 2002.

Deshpande, G. P., ed. *Selected Writings of Jotirao Phule*. Translated by Aniket Jawaare. New Delhi: LeftWord Books, 2002.

Deshpande, Prachi. "Caste as Maratha: Social Categories, Colonial Policy and Identity in Early Twentieth-Century Maharashtra." *Indian Economic and Social History Review* 41, 1 (Jan.–March 2004): 7–32.

Creative Pasts: Historical Memory and Identity in Western India, 1700–1960. New York: Columbia University Press, 2007.

Devji, Faisal. "The Minority as Political Form." In *From the Colonial to the Post-Colonial: India and Pakistan in Transition*, edited by Dipesh Chakrabarty, Rochona Majumdar, and Andrew Sartori, 85–95. New Delhi: Oxford University Press, 2007.

Dewey, Clive. "The Influence of Sir Henry Maine on Agrarian Policy in India." In *The Victorian Achievement of Sir Henry Maine: A Centennial Reappraisal*, edited by Alan Diamond, 353–375. Cambridge: Cambridge University Press, 1991.

Diamond, Alan, ed. *The Victorian Achievement of Sir Henry Maine: A Centennial Reappraisal*. Cambridge: Cambridge University Press, 1991.

Dirks, Nicholas B. *The Hollow Crown: Ethnohistory of an Indian Kingdom*. Cambridge South Asian studies. Cambridge: Cambridge University Press, 1987.

Castes of Mind: Colonialism and the Making of Modern India. Princeton, NJ: Princeton University Press, 2001.

The Scandal of Empire: India and the Creation of Imperial Britain. Cambridge, MA: Harvard University Press, 2006.

Dobbin, Christine. *Urban Leadership in Western India: Politics and Communities in Bombay City, 1840–1885*. London: Oxford University Press, 1972.

Dumont, Louis. *Affinity as a Value*. Chicago: University of Chicago Press, 1984.

Engineer, Asghar Ali. *The Muslim Communities of Gujarat: An Exploratory Study of Bohras, Khojas and Memons*. Delhi: Ajanta Publications, 1989.

Esmeir, Samera. "At Once Human and Not Human: Gender, Law, and Becoming in Colonial Egypt." *Gender & History* 23, 2 (Aug. 2011): 235–249.

Fanon, Franz. *The Wretched of the Earth*. Translated by Richard Philcox. New York: Grove Press, 2004 (orig. 1961).

Feldhaus, Anne. *Images of Women in Maharashtrian Society*. Albany: State University of New York Press, 1998.

Forbes, Geraldine. *Women in Modern India*. Cambridge: Cambridge University Press, 1996.

Foucault, Michel. *The History of Sexuality*, Vol. 1. Trans. Robert Hurley. New York: Vintage Books, 1990.

"Governmentality." In *The Foucault Effect: Studies in Governmentality, with Two Lectures by and an Interview with Michel Foucault*, edited by Graham Burchell, Colin Gordon, and Peter Miller, 87–104. Chicago: University of Chicago Press, 1991.

Fraser, Nancy, and Linda Gordon. "A Genealogy of Dependency: Tracing a Keyword of the U.S. Welfare State." *Signs* 19, 2 (1994): 309–336.

Frietag, Sandria. *Collective Action and Community: Public Arenas and the Emergence of Communalism in North India.* Berkeley: University of California Press, 1989.

Fukazawa, Hiroshi. *The Medieval Deccan: Peasants, Social Systems and States, Sixteenth to Eighteenth Centuries.* Delhi: Oxford University Press, 1991.

Fyzee, Asaf A. A. *Outlines of Muhammadan Law.* 2nd ed. London: Oxford University Press, 1955.

———. *Cases in the Muhammadan Law of India and Pakistan.* London: Oxford University Press, 1974.

Galanter, Marc. "Justice in Many Rooms: Courts, Private Ordering, and Indigenous Law." *Journal of Legal Pluralism and Unofficial Law* 19 (1981): 1–47.

———. *Law and Society in Modern India.* Edited and with an introduction by Rajeev Dhavan. Delhi: Oxford University Press, 1989.

Ganguli, B. N. *Indian Economic Thought: Nineteenth-Century Perspectives.* New Delhi: Tata McGraw-Hill Publishing Co., 1977.

Garzilli, Enrica. "Stridhana: To Have and to Have Not." *Journal of South Asian Women's Studies* 2, 1 (Jan. 1996): 37–56.

Geetha, V. "Periyar, Women and an Ethic of Citizenship." In *Gender and Caste,* edited by Anupama Rao, 180–203. New Delhi: Kali for Women, 2003.

Gidwani, Vinay. *Capital, Interrupted: Agrarian Development and the Politics of Work in India.* Minneapolis: University of Minnesota Press, 2008.

Gill, Kulwant. *Hindu Women's Right to Property in India.* Delhi: Deep & Deep, 1986.

Glushkova, Irina, and Anne Feldhaus, eds. *House and Home in Maharashtra.* Delhi: Oxford University Press, 1998.

Glushkova, Irina, and Rajendra Vora, eds. *Home, Family, and Kinship in Maharashtra.* Delhi: Oxford University Press, 1999.

Goody, Jack. *The Oriental, the Ancient and the Primitive: Systems of Marriage and the Family in the Pre-Industrial Societies of Eurasia.* Cambridge: Cambridge University Press, 1990.

Goody, Jack, and S. J. Tambiah. *Bridewealth and Dowry.* Cambridge Papers in Social Anthropology, no. 7. Cambridge: Cambridge University Press, 1973.

Goodyear, Sara Suleri. *The Rhetoric of English India.* Chicago: University of Chicago Press, 1992.

Gooptu, Nandini. *The Politics of the Urban Poor in Early Twentieth-Century India.* Cambridge: Cambridge University Press, 2001.

Gordley, James. *The Philosophical Origins of Modern Contract Doctrine.* Oxford: Clarendon Press, 1991.

Gordon, Stewart. *The Marathas, 1600–1818.* The New Cambridge History of India, II, 4. Cambridge: Cambridge University Press, 1993.

———. *Marathas, Marauders, and State Formation in Eighteenth-Century India.* Delhi: Oxford University Press, 1994.

Goswami, Manu. *Producing India: From Colonial Economy to National Space.* Chicago: University of Chicago Press, 2004.

Griffiths, John. "What Is Legal Pluralism?" *Journal of Legal Pluralism and Unofficial Law* 24 (1986): 1–55.

Guha, Ranajit. *A Rule of Property for Bengal: An Essay on the Idea of Permanent Settlement*. Paris: Mouton & Co., 1963. Reprint, Durham, NC: Duke University Press, 1996.

——— *Elementary Aspects of Peasant Insurgency in Colonial India*. Delhi: Oxford University Press, 1983.

——— "The Prose of Counter-Insurgency." In *Subaltern Studies, Vol. II: Writings on South Asian History and Society*, edited by Ranajit Guha. Delhi: Oxford University Press, 1983

Guha, Ranajit, and Gayatri Chakravorty Spivak. *Selected Subaltern Studies*. New York: Oxford University Press, 1988.

Guha, Sumit. *The Agrarian Economy of the Bombay Deccan, 1818–1941*. Delhi: Oxford University Press, 1985.

——— "Society and Economy in the Deccan, 1818–1850." In *The Making of Agrarian Policy in British India, 1770–1900*, edited by Burton Stein, 187–214. Delhi: Oxford University Press, 1992.

——— "An Indian Penal Régime: Maharashtra in the Eighteenth Century." *Past and Present* 147 (May 1995): 101–126.

——— "Wrongs and Rights in the Maratha Country: Antiquity, Custom and Power in Eighteenth-Century India." In *Changing Concepts of Rights and Justice in South Asia*, edited by Michael R. Anderson and Sumit Guha, 14–29. Delhi: Oxford University Press, 1998.

——— "Weak States and Strong Markets in South Asian Development, c. 1700–1970." *Indian Economic and Social History Review* 36, 3 (1999): 335–353.

——— "Claims on the Commons: Political Power and Natural Resources in Pre-Colonial India." *Indian Economic and Social History Review* 39, 2–3 (2002): 181–196.

——— "Civilisations, Markets and Services: Village Servants in India from the Seventeenth to the Twentieth Centuries." *Indian Economic and Social History Review* 41, 1 (2004): 79–101.

Gune, V. T. *The Judicial System of the Marathas, a Detailed Study of the Judicial Institutions in Maharashtra, from 1600–1818, Based on Original Decisions Called Mazhars, Nivadpatras, and Official Orders*. Pune: Deccan College Postgraduate and Research Institute, 1953.

Gupta, Charu. *Sexuality, Obscenity and Community: Women, Muslims and the Hindu Public in Colonial India*. New York: Palgrave, 2002.

Habib, Irfan. *The Agrarian System of Mughal India, 1556–1707*. London: Asia Publishing House, 1963.

Hart, H. L. A. *The Concept of Law*. 2nd ed. Clarendon Law Series. Oxford: Oxford University Press, 1997.

Hasan, Zoya, ed. *Forging Identities: Gender, Communities and the State in India*. Boulder, CO: Westview Press, 1994.

Hatekar, Neeraj. "Information and Incentives: Pringle's Ricardian Experiment in the Nineteenth Century Deccan." *Indian Economic and Social History Review* 33, 4 (1996): 437–457.

Haynes, Douglas and Gyan Prakash, eds. *Contesting Power: Resistance and Everyday Social Relations in South Asia*. Delhi: Oxford University Press, 1991.

High Court at Bombay. *The High Court at Bombay, 1862–1962.* Bombay: Government Central Press, 1962.

Hirschon, Renée. *Women and Property – Women as Property.* London: Croon Helm, 1989.

Holcombe, Lee. *Wives and Property: Reform of the Married Women's Property Law in Nineteenth-Century England.* Toronto: University of Toronto Press, 1983.

Hont, Istvan, and Michael Ignatieff. "Needs and Justice in the Wealth of Nations: An Introductory Essay." In *Wealth and Virtue: The Shaping of Political Economy in the Scottish Enlightenment.* Cambridge: Cambridge University Press, 1983.

Hooker, M. B. *Legal Pluralism: An Introduction to Colonial and Neo-Colonial Laws.* London: Oxford Clarendon Press, 1975.

Hussain, Nasser. *The Jurisprudence of Emergency: Colonialism and the Rule of Law.* Ann Arbor: University of Michigan Press, 2003.

Islam, Sirajul. *The Permanent Settlement in Bengal: A Study of Its Operation, 1790–1819.* Dacca: Bangla Academy, 1979.

Jacobsohn, Gary Jeffrey. *The Wheel of Law: India's Secularism in Comparative Constitutional Perspective.* New Delhi: Oxford University Press, 2003.

Jagirdar, P. J. "Ranade and the Historical School of Economics." *Indian Journal of Economics* 34, 3 (January 1954): 195–201.

Jalal, Ayesha. *The Sole Spokesman: Jinnah, the Muslim League, and the Demand for Pakistan.* Cambridge: Cambridge University Press, 1985.

John, Mary E., and Janaki Nair, eds. *A Question of Silence? The Sexual Economies of Modern India.* New Delhi: Kali for Women, 1998.

Jones, Kenneth. *Arya Dharm: Hindu Consciousness in Nineteenth-Century Punjab.* Berkeley: University of California Press, 1976.

Kadam, V. S. "The Institution of Marriage and Position of Women in Eighteenth-Century Maharashtra." *Indian Economic and Social History Review* 25, 3 (July–Sept. 1988): 341–370.

Kaiwar, Vasant. "Property Structures, Demography and the Crisis of the Agricultural Economy of Colonial Bombay Presidency." *Journal of Peasant Studies* 19, 2 (Jan. 1992): 255–300.

Kannabiran, Kalpana. "Judiciary, Social Reform and Debate on 'Religious Prostitution' in India." *Economic and Political Weekly* 30, 43 (Oct. 28, 1995): WS59–WS-69.

Kannabiran, Kalpana, and Vasanth Kannabiran. "Caste and Gender: Understanding Dynamics of Power and Violence." In *De-Eroticizing Assault: Essays on Modesty, Honour and Power.* Calcutta: Stree, 2002.

Kantorowitz, Ernst. *The King's Two Bodies: A Study in Medieval Political Theology.* Princeton, NJ: Princeton University Press, 1957.

Kapur, Ratna, and Brenda Cossman. *Subversive Sites: Feminist Engagements with Law in India.* New Delhi: Sage Publications, 1996.

Karve, Irawati. *Kinship Organization in India.* Pune: Deccan College Post-Graduate and Research Institute, 1953.

Kasturi, Malavika. *Embattled Identities: Rajput Lineages and the Colonial State in Nineteenth-Century North India.* New Delhi: Oxford University Press, 2002.

Kaviraj, Sudipta. "The Imaginary Institution of India." *Nehru Memorial Museum and Library, Occasional Papers on History and Society,* 2nd ser., 42 (Aug. 1991): 1–113.

"Modernity and Politics in India." *Daedalus* Special Issue on Multiple Modernities 129, 1 (Winter 2000): 137–162.

Kaviraj, Sudipta, and Sunil Khilnani. "Introduction: Ideas of Civil Society." In *Civil Society: History and Possibilities,* edited by Sudipta Kaviraj and Sunil Khilnani, 1–6. Cambridge: Cambridge University Press, 2001.

Keer, Dhananjay. *Mahatma Jotirao Phooley: Father of the Indian Social Revolution.* Bombay: Popular Prakashan, 1974. Reprint, 1997.

Kellock, James. "Ranade and After: A Study of the Development of Economic Thought in India." *Indian Journal of Economics* 2, 3 (Jan. 1942): 245–260.

Kishwar, Madhu. "Dowry and Inheritance Rights." *Economic and Political Weekly* 24, 12 (March 19, 1989): 586–587.

"Continuing the Dowry Debate." *Economic and Political Weekly* 24, 49 (December 9, 1989): 2738–2740.

Kodoth, Praveena. "Courting Legitimacy or Delegitimizing Custom? Sexuality, Sambandham, and Marriage Reform in Late Nineteenth-Century Malabar." *Modern Asian Studies* 35, 2 (May 2001): 349–384.

Kolsky, Elizabeth. *Colonial Justice in British India: White Violence and the Rule of Law.* Cambridge: Cambridge University Press, 2010.

"Codification and the Rule of Colonial Difference: Criminal Procedure in British India." *Law and History Review* 23, 3 (Aug. 2010): 631–683.

Kosambi, Meera. "Girl-Brides and Socio-Legal Change: Age of Consent Bill (1891) Controversy." *Economic and Political Weekly* 26, 31–32 (August 3–10, 1991): 1857–1868.

"Gender Reform and Competing State Controls over Women: The Rakhmabai Case (1884–1888)." *Contributions to Indian Sociology,* n.s., 29, 1–2 (1995): 265–290.

"Life after Widowhood: Two Radical Reformist Options in Maharashtra." In *Intersections: Socio-Cultural Trends in Maharashtra,* edited by Meera Kosambi, 92–114. Hyderabad: Orient Longman, 2000.

Kotani, Hiroyuki. *Western India in Historical Transition: Seventeenth to Early Twentieth Centuries.* Delhi: Manohar, 2002.

Kozlowski, Gregory. *Muslim Endowments and Society in British India.* Cambridge: Cambridge University Press, 1985.

"Muslim Women and the Control of Property in North India." In *Women in Colonial India: Essays on Survival, Work and the State,* edited by J. Krishnamurty, 163–181. Delhi: Oxford University Press, 1989. Reprint, 1999.

Krishnamurty, J., ed. *Women in Colonial India: Essays on Survival, Work and the State.* Delhi: Oxford University Press, 1989. Reprint, 1999.

Kugle, Scott. "Framed, Blamed, and Renamed: The Recasting of Islamic Jurisprudence in Colonial South Asia." *Modern Asian Studies* 35, 2 (May 2001): 257–314.

Kulkarni, A. R. "Source Material for the Study of Village Communities in Maharashtra." *Indian Economic and Social History Review* 13, 4 (1976): 513–523.

"The Mahar Watan: A Historical Perspective." In *Intersections: Socio-Cultural Trends in Maharashtra*, edited by Meera Kosambi, 121–140. Hyderabad: Orient Longman, 2000.

Kulkarni, A. R., and N. K. Wagle, eds. *Region, Nationality and Religion*. Bombay: Popular Prakashan, 1999.

Kumar, Ravinder. *Western India in the Nineteenth Century: A Study in the Social History of Maharashtra*. London: Routledge & Kegan Paul, 1968.

Kuper, Adam. "The Rise and Fall of Maine's Patriarchal Theory." In *The Victorian Achievement of Sir Henry Maine: A Centennial Reappraisal*, edited by Alan Diamond, 99–110. Cambridge: Cambridge University Press, 1991.

Larson, Gerald James, ed. *Religion and Personal Law in Secular India: A Call to Judgment*. Bloomington: Indiana University Press, 2001.

Lester, V. Markham. *Victorian Insolvency: Bankruptcy, Imprisonment for Debt, and Company Winding-up in Nineteenth-Century England*. New York: Oxford University Press, 1995.

Levy, Harold Lewis. "Lawyer-Scholars, Lawyer-Politicians and the Hindu Code Bill, 1921–1956." *Law and Society Review* 3, 2–3 (Nov. 1968–Feb. 1969): 303–316.

Lieberman, David. *The Province of Legislation Determined: Legal Theory in Eighteenth-Century Britain*. Cambridge: Cambridge University Press, 1989.

"Property, Commerce, and the Common Law: Attitudes to Legal Change in the Eighteenth Century." In *Early Modern Conceptions of Property*, edited by John Brewer and Susan Staves, 144–158. London: Routledge, 1995.

Low, D. A. *Britain and Indian Nationalism, 1929–1942: The Imprint of Ambiguity*. Cambridge: Cambridge University Press, 1997.

Majumdar, Rochona. *Marriage and Modernity: Family Values in Colonial Bengal*. Durham, NC: Duke University Press, 2009.

Mamdani, Mahmood. *Citizen and Subject: Contemporary Africa and the Legacy of Late Colonialism*. Princeton, NJ: Princeton University Press, 1996.

Mani, Lata. *Contentious Traditions: The Debate on Sati in Colonial India*. Berkeley: University of California Press, 1998.

Mantena, Karuna. "Law and 'Tradition': Henry Maine and the Theoretical Origins of Indirect Rule." In *Law and History*, edited by Andrew Lewis and Michael Lobban, 159–188. Oxford: Oxford University Press, 2004.

"The Crisis of Liberal Imperialism." In *Victorian Visions of Global Order: Empire and International Relations in Nineteenth-Century Political Thought*, edited by Duncan Bell, 113–135. Cambridge: Cambridge University Press, 2007.

Alibis of Empire: Henry Maine and the Ends of Liberal Imperialism. Princeton, NJ: Princeton University Press, 2010.

Marglin, F. A. *Wives of the God-King: The Rituals of the Devadasis of Puri*. Delhi: Oxford University Press, 1985.

Marshall, Peter J. *Bengal: The British Bridgehead, 1740–1828*. The New Cambridge History of India, II, 2. Cambridge: Cambridge University Press, 1988.

Masselos, Jim. "The Khojas: The Defining of Formal Membership Criteria during the Nineteenth Century." In *Caste and Social Stratification among Muslims in India*, edited by Imtiaz Ahmed, 97–116. Delhi: Manohar, 1978.

Maurer, Bill, and Gabrielle Schwab, eds. *Accelerating Possession: Global Futures of Property and Personhood*. New York: Columbia University Press, 2006.

Mauss, Marcel. *The Gift: Forms and Functions of Exchange in Archaic Societies*. Translated by Ian Cunnison. Glencoe, IL: Free Press, 1954.

Mazower, Mark. "The Strange Triumph of Human Rights, 1933–1950." *Historical Journal* 47, 2 (2004): 379–398.

McKeon, Michael. *The Secret History of Domesticity: Public, Private, and the Division of Knowledge*. Baltimore: The Johns Hopkins University Press, 2005.

Mehta, Uday Singh. *Liberalism and Empire: A Study in Nineteenth-Century British Liberal Thought*. Chicago: University of Chicago Press, 1999.

Members of the Subcommittee of the Khoja Sunnat Summat. *An Account of The Khoja Sunnat Jamat*. Bombay, 1969.

Menon, Nivedita. *Recovering Subversion: Feminist Politics beyond the Law*. New Delhi: Permanent Black, 2004.

Merry, Sally Engle. "Legal Pluralism." *Law and Society Review* 22, 5 (1988): 869–896.

Meschievitz, Catherine. *Panchayat Justice: State-Sponsored Informal Courts in Nineteenth- and Twentieth-Century India*. Institute for Legal Studies Working Papers Series 8: 1. Madison: University of Wisconsin, Madison Law School, 1987.

Metcalf, Barbara Daly. *Islamic Revival in British India: Deoband, 1860–1900*. Princeton, NJ: Princeton University Press, 1982.

  Perfecting Women: Maulana Ashraf 'Ali Thanawi's Bihishti Zewar. Berkeley: University of California Press, 1990.

Metcalf, Thomas. "The British and the Moneylender in Nineteenth-Century India." *Journal of Modern History* 34, 4 (Dec. 1962): 390–397.

  The Aftermath of Revolt: India, 1857–1870. Princeton, NJ: Princeton University Press, 1964.

  Land, Landlords and the British Raj: Northern India in the Nineteenth Century. Berkeley: University of California Press, 1979.

  Ideologies of the Raj. The New Cambridge History of India, III, 4. Cambridge: Cambridge University Press, 1994.

Mines, Mattison. "Courts of Law and Styles of Self in Eighteenth-Century Madras: From Hybrid to Colonial Self." *Modern Asian Studies* 35, 1 (2001): 33–74.

Misra, B. B. *The Central Administration of the East India Company, 1773–1834*. Manchester: Manchester University Press, 1959.

  The Administrative History of India, 1834–1947, General Administration. New Delhi: Oxford University Press, 1970.

Mitchell, Timothy. *Colonizing Egypt*. Cambridge: Cambridge University Press, 1988.

  ed. *Questions of Modernity*. Minneapolis: University of Minnesota Press, 2000.

  Rule of Experts: Egypt, Techno-Politics, Modernity. Berkeley: University of California Press, 2002.

Mommsen, W. J., and J. A. de Moor, eds. *European Expansion and Law: The Encounter of European and Indigenous Law in Nineteenth- and Twentieth-Century Africa and Asia*. Oxford: Berg Press, 1992.

Moore, Sally Falk. "Law and Social Change: The Semi-Autonomous Social Field as an Appropriate Subject of Study." *Law and Society Review* 7, 4 (Summer 1973): 719–746.

Social Facts and Fabrications: "Customary" Law on Kilimanjaro. Cambridge: Cambridge University Press, 1986.

Mufti, Aamir. *Enlightenment in the Colony: The Jewish Question and the Crisis of Postcolonial Culture*. Princeton, NJ: Princeton University Press, 2007.

Mukherjee, Mithi. "Justice, War, and the Imperium: India and Britain in Edmund Burke's Prosecutorial Speeches in the Impeachment Trial of Warren Hastings." *Law and History Review* 23, 3 (Fall 2005): 589–630.

India in the Shadows of Empire: A Legal and Political History, 1774–1950. New Delhi: Oxford University Press, 2010.

Mukhopadhyay, Maitrayee. *Legally Dispossessed: Gender, Identity and the Process of Law*. Calcutta: Stree, 1998.

Nair, Janaki. "The Devadasis, Dharma and the State." *Economic and Political Weekly* 29, 50 (Dec. 10, 1994): 3157–3167.

"Prohibited Marriage: State Protection and the Child Wife." *Contributions to Indian Sociology*, n.s., 29, 1–2 (1995): 157–186.

Women and Law in Colonial India: A Social History. New Delhi: Kali for Women, 1996.

Nagar, V. D., and K. P. Nagar. *Economic Thought and Policy of Dr. Ambedkar*. New Delhi: Segment Books, 1992.

Naregal, Veena. *Language Politics, Elites and the Public Sphere: Western India under Colonialism*. New Delhi: Permanent Black, 2001.

Newbigin, Eleanor. "A Post-Colonial Patriarchy? Representing Family in the Indian Nation-State." *Modern Asian Studies* 44, 1 (2010): 121–144.

Ocko, Jonathan and David Gilmartin. "State, Sovereignty and the People: A Comparison of the Rule of Law in China and India." *Journal of Asian Studies* 68, 1 (February 2009): 55–133.

O'Hanlon, Rosalind. *Caste, Conflict and Ideology: Mahatma Jotirao Phule and Low Caste Protest in Nineteenth-Century Western India*. Cambridge: Cambridge University Press, 1985.

"Issues of Widowhood: Gender and Resistance in Colonial Western India." In *Contesting Power: Resistance and Everyday Social Relations in South Asia*, edited by Douglas Haynes and Gyan Prakash, 62–108. Delhi: Oxford University Press, 1991.

A Comparison between Women and Men: Tarabai Shinde and the Critique of Gender Relations in Colonial India. New York: Oxford University Press, 1994.

Oldenburg, Veena Talwar. "Lifestyle as Resistance: The Case of the Courtesans of Lucknow." In *Contesting Power: Resistance and Everyday Social Relations in South Asia*, edited by Douglas Haynes and Gyan Prakash, 23–61. Delhi: Oxford University Press, 1991.

Dowry Murder: The Imperial Origins of a Cultural Crime. New York: Oxford University Press, 2002.

Orsini, Francesca. *The Hindi Public Sphere, 1920–1940: Language and Literature in the Age of Nationalism.* New Delhi: Oxford University Press, 2002.

Outhwaite, R. B. *The Rise and Fall of the English Ecclesiastical Courts, 1500–1800.* Cambridge Studies in English Legal History, edited by J. H. Baker. Cambridge: Cambridge University Press, 2006.

Pandey, Gyanendra. *The Construction of Communalism in Colonial North India.* Delhi: Oxford University Press, 1990.

Parashar, Archana. *Women and Family Law Reform in India: Uniform Civil Code and Gender Equality.* New Delhi: Sage Publications, 1992.

Pateman, Carole. *The Sexual Contract.* Stanford, CA: Stanford University Press, 1988.

"Self-Ownership and Property in the Person: Democratization and a Tale of Two Concepts." *Journal of Political Philosophy* 10, 1 (2002): 20–53.

Patterson, Maureen L. P. "Chitpavan Brahman Family Histories: Sources for a Study of Social Structure and Social Change in Maharashtra." In *Structure and Change in Indian Society,* edited by Milton Singer and Bernard S. Cohn, 397–411. Chicago: Aldine Publishing Co., 1968.

Paul, John Jeya. *The Legal Profession in Colonial South India.* Bombay: Oxford University Press, 1991.

Peck, Lisa Levy. "Kingship, Counsel and Law in Early Stuart Britain." In *The Varieties of British Political Thought, 1500–1800,* edited by J. G. A. Pocock, 80–115. Cambridge: Cambridge University Press, 1993.

Perlin, Frank. "Of White Whale and Countrymen in the Eighteenth-Century Maratha Deccan: Extended Class Relations, Rights, and the Problem of Rural Autonomy under the Old Regime." *Journal of Peasant Studies* 5, 2 (1978): 170–237.

Pierce, Stephen. *Farmers and the State in Colonial Kano: Land Tenure and the Legal Imagination.* Bloomington: Indiana University Press, 2005.

Pincus, Steve. "Neither Machiavellian Moment Nor Possessive Individualism: Commercial Society and the Defenders of the English Commonwealth." *American Historical Review* 103, 3 (June 1998): 705–737.

Pinney, Christopher. *'Photos of the Gods': The Printed Image and Political Struggle in India.* London: Reaktion Books, 2004.

Pocock, J. G. A. *The Machiavellian Moment: Florentine Political Thought and the Atlantic Republican Tradition.* Princeton, NJ: Princeton University Press, 1975.

Virtue, Commerce, History: Essays on Political Thought and History. Cambridge: Cambridge University Press, 1985.

Poovey, Mary. *Uneven Developments: The Ideological Work of Gender in Mid-Victorian England.* Chicago: University of Chicago Press, 1988.

Making a Social Body: British Cultural Formation, 1830–1864. Chicago: University of Chicago Press, 1994.

A History of the Modern Fact: Problems of Knowledge in the Sciences of Wealth and Society. Chicago: University of Chicago Press, 1998.

"The Liberal Civil Subject and the Social in Eighteenth-Century British Moral Philosophy." In *The Social in Question: New Bearings in History and the Social Sciences*, edited by Patrick Joyce, 44–61. London: Routledge, 2002.

Pottage, Alain. "Our Original Inheritance." In *Law, Anthropology, and the Constitution of the Social: Making Persons and Things*, edited by Alain Pottage and Martha Mundy, 249–284. Cambridge: Cambridge University Press, 2004.

Povinelli, Elizabeth. *The Cunning of Recognition: Indigenous Alterities and the Making of Australian Multiculturalism.* Durham, NC: Duke University Press, 2002.

Prakash, Gyan. *Bonded Histories: Genealogies of Labor Servitude in Colonial India.* Cambridge: Cambridge University Press, 1990.

"Writing Post-Orientalist Histories of the Third World: Perspectives from Indian Historiography." *Comparative Studies in Society and History* 32, 2 (1990): 383–408.

"The Colonial Genealogy of Society: Community and Political Modernity in India." In *The Social in Question: New Bearings in History and the Social Sciences*, edited by Patrick Joyce, 81–96. London: Routledge, 2002.

Price, Pamela. *Kingship and Political Practice in Colonial India.* Cambridge: Cambridge University Press, 1996.

Punacha, Veena. "Redefining Gender Relationships: The Imprint of the Colonial State on the Coorg/Kodava Norms of Marriage and Sexuality." *Contributions to Indian Sociology*, n.s., 29, 1–2 (1995): 39–63.

Radin, Margaret. *Reinterpreting Property.* Chicago: University of Chicago Press, 1993.

Rai, Kailash. *History of the Courts, Legislature and Legal Profession in India.* Reprint of 2nd ed. Faridabad, Haryana: Allahabad Law Agency, 2000.

Raj, K. N., Neeladri Bhattacharya, Sumit Guha, and Sakti Padhi, eds. *Essays on the Commercialization of Indian Agriculture.* Delhi: Oxford University Press, 1985.

Rao, Anupama, ed. *Gender and Caste.* New Delhi: Kali for Women, 2003.

The Caste Question: Dalits and the Politics of Modern India. Berkeley: University of California Press, 2009.

Raychaudhuri, Tapan. "The Agrarian System of Mughal India: A Review Essay." In *The Mughal State, 1526–1750*, edited by Muzaffar Alam and Sanjay Subrahmanyam, 259–283. Delhi: Oxford University Press, 1998.

Rege, Sharmila. "The Hegemonic Appropriation of Sexuality: The Case of the Lavani Performers of Maharashtra." *Contributions to Indian Sociology*, n.s., 29, 1–2 (Jan. 1995): 23–38.

Rothschild, Emma. *Economic Sentiments: Adam Smith, Condorcet and the Enlightenment.* Cambridge, MA: Harvard University Press, 2001.

Roulet, Marguerite. "Dowry and Prestige in North India." *Contributions to Indian Sociology*, n.s., 30, 1 (1996): 89–107.

Rubin, G. R. "Law, Poverty and Imprisonment for Debt, 1869–1914." In *Law, Economy and Society, 1750–1914: Essays in the History of English Law,* edited by G. R. Rubin and David Sugarman, 241–299. Abingdon: Professional Books, 1984.

Sangari, Kumkum. "Politics of Diversity: Religious Communities and Multiple Patriarchies." *Economic and Political Weekly* 30, 51–52 (Dec. 23–30, 1995): 3287–3305, 3381–3389.

"Gender Lines: Personal Laws, Uniform Laws, Conversion." *Social Scientist* 27, 5–6 (May–June 1999): 17–61.

Sangari, Kumkum, and Sudesh Vaid. *Recasting Women: Essays in Indian Colonial History*. New Brunswick, NJ: Rutgers University Press, 1990.

Santos, Boaventura de Sousa Santos. "Law: A Map of Misreading. Toward a Postmodern Conception of Law." *Journal of Law and Society* 14, 3 (Autumn 1987): 279–302.

Sarkar, Tanika. "Rhetoric against Age of Consent: Resisting Colonial Reason and the Death of a Child-Wife," *Economic and Political Weekly* 28, 36 (Sept. 4, 1993): 1869–1878.

"A Pre-History of Rights: The Age of Consent Debate in Colonial Bengal." *Feminist Studies* 26, 3 (Autumn 2000): 601–622.

Hindu Wife, Hindu Nation: Community, Religion, and Cultural Nationalism. Bloomington: Indiana University Press, 2001.

Sartori, Andrew. *Bengal in Global Concept History: Culturalism in the Age of Capital*. Chicago: University of Chicago Press, 2008.

Schmitthener, Samuel. "A Sketch of the Development of the Legal Profession in India." *Law and Society Review* Special Issue Devoted to Lawyers in Developing Societies with Particular Reference to India 3, 2–3, (Nov. 1968–Feb. 1969): 337–382.

Scott, David. "Colonial Governmentality." *Social Text* 43 (Autumn 1995): 191–220.

Scott, David and Charles Hirschkind, eds. *Powers of the Secular Modern: Talal Asad and His Interlocutors*. Stanford, CA: Stanford University Press, 2006.

Scott, Joan. *Gender and the Politics of History*. New York: Columbia University Press, 1988.

Only Paradoxes to Offer: French Feminists and the Rights of Man. Cambridge, MA: Harvard University Press, 1996.

Sen, Samita. "Offences against Marriage: Negotiating Custom in Colonial Bengal." In *A Question of Silence? The Sexual Economies of Modern India*, edited by Mary E. John and Janaki Nair, 77–110. New Delhi: Kali for Women, 1998.

Sen, Sudipta. *Empire of Free Trade: The East India Company and the Making of the Colonial Marketplace*. Philadelphia: University of Pennsylvania Press, 1998.

Seth, Sanjay. "Rewriting Histories of Nationalism: The Politics of 'Moderate Nationalism' in India, 1870–1905." *American Historical Review* 104, 1 (Feb. 1999): 95–116.

Shanley, Mary Lyndon. *Feminism, Marriage and the Law in Victorian England, 1850–1895*. Princeton, NJ: Princeton University Press, 1989.

Sheel, Ranjana. *The Political Economy of Dowry: Institutionalization and Expansion in North India*. Delhi: Manohar Press, 1999.

Shirgaonkar, Varsha. *Social Reforms in Maharashtra and V. N. Mandlik*. New Delhi: Navrang, 1989.

Shodhan, Amrita. *A Question of Community: Religious Groups and Colonial Law.* Calcutta: Samya Press, 2001.

Siddiqi, N. A. *Land Revenue Administration under the Mughals, 1700–1750.* New York: Asia Publishing House, 1970.

Singh, Meera. *British Revenue and Judicial Policies in India: A Case Study of Deccan, 1818–1826.* New Delhi: Har-Anand Publications, 1994.

Singha, Radhika. "Making the Domestic More Domestic: Criminal Law and the 'Head of the Household,' 1772–1843." *Indian Economic and Social History Review* 33, 3 (1996): 309–343.

   A Despotism of Law: Crime and Justice in Early Colonial India. Delhi: Oxford University Press, 1998.

Sinha, Chittaranjan. *The Indian Judiciary in the Making, 1800–1833.* New Delhi: Munshiram Manoharlal, 1971.

Sinha, Mrinalini. *Specters of Mother India: The Global Restructuring of an Empire.* Durham, NC: Duke University Press, 2006.

Smith, K. J. M. *James Fitzjames Stephen: Portrait of a Victorian Rationalist.* Cambridge: Cambridge University Press, 1988.

Smith, Richard Saumarez. *Rule by Records: Land Registration and Village Custom in Early British Panjab.* Delhi: Oxford University Press, 1996.

Sontheimer, Günther-Dietz. *The Joint Hindu Family: Its Evolution as a Legal Institution.* New Delhi: Munshiram Manoharlal, 1977.

Spellman, Elizabeth. "The Heady Political Life of Compassion." In *Reconstructing Political Theory: Feminist Perspectives,* edited by Mary Lyndon Shanley and Uma Narayan, 128–143. University Park: The Pennsylvania State University Press, 1997.

Sreenivas, Mytheli. "Conjugality and Capital: Gender, Families and Property under Colonial Law in India." *Journal of Asian Studies* 63, 4 (Nov. 2004): 937–960.

   Wives, Widows and Concubines: The Conjugal Family Ideal in Colonial India. Bloomington: Indiana University Press, 2008.

Srinivas, M. N. *Some Reflections on Dowry.* J. P. Naik Memorial Lecture, 1983. Delhi: Oxford University Press, 1984.

Srinivasan, Amrit. "Reform and Revival: The Devadasi and Her Dance." *Economic and Political Weekly* 20, 44 (Nov. 2, 1985): 1869–1876.

Srivastava, Ramesh Chandra. *Development of Judicial System in India under the East India Company, 1833–1858.* Lucknow: Lucknow Publishing House, 1971.

Stevens, Jacqueline. *Reproducing the State.* Princeton, NJ: Princeton University Press, 1999.

Stokes, Eric. *The English Utilitarians and India.* Oxford: Clarendon Press, 1959.

   "The Land Revenue Systems of the North-Western Provinces and Bombay Deccan 1830–1880: Ideology and the Official Mind." In *The Making of Agrarian Policy in British India, 1770–1900,* edited by Burton Stein, 84–112. Delhi: Oxford University Press, 1992.

Stoler, Ann Laura. *Along the Archival Grain: Epistemic Anxieties and Colonial Common Sense.* Princeton, NJ: Princeton University Press, 2009.

Stoler, Ann Laura, and Frederick Cooper, eds. *Tensions of Empire: Colonial Cultures in a Bourgeois World.* Berkeley: University of California Press, 1987.

Stone, Lawrence. *Family, Sex and Marriage in England, 1500–1800*. New York: Harper & Row, 1977.

Strathern, Marilyn. *After Nature: English Kinship in the Late Twentieth Century*. Cambridge: Cambridge University Press, 1992.

Property, Substance and Effect: Anthropological Essays on Persons and Things. London: Athlone Press, 1999.

Sunder Rajan, Rajeswari. "Rethinking Law and Violence: The Domestic Violence (Prevention) Bill in India, 2002." *Gender and History* 16, 3 (November 2004): 769–93.

The Scandal of the State: Women, Law and Citizenship in Postcolonial India. Durham, NC: Duke University Press, 2003.

Sunthankar, B. R. *Nineteenth-Century History of Maharashtra*. Vol. 1, *1818–1857*. Pune: Shubhada-Saraswat Prakashan, 1988.

Maharashtra 1858–1920. Bombay: Popular Book Depot, 1993.

Tambe, Ashwini. "Brothels as Families: Reflections on the History of Bombay's *Kothas*." *International Feminist Journal of Politics* 8, 2 (June 2006): 219–242.

Codes of Misconduct: Regulating Prostitution in Late Colonial Bombay. Minneapolis: University of Minnesota Press, 2009.

Taylor, Charles. "The Politics of Recognition." In *Multiculturalism: Examining the Politics of Recognition*, edited by Amy Gutmann, 25–74. Princeton: Princeton University Press, 1994.

Teubner, Gunther. "The Two Faces of Janus: Rethinking Legal Pluralism." *Cardozo Law Review* 13 (1992): 1443–1462.

Thomas, Nicholas. *Entangled Objects: Exchange, Material Culture and Colonialism in the Pacific*. Cambridge, MA: Harvard University Press, 1991.

Thompson, E. P. *Whigs and Hunters: The Origins of the Black Act*. New York: Pantheon Books, 1975.

Trautmann, Thomas. *Lewis Henry Morgan and the Invention of Kinship*. Berkeley: University of California Press, 1987.

Travers, Robert. "'The Real Value of the Lands': The Nawabs, the British and the Land Tax in Eighteenth-Century Bengal." *Modern Asian Studies* 38, 3 (2004): 517–558.

Ideology and Empire in Eighteenth-Century India: The British in Bengal. Cambridge: Cambridge University Press, 2007.

Tuck, Richard. *Natural Rights Theories: Their Origin and Development*. Cambridge: Cambridge University Press, 1979.

Uberoi, Patricia, ed. *Family, Kinship, and Marriage in India*. Delhi: Oxford University Press, 1993.

"When Is a Marriage Not a Marriage: Sex, Sacrament, and Contract in Hindu Marriage." *Contributions to Indian Sociology*, n.s., 29, 1–2 (1995): 319–345.

Upadhya, Carol Boyack. "Dowry and Women's Property in Coastal Andra Pradesh." *Contributions to Indian Sociology*, n.s., 24, 1 (1990): 29–59.

Vachha, P. B. *Famous Judges, Lawyers and Cases of Bombay: A Judicial History of Bombay during the British Period*. Bombay: N. M. Tripathi, 1962.

Valenze, Deborah. *The Social Life of Money in English Past*. Cambridge: Cambridge University Press, 2006.

van der Veer, Peter. *Religious Nationalism: Hindus and Muslims in India*. Berkeley, CA: University of California Press, 1994.

ed. *Conversion to Modernities: The Globalization of Christianity*. New York: Routledge, 1996.

Viswanathan, Gauri. *Outside the Fold: Conversion, Modernity and Belief*. Princeton, NJ: Princeton University Press, 1998.

Wagle, Narendra K. "A Dispute between the Pancal Devajna Sonars and the Brahmanas of Pune Regarding Social Rank and Ritual Privileges: A Case-Study of the British Administration of Jati Laws in Maharashtra, 1822–1825." In *Images of Maharashtra: A Regional Profile of India*, edited by Narendra K. Wagle, 129–159. Toronto: Curzon Press, 1980.

"Women in the Kotwal's Papers: Pune 1767–1791." In *Images of Women in Maharashtrian Society*, edited by Anne Feldhaus, 15–60. Albany: State University of New York Press, 1998.

ed. *Writers, Editors and Reformers: Social and Political Transformations of Maharashtra, 1830–1930*. New Delhi: Manohar, 1999.

"Three Letters of Govind Babaji Joshi on Inter-Jati Marriage in Nineteenth-Century Maharashtra." In *Writers, Editors and Reformers: Social and Political Transformations of Maharashtra, 1830–1930*, edited by Narendra K. Wagle, 200–217. New Delhi: Manohar, 1999.

"The Government, the Jati, and the Individual: Rights, Discipline, and Control in the Pune Kotwal's Papers, 1766–1794." *Contributions to Indian Sociology* 34, 3 (Sept.–Dec., 2000): 321–360.

Walkowitz, Judith. *Prostitution and Victorian Society: Women, Class and the State*. Cambridge: Cambridge University Press, 1980.

City of Dreadful Delight: Narratives of Sexual Danger in Late-Victorian London. Chicago: University of Chicago Press, 1992.

Washbrook, David A. "Law, State and Agrarian Society in Colonial India." *Modern Asian Studies* 15, 3 (1981): 649–721.

"India, 1818–1860: The Two Faces of Colonialism." In *The Oxford History of the British Empire, The Nineteenth Century*, edited by Andrew Porter, 395–421. Oxford: Oxford University Press, 1999.

Watson, James L. "Transactions in People: The Chinese Market in Slaves, Servants, and Heirs." In *Asian and African Systems of Slavery*, edited by James L. Watson. Berkeley: University of California Press, 1980.

Weber, Max. *Essays in Sociology*. Translated and edited by H. H. Gerth and C. Wright Mills. New York: Oxford University Press, 1953.

Economy and Society. 2 vols. Edited by Guenther Roth and Claus Wittich. Translated by Ephraim Fischoff, Hans Gerth, et al. Berkeley: University of California Press, 1978 (orig. 1922).

Weiner, Annette. *Inalienable Possessions: The Paradox of Keeping-While-Giving*. Berkeley: University of California Press, 1992.

Weintraub, Jeff, and Krishan Kumar. *Public and Private in Thought and Practice: Perspectives on a Grand Dichotomy*. Chicago: University of Chicago Press, 1997.

Williams, Patricia. *The Alchemy of Race and Rights: Diary of a Law Professor.* Cambridge, MA: Harvard University Press, 1991.

Wink, André. *Land and Sovereignty in India: Agrarian Society and Politics under the Eighteenth-Century Maratha Svarajya.* Cambridge: Cambridge University Press, 1986.

Cases Cited

The Advocate General ex relatione Daya Muhammad v. Muhammad Husen Huseni (1867) Bom HCR 203.

Advocate General of Bombay v. Jimbabai (1917) ILR 41 Bom 181.

Advyapa v. Rudrava (1879) ILR 4 Bom 104.

Amarendra Mansigh v. Sanatan Singh (1933) 12 Pat 642.

Anandi v. Hari Suba Pai (1909) ILR 33 Bom 404.

Anandibai v. Rajaram Chintaman Pethe (1897) ILR 22 Bom 984.

Anandrao Vinayak v. The Administrator General of Bombay (1895) ILR 20 Bom 45

Ananta v. Ramabai (1877) ILR 1 Bom 554.

Annaji Dattatraya v. Chadrabai (1892) ILR 17 Bom 503.

Appaya v. Padappa (1899) ILR 23 Bom 122.

Babubhai Girdharlal v. Girdharlal Hargovandas (1937) ILR 61 Bom 708.

Bai Jivi v. Narsingh (1926) ILR 51 Bom 329.

Bai Lakshmi v. Lakhmidas Gopaldas (1863) 1 Bom 13.

Bai Mamubai v. Dossa Morarji (1890) ILR 15 Bom 443.

Bai Mangal v. Bai Rukhmini (1898) ILR 23 Bom 291.

Bai Parwati v. Ghanchi Mansukh Jetha (1920) ILR 44 Bom 972.

Bai Vijli v. Nansanagar (1885) ILR 10 Bom 152.

Bala Anna Gurav v. Akubai (1926) ILR 50 Bom 722.

Balu Sakharam Powar v. Lahoo Sambhaji Tetgura (1936) ILR 61 Bom 508

Bhaeeshunker Nurbheram v. Baee Ruttun (1860) Bom SDA Rep. Vol. VIII, 106.

Bhagirthibai v. Kahnujirav (1886) ILR 11 Bom 285

Bhaidas Shivdas v. Bai Gulab (1921) ILR 46 Bom 153.

Bhala Nahana v. Parbhu Hari (1877) ILR 2 Bom 67.

Bhaskar Purshotam v. Sarasvatibai (1892) ILR 17 Bom 486.

Bhau bin Abaji Gurav v. Raghunath Krishnagurav (1905) ILR 30 Bom 229.

Bhikaji v. Secretary of State (1925) ILR 49 Bom 554.

Bhikubai v. Hariba (1924) ILR 49 Bom 459.

Bhimabai v. Gurunathgouda Khandappagouda (1932) ILR 57 Bom 157.

Bhimawa v. Sangawa (1896) ILR 22 Bom 206.

Bhugwunt v. Goozabaee (1860) 8 Bom HCR 120.

Chandrabhagabai v. Kashinath Vithal (1866) 2 Bom HCR 323.

Chitko v. Janaki (1873) 11 Bom HCR 199.

Chunilal Prashankar v. Surajram Haribhai; Bhogilal Valabhram v. Surajram Haribhai (1909) ILR 33 Bom 433.

Collector of Madura v. Mootoo Ramalinga Sathupathy (1868) 12 MIA 397.

Dadaji Bhikaji v. Rukhmabai (1886) ILR 9 Bom 529.

Dalsukhram v. Lallubhai (1883) ILR 7 Bom 282.

Damodhar Madhowji v. Purmanandas Jeewandas; Purmanandas Jeewandas v. Damodhar Madhowji (1883) ILR 7 Bom 155.

Damodhar Vithal Khare v. Damodhar Hari Soman (1863) 1 Bom HCR 182.

Dewarkur Josee v. Naroo Keshoo Goreh (1837) Bom Sel. SDA Rep. 1820–1840, 190.

Dholidas Ishvar v. Fulchand Chhagan (1897) ILR 22 Bom 661.

Dhondi Dnyanoo Sinde v. Rama Bala Sinde (1935) ILR 60 Bom 82.

Dulari v. Vallabdas Pragji (1888) Ind. Dec. NS 7 Bom 84 (corresponding to ILR 13 Bom 126).

Dundappa Basappa Yedal v. Bhimawa (1920) 45 Bom 557.

Duttoo Wullud Essujee, Patil v. Mulkappa bin Mullappa, Patil (1848) Bom Sel. SDA Rep., 1840–1848, 88.

Empress v. Umi (1882) ILR 6 Bom 126.

Fakirgowda Basangowda Patil v. Dyamawa (1932) ILR 57 Bom 488.

Gadadhar Bhat v. Chandrabhagabai (1892) ILR 17 Bom 690.

Gangabai v. Hari Ganesh Joshi (1921) ILR 45 Bom 1167.

Gangabai v. Thavar Mulla (1863) 1 Bom HCR 71.

Ghelabhai Mulchand v. Bai Mancha (1883) ILR 7 Bom 491.

Girianna Murkunki Naik vs. Honama (1890) 15 Bom 236.

Gundo Mahadev v. Rambhat bin Bhaubhat (1863) 1 Bom HCR 39.

Gungbae v. Sonabae (1847) Perry OC 110.

Gurushiddappa v. Parwatewwa (1936) ILR 61 Bom 113.

Hanmant Ramchandra Kulkarni v. Secretary of State (1929) ILR 54 Bom 125.

Haridas Narayandas Bhatia v. Devkuvarbai Bhratar Mulji (1926) ILR 50 Bom 443.

Hira v. Hansji Pema (1912) 37 Bom 299.

Hirbae v. Sonabae (1847) Perry OC 110.

Hirbai v. Gorbai (1875) 12 Bom HCR 294.

Honamma v. Timmanabhat (1877) ILR 1 Bom 559.

Hurbujee Raojee v. Hurgovind Trikumdass (1847) Sel. SDA Rep., 1840–1848, 76.

In re: Bulakidas (1898) ILR 23 Bom 485.

In re: Gulabdas Bhaidas (1891) ILR 16 Bom 269.

In re: Kalidas Mansukram (1878) Criminal Revision No. 119 of 1878.

In re: Padmavati (1870) 5 Bom HCR 415.

Ishwar Dadu Patil v. Gajabai kom Babaji Patil (1925) ILR 50 Bom 468.

Jagannath Raghunath v. Narayan Shethe (1910) ILR 34 Bom 553.

Javerbai v. Kablibai (1890) ILR 15 Bom 326.

Janaki Ammal v. Narayanasami Aiyer (1916) LR 43 IA 207, s.c. 39 Mad 634.

Jan Mahomed v. Datu Jaffer (1915) ILR 38 Bom 449.

Jinnappa Mahadevappa Kundachi v. Chimmava (1934) ILR 59 Bom 459.

Jugmohandas Mangaldas v. Sir Mangaldas Nathubhoy (1886) ILR 10 Bom 528.

Kalo Nilkanth v. Lakshmibai (1878) ILR 2 Bom 637.

Kalu v. Kashibai (1882) ILR 7 Bom 127.

Kamalam v. Sadagopa Sami (1878) 1 Mad 356.

Karbasappa v. Kallava (1918) ILR 43 Bom 66.

Kasturbai v. Shivatiram (1879) ILR 3 Bom 372.

Keshav Hargovan v. Bai Gandi (1915) ILR 39 Bom 538.

Krishnanath Narayan v. Atmaram Narayan (1891) ILR 15 Bom 543.

Krishnarao Ramchandra v. Benabai (1895) ILR 20 Bom 571.

Kuverji v. Babai (1886) ILR 19 Bom 374.

Lakshman v. Satyabhamabai (1877) ILR 2 Bom 494.

Lakshman Dada Naik v. Ramchandra Dada Naik and Ramchandra Dada Naik v. Lakshman Dada Naik (1876), ILR 1 Bom 561.

Lakshmibai v. Hirabai (1886) ILR 11 Bom 69.

Lakshmibai v. Ramchandra (1896) ILR 22 Bom 590.

Lallu v. Jagmohan (1896) ILR 22 Bom 409.

Lulpotee Moonomy v. Tikha Moodoi (1870) 13 Cal WR 52 Criminal Rulings.

Luximan Narayan v. Jamnabai (1882) ILR 6 Bom 225.

Mahableshvar Fondba v. Durgabai (1896) ILR 22 Bom 199.

Mahomed Sidick v. Haji Ahmed (1886) ILR 10 Bom 1.

Malgauda Paragauda Patil v. Babaji Dattu Bhakare (1912) ILR 37 Bom 107.

Mancharam Bhiku Patil v. Dattu (1919) 44 Bom 166.

Manilal v. Bai Tara (1892) ILR 17 Bom 398.

Manilal Rewadat v. Bai Rewa (1892) ILR 17 Bom 753

Mathura Naikin v. Esu Naikin (1880) ILR 4 Bom 545.

Mithibai v. Meherbai (1921) ILR 46 Bom 162.

Mohanlal Khubchand v. Jagjivan Anandram (1937) ILR 62 Bom 292.

Moolji Lilla v. Gokuldas Vulla (1883) ILR 8 Bom 154.

Moolchund Bhaeechund v. Dhurmlal Deepalal (1861) Bom Sel. SDA Rep., Vol. VIII, 9–11.

Mordaunt v. Mordaunt (1870) LR 2 Pro. and Div. 103.

Motilal Lalubhai v. Ratilal Mahipatram (1895) ILR 21 Bom 170.

Muktabai v. Antaji (1899) ILR 23 Bom 39.

Mulji Thakersey v. Gomti and Kastur (1887) ILR 11 Bom 412.

Murarji Gokuldas. v. Parvatibai (1877) ILR 1 Bom 177.

Narbadabai v. Mahadeo Narayan (1880) ILR 5 Bom 99.

Panachand Chhotalal v. Manoharlal Nandlal (1917) ILR 42 Bom 136.

Parami v. Mahadevi (1909) ILR 34 Bom 278.

Parekh Ranochor v. Bai Vakhat (1886) ILR 11 Bom 119.

Parvati v. Kisansing (1882) ILR 6 Bom 567.

Pitamber Ratansi v. Jagjivan Hansraj (1884) ILR 13 Bom 131.

Pitamber Ratansi v. Jagjivan Hansraj (1884) Ind. Dec. NS 7 Bom 88 (corresponding to ILR 13 Bom 131) appended to 13 Bom 126, Pauper Petition, No. 20 of 1,888.

Pragji v. Govind (1886) ILR 11 Bom 534.

Pranjivandas Tulsidas v. Devkuvarbai (1859) 1 Bom HCR 130.

Prashankar v. Prannath (1863) 1 Bom HC, AC 12.

Purshotamdas Maneklal v. Bai Mani (1896) 21 Bom 610.

Rahimatbae v. Hadji Jussap (1847) Perry OC 110.

Ramlakshmi Ammal v. Sivanantha 7 Mad HCR 250; Ramalakshmi Ammal v. Sivanantha (1872) 14 MIA 570

Rambhat v. Timmayya (1892) ILR 16 Bom 673.

Ramchandra Bhagavan v. Mulji Nanabhai (1896) ILR 22 Bom 558.

Ramchandra Dada Naik v. Dada Mahadev Naik (1861) 1 Bom HCR, Appendix, lxxvi.

Rango v. Yamunabai (1878) ILR 3 Bom 44.

Ravji Vinayakrav v. Lakshmibai Shankarsett (1887) ILR 11 Bom 381.

Reg. v. Jaili Bhavin (1869) 6 Bom HCR 60.
Reg. v. Karsan Goja and Reg. v. Bai Rupa (1864) 2 Bom HCR 124.
Reg v. Manohar (1868) 5 Bom HCR 17 (Part I).
Reg. v. Sambhu Raghu (1876) ILR 1 Bom 347.
Sakvarbai v. Bhavanji Raje Ghatge Zanjarrav Deshmukh (1864) 1 Bom 197.
Sankaralingam Chetti v. Subban Chetti (1894) ILR 17 Mad 479.
Savitribai v. Luximibai (1878) ILR 2 Bom 573.
Sewram Moreshwar Pettae v. |illegible|, Widow of Moro Mahadarow Pettae (1830) MSA, RD 1831, 26/354.
Shankar Vinayak Nigade v. Ramrao Sahebrao Nigade (1935) ILR 60 Bom 89.
Shivabasava v. Sangappa (1904) ILR 29 Bom 1.
Shivji Hasam v. Datu Mavji Khoja (1874) 12 Bom HCR 281.
Sidlingapa v. Sidava (1878) ILR 2 Bom 624.
Sitabai v. Govindrao Ramrao Deshmukh (1926) ILR 51 Bom 217.
Sitabai v. Secretary of State (1925) ILR 49 Bom 554
Sivanananja Perumal v. Muttu Ramalinga (1866) 3 Mad HCR 75.
Sri Sunkar v. Sidha (1845) 2 Bom 473.
Sundrabai v. Hanmant (1931) ILR 56 Bom 298.
Surajname v. Rabi Nath (1903) 25 All 355.
Tara v. Krishna (1907) ILR 31 Bom 495.
Tara Naikin v. Nana Lakshman (1889) 14 Bom 90.
Timmappa Bhat v. Parmeshriamma (1868) 5 Bom HCR 130.
Treebhowan Khooshal v. Lulloo Soorchund (1861) Bom SDA Rep. Vol. VIII, 198.
Tukaram v. Ramchandra (1869) 6 Bom HCR 247.
Udaram Sitaram v. Sonkabai (1873) 10 Bom HCR 483.
Umabai v. Bhavu Padmanji (1877) ILR 1 Bom 557.
Umabai v. Nani (1935) ILR 60 Bom 102.
Valu v. Ganga (1882) ILR 7 Bom 84.
Vasudev Bhat v. Venkatesh Sambhav (1873) 10 Bom HCR 139.
Vijaysingji Chhatrasangji v. Shivsangji Bhimsangji (1935) ILR 59 Bom 360.
Vithu v. Govinda (1896) ILR 22 Bom 321.
Yamunabai v. Manubai (1899) ILR 23 Bom 394.

Theses and Dissertations

Conlon, Frank. "The Khojas and the Courts: A Study of the Impact of British Justice in India upon the Social and Religious Life and Institutions of a Muslim Community." M.A. thesis, University of Minnesota, 1963.
Hickling, Carissa. "Disinheriting Daughters: Applying Hindu Laws of Inheritance to the Muslim Khoja Community of Bombay, 1847–1937." M.A. thesis, University of Manitoba, 1998.
Khan, Fareeha. "Traditionalist Approaches to Shari'ah Reform: Maulana Ashraf 'Ali Thanawi's Fatwa on Women's Right to Divorce." Ph.D. diss., University of Michigan, 2008.
Levy, Harold Lewis. "Indian Modernization by Legislation: The Hindu Code Bill." Ph.D. diss., University of Chicago, 1973.

Solanki, Gopika. "Adjudication in Religious Family Laws: Cultural Accommodation, Legal Pluralism, and Women's Rights in India." Ph.D. diss., McGill University, 2007.

Sturman, Rachel. "Family Values: Refashioning Property and Family in Colonial Bombay Presidency, 1818–1937." Ph.D. diss., University of California, Davis, 2001.

Index

Abdulla, H. M., 212, 215–216
abstract human universality, 4, 105, 195
abstract politico-legal subjecthood, 10, 25, 110, 138, 172, 223, 237
abstract rights, 5, 24
Act XI of 1843, 99n
adjectival law, 215
adoption, 142–146, 156, 237
adultery, 160
  see also bigamy
Advocate General of Bombay v. Jimbabai, 208
affective claim, 40, 133, 136n
Aga Khan, 201, 204
"Aga Khan case," 203
Age of Consent Act (1891), 187n
agency, 145–146, 227
  see also Hindu widows, legal agency of; women, legal agency of
agricultural indebtedness, 75
  see also debt; rural society, and indebtedness
agricultural productivity, 92
  agriculturalists, 77, 80, 83, 87
  see also cultivators; peasants
agriculture, 40–41
  and colonial political economy, 39, 45–50, 77–88
Ahmednagar District, 78
alienability of property
  see property, alienability of
All-India Muslim League, 196–197, 212–213

All India Women's Conference (AIWC), 196n, 211
Ambar, Malik, 48
Ambedkar, B. R., 95, 222, 226–233
Anagol, Padma, 128n, 140, 160n, 184n, 185n
ancestral property
  see joint family property
ancient law, 19, 93
  see also Maine, Henry Sumner
Aney, M. S., 216
anti-caste politics, 89–91, 196–197, 222–231
anti-dedication campaign, 172–173, 175–176, 178–182
  see also temple dedication
antiquity, 39, 93, 154
  as origin of right, 42
  as source of law, 21, 26, 63
  see also law, sources of
Arendt, Hannah, 25, 71n, 111n
Arnould, Justice, 203
arranged marriage
  see marriage, arranged
Asiatic despotism, 42
  see also state, as universal landlord
Asura marriage, 166–170, 180
  see also bride-price
Austin, John, 21, 157n
autonomy, 41, 72–73, 84, 86n, 92, 96, 105, 110, 113–114, 116, 122–124, 126, 130, 132, 147, 220–221, 236
  see also non-autonomy

Other titles in the series